INTERTEXTU
IN AMERICAN
DRAMA

KU-329-539

Critical Essays on Eugene O'Neill,
Susan Glaspell, Thornton Wilder,
Arthur Miller and Other
Playwrights

Edited by Drew Eisenhauer *and*
Brenda Murphy

McFarland & Company, Inc., Publishers
Jefferson, North Carolina, and London

UNIVERSITY OF WINCHESTER
LIBRARY

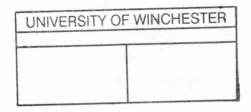

LIBRARY OF CONGRESS CATALOGUING-IN-PUBLICATION DATA

Intertextuality in American drama : critical essays on Eugene
   O'Neill, Susan Glaspell, Thornton Wilder, Arthur Miller
   and other playwrights / edited by Drew Eisenhauer and
   Brenda Murphy.
       p.   cm.
   Includes bibliographical references and index.

   ISBN 978-0-7864-6391-6
   softcover : acid free paper ∞

   1. American drama — 20th century — History
and criticism.   2. O'Neill, Eugene, 1888–1953 —
Criticism and interpretation.   3. Glaspell, Susan,
1876–1948 — Criticism and interpretation.
4. Wilder, Thornton, 1897–1975 — Criticism
and interpretation.   5. Miller, Arthur, 1915–2005 —
Criticism and interpretation.   6. Intertextuality.
I. Eisenhauer, Drew.   II. Murphy, Brenda, 1950–
PS350.I58 2013
812'.509 — dc23   2012038662

BRITISH LIBRARY CATALOGUING DATA ARE AVAILABLE

© 2013 Drew Eisenhauer and Brenda Murphy.
All rights reserved

*No part of this book may be reproduced or transmitted in any form
or by any means, electronic or mechanical, including photocopying
or recording, or by any information storage and retrieval system,
without permission in writing from the publisher.*

Front cover image © 2013 Shutterstock

Manufactured in the United States of America

McFarland & Company, Inc., Publishers
  Box 611, Jefferson, North Carolina 28640
  www.mcfarlandpub.com

Table of Contents

Part II: Cultural Intertextuality

Introduction

What Is "Intertextuality" and
Why Is the Term Important Today?

DREW EISENHAUER

This volume is a unique effort that brings together essays interpreting the work of diverse American dramatists through the lens of intertextuality, a critical concept not often used in connection with drama.[1] That critics have been reticent to use this popular term is undoubtedly related to the persistent question as to whether or not works of theatre or performance are, in fact, "texts" at all. The dramatic text is often seen as only an element in the theatre — the bluprint of a play — and a written text is sometimes absent completely in avant-garde or art performance. However represented, though, performed works are cultural "texts" and very often linguistic ones as well, in the sense that there is an informed use of language — whether written, spoken, projected, or deconstructed — deserving of the same criticism, analysis, interpretation and scholarship as the language of other literary and artistic genres. Dramatic texts are connected to other works within the medium of theatre but also to a myriad of other writings, media, and cultural references through processes linguistic, aesthetic, historical, visual, technological, and epistemological. Thus the present collection fills an important conceptual gap in contemporary criticism. Originially an outcome of a collaborative exchange project among five member societies of the American Literature Association — the American Theatre and Drama Society (ATDS), the Arthur Miller Society, the Eugene O'Neill Society, the Susan Glaspell Society, and the Thornton Wilder Society — the incisive and diverse approaches to intertextuality presented here testify to the continuing vitality of research in American drama and performance.

The term intertextuality was originally coined by the Bulgarian theorist Julia Kristeva, working in her adopted city and intellectual milieu of turbulent 1960s Paris; it was initially employed by post-structuralists, although the term soon came into wider usage and began to include a variety of theoretical and ideological perspectives on textual meaning. Kristeva began with a critique of Ferdinand de Saussure's synchronic model of language as a complete system. Introducing the West to the works of Russian literary theorist Mikhail Bakhtin, Kristeva applied to textual interpretation Bakhtin's claim that language is always used within real historical circumstances and situations and is affected by the cultural and ideological structures of society. She also emphasized Bakhtin's concept that any instance of language use bears with it the traces of all previous utterances of the same words and phrases (Allen 17). Kristeva argued, therefore, that meaning is always mediated through the multitude of other texts that lie behind the writer and the reader's use and decoding of meaning: "any text is constructed as a mosaic of quotations; any text is the absorption and transformation of another" (Kristeva 66). Kristeva also defined two types or "axes" of intertextuality, a *horizontal axis* between the writer and reader of a text, and a *vertical axis*, which connects the text to other texts (Kristeva 69).

Perhaps the most famous outcome of Kristeva's work was the 1967 essay by her mentor, Roland Barthes, "The Death of the Author." Arguing "the text is a tissue of citations, resulting from the thousand sources of culture," Barthes explains the author as simply an empty site for the collection of texts: "[the] utterance in its entirety is a void process, which functions perfectly without requiring to be filled by the person of the interlocutors."

If poststructuralists offered a precise definition of intertextuality, the term spread rapidly and developed a variety of uses often absorbing conventional concepts such as allusion and influence. This trend, in turn, led some critics on both the left and the right, including Kristeva herself, to distance themselves from the term. In a 1991 survey of the debate, H.P. Mai determined that while poststructuralists use the term as a "springboard for associative speculations about semiotic and cultural matters ... on the other hand, traditional literary studies have seized upon the term to integrate their investigative interests in structures and interrelations of literary texts" (51). Today this theoretical controversy has settled down to some extent, and intertextuality as variously defined appears to be here to stay, a ubiquitous term in the contemporary critical vocabulary. It remains remarkably malleable and useful for discussing relationships among texts of all types.

Critics in a variety of fields today use intertextuality to discuss the many sources that form, influence, impinge on, limit, and expand the meaning of a text. Such influences can range from something as small as a word, phrase or traditional literary allusion to interactions between genres, the inter-relationship between different texts in a single author's canon, or the interdependencies between a text's meaning and entire schemas of social and historical context. For the purposes of our collection, we have considered intertextuality in its broadest sense, with each contributor seeking to uncover the relations between dramas or performances and not only literary and philosophical texts, but theatrical, visual, cinematic and material culture as well.

The contributors' backgrounds are as diverse as their critical approaches. *Intertextuality in American Drama* includes the work of researchers at every stage of their careers — from emerging scholars to distinguished researchers — and representing three continents and five countries: India, Canada, France, Italy and the United States. These scholars practice an intertextuality between media and genres as diverse as their approaches in this volume. Several are accomplished in multiple fields, such as Rupendra Guha Majumdar, a published poet and visual artist as well as an internationally known scholar of Eugene O'Neill; Herman Daniel Farrell III, an accomplished playwright and screenwriter as well as scholar; Michael Winetsky, a prize-winning scholar of playwright Susan Glaspell and an emerging playwright himself; and Lisa Hall Hagen, who can claim degrees in playwriting and performance in addition to a critical volume on gender and theatre, to name just a few on the list.

Reflecting the popularity and diverse uses of the term in contemporary scholarship, the contributors to *Intertextuality in American Drama* offer the widest array of possible interpretations of intertextuality and, ultimately, of dramas and performances. We have suggested, rather than imposed, a loose structure to organize the book, which we derived from the submissions themselves. We divide the various approaches of our contributors into two major parts: "Literary Intertextuality" and "Cultural Intertextuality." "Literary" seemed the ideal heading under which to feature a series of articles that explore plays for their intertextual relationships to two of the major literary genres: thus this section is comprised of "Poets" and "Playwrights and Performance Texts." As our contributors show, the traces of meaning left by American playwrights' reading of other literary writers proves both more profound and, at times, more destabilizing than might be imagined. The section on poets begins with two equally compelling but in many ways contrasting essays about Eugene O'Neill's 1924 adaptation of Samuel Taylor Coleridge's "The Rime of the Ancient Mariner." Herman Daniel Farrell III argues from a structural perspective that O'Neill's encounter with Coleridge afforded him the opportunity to experiment, once in his career, with the death of the author, that it was "a particular moment in O'Neill's development, an intertextual epiphany in which the playwright permitted the near obliteration of his agency." Rupendra Guha Majumdar argues that although "The Rime of the Ancient Mariner" is not normally thought a great O'Neill work, O'Neill's encounter with the Coleridge text was profound, creating a "poetical resource that would gradually acquire a mythic significance" for the playwright, and ultimately contribute to "a new romantic lyricism" in O'Neill's late, critically acclaimed plays. Like

Farrell and Majumdar, Aurélie Sanchez demands we recognize that the importance of O'Neill's encounter with other poetic texts has been heretofore under-
estimated. Sanchez argues that "the comic action and the characterization of
A Moon for the Misbegotten," the third of O'Neill's late acclaimed works, are
"permeated by numerous intertextual echoes," particularly with "Shakespeare's
archetypal festive comedy, *A Midsummer Night's Dream*, and romantic symbolism in the form of references to the moonlight in Keats's odes."

It is appropriate for a study of works of American drama to begin with
analyses of Eugene O'Neill, but it is equally fitting that the last two essays in
the first section focus on American playwright Susan Glaspell. Glaspell, whose
fifteen plays presented at the Provincetown Playhouse were often more critically acclaimed than O'Neill's, also wrote 9 novels and more than 50 short
stories. After her one-act play *Trifles* was rediscovered by feminist critics in
the 1970s, a flurry of critical books and articles appeared on her works. Here,
Michael Winetsky treats Glaspell as playwright and novelist whose work
reveals not only her own reading of American and English romantic poets,
such as Wordsworth and Whitman, but which traces the historial relationship
between intellectual and literary texts and American culture. Winetsky shows
Glaspell as perhaps as aware of intertextuality as Kristeva's generation, a recognition that the meaning of cultural texts is read by and into historical contexts.
"Glaspell's echoes of Romanticism," Winetsky claims, reflect "at first ... the
wild hope that a religion of humanity might integrate the culture of the university seamlessly into popular American ethics. At last, this intertextuality
reflects a sense of loss as ... an intellectual elite pulls away from engagement
with popular concerns." Noelia Hernando-Real further explores Glaspell's
reading of poetry, explicating her 1931 drama *Alison's House*, which won the
Pulitzer Prize, for its echoes of Emily Dickinson in Glaspell's gender politics.
As Hernando-Real informs us, for Glaspell in this play "Dickinson not only
serves as a model for one character but ... the poet's words also reverberate
quite overtly ... the Amherst poet encapsulated women's need to be considered
individuals, one of the main themes in Glaspell's *oeuvre*."

In the next section, "Playwrights and Performance Texts," two new studies focus on the interrelationships *between* canonical American playwrights.
Kristin Bennett and Stephen Marino shed light on the influences, layered over
time, in the work of Thornton Wilder and Arthur Miller, respectively. Bennett
demonstrates that, despite the fact that Wilder is not generally seen in contemporary criticism to have a political agenda, his awareness of the social
construction of gender roles "presenting individuals who unconsciously perform behaviors that have been rehearsed, or abided by, over time" is precisely
critical of an incipient type of intertextuality, where human identities, particularly those of women, "are hidden beneath decades of tradition." Thus,

she argues, "Wilder anticipates the idea of gender as performance suggesting Judith Butler's theory of performativity." Stephen Marino reminds us that for Arthur Miller, whose work has been interpreted from various perspectives, including the political, the plays of Thornton Wilder seem unlikely intertexts. However, as Marino proves, Wilder in fact "had a strong influence ... on Miller's theory of the poetic social drama ... particularly during the ... early part of Miller's seventy-year career — when his views about how form and structure, aesthetics, themes, poetry and poetic language operate in drama were evolving." The final essay in this section explores not close readings of stable dramatic or poetic texts by an individual canonical author, but performances as they occur at specific moments in history, evolving to meet or sometimes resist changing definitions of American ideas. Jason Shaffer argues that America's reliance on central narratives has always been unstable — even in the nineteenth century when values were supposed to be durable, and the death of the author a theory far in the future. Shaffer claims: "In an era when ghost-written celebrity memoirs, fan fiction, and viral video have all contributed to a gradual erosion of the integrity of the relationship between a narrative and its putative creator, it offers some comfort to consider that even the most archetypal of stories have suffered from similar contingencies." Shaffer demonstrates the revisionary history of a great American text on stage: *Rip Van Winkle*.

In "Cultural Texts," the first section in Part II, which covers cultural intertextuality, four scholars present effective commentaries on political, sociological, historical, religious, and psychological intertexts that informed or were anticipated by the work of American playwrights Eugene O'Neill and Susan Glaspell and have been previously overlooked. Franklin J. Lasik explores connections between Charlotte Perkins Gilman's feminist novel *Herland* and Glaspell's presentation of the search for "a female utopia." Lasik points out, "Gilman spoke out on issues relevant to the role of women in American society, especially issues of work, education, and health care." He identifies the frustrations of a similar quest on the part of Glaspell's heroine Claire Archer in her expressionist play *The Verge* (1921). Sarah Withers, in her prize-winning essay, considers ideas about "the intersection of performance, loss, and cultural memory" by looking at Susan Glaspell's 1921 play *Inheritors*, "in which the ephemerality of history itself comes under examination" by Glaspell in her multi-generational story of a midwestern family and college town.

Annalisa Brugnoli explores the leit-motif of "divine hiddenness," the *deus absconditus* originally from Isaiah "as it appears as a recurring intertextual reference in Eugene O'Neill's published, unpublished, fictional and non-fictional work." Brugnoli argues "the idea of God's deliberate absence or unbridgeable distance from the human world subtends a wide and comprehensive transcultural tradition," which involves not only biblical but Greek references and in O'Neill anticipates the late work of Carl Jung. Emeline Jouve also tackles Glaspell's complex avant-gardism in *The Verge*, particularly a long-outstanding issue in Glaspell criticism — whether her heroine is sane or insane at the conclusion of the play. "Intertextual Insanities," Jouve explains, investigates "this seemingly paradoxical correlation between 'craziness' and 'sanity'" on which Glaspell insists in a prose essay, and it "resonates" with *The Verge*, in which "Glaspell has her heroine, Claire Archer, declare that 'madness ... is the only chance for sanity'" (251). Jouve further ties Glaspell's work in this play to her statement that in a book, "the different elements ... must not be detached things, but thread held together, as a weaving pattern," a metaphor, one might point out, also used by Kristeva to explain intertextuality.

The final section of this collection, "Cultural Context," features five essays on American plays and playwrights whose work must be seen differently in different cultural, historical, and national contexts. The scholars in this section look at how the reception of plays and our knowledge about given playwrights, often thought to be permanent, universal, and well-established, in fact change in direct proportion to the cultural intertexts of which they become a part. Lisa Hall Hagen points out that for all three early twentieth-century women playwrights in her study — Maurine Dallas Watkins, Susan Glaspell and Sophie Treadwell — it is precisely their previous writings or observations as journalists that contribute to the recognition of their most well-known plays. Hagen suggests that this is not coincidental but tied to the fact that the origins of these plays as true crime stories legitimated them to contemporary audiences and reviewers. In addition to the journalism, the actual courtrooms in which the women were tried formed the public's understanding of the texts used by the writers and ultimately constrain the subversive nature of these playwrights' feminism.

Jeffrey Eric Jenkins suggests that Thornton Wilder's intentions in *Our Town* depended less on a nostalgia for small town America — fixed in time, having a sense of certainty — than on an interaction between the play and memory, shedding new light on Wilder's view of audience. Jenkins discusses how the play came into being, drawing parallels between this play and the work of archaeology. Jenkins quotes Wilder as asking in *Our Town*, "What is the relation between the countless 'unimportant' details of our daily life, on the one hand, and the great perspectives of time, social history and current religious ideas on the other?"[2]

Ramón Espejo Romero similarly re-examines one of the most canonical works in American drama, Arthur Miller's *Death of Salesman,* and he finds numerous particularities for the work's reception in Spain. He asks whether or not there can be "such a thing as a universal, timeless audience" for the play, especially for "a foreign audience, from whom the play is screened by a translation," which is unlikely to be aware of the author's subtle distinctions in word choice or even in references to things, events, and personalities well-known in the play's native context, e.g., 1950s Brooklyn. Espejo Romero thus traces the history of his efforts in publishing a new translation of *Salesman*. "The more I delved into the text, the more convinced I became of its take on a given time and place," he explains. He thus developed a system for cataloguing what he terms Miller's "meaningful references," identifiying three major groups: "those understandable across cultures; those that are self-explanatory; and those that are somewhat inaccessible" from an audience removed in time and place from the original cultural context of the play.

Graham Wolfe presents one of the most theoretically challenging studies in the collection, examining what he calls "Intertextual Seduction" in John Guare's play of postmodern inter-relationships *Six Degrees of Separation*. Wolfe comments on the plays's titular reference to the interconnections among everyone on the globe as ultimately "comforting" in "the implication that gaps between people are *contingent* rather than fundamental. Wolfe examines Guare's central motif as itself a self-conscious exploration of intertextuality, arguing the play "encourages us to explore both our desire for connections and the complex ways in which connections evoke desire." This recognition demands, as Wolfe proves, an interpretation employing tools of psychoanalysis and critical theory from Slavoj Žižek and Jaques Lacan "to show how an intertextual approach to *Six Degrees of Separation* enables and encourages us to complicate existing assessments of its engagement with social unity, interconnection, and love in a fractured world."

Having begun this collection with auspicious essays on the founder of the modern American theatre, Eugene O'Neill, it seems appropriate to close the collection with a study about his colleague from the Provincetown Players, Susan Glaspell. Sharon Friedman provides an extended interpretation of Glaspell's treatment of American nationalism, showing how the political and social contexts of American xenophobia just after the First World War prove to be radical intertexts for the playwright. Friedman notes the presence in Glaspell's work of three major waves of ideologies: "nativism and the eugenics movement, which fomented anti-immigrant sentiment; assimilation and "Americanization," which demanded undivided loyalty to nation; and cultural pluralism, which sought unity in difference." Friedman argues effectively that Glaspell's response to these discourses is "rendered metaphorically" in a number of her short stories that were published in *Harper's* magazine, and although less well-known today than her drama, frequently featured characters and themes responding to reactionary ideologies which can then be seen "expressed more explicitly in her drama, culminating in her scathing indictment of nativism and repressive American nationalism in her full-length (1921) play *Inheritors*."

Notes

1. One notable previous collection discussing intertextuality in relation to the work of an American playwritght is *Disclosing Intertextualities: The Plays, Novels, and Short Stories of Susan Glaspell*, edited by Barbara Ozieblo and Martha Carpentier (Amsterdam: Rodopi, 2005). Glaspell's work is well represented in the present edition.
2. Wilder, "A Preface for *Our Town*," *New York Times* 13 Feb. 1938: p. X:1.

Works Cited

Allen, Graham. "Introduction." *Intertextuality: The New Critical Idiom*. London: Routledge, 2000. Print.

Barthes, Roland. "The Death of the Author." Trans. Richard Howard. (1967). The Brown University Wiki Service. n. pg. Web. July 21, 2011.

Irwin, William. "Against Intertextuality." *Philosophy and Literature* 28.2 (2004): 227–243.

Kristeva, Julia. "Word, Dialogue, and Novel." *Desire in Language*. New York: Columbia University Press, 1980. 64–91. Print.

Mai, Hans-Peter. "Bypassing Intertextuality. Hermeneutics, Textual Practice, Hypertext." *Intertextuality*. Ed. Heinrich F. Plett. Berlin: Walter de Gruyter, 1991. 30–59. Print.

PART I
Literary Intertextuality

Section One: Poets

The Ancient Mariner and O'Neill's Intertextual Epiphany

HERMAN DANIEL FARRELL III

In 1923, Eugene O'Neill adapted Samuel Taylor Coleridge's epic poem, "The Rime of the Ancient Mariner," for the stage. That same year and into the next, O'Neill contemplated and worked on other adaptations. One was derived from Mark Twain's novel *The Gilded Age* (Bogard and Breyer 178) and another was based on *The Revelation of St John the Divine*[1] (Ranald 615). In a letter to Kenneth Macgowan in June of 1923, after noting his preliminary work on *Marco Millions* and an outline for a never completed play called *Homo Sapiens*, O'Neill contextualized his work on the adaptations: "I'm sort of 'off' everything else original for the moment" (Bogard and Bryer 178).

This article will examine this particular moment in O'Neill's writing career wherein he willingly diminished his authorial originality in deference to the construction of a "dramatic arrangement of Coleridge's poem" (Bogard, *Unknown O'Neill* 169). This experiment in theatrical devising, directed and designed by Robert Edmond Jones, was concocted of a mash-up of texts incorporating Coleridge's poem, Noh Drama images, cinematic reference, pageant form, the use of masks and music structure. I will demonstrate that this confluence in O'Neill's dramaturgy, wherein he deliberately sought out inspiration from extant sources and played with a variety of forms in one play was of a particular moment in O'Neill's development, an intertextual epiphany in which the playwright permitted the near obliteration of his agency.

I adopt the structuralist approach to intertextual criticism. Susan Stanford Friedman in "Weavings: Intertextuality and the (Re)Birth of the Author" notes "a tendency in American intertextual criticism to ignore or refuse the 'death of the author' as a precondition of intertextual readings" (155). This article does not completely ignore or refuse the Barthesian notion, but it maintains that the choice of "death" of authorial agency remains in the hands of the playwright. This position stands in contrast to the poststructuralist approach of Barthes and Kristeva that "posits the notion of a text which is a 'mosaic' or 'tissue' of quotation without quotation marks, without a preexistent author exercising agency in the construction of that text" (149). This article examines the mosaic or tissue of texts that make up the "dramatic arrangement" (Bogard 169) known as *The Ancient Mariner* while also acknowledging the voluntary diminution of agency by the author in the construction of the text.[2]

Eugene O'Neill acknowledged that his Coleridge adaptation was a pastiche, describing it in the letter to Macgowan in June of 1923 as "a novel form of recitative, pantomime, expressionistic set drama and Norse saga" (Bogard and Breyer 178). *The Ancient Mariner* was O'Neill's first produced adaptation (Wainscott 138), but it was not his initial attempt at a derivative work. At the dawn of his writing career in 1912, O'Neill crafted poems for the New London *Telegraph* that were based on or drawn from poems of well-known writers. The fledgling poet and journalist disclosed the source of his inspiration in the titles of his poems. For example, "'For the Waterways Convention's in the Morning' (With apologies to Rudyard K[ipling]'s 'Danny Deever')" and "'The Waterways Convention, A Study in Prophecy' (With apologies to [Longfellow's] Hiawatha)" (*Poems* 2–6). Travis Bogard, in his study of O'Neill's *Ancient Mariner*, remarked that O'Neill's early one-act plays *Thirst* and *Fog* were written "under the spell of the poem" (Bogard, *Unknown O'Neill* 167).

Throughout the 1920s and into the early 1930s, O'Neill would pen several plays that were based on or inspired by extant literary and/or historical texts. From 1921 to 1922, O'Neill wrote *The Fountain* (Ranald 238), an epic drama loosely tethered[3] to historical accounts of Juan Ponce de León (227). He drafted *Marco Millions* from 1923 to 1924, based on *The Travels of Marco Polo*, "the historical hero's actual account of his journey to the East" (Floyd 57). *Lazarus Laughed*, derived from the New Testament and "Roman history and books on mythology" was researched and created from 1925 to 1926 (Floyd 98). Further, from 1929 to 1931, O'Neill crafted *Mourning Becomes Electra,* inspired by *The Oresteia* by Aeschylus and *Electra* by Sophocles.

The adaptation of the Coleridge poem, however, is particularly unique because of the manner in which O'Neill constructed the work. The text of the play is fashioned from a book containing the poem with stage directions inserted here and there in the margins by O'Neill.

Donald Gallup, who was curator of the Yale Collection of American Literature at the Beinecke Rare Book and Manuscript Library, stated that *The Ancient Mariner* was not published during O'Neill's lifetime (Gallup 62). Indeed, it was first published in 1960 in the *Yale University Library Gazette* in an edition of the text put together by Gallup (Bogard, *Unknown O'Neill* 168).[4]

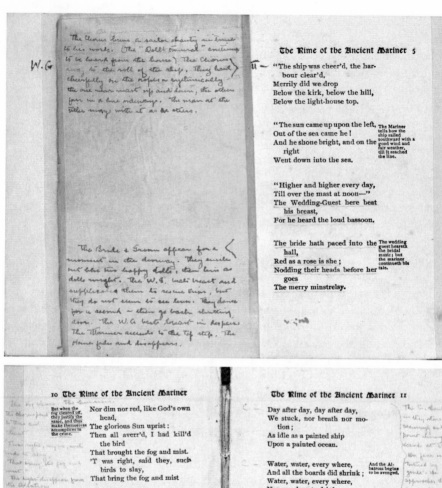
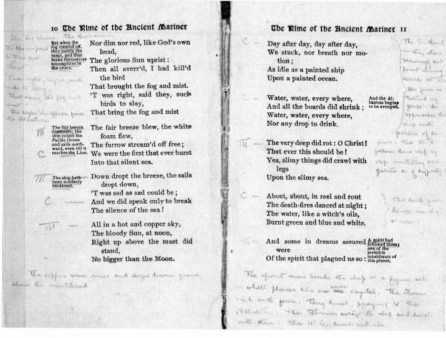

The Ancient Mariner by Eugene O'Neill (Yale Collection of American Literature, Beinecke Rare Book and Manuscript Library, Yale University).

Gallup provided details of the makeup and purpose of O'Neill's marginalia:

> Using a copy of *The Rime of the Ancient Mariner and Christabel* (New York and London, G.P. Putnam's Soons, The Knickerbocker Press [n.d.]) purchased from the Gotham Book Mart, O'Neill pasted in at the beginning two blank leaves and on them in red ink wrote his opening stage directions. In the text of the poem he added further directions in the margins in red, underlined occasional passages for use as supplementary stage directions, indicated speakers' initials in blue or red, and cancelled in red the passages of the poem to be omitted.... [E]xcerpts printed in the *Times* [review by John Corbin] are prefaced by a statement "O'Neill had added no spoken word to 'The Ancient Mariner' in making his 'dramatic arrangement' of that poem." Although this is not strictly true, the additional dialogue amounts altogether to a fewer than a dozen words, plus an occasional repetition of a phrase from the poem, and O'Neill's writing may be said to have been confined to stage directions [62].

Thus, Eugene O'Neill created his only completed and produced stage adaptation in 1923 by merely marking up his copy of the famous Coleridge poem and handing it to Bernard Simon, who was tasked with typing up a working script for the actors. Simon noted to Arthur and Barbara Gelb: "I was one of the few people at the Provincetown who could run a typewriter and also read O'Neill's handwriting" (557). The typed script, apparently, has not survived.

The short dramatic piece, *The Ancient Mariner*, opened on April 6, 1924, at the Provincetown Playhouse and ran for 33 performances, according to Ronald Wainscott in *Staging O'Neill: The Experimental Years, 1920–1934* (138). This relatively short run was due to dreadful reviews and the need to make way for the revival of O'Neill's *The Emperor Jones* that would showcase the rising star, Paul Robeson. *The Ancient Mariner* was placed into the season as a last minute substitute, filling a slot originally planned for O'Neill's *All God's Chillin Got Wings* that would also feature Robeson. That play had suffered from the loss of its other lead, Mary Blair, to illness and was embroiled in controversy throughout the early months of 1924. Conservative reactionaries and the tabloid press were having a field day with the subject of O'Neill's drama: interracial marriage (Gelb and Gelb 551–52). The infamous staged kiss between Mary Blair and Paul Robeson would have to wait until May 15, 1924, after *The Ancient Mariner* and *Emperor Jones* closed at the Provincetown (Wainscott 147).

This was not the same Provincetown entity that had discovered O'Neill in 1916 on Cape Cod and subsequently produced his plays on MacDougal Street in Greenwich Village. That company, including O'Neill as one of its members and headed by George Cram "Jig" Cook and Susan Glaspell, took a break from producing after the 1921-22 season in New York (Williams 166) and ceased operating in June of 1923 when Cook, writing from Greece to Edna Kenton, acquiesced to the termination of the producing organization known as The Provincetown Players. Lamenting the demise of the troupe that he had abandoned in order to pursue Dionysus in the land of the ancient Greek Gods, Cook eulogized

> I am forced to confess that our attempt to build up, by our own life and death, in an alien sea, a coral island of our own, has failed.... Since we have failed spiritually in the elemental things, and the result is mediocrity, what one who has loved it wishes for it now is euthanasia — a swift and painless death [Gelb and Gelb 524].

O'Neill was actually pleased with the demise (Gelb and Gelb 525). He had grown tired of the company's (ostensibly) democratic orientation (Bogard and Bryer 179) and its decidedly amateur orientation.

> In 1923, a new group formed, The Experimental Theatre, Incorporated, using the Provincetown Playhouse. The intent of its leaders — O'Neill, Kenneth Macgowan and Robert Edmond Jones, was to replace Cook's blend of communalism and paternalism with professionally finished productions of a wide range of plays, including new American works, under the new art theatre aesthetic [Williams 166].

O'Neill embraced the notion of hierarchy in theatre — even to the point of supporting dictatorships. He looked forward to working with Kenneth Macgowan and Robert Edmond Jones where he welcomed the idea that Macgowan would act as a dictator in disputes between the playwright and designer (Gelb and Gelb 525). Macgowan described his desired role in the partnership that he hoped would be more akin to an arbitrator than a tyrant: "[O'Neill] suggested that I be the dictator, but I said no, let's have a triumvirate of you, Bobby and myself, and if there's a disagreement, I'll settle it" (525). O'Neill, Macgowan and Jones would indeed come to be known as the "Triumvirate." As Wainscott notes, they would be the most significant experimental theatre organization in the 1920s, only to be rivaled by the celebrated Group Theatre in the 1930s (147).

In January of 1924, the new leadership took over the Provincetown Playhouse on MacDougal Street and launched its inaugural season with *The Spook Sonata* by August Strindberg. O'Neill wrote to his teenage son Eugene O'Neill, Jr., who was attending The Horace Mann School in the Bronx and invited him to attend the classic by "one of the great moderns" proclaiming it "an unusual play unusually produced in an unusual theatre" (Bogard and Bryer 185).

A month later, *Fashion*, the 1845 light comedy by Ana Cora Mowatt, directed by Robert Edmond Jones, was staged by the virgin company and became an unexpected hit. This was the other significant cause for the bumping of *All God's Chillun Got Wings* from its original start date. *Fashion* held over at the Provincetown until it could move to the Greenwich Street Theatre and later uptown to the Cort Theater where it would run until August of that year 1924 (Gelb and Gelb 546). According to Stella Hanau and Helen Deutsch, chroniclers of the history of the Provincetown, *Fashion*'s success sparked a "vogue for revivals" causing nineteenth century American melodramatic war horses to be trotted out, with some success, for much of the rest of the decade (103–04). After *Fashion*, the double bill in early April featured *George Dandin* by Molière and O'Neill's "dramatic arrangement" of Coleridge's epic poem.

O'Neill had two clear aims when forming the partnership with Macgowan and Jones. The first goal was to wield more influence in the production side of his work. In a letter to George Jean Nathan in December 1923, O'Neill playfully queried: "What do you think of our new group? I think we're going to do some really original stuff in the way of production. My ideas are playing an active part here — not like the old P.P. [Provincetown Players] where I simply handed in plays but kept out otherwise" (Roberts and Roberts 52).

O'Neill stated similar thoughts to Macgowan in the correspondence of June 1923 wherein he discussed the scope of and his hope for their new company:

> I'd like to take as active an interest as my work —(meaning actual writing time)— permits. This would mean a good deal more active interest than I ever showed in the old P.P. except during the first year — and even then my participation was alcoholically erratic. Physically and every other way, I feel up to more in a cooperative sense than I believe I ever have before — constructively speaking [Bogard and Bryer 178].

O'Neill's second objective, as suggested by Ranald, was to encourage the work of the directors and designers of the company.

> *The Ancient Mariner* was part of a deliberate experiment in the development of a theatrical experience resulting from the joint skills of designer, director and playwright to create spectacle and a total involvement of the senses of the audience without dependence on the actor or on the text. In effect, then, the playwright would provide a scenario on which the director would exercise his skills, together with those of his costume and set designers [23].

O'Neill elaborated to Macgowan:

> My greatest interest in this venture, as I guess you know from what I've said, would be as a person with ideas about the how and what of production rather than original writing — I mean there are so many things outside of my own stuff that I have a creative theatre hunch about as being possibilities for experiment, development, growth for all concerned in working them out. Perhaps I'm mistaken about myself in this capacity. At any rate, I'm willing to work these out with whoever is interested & pass them on to whoever is interested to act as one part of an imaginative producing scheme [Bogard and Bryer 178–79].

The designer Robert Edmond Jones and the director James Light, acting as co-directors, proceeded with the production of *The Ancient Mariner* under the aegis of O'Neill's "creative theatre hunch" and "imaginative producing scheme."

Jones noted in the program for the show: "The director of today thinks in terms of sculpture and arranges his actors in powerfully expressive groups as a sculptor might wish to arrange them.... The scene designer models with light" (Wainscott 140). And in an article appearing in *Theatre Arts Monthly* in May of 1924, Jones professed his own vision for the future of playmaking wherein the innovative, multi-talented, multi-disciplinary, theatre artist, capable of drawing from multiple media, reigns supreme.

> The theatre cries out to be delivered from the tyranny of the writer, the maker of words. The poet of the future (I see him as a solitary visionary — a motion-picture caption-writer expressing himself in free verse, who has brooded over the inner significance of sound, learned to play the oboe, spoken long with Isadora Duncan and Rodin, visited Russia under the Revolution, and lived in the clear sunlight of the desert) will see in his ecstatic vision the immense, brooding, antithetical self of the world, a completion of everyday incompleteness, the unconscious awakening from the dream of life into a perception of living spiritual reality (as do the modern artists who perceive what is called *significant form* existing, by itself, in space) and this vision will mirror itself in him — whose every effort is indeed to make of himself a transparent mirror — not in a representation of the actual world about him, but in a presentation of light, color, moving form and sound, an abstract evocation and release of desire, a dream that is living with "life beyond life." Through the art of this new Blake, this new Shelley, this new Cézanne, this new Griffith, the vision of the living soul of the world will express itself in a new dramatic form utterly apart from any theatric experience we have known [Jones 323–24].

Without using the phraseology, the process that Ranald, O'Neill and Jones are describing, involving a co-equal joint effort amongst director, designer and playwright, where the playwright contributes "ideas about the how and why of production rather than original writing" and wherein the "tyranny of the writer" is overthrown, is defined in our current theatrical milieu as devising.

In *Making a Performance: Devising Histories and Contemporary Practices* (2007), the authors offer a definition of the term "devising" and identify its genesis:

> In the first book published with an explicit focus on the subject, Alison Oddey's *Devising Theatre: A Practical and Theoretical Handbook* (1994), devising is described in terms that emphasise the oppositional intentions of artists and how their aspirations were translated into creative processes and affected collaborations:
>> Devised work is a response and a reaction to the playwright-director relations, to text-based theatre, and to naturalism, and challenges the prevailing ideology of one person's text under another person's direction. Devised theatre is concerned with the collective creation of art (not the single vision of the playwright), and it is here that the emphasis has shifted from the writer to the creative artist (Oddey 1994: 4) [Govan, Nicholson and Normington 5].

Thus, in the devising process, the traditional playwright-privileged hierarchy is transformed to allow the director and designers more authority in the play construction. It appears that in the process of creating *The Ancient Mariner*, Eugene O'Neill participated in a collaborative effort akin to contemporary devising practices. O'Neill's willingness to subsume his own authority, that is, to diminish his agency as sole author of the piece, is evidenced in his letter to Macgowan where he states his willingness to transcend his "original writing" and work collaboratively "with whoever is interested to act as one part of an imaginative producing scheme" (Bogard and Bryer 179).

Jones made a noble attempt to bring his ideas, as well as the scenic requirements of O'Neill's dramatization, to life in his work as designer and co-director of *The Ancient Mariner*. Only one image of the production survives, a sketch of the mariner's ill-fated boat cowering below what appears to be the skeletal poltergeist of the ominous albatross.

O'Neill's detailed set description and stage directions begin:

> Night — A background of sky and sea. On the right, a screen indicates a house. A door with three steps leading up. A lighted ship's lantern over door. A large window with a semi-transparent white shade. Music from within — Tchaikovsky, "Doll's Funeral March," to which guests are dancing. The shadows come and go on the window like shadowgraphs [Bogard, *Unknown O'Neill* 169].

Wainscott informs us that Jones had extended the Provincetown stage for the production of *Fashion* and notes that the dome constructed by "Jig" Cook for the initial celebrated production of *The Emperor Jones* in 1920, remained. "Jones enlarged the downstage playing area a few feet by extending the apron as far as possible towards the seats. In addition, he added curtained proscenium doors to each side of the stage, a device which he put to full use, especially in *Fashion* and *The Ancient Mariner*" (144). Bogard provides his own illustration of the scenography. "The staging of *The Ancient Mariner* at the playhouse was made stylistically possible by virtue of the plaster dome.... Against the conclave half-dome at the back of the stage, light played freely and actors were to be seen in partial or total silhouette.... Light and shadow, actors in chiaroscuro..." (Bogard, *Unknown O'Neill* 167–68).

Wainscott also states that the light design by Jones was revered by theatre critics for its ability to "surround the actors 'in a luminous, shadowless aether,' an environment in which the characters might sometimes seem 'self-luminous and radiant — important, heroic'" (145). A screen was used for the projection of images of a wedding party within (144).

O'Neill's initial stage directions introduce the use of masks by actors and describe the puppet-like gestures of most of the characters of this play:

> The Mariner stands at foot of steps. His long hair and beard are white, his great hollow eyes burn with fervor. His hands are stretched up to the sky, his face is rapt, his lips move in prayer. He is like a prophet out of the Bible with the body and dress of a sailor.

> The three Wedding Guests enter arm in arm. They are all dressed identically in their festive, proper best. All are comparatively young. Two of them have mask-like faces of smug, complacent, dullness; they walk like marionettes. The third, with the same type of face, is nevertheless naturally alive — a human being [Bogard, *Unknown O'Neill* 169].

Masks, created by James Light, were worn by the actors. They were "inspired by the enigmatic Japanese Noh masks. Light tried to build masks which seemed to alter expression when the angle of lighting was changed" (Wainscott 142).

In the play's program notes, Light stated: "We are using masks in *The Ancient Mariner* for this reason: that we wish to project certain dramatic motifs through that spiritual atmosphere which the mask peculiarly gives.... We are trying to use it to show the eyes of tragedy and the face of exaltation" (Clark 103).

Wainscott notes:

> Macgowan called the production "an attempt to formalize the stage almost to the point of the Japanese No drama." Something of this goal was discernible to [the New York *Herald Tribune* critic Frank] Vreeland, who acknowledged "an almost Chinese simplicity and transparency" in the production's presentation and style [143].

Setting aside the early 20th century American critic's inability to distinguish the differences between traditional Japanese and Chinese theatrical forms, Macgowan's reference to Japanese No drama provides us with some insight as to the rationale by the designers for the use of the masks in the production. Bogard, however, describes O'Neill's own rationale and places this prominent use of masks in its proper context in O'Neill's oeuvre.

> The masks for the chorus, designed by the director, James Light, were O'Neill's first significant use of a device for which he was ultimately to demonstrate a perhaps inordinate fondness. A year earlier, in *The Hairy Ape*, masks had served to dehumanize the mannequin-like denizens of the Fifth Avenue scenes. Their use was suggested by Blanche Hays, the Provincetown costumer, and O'Neill was excited by their effectiveness. He was later to feel that from the opening of the fourth scene, Yank, the titular "ape," should enter a masked world. Masks were to play a large role, not only in his stagecraft but in his understanding of the complexities of human nature as *All Gods Chillun Got Wings* (1924), *The Great God Brown* (1926), *Lazarus Laughed* (1928), and drafts of *Mourning Becomes Electra* (1931) were to demonstrate [Bogard, *Unknown O'Neill* 168].

By way of sound, the audience heard "celestial chords" and "sea chanties" (143) by a six-man chorus — the "first use of a declared chorus" in an O'Neill play, according to Wainscott (142). "The script ... called for [the chorus] to 'sway to the roll of the ship,' 'sing a hymn to a sort of chanty rhythm,' and 'after one staccato scream of horror, fall on their faces'" (142). Bogard, in *The Eugene O'Neill Songbook*, describes how O'Neill incorporated music into the "dramatic arrangement."

[A]lthough O'Neill evidently had a musical plan in mind, his text does not provide specific musical details. He calls for a number of choral effects by the chorus of drowned sailors: a sailor chanty, a "hymn to a chanty rhythm," a hymn for the Hermit, and chants to serve at various points.... No music is specified by title except for that heard at the beginning and end of the play, a small piano piece from Tchaikovsky's *Children's Album*, "The Doll's Funeral March...." The march, whose tempo marking is *grave*, is not music for dancing, but perhaps its lugubrious melody matched O'Neill's conception of the mood of the scene [Bogard, *O'Neill Songbook* 1].

Early in the play, O'Neill introduces the chorus:

[S]ix old sailors wearing the masks of drowned men — bring in the ship from left. Two sections to indicate the bow — two, the bulwarks of sides — one the mast on which a white sail — and one, the tiller.... The Chorus hums a sailor chanty in time to [the Ancient Mariner's] words. (The "Doll's Funeral" continues to be heard from the house.) The chorus sways to the roll of the ship. They haul cheerfully on the ropes — rhythmically — the one near mast up and down, the other four in a line sideways. The man at the tiller sways with it as he steers [Bogard, *Unknown O'Neill* 169–70].

Wainscott paints a picture of the movement of the chorus derived from observers and critics of the 1924 production:

Jones and Light kept the chorus busy with often dancelike "pantomimic accompaniment" as they "acted with macabre postures" the Mariner's tale. Deutsch reported that the chorus "grouped and regrouped about the tall mast of the phantom ship," supplying, in Vreeland's words, "much of the half-world undercurrent of the piece." Hornblow found "much beauty of motion in the rhythmic movements" [142–43].

The play contained seven episodes and each one faded out like a movie, Wainscott informs us, relying on the account of a reviewer (145). Timo Tiusanen writing in *O'Neill's Scenic Images* also noted that the "sequences" were like a "slow motion picture" (174).

The use of a narrator in the play was a first for O'Neill (Wainscott 141). Observers of the production criticized the mixed style of presentation, complaining that the shifts in narrative point of view went from gradual to sudden making it unclear whether they were witnessing "dramatic narration or narrative drama" (141). Tiusanen weighed in with his own critique: "there is a confusion of the past tense of the action and the present tense of the stage" (174).

Perhaps O'Neill, in his romp through the fields of intertextual sourcing, was layering in yet one more text: the popular pageant-play form of early 20th century America. The use of a narrator describing simultaneous action in conjunction with "interludes of allegorical action using symbolic figures or devices" (Moe, Parker and McCalmon 92–92) was a staple of American pageant drama before and during the time that O'Neill and Jones devised *The Ancient Mariner*. Frank Cunningham, has, indeed, categorized O'Neill's dramatization of Coleridge's poem as "a pageant-play" (1).

The co-director and designer of the production, Robert Edmond Jones,

had experience in the form, having worked on several celebrated and even notorious pageant-plays over the previous decade. Fresh out of Harvard College,
Jones teamed with his classmate John Reed in the staging of the controversial
Pageant of the Paterson Strike at Madison Square Garden in 1913 (Kornbluh 201)
that featured live on stage one thousand silk workers who had marched over to
New York from Paterson, New Jersey, in order to present "a stylized re-enactment
of events in the[ir] on-going strike" (McLaughlin 6). In 1916, Jones designed
with Joseph Urban the sets and costumes for the pageant-play *Caliban of the
Yellow Sands* that was presented in Lewissohn Stadium at City College in New
York City, featuring a cast of 1500, including Isadora Duncan and revived a
year later on a similarly grand scale at Harvard Stadium (Pendleton 148–49).
And Jones designed the costumes for *The Will of the Song* "a two dramatic service
of community singing by Percy Mackaye" (the renowned pageant master) that
was staged at the Armory in Orange, New Jersey, in 1919 (152).

In its time the pageant form, now dismissed for its stilted and prosaic
quality, was embraced by avant-garde theatre artists, according to recent commentators. Rosemary McLaughlin states in her study of the connection
between the silk strike pageant play and leaders of the Provincetown Players:
"the staging of the Pageant anticipates 'epic theatre,' as conceived by Piscator
and Brecht. Before coming to New York, Jones had worked with Max Rein-
hardt, and met with Mabel Dodge's old friend, Gordon Craig. Avant-garde
theatre ideas were in the air..." (6).

David Glassberg, writing in *American Historical Pageantry: The Uses of
Tradition in the Early Twentieth Century* goes further:

> Some dramatists interested in pageantry as a form of experimental theater also
> favored the use of abstract symbolic dance, citing its kinship with the trans-atlantic
> avant-garde theater of Edward Gordon Craig, Isadora Duncan, and Robert
> Edmund Jones, which eschewed realistic representations in favor of presenting the
> emotional essence of a scene [120].

O'Neill was aware of the pageant-play form. His mentor George Pierce
Baker was "active in the pageantry movement" (259) and was the creator of
The Pilgrim Spirit, the Pilgrim tercentenary pageant that was presented in
Plymouth, Massachusetts, in 1921 (264–65). O'Neill's familiarity with this
popular form that was being embraced by the avant-garde may have fostered
his willingness to allow Jones to apply many of the established pageant-play
techniques in the scenography and staging of *The Ancient Mariner*.

As to the writing, or "dramatic arrangement" of the piece, it is not too great
a leap to consider that O'Neill may have consciously or unconsciously incorporated the pageant form's mixed style of narrative presentation into his text.

The pageant form, according to the authors of *Creating Historical Drama*
(2005) very often featured a variety of narration and presentation devices that

they identify as "connective frames" (Moe, Parker and McCalmon 92). This mixed style of presentation is apparent in O'Neill's dramaturgy. One connective frame consists of "interludes of allegorical action using symbolic figures or devices" (92). In Part Two of *The Ancient Mariner* O'Neill introduces a symbolic figure: "The Spirit rises beside the ship — a figure all in white planes like a snow crystal" (Bogard *Unknown O'Neill* 175). Another "connective frame consists of realistic action interludes" (Moe, Parker and McCalmon 93). The opening sequence of the play wherein the Mariner confronts the Wedding Guests is an episode that is steeped in realism. A "third type of connective frame is narration by one who may be realistic or abstract or allegorical, seen or unseen" (93). The Chorus of "six old sailors wearing the masks of drowned men" (Bogard, *Unknown O'Neill* 169) act as narrators and allegorical figures throughout the play.

In light of Robert Edmond Jones's active engagement with the pageant form prior to his work on *The Ancient Mariner* and O'Neill's familiarity with the form, it is not too forward to suggest that O'Neill introduced the mixed style of narrative and presentation of the pageant form into *The Ancient Mariner*.

I would argue that perhaps the inclusion of this particular ingredient in the intertextual melting pot known as *The Ancient Mariner* was greatly responsible for the bad taste left lingering for audience members and critics alike who attended the production in 1924. Pageant plays went away for a reason. They, as Timo Tiusanen notes: "[L]ack 'the life blood of drama'" (142). The pageant play form tends to dissipate the prototypical tension inherent in drama in its overuse of narration and blatant exposition in its visual presentation.

The critics of O'Neill's multi-media experiment were blunt and brutal. Heywood Broun called it "base metal from a cracked test tube in the Provincetown lab" (Geb and Gelb 546). Alexander Woolcott said it was "childish" — a "nursery entertainment" (Bogard, *Contour* 231). The *New York Herald Tribune* headline read: "Ancient Mariner Made Vivid Even for School Boys" (Wainscott 142, note 124). O'Neill's friend George Jean Nathan could not restrain himself from stating that the playwright had deluded himself that he had "made a dramatization, what Eugene O'Neill actually made was a motion picture." Nathan continued: "The weakness of the Provincetown Theatre group, as with the majority of semi-amateur organizations, lies in its preoccupation with lighting and scenery at the expense of drama." Nathan's most salient point was with regard to the pantomime and acting out of the text of the poem. "O'Neill's theory of dramatizing the Coleridge ululation reposed in the typical cinema notion of leaving nothing to the imagination" (Cargill 166). Two months after the show closed, Arthur Hornblow summed up the collective critical opinion: "The haunting beauty of Coleridge's poem is destroyed by dramatization" (19).

This criticism has been echoed by Wainscott and Tiusanen. Wainscott surmised that in the small Provincetown Theatre "the Mariner's visions seemed to shrink almost to pettiness" (147). There was a "too exacting correlation of description and action." Wainscott concludes that the production "zealously tried to literalize much of the fantasy in the poem, to prevent events verbatim rather than through suggestion" (146).

Tiusanen suggests that these experimenters in theatricality, Jones and O'Neill, "presumably believed in the beautifying power of their theatre machinery: it was possible to realize verbal images on the stage, because the masks and lights would 're-spiritualize' them" (173). Tiusanen laments that O'Neill's "basic error was in ignoring the fact that verbal images cannot, without damage, be translated directly into scenic images. When the poem and the Mariner on the stage speak of moonlight and a moonlight is, eureka! created by the light technician, nothing is achieved except a naïve demonstration, an over-pictorialization, disastrous to poetry" (173).

So, *The Ancient Mariner* was a failure, but not a complete one. O'Neill's response to such critical and artistic blowback often entailed perseverance tempered with reassessment. At some point during the year he decided to scrap the Mark Twain and St. John the Divine adaptations and then he turned back to his own original narratives by penning *Desire Under the Elms*. But he did not completely give up his "derivative aestheticism" (149) as Tiusanen describes O'Neill's intertextual interest. "What might be called his adaptations of older plays are really recreations of an ancient theme (*Mourning Becomes Electra*), or 'counter-sketches,'" Tiusanen writes, "they are original plays influenced by more or less distant models" (170).

Providing much more than mere stage directions to the diaries of the infamous sojourner Marco Polo, the biblical passages of the resurrected Lazarus and the historical record of the quixotic Juan Ponce de León, O'Neill would reassert his agency in the process of playmaking as he continued to mine the intertextual field with the development, production and writing of the full length epic plays, *Marco Millions*, *Lazarus Laughed* and *The Fountain*. Learning a lesson from the *Mariner* experiment, in these theatrically grandiose works O'Neill moved away from blatant, overstated correlations between word and image. Indeed, as his career progressed, O'Neill would come to rely less and less on scenic imagery and more and more on poetic language to paint his stage. In the last days of the playwright's progress, O'Neill would evoke the images of his personal epiphany at sea, not by representing a sailing vessel upon the stage but by the mere words spoken by his doppelganger Edmund Tyrone while seated at a table:

> When I was on the Squarehead square rigger, bound for Buenos Aires. Full moon in the Trades. The old hooker driving fourteen knots. I lay on the bowsprit, facing

astern, with the water foaming into a spume under me, the masts with every sail white in the moonlight, towering high above me. I became drunk with the beauty and singing rhythm of it, and for a moment I lost myself ... [O'Neill, *Long Day's Journey into Night*, Act IV].

In these plays, O'Neill was engaging in, what has been termed in the context of film criticism, horizontal intertextuality, wherein an author references texts of another genre (Fiske 87). Here, a writer of drama borrows from and relies on works of history and literature. O'Neill would later try his hand at vertical intertextuality (95), feasting at the same table of fellow playwrights Aeschylus and Sophocles with his pointed allusions to *The Oresteia* and *Electra* in his play *Mourning Becomes Electra*. To riff on this geometric theme, it could be argued that O'Neill's writing in his final years morphed from a reliance on the vertical or the horizontal to an intertextuality that was decidedly interstitial and infinitely recursive. That is, rather than drawing on texts from above, below or beside — he would also interweave texts from within. By the time the Nobel Prize winning playwright arrived at Tao House in Danville, California, in the late 1930s, O'Neill would rely upon a distinct text for one of his greatest dramatic arrangements. The text was his past and the drama would be *Long Day's Journey into Night*.

Notes

1. Eisen briefly describes the unfinished biblical adaptation: "This work begins with the fall of Babylon, concludes with the advent of the New Jerusalem and features such apocalyptic imagery as the Four Horsemen; it combines the stagy lyricism of 'The Ancient Mariner' with the schematized pageantry of *Lazarus Laughed*" (218).

2. This essay is the third in a series that I have written that focus on obscure O'Neill works that were considered to be "failures" at their inception but nonetheless played a critical role in his development as an artist. The paper "Catholic Boyhood: O'Neill's Brief Respite from a Tragic Sense of Life" that examined O'Neill's *Days Without End* was presented at the Seventh International Conference on Eugene O'Neill at Tao House, Danville, California, in June of 2008. The paper "Masking the Truth: The Destruction of Eugene O'Neill's *Exorcism*" was presented at the Sixth International Conference on Eugene O'Neill in Provincetown, Massachusetts, in June of 2005.

3. Ranald notes: "O'Neill takes conscious liberties with historical facts throughout" *The Fountain* (227). And Sheaffer astutely observes that O'Neill was "more concerned with 'the truth' behind Ponce de León's career than with historical accuracy..." (52).

4. The original work, housed at the Beinecke Library, "was acquired by the Yale Library with income from the Eugene O'Neill fund established by the dramatist's widow Carlotta Monterey O'Neill" (Gallup 62).

Works Cited

Black, Stephen A. *Eugene O'Neill: Beyond Mourning and Tragedy*. New Haven: Yale University Press, 1999. Print.
Bogard, Travis. *Contour in Time: The Plays of Eugene O'Neill*. Rev. ed. New York: Oxford University Press, 1972, 1988. Print.

_____, ed. *The Eugene O'Neill Songbook.* 1993. *eOneill.com.* Web. 26 Nov. 2010.

_____, ed. *The Unknown O'Neill: Unpublished or Unfamiliar Writings of Eugene O'Neill.* New Haven: Yale University Press, 1988. Print.

_____, and Jackson R. Bryer, eds. *Selected Letters of Eugene O'Neill.* New Haven: Yale University Press, 1988. Print.

Cargill, Oscar, ed. *O'Neill and His Plays, Four Decades of Criticism.* New York: New York University Press, 1961. Print.

Clark, Barrett H. *Eugene O'Neill: The Man and His Plays.* New York: Dover, 1947. Print.

Eisen, Kurt. *The Inner Strength of Opposites: O'Neill's Novelistic Drama and the Melodramatic Imagination.* Athens: University of Georgia Press, 1994. Print.

Estrin, Mark W. ed. *Conversations with Eugene O'Neill.* Jackson: University Press of Mississippi, 1990. Print.

Fiske, John. *Television Culture.* London: Methuen, 1987. Print.

Floyd, Virginia, ed. *Eugene O'Neill at Work: Newly Released Ideas for Plays.* New York: Frederick Ungar, 1981. Print.

Friedman, Susan S. "Weavings: Intertextuality and the (Re)Birth of the Author." *Influence and Intertextuality in Literary History.* Ed. Jay Clayton and Eric Rothstein. Madison: University of Wisconsin Press, 1991. 146–180. Print.

Gelb, Arthur, and Barbara Gelb. *O'Neill.* New York: Harper & Row, 1960, 1962, 1973. Print.

Glassberg, David. *American Historical Pageantry: The Uses of Tradition in the Early Twentieth Century.* Chapel Hill: University of North Carolina Press, 1990. Print.

Govan, Emma, Helen Nicholson, and Katie Normington. *Making a Performance: Devising Histories and Contemporary Practices.* New York: Routledge, 2007. Print.

Hornblow, Arthur. "Mr. Hornblow Goes to the Play." *Theatre Magazine,* June 1924. Print.

Jones, Robert Edmond. "Notes on the Theatre." *Theatre Arts Monthly,* May 1924: 323–325. Print.

Kornbluh, Joyce L., ed. *Rebel Voices: An I.W.W. Anthology.* Ann Arbor: University of Michigan Press, 1964. Print.

McLaughlin, Rosemary. "From Paterson to P'Town: How a Silk Strike in New Jersey Inspired the Provincetown Players." *Laconics* 1 (2006): 1–23. *eOneill.com.* Web. 26 Nov. 2010.

Moe, Christian H., Scott J. Parker, and George McCalmon. *Creating Historical Drama.* Carbondale: Southern Illinois University Press, 1965, 2005. Print.

O'Neill, Eugene. *Long Day's Journey into Night.* New Haven: Yale University Press, 1955. Print.

_____. *Poems: 1912–1942 (A Preliminary Edition).* New Haven: Yale University Library. 1979. Print.

Pendleton, Ralph, ed. *The Theatre of Robert Edmond Jones.* Middletown, CT: Wesleyan University Press, 1958. Print.

Ranald, Margaret Loftus. *The Eugene O'Neill Companion.* Westport: Greenwood Press, 1984, Print.

Roberts, Arthur, and Nancy L. Roberts, eds. *"As ever, Gene": The Letters of Eugene O'Neill to George Jean Nathan.* Rutherford: Fairleigh Dickinson University Press, 1987. Print.

Sheaffer, Louis. *O'Neill: Son and Artist.* Boston: Little, Brown, 1973. Print.

Tiusanen, Timo. *O'Neill's Scenic Images.* Princeton: Princeton University Press, 1968. Print.

Wainscott, Ronald H. *Staging O'Neill: The Experimental Years, 1920–1934.* New Haven: Yale University Press, 1988. Print.

Williams, Gary Jay. "Turned Down in Provincetown: O'Neill's Debut Re-examined." *Theatre Journal* 37.2 (1985): 155–166. *JSTOR.* Web. 26 Nov. 2010.

"Deep in my silent sea"

Eugene O'Neill's Extended Adaptation of Coleridge's The Ancient Mariner

Rupendra Guha Majumdar

This essay examines the genesis of O'Neill's apparently "unsuccessful" adaptation of a powerful Romantic text, Coleridge's *The Rime of the Ancient Mariner* (1798–1834), staged at the Provincetown Playhouse[1] in New York beginning on 6 April 1924 and closing abruptly on the 26th, with a brief run of thirty-three performances. The "failure," I feel, is deceptive — the tip of an iceberg — for, it points to the potential of a poetical resource that would gradually acquire a mythic significance of sorts in O'Neill's imagination. He seems to have continued to identify with this gothic ballad[2] about a voyager far beyond the 1920s, at several levels of consciousness and form, vindicating his tragic vision of life with a new romantic lyricism in his last plays.

In responding to Coleridge's central poetical statement in his own way, O'Neill acted with characteristic sensitivity, reiterating his position with respect to other similar, messianic evocations like Frances Thompson's *The Hound of Heaven* (1889) and Friedrich Nietzsche's *Thus Spake Zarathustra* (1885). From these works he culled the outlines of conflicts and epiphanies that would reinforce his own creative outlook as a modern American playwright. O'Neill's alienation from orthodox Christianity, his suffering, guilt and prodigal return to a faith reborn through universal compassion, are brought alive in his projection, in different degrees, of the three nineteenth-century texts. But of these three, it is *The Ancient Mariner* whose poetical influence is the most persistent and mesmerizing, something that O'Neill, like Coleridge's Wedding Guest, could not help but acknowledge and manifest.

The Mariner's voyage reveals the cycle of the soul-searching journey through an epic vista of ocean and the subsequent reconciliation with the miraculous life of blessed creatures.[3] O'Neill, too, experienced such a cycle of dispossession and regeneration of faith as his plays reveal. He could perhaps project himself into the personae of both the Mariner and the Wedding Guest in a poised dialectic. The Mariner, a prototype of the Wandering Jew, is like a non-tragic Ahab or Hamlet, compelled to venture to the brink of the chasm of knowledge and to return to live in a hell of memories. The Wedding Guest is like Horatio or Ishmael, drawn into temptation to a lesser degree and delegated to chronicle, in a sublimation of language, the frontier experience of the mentor: "Absent thee from felicity awhile,/ And in this harsh world draw thy breath in pain/ To tell my story" (*Hamlet*, V.ii.346). The tendency to present social and poetical states of being dialectically is common to both Coleridge and O'Neill and for the latter is embodied in his theory of masks.[4]

Three decades after Donald Gallup had first published O'Neill's adaptation of *The Ancient Mariner* in 1960 in the *Yale University Library Gazette*, Travis Bogard re-published it in *The Unknown O'Neill* (1988). An understated yet persistent interest in the influence of Coleridge's poem upon O'Neill is revealed in Bogard's *Contour in Time* (1972) which augments the above two editions of the adapted poem through a number of keen observations. The adaptation, Bogard feels, comprises "a silent acknowledgment" to Coleridge from the time of *Fog* and *Thirst*, marking the "first use of a declared chorus" wearing masks in an anticipation of *Lazarus Laughed* (142). And along with *The Fountain* and an unfinished play *The Revelation of John the Divine*, O'Neill had placed *The Ancient Mariner* in the category of "aesthetic" drama.[5]

But it is one comment of Bogard that draws my interest most: "After 1922 the year of his mother's death with the single exception of *The Ancient Mariner*, all the plays reveal some direct autobiography" (*Contour*, 444). It is this "gap" in autobiography, the inverse implication, which interests me as an autobiographical index. While O'Neill's version of *The Ancient Mariner* may not indicate any "direct" autobiography in 1924, a lifelong absorption of the poem's influence is metaphorically manifested in his plays, especially in *Long Day's Journey into Night*, his central autobiographical work.

*   *   *

The influence of *The Ancient Mariner* on O'Neill is by virtue of its combined dramatic, visual and symbolic richness. Most of his one-act sea-plays, those in the *Glencairn* cycle and *Ile, Fog, Thirst, Gold, Where the Cross Is Made*, reflect features of the *Mariner* quite literally — in the atmosphere, characters, images, words, ideas, and the supernatural including ghost ships and walking corpses. The whaling ship trapped in an icy impasse for one year, the predicament of overwhelming thirst in the middle of an ocean and the resulting madness are evident in *Ile, Thirst* and *Gold*. There is also the compulsion of protagonists under trial to unburden the deep guilt of their stifled hearts and minds. "I been eatin' my heart to tell someone — someone who would believe" (*Gold*, 186), exclaims Captain Isaiah Bartlett to his son Nat who, like the Wedding Guest, finally does come to believe but for the wrong reasons. In *Thirst* and *Fog*, O'Neill introduces one of his classic metaphors, the "fog," which was to gain almost a metaphysical lyricism years later in *Long Day's Journey*, an extended memory, perhaps, of Coleridge's poem. Referring to *Fog*, Bogard comments on the poetic anxiety involved: "Coleridge's recreation of the sea's mystery enables O'Neill to project something of the inner quality of the experience he is narrating and to create an appropriate setting for his death ridden Poet" (*Contour*, 27).

It is the Ancient Mariner's compulsive narrative of a Dantesque[6] journey that sublimates the guilt of his killing of the beatific albatross. Such a discourse of dramatic accountability is found in O'Neill's plays as well. He too dramatizes the process of guilt and expiation of protagonists regarding the murder of innocents. Two early plays of his, *Gold* (1921) and *Where the Cross Is Made* (1918), relate, through the story of Captain Bartlett, several ideas and images of *The Ancient Mariner* in a refracted or melodramatic manner. The Captain's gaunt appearance and *"the obsessed glare of his somber dark eyes"* fit in with the description of the Ancient Mariner that O'Neill provides in his introduction to his adaptation: *"He is like a prophet out of the Bible with the body and dress of a sailor"* (O'Neill, *The Ancient Mariner*, 169). Many of O'Neill's protagonists bear this combination of Biblical name and maritime or pioneering appearance — Captain Isaiah Bartlett, Captain David Keeney, Ephraim Cabot and of course, Lazarus.

The Captain in a moment of greed and self delusion commits the sin of compliance in the murder of two innocent deck-hands. His loving wife Sara, devastated by his crime and imminent damnation and insisting that he confess his sins to seek redemption, fatally succumbs to the tension and onslaught of his anger. The idea of a formidable father-figure being responsible for the alienation or madness/death, of a spouse/mother figure — is an autobiographical as well as an Oedipal idea that runs throughout O'Neill's plays. "Would you murder me too Isaiah?" (*Gold*, 176), cries Sarah Bartlett disbelievingly, as her husband, pressed by her relentless moralizing, raises his fist to strike her.

Ephraim Cabot in *Desire Under the Elms* is held responsible for the premature death of his second wife, Eben's mother. Captain Keeney in *Ile* drives his wife to madness by following his own dream. Hickey's murder of his wife Evelyn in *The Iceman Cometh* provides him, it seems, the macabre cause of "authorship" of his own self-enacted play of expiation before he is led to the electric chair. And Mary Tyrone's twilight state of mind and addiction in *Long Day's Journey* is rooted in the conscious lapses of her actor husband. From the fictional murder of innocence, O'Neill returns again and again to his family's inclement hearth.

Coleridge's central symbol of the albatross in the poem, image of innocence, martyrdom and grace, provides O'Neill the metaphorical link between autobiography and an objective dramatic discourse. After all, biographical interpretations of *The Ancient Mariner* have seen the albatross as a loved one —

Sara Coleridge,[7] Sara Hutchinson or even Dorothy Wordsworth — and the Mariner as Coleridge himself. "So I killed her" (241), Hickey declares with grim finality to his mates at the bar. His statement echoes the Mariner's abrupt declaration to the Wedding Guest, "I shot the albatross" (172). In both instances, the adaptation and *Iceman*, the audience shrinks away in horror on hearing the candid confession.

The Mariner's sufferings have also been read as Coleridge's opium addiction and moral collapse that was set right by his return to the harbor of his poetry. O'Neill's lifelong guilt regarding his mother's drug addiction and suffering in connection with his own birth and his father's miserliness could likewise be symbolized in the unjustified and cruel demise of the albatross on the high seas. Ella Quinlan O'Neill could be seen in the same light. The idea of her or O'Neill's (or his brother Jamie's) "return" to a harbor of peace is more wishful thinking than a reality; and yet it is this thought that provides the tragic impetus behind the language and vision of his last plays.

However, the Mariner's Christian path of returning to the harbor before being shrived by the Hermit is not emulated by O'Neill's Captain Isaiah Bartlett. On the contrary, the latter plunges deeper into the abyss his wife had foreseen ("You be lost Isaiah — no one can stop you!" [*Gold*, 157]). He does not ask "pardon o' God or man." In his demonic journey, the captain in his culpability can be seen as connected to the Ancient Mariner on one side, and on the other, anticipating the self-destructive, nihilistic goal of Hickey in *The Iceman Cometh*.

In his conflict between the religious and the atheistic, Bartlett desperately attempts a proxy redemption regarding the fruits of sin he will not let go. He forces his wife Sara to christen his schooner with her own name before it sails to fetch the sinful "treasure," so as to negate the evil eye and solicit a superior force to lead it to fulfillment. O'Neill portrays the irony of the captain's joy and optimism at the miracle of christening his ship by his wife, in the language and imagery of *The Ancient Mariner*: "And when she christened the schooner — just to the minute mind ye! — a *fair breeze* sprung up and come down to blow her out to sea" (emphasis mine; *Gold*, 165); but Bartlett's trials are far from over despite nature's sanction of a speedy, forward motion. Coleridge's mariner also projects a premature optimism, since many hurdles yet block his path:

> The fair breeze blew
> The white foam flew
> The furrow followed free;
> We were the first that ever burst
> Into the silent sea [*Mariner*, II, 103–6].

For both Bartlett and the Mariner, the "fair breeze" indeed blows the ship onward, but ironically for Bartlett to its doom or further trial rather than its homecoming.

In the sequel, *Where the Cross Is Made*, Nat Bartlett's view of life ("Deep under the sea! I've been drowned for years!" [*Cross*, 570]) finally succumbs to the delusion of his father, and they (along with the audience) witness the ghosts of three drowned sailors, water and sea-weed dripping from their rotten clothes, appear before them in the same manner as the dead sailors stood on the deck of the ship, glaring at the Ancient Mariner ("All fixed on me their stony eyes/ that in the moon did glitter" [*Mariner*, VI, 435–6]). In his play, O'Neill projects the Coleridgean atmosphere of the supernatural through the prism of Expressionism that he had featured in the Emperor Jones's mind[8] as the little Formless Fears that confront him in the forest. It is interesting to note in passing that the conceptual resemblance of Nat Bartlett in *Gold* to the Mariner in the adaptation may have prompted the directors[9] of the original production to choose the same actor, E.J. Ballantine, to play both the roles.

"Dead" men walking discontentedly on the stage henceforth becomes a viable metaphor in O'Neill's repertoire as it had been in Gorky's *Lower Depths* (1902) and in the Virgilian atmosphere of *The Waste Land* (1922) with the untimely drowned Phlebas the Phoenecian whom the poet recalls from the depths of myth. An urbanized and existential view of the same metaphor appears with gothic rigor in *The Iceman Cometh* in which, "in the wake of Hickey's teaching," as Travis Bogard observes, "men are left as walking corpses wandering in an icy hell" (*Contour*, 415).

*   *   *

O'Neill's propensity for the Gothic[10] as a dramatic mode is revealed through his intuitive attitude to Coleridge's revised versions of *The Ancient Mariner*. In the portrayal of the approaching spectral ship and its grim inmates in Part III, O'Neill moves counter to the editing scheme executed by Coleridge by choosing to include the very stanza that the latter had deleted in the 1817 and all subsequent versions until 1834 — the one describing the *male*, skeletal figure of Death, preceding the one about the *female* Life-in-Death:

> *His bones were black with many a crack,*
> *All black and bare, I ween*
> *Jet-black and bare, save where with rust*
> *Of mouldy damps and charnel crust*
> *They were patch'd with purple and green* [(III, 181–185), 1798].

> Her lips were red, her looks were free,
> Her locks were yellow as gold;
> Her skin was as white as leprosy,
> The Night-mare Life-in-Death was she,
> Who thicks man's blood with cold [(III, 190–194), 1834].

Coleridge had made the revision to shift the emphasis from Death to Life-in-Death who defeats the Ancient Mariner in the dice game. The shift implied a move away from the conventional Gothic horror ballad to a deeper form of symbolism of the inner psyche, projecting a trying, existential ambivalence of being, the long day's journey into night, a joint attestation of beauty, hope and liberation within the vice of enervating materialism, of "death." This is O'Neill's configuration of tragedy in modern terms. By reincarnating this buried stanza from the 1800 version of the poem, O'Neill reiterates the stress on Gothic dread — a characteristic trend in his early Expressionist works like *The Emperor Jones, Desire Under the Elms* and *All God's Chillun Got Wings*. Coleridge's transcendental vision is a goal that is resolved poetically by O'Neill in his last plays.

* * *

O'Neill's confessional mode reaches gothic intensity through the final dramatic exposition of Hickey in *The Iceman Cometh*. Hickey's self-indictment of the heinous murder of his own wife, Evelyn, is presented with the flair of a seasoned salesman on his last beat. Like the Ancient Mariner ("I know the man that must hear me" [VII, 590]), Hickey returns to the living world of festivity and frolic to find the singular audience for his confession ("I had hell inside me, I can spot it in others" [*Iceman*, 117]), and his deathly visage is recognized by Larry Slade: "I am damned sure he's brought death here with him" (116). In a Nietzschean cycle of "eternal recurrence," Lazarus, Cabot, Edmund ("a ghost belonging to the fog") in *Journey*— all "return" from their respective frontiers of death and despair to be reborn, reflecting O'Neill's return from death — TB and a botched suicide — in his early twenties to narrate his own life-story on the stage.

The setting of the confession in *Iceman* is, ironically, a birthday party, paralleling the wedding feast in *The Ancient Mariner* and the overall structure of chivalric romances in which arduous trials conclude with ritual feasting. It is "the Feast of all Fools, with the brass bands playing!" while "ships will come in loaded to the gunwales" (I, 9). The idea of a "wedding" is cryptically endorsed in the derivation of the title from Matthew 25:6 which, as Bogard observes, parodies the description of the coming of the Savior: "But at midnight there was a cry made, / Behold the bridegroom cometh!" (*Contour*, 413).

In *Iceman*, O'Neill descends into the depths of a suicidal despair that would induce "any lover of liberty" to "be relieved to die" (O'Neill qtd. in Bogard 418),[11] as Parritt and Hickey so grimly demonstrate. Larry has reached a state where all things signify to him the same meaningless joke, for they "grin" at him through "the one skull of death." The acute alienation of the playwright in a Nietzschean, godless universe, is paralleled in the Mariner's penultimate realization:

> O Wedding Guest! This soul hath been
> Alone in a wide wide sea
> So lonely 'twas that God himself
> Scarce seemed there to be [VII, 597–600].

But in the last two stanzas the Wedding Guest reconciles himself to the severe but uplifting Christian conviction of the Mariner, then turns disenchanted from the feast, goes to bed, and awakes on the morrow a different man:

> The Mariner, whose eye is bright,
> Whose beard with age is hoar,
> Is gone: and now the Wedding-Guest
> Turned from the bridegroom's door.

> He went like one that hath been stunned,
> And is of sense forlorn:
> A sadder and wiser man,
> He rose to the morrow morn [VII, 618–625].

These last two stanzas O'Neill deletes in his adaptation. Why? He prefers a burlesque but pessimistic ending, in which his Wedding Guest, like the denizens of Harry Hope's bar, reverts to the bonhomie and pipe dreams that he had been pulled away from — he "*bolts into the house as if running from the devil*" (190), literally turns into a shadow on the window screen and "dances with the bride," marionette-like, as the curtain falls. The false optimism anticipates the ending of *Iceman Cometh*: "Bejees, let's sing! Let's celebrate! It's my birthday party!" cries Harry Hope (IV, 259), just as the shadow-dance of O'Neill's Mariner recalls the atmosphere of Strindberg's *Dance of Death* and *The Spook Sonata*,[12] plays which reiterate the common image of the unfulfilled hearth. In Act Four of *Long Day's Journey* Jamie quotes from Oscar Wilde's *The Harlot's House*: "The dead are dancing with the dead./ The dust is whirling with the dust."

In the end, Larry Slade becomes identified with his mentor's terminal vision ("I'm the only real convert to death Hickey made here" [258]) just as the Wedding Guest, with a newly discovered seriousness, endorses the Mariner's tale. But Hickey's vision is one of death not of life, a legacy that Larry will manifest in a perversion of the idea of compassion — in his solicited endorsement of Parritt's death-wish.

* * *

In *Long Day's Journey,* Edmund's rhapsody before his father after he returns from his walk in the fog transports him across a vast imaginary ocean reminiscent of the surreal account of Coleridge's Mariner: "I didn't meet a soul. Everything looked and sounded unreal.... It was like walking on the bottom of the sea. As if I had drowned long ago. As if I was a ghost belonging to the fog and the fog was the ghost of the sea" (131). In Part V of *The Ancient Mariner*, the poet writes:

> "I moved and could not feel my limbs:
> I was so light — almost
> I thought I had died in my sleep,
> And was a blessed ghost."

Edmund's lyrical fantasizing in the Coleridgean idiom could be seen as a recapitulation of O'Neill's nascent romanticism revealed in his early sea-plays. Ironically, the sublime, liberating fog becomes alienating when Edmund's mother takes recourse to the same insulation of identity — "a bank of fog in which she hides and loses herself. Deliberately, that's the hell of it! to get beyond our reach ... to forget we are alive!" (139).

It is this inscrutable nature of the fog-as-veil that can one moment reveal the beatific truth of the self and in the next obliterate a loved one that O'Neill, like Coleridge in *Ancient Mariner,* develops powerfully in *Journey.* The Mariner visualizes the albatross:

> In mist or cloud, on mast or shroud/
> It perched for vespers nine; /
> Whiles all the night, through fog-smoke white/
> Glimmered the white moonshine" [I, 75–78].

The fog, like the white albatross, symbolizes the mystery of creation. And in the very next stanza, the Mariner shoots the bird dead in order to penetrate the same mystery, the fog, and the spirit that he literally and metaphysically wishes to identify with. Edmund in *Long Day's Journey into Night* talks about the inscrutableness of a transcendent vision in terms of the fog imagery — "like a saint's vision of beatitude" which simultaneously uncovers and lets fall the "veil of things" to mark his loneliness, "lost in the fog again" (IV,153).

It is the same unworldly, non-gravitational ambience of the fog that makes Edmund prefer the "sea gull or a fish" as his fantasy models of happiness and self incarnation. The sea gull of course brings to mind the albatross which still soars in O'Neill's sky. The conflicts introduced in the early sea-plays are tragically resolved in *Long Day's Journey into Night,* in which father and sons, in the length of one long night, come to terms with their lapses and illusions and are together drawn into the whirlpool of a common fate. The autobiographical poignancy of O'Neill is underscored here as the "return" of the Ancient Mariner from his hallucinatory journey back to his "kirk" and country may denote for the former his wishful thinking about the futile hopes of his mother's recovery from addiction. Her forfeited "return" to her adolescent ideals and her articulation (as Mary) of her loss are revealed in a haunting speech at the end of the play.

I play so badly now. I'm all out of practice. Sister Theresa will give me a dreadful scolding. She'll tell me it isn't fair to my father when he spends so much money for extra lessons. She's quite right, it isn't fair, when he's so good and generous, and so proud of me. I'll practice every day from now on. But something horrible has happened to my hands. The fingers have gotten so stiff — (*she lifts her hands to examine them with a frightened puzzlement*). The knuckles are all swollen. They're so ugly. I'll have to go to the infirmary and show Sister Martha (*With a sweet smile of affectionate trust*). She's old and cranky, but I love her just the same, and she has things in her medicine chest that'll cure anything. She'll give me something to rub on my hands, and tell me to pray to the Blessed Virgin, and they'll be well again in no time (*She forgets her hands and comes into the room, the wedding gown trailing on the floor. She glances around vaguely, her forehead puckered again*). Let me see. What did I come here to find? It's terrible how absentminded I've become... [171].

The game of cards between James Tyrone and Edmund while they sift through the history, cause and accountability of the critical predicaments of both Edmund (in the shadow of TB) and Mary (her potential death through induced addiction) obliquely recalls the game of dice on the ghost ship in *The Ancient Mariner* in which the marginal gloss notes: "*Death and Life-in-Death have diced for the ship's crew and the latter winneth the ancient Mariner*" (III, 15). Edmund, the poet, the sufferer, plays for similar stakes. And so does O'Neill.

* * *

In his protracted engagement with *The Ancient Mariner* through the corpus of his own work, O'Neill may be seen in the context of the Coleridge connection which began a hundred years earlier in the New England Transcendentalist movement in the 1830s. The influence of the Romantic poet on the Transcendentalists Ralph Waldo Emerson, William Ellery Channing and others was initially established through the American publication of his philosophical essays *Aids to Reflection* in 1829 and *The Friend* in 1833 both of which made the crucial distinction between "Reason" and "Understanding." And *The Ancient Mariner* too found a cryptic embodiment on American soil in Edgar Allan Poe's short stories — "Ms. Found in a Bottle" (1831)[13] and "A Descent Into the Maelstrom."

The idea of a sailor returning from the whirlpool of death to achieve a catharsis of confession reaches a pitch in Poe's gothic tale, wherein we register with horror in the end that the narration, in the present tense, is given through the voice of a drowned man whose spirit has hopefully gained peace. The same concern for an expiating peace for their respective protagonists links, through thought and imagery, Coleridge's poem with O'Neill's last two plays. O'Neill's tragic dream for a wishful but impossible rest for his late mother is projected into a prayer — through Josie's lips — for a similar serenity for his wayward brother in *A Moon for the Misbegotten*:

JOSIE: (*Her face sad, tender and pitying—gently*): May you have your wish and die in your sleep soon, Jim, darling. May you rest forever in forgiveness and peace [115].

The universal compassion that O'Neill elicits for the redemption of his misbegotten soul Jamie is similar to that Coleridge bestows on his Mariner; and in each case the dominant symbol of that love and compassion is the *moon*. As the Mariner looks at the moonscape, the sea creatures that he had earlier despised ("the thousand slimy things") become transformed with grace and he blesses them "unaware" after "a spring of love gushed from [his] heart" (IV, 21). The gloss in the margin states, *"By the light of the moon he beholdeth God's creatures of the great calm.'"* In the next moment he can pray and the albatross falls off from his neck in a sign of absolution. The curse is expiated and the moon is viewed as the eternal love of god.

In *A Moon for the Misbegotten*, O'Neill brings the balm of compassion to an exhausted and disillusioned Jamie through Josie Hogan. She finally realizes the import of her role in the moonlight that becomes identified with her. She, the earth mother, has the power to "raise" the dead through her love: "It was my mistake. I thought there was still hope. I didn't know he'd died already — that it was a damned soul coming to me in the moonlight to confess and be forgiven and find peace for a night" (104). She bestows that blessing on Jamie as he departs down the moonlit road.

As with the Ancient Mariner, the Wedding Guest and Jamie Tyrone, O'Neill himself wanted such peace and benediction beyond the passion of urban modernity, and he expressed this need in a poem that he wrote in Tao House, Danville, in 1942. He refers to himself as a "quiet" man who lives quietly

> Among the visions of my drowned
> Deep in my *silent sea* [italics mine, *Poems*, 114].

It is a state of being that he had partially discovered and cherished two decades earlier in Coleridge's ballad of *The Ancient Mariner*.

Notes

1. James Light and Robert Edmond Jones staged the work produced by Kenneth Macgowan. Critics like George Jean Nathan and Alexander Woollcott noted the childishness of the production.

2. "It is a late manifestation of the Gothic revival," observes Harold Bloom regarding the poem (207). O'Neill develops his version of the American Gothic mode in relation to the Romantic antecedent.

3. "Blessed creatures" would imply the "goodly company" of innocent beings (like the Wedding Guest), including those redeemed from sin, with whom the Ancient Mariner could share his tale and his necessary prayers, following his mythic trial on the high seas.

4. In his essay "Memoranda on Masks" and in plays like *The Great God Brown, Lazarus Laughed*, and others. A "study in masks" reveals "a drama of souls" of inner reality, constituting "the new psychological insight into human cause and effect ... an exercise in unmasking."

5. The kind of dramatic synthesis achieved that was able to combine the collaborative efforts of designer, director and playwright as ideally visualized by the pioneers: Kenneth Macgowan, Gordon Craig, Robert E. Jones. It was expected to develop a sense of rhythm that affected the audience "much as music does" (Bogard, *Contour*, 424).

6. John Spencer Hill mentions that "the basic pattern of the spiritual voyage from ignorance to self knowledge" in *The Ancient Mariner* is one which is "inspired and sustained by the example of Homer, Virgil and especially Dante" (151).

7. Richard Holmes writes about the absurdities of literal interpretation by citing the Ken Russel psycho-biographic film on Coleridge made in 1977 in which the albatross is depicted as Mrs. Coleridge draped around the poet's neck!

8. O'Neill, *The Emperor Jones* (1921).

9. Homer Saint-Gaudens and James Light. Ostensibly the British actor Ballentine was not featured in any other O'Neill play.

10. Edgar Allan Poe also maximized the Gothic component of Coleridge's influence in his *Ms. Found in a Bottle*, referred to later in this paper.

11. O'Neill's letter to Langer from Tao House, 11 September 1939 (qtd. in Bogard 418).

12. O'Neill refers to *The Spook Sonata* in his essay on Strindberg and the Theatre (1923): "One of the most difficult of Strindberg's "behind-life" (if I may coin the term) plays to interpret with insight and distinction — but the difficult is properly our special task, or we have no good reason for existing. Truth, in the theatre as in life, is eternally difficult, just as the easy is the everlasting lie." The mystery of life emerges through the ongoing differentiation between illusion and reality, the kind of narrative that hypnotically draws the Wedding Guest to the Mariner in the minds of both O'Neill and Coleridge.

13. "At times we gasped for breath at an elevation beyond the albatross — at times became dizzy with the velocity of our descent into some watery hell"; and the crew "glide to and fro like the ghosts of buried centuries" (Poe 43).

Works Cited

Barth, J. Robert. *Coleridge and Christian Doctrine*. Boston: Harvard University Press, 1969. Print.

Bloom, Harold. *The Visionary Company*. Ithaca: Cornell University Press, 1961. Print.

Bogard, Travis. *Contour in Time*. New York: Oxford University Press, 1972. Print.

Coleridge, Samuel Taylor. *The Rime of the Ancient Mariner*. Ed. Royal A. Gettmann. San Francisco: Wadsworth, 1961. Print.

Hill, John Spencer. *A Coleridge Companion*. Boston: Macmillan, 1983. Print.

Holmes, Richard. *Coleridge*. Oxford: Oxford University Press, 1982. Print.

Jasper, David. *Coleridge as Religious Thinker*. London: Macmillan, 1985. Print.

O'Neill, Eugene. *The Ancient Mariner. The Unknown O'Neill*. Ed. Travis Bogard. New Haven: Yale University Press, 1988. Print.

_____. *The Iceman Cometh*. New York: Vintage, 1967. Print.

_____. *Long Day's Journey into Night*. New Haven: Yale University Press, 1955. Print.

_____. "Memoranda on Masks." *European Theories of the Drama*. Ed. Barrett H. Clark. New York: Crown, 1965. Print.

_____. *A Moon for the Misbegotten*. New York: Vintage, 1974. Print.

_____. *Poems: 1912–1942*. Ed. Donald Gallup. New Haven: Yale University Library, 1979. Print.

_____. *Six Short Plays of Eugene O'Neill*. New York: Vintage, 1951. Print.

_____. "Strindberg and the Theatre." *Provincetown Playbill*, 1923. Imagination.com. Dec. 4, 2011. Web.

_____. *Work Diary: 1924–1943*. Ed. Donald Gallup. New Haven: Yale University Library, 1981. Print.

Poe, Edgar Allan. *Tales of Mystery and Imagination*. London: Wordsworth, 1995. Print.

Strindberg, August. *A Dream Play and Four Chamber Plays*. New York: Norton, 1973. Print.

Thompson, Frank T. "Emerson's Indebtedness to Coleridge." *Studies in Philology* 22, no. 1 (Jan. 1926): 55–76. Print.

Wainscott, Ronald H. *Staging O'Neill*. New Haven: Yale University Press, 1988. Print.

UNIVERSITY OF WINCHESTER
LIBRARY

A Multi-Faceted Moon

Shakespearean and Keatsian Echoes in Eugene O'Neill's A Moon for the Misbegotten

Aurélie Sanchez

Eugene O'Neill's last extant play, *A Moon for the Misbegotten*, is often discussed as the sequel to *Long Day's Journey into Night*, the playwright's tragic masterpiece. In *Long Day's Journey into Night*, O'Neill revealed the dark secrets of his family, which enabled him to deal with the demons of his past, turning the stage into a place of forgiveness and absolution for Ella, James and Jamie O'Neill, as is shown in the often-quoted dedication to his wife Carlotta. This dedication evokes all the members of the family[1] but O'Neill wrote *A Moon for the Misbegotten* to focus more specifically on his brother's destiny. Indeed, the play stages the last day in the life of Jim Tyrone, Jamie O'Neill's fictional double. Jim is presented as guilt-ridden, consumed by alcohol and remorse because he had defiled the memory of his mother by consorting with a prostitute on the train bringing him and her coffin from the West Coast to New England. Jim seeks comfort and forgiveness in the arms of Josie, a poor farm girl who lives with her father on the Tyrones' stony land and who likes to pretend she has had a lot of lovers. In one fall night, bathed by the moonlight, Jim confesses his sin to Josie, while the latter reveals that she is still a virgin and that she is in love with him. However, this moment of redemption is ephemeral, as Jim already shows signs of premature death. His physical disintegration is noted both in the dialogue, as Josie describes him as "a dead man walking slow behind his own coffin" (23), and in the stage directions.[2] The dialogues in Act IV are regularly peppered with references to religion and with expressions which are usually used during funeral rites, thus foreshadowing Jim's imminent death.[3]

In spite of this tragic epiphany, however, the tone of the play is different from that of *Long Day's Journey into Night*. Indeed, *A Moon for the Misbegotten* opens with a series of comic scenes that last until the end of Act II and only then give way to tragic revelations. O'Neill borrows from different comic genres and offers a multitude of metatheatrical references to the spectator, using farce, New Comedy and the carnival.[4] The comic action and the characterization of *A Moon for the Misbegotten* are also permeated by numerous intertextual echoes. Each of these echoes deserves to be developed, but this article will focus specifically on the structure of the play, through a comparison with William Shakespeare's archetypal festive comedy, *A Midsummer Night's Dream*, and romantic symbolism in the form of references to the moonlight in Keats's odes.

In spite of the realistic fabric of O'Neill's play, one finds echoes of Shakespeare in *A Moon for the Misbegotten*. Like *Midsummer Night's Dream*, O'Neill's play is characterized by comic reversals and metamorphoses, and in both works the moon plays a central role, pinpointing the instability of the plot and of the characters. The *chiaroscuro* of the night and the moonlight crystallizes the tension between slice-of-life realism and uncanny defamiliarization. It reveals the characters' prosaic desires, but also their hidden, intimate secrets. The dim light of the moon has a suggestive power and transports the characters out of everyday life. It transforms the stage into a strange realm and into a poetic shelter where time is suspended and where the spectators are invited to see through darkness and through the characters' appearances. In this respect, the night and the moon conjure up a melancholy mood that is reminiscent of John Keats's romantic vision. Keats's poetry is quoted once, but its influence can be felt throughout the play. The protean function of the moon and the intermingling of light and darkness accompany the shift from comedy to melancholy that characterizes *A Moon for the Misbegotten*. Furthermore, the central position of the moon and the defamiliarizing process that one finds in Shakespeare's and O'Neill's plays are also present in Keats's odes, such as "Ode to a Nightingale":

> ... tender is the night,
> And haply the Queen-Moon is on her throne,
> Cluster'd around by all her starry Fays;
> But here there is no light,
> Save what from heaven is with the breezes blown
> Through verdurous glooms and winding mossy ways [217].

Through the moonlight, the echoes of the Shakespearean pastoral are distorted and transformed into Keatsian "verdurous glooms." O'Neill's interstice between comedy and melancholy is thus illustrated by the passing from light to darkness.

A Moon for the Misbegotten is defined by a generic oscillation that Barbara Gelb expresses in the following terms:

> Rather than inhabiting the realistic setting of "Long Day's Journey," which closely mirrors the life of O'Neill's brother, the Jim Tyrone of "A Moon for the Misbegot-

ten" materializes amid a twisted fable that is part tragedy, part raucous comedy and part miracle play ["A Second Look"].

Shakespeare's mechanicals give an oxymoronic definition of the play-within-the-play they have to perform, *Pyramus and Thisby*. Their definition can apply not only to *A Midsummer Night's Dream* as a whole, but also to *A Moon for the Misbegotten*:

> QUINCE. Marry, our play is — the most lamentable comedy, and most cruel death of Pyramus and Thisby [I, 2].
> PHILOSTRATE. Merry and tragical! Tedious and brief! That is, hot ice and wondrous strange snow! [V, 1].

The blending of comedy and tragedy evoked by the mechanicals echoes O'Neill's view of the comic. According to the American playwright, comedy bears the seeds of tragedy and constitutes a prelude to a blunt, uncompromising unraveling of the truth:

> It's struck me as time goes on, how something funny, even farcical, can suddenly without any apparent reason, break up into something gloomy and tragic.... I think I'm aware of comedy more than I ever was before, a big kind of comedy that doesn't stay funny very long [Gelb *O'Neill*, 871].

In spite of the first two comic acts, *A Moon for the Misbegotten* seems to shift toward a more somber view of the world. As darkness falls on stage, the emergence of the moon triggers the appearance of Jim's ghosts from the past and provokes the characters' confessions. According to Laurin Porter, the outpouring of guilt and sorrow leads to a form of redemption:

> O'Neill employs the rite of confession to shape the scene and chooses language with religious overtones. In [*A Moon for the Misbegotten*] the pattern of confession and absolution moves toward a cosmogony, the creation of a new order.... A death-resurrection archetype underlies the climax of *A Moon for the Misbegotten* [100–01].

Although the vocabulary used by the dramatist does point to a redemption, the end of *A Moon for the Misbegotten* can also be interpreted in the light of the Romantic definition of melancholy, edging what Porter calls a "new order" into the realm of spleen and black humor. In fact, the "death–resurrection archetype" outlined by Porter can be viewed as a form of resurrection through poetry, and is similar to that expressed in Keats's romanticism, particularly "Ode to a Nightingale."[5] Thus O'Neill employs the religious terminology to depict a Romantic experience.

The imagery of miracle plays is also present in *A Moon for the Misbegotten*, as the position of the characters in Act III and IV is reminiscent of a *pietà*, with Josie tenderly holding a weakened and suffering Jim in her arms.[6] However, the disappearance of God, marked by Mike Hogan's departure at the beginning of the play,[7] and the connection with nature and with the moon are redolent with images of the Romantic period. According to Denis Bonnecase, "'inhabiting the world' poetically was ... one of the major preoccupations of the Romantics in their phenomenological quest for at-oneness with Nature" (44).[8] Jim's link with the moon illustrates Bonnecase's definition of Romanticism as a fusion of man, poetry and nature that eventually leads to the dissolution of the "I" in the immensities of the world. Under the influence of the moon, the comic metamorphosis of the characters in the Shakespearean first half of the play gives way to a melancholic reversal and to a strangely motionless and almost imperceptible transformation of the protagonists by the romantic end of the play.

A Midsummer Night's Dream is an example of Northrop Frye's definition of "the drama of the green world":

> Shakespeare's type of romantic comedy may be called the drama of the green world, its plot being assimilated to the ritual theme of life and love over the waste land.... The action of comedy begins in a world represented as a normal world, moves into the green world, goes into a metamorphosis there in which the comic resolution is achieved, and returns to the normal world [302].

The pastoral and the green world described by Frye belong to a literary tradition that influences what François Laroque defines as "festive comedy." Festive comedies are comedies of love that stage the meandering of young couples who escape the oppressive patriarchal atmosphere of the city. They enter a pastoral world — most often a forest — where natural, social and family rules are upside down, before eventually abiding by the rules and getting married. The green world is an enchanted, maze-like place where the characters follow a spatial and mental progression (Laroque 205). In *A Midsummer Night's Dream*, the night and the forest witness the adventures of two couples — Hermia and Lysander and Helena and Demetrius. As the two pairs of lovers are interchanged through the tricks of the king of fairies, Oberon, the human world also blends with the fantastic world of supernatural creatures. The structure of Shakespeare's play also relies on reversal and *mise-en-abyme*, through the mechanicals' performance of their play-within-the-play.

Both *A Moon for the Misbegotten* and *A Midsummer Night's Dream* rely on comic metamorphoses and theatrical illusion. The characters in O'Neill's play seem to be part of an elaborate play-within-the-play and act roles they have defined for themselves. Act I stages a series of duets in which Josie, Hogan and Jim alternatively play different parts while one of them stands as the audience. There seems to be no end to illusion as there is a *mise-en-abyme* of lies and pretense, as is shown by Josie's statement to her father: "You've always a trick hidden behind your trick" (17). One after the other, the characters play little scenes, using theatrical codes. The first two acts of the play are permeated with references to farce for example. The sham violence between

Josie and her father, the use of props such as the broomstick in Act II, or the characters' movements that resemble choreography are in keeping with Albert Bremel's definition of farcical acting:

> Comic actors try to appear natural.... No overacting.... [F]arcical acting has little use for such restraint. Because his capital effects are physical, the farceur quickly learns to act unabashedly with his entire body. His acting looks heightened to the point of caricature [Bremel 56].

In *A Moon for the Misbegotten*, the characters' performances always appear as *artifacts*, and the three main characters are akin to amateur actors who cannot produce a perfect theatrical illusion and who are aware of it, as is revealed by Hogan when Josie tries to dismiss her father's acting skill as amateurism:

> JOSIE. [Jim's father] ... always saw through your tricks.
> HOGAN. Didn't I know he would? Sure, all I wanted was to give him the fun of seeing through them so he couldn't be hard-hearted. That was the real trick [17].

In this respect, Hogan is akin to Shakespeare's mechanicals, who cannot perform *Pyramus and Thisby* properly because of their clumsiness — even though O'Neill's character only feigns to be a bad actor. However, whether the characters are unable to act or simply pretend not to be able, illusion is clearly presented as an artifact in both cases and the description of a mock-theatrical creation participates in the comic mood of the play. Even if this inability to perform is accepted, and even exploited by Josie's father — as opposed to the mechanicals, who are mocked at by their spectators — the failure of both O'Neill's and Shakespeare's characters provokes laughter in the audience. Indeed, according to C.L. Barber in his analysis of *A Midsummer Night's Dream*, "the clowns provide a broad burlesque of the mimetic impulse to become something by acting it..." (148). In *A Moon for the Misbegotten*, each character plays at being someone else. Josie poses as a free woman and lover while her father and Jim fake a stereotypical owner/tenant relationship when Tyrone makes his entrance in Act I.

Comic reversals are brought forth by Hogan's attitude towards Harder. As the rich neighbor comes to complain about Hogan's pigs, the farmer completely turns the situation upside down, accusing Harder of trying to kill his pigs and turning the oppressor, Harder, into the oppressed. He also confuses his neighbor by changing the meaning of his sentences, as in the following passage:

> HARDER. Listen to me Hogan! I didn't come here...
> HOGAN. What? What's that you said? You didn't come here? Did you hear that Josie? Well, that's a puzzle surely. How d'you suppose he got here? [38].

Thus, Hogan provokes a three-fold reversal: a social one, a linguistic one, and a reversal of situation. He recalls the Shakespearean clown, who, according to François Laroque, "turns the world upside down":

The distinctive characteristic of [the clown's] language relies on its parodic power and its tendency to turn the world upside down.... All those reversals or changes of meaning that usually signal a lack of understanding ... show here, on the contrary, the presence of a nagging witty spirit that contradicts the official or the sacred discourse [49].[9]

If Hogan appears as a clown or as an amateur actor, he nevertheless cunningly stages the meeting between his daughter and Jim. He is a shifty character and he embodies several Shakespearean figures at the same time. If he is first reminiscent of one of the mechanicals, then he turns into a Puck-like figure, oscillating between mirth and mischievousness. He embodies the duplicity of magic creatures in *A Midsummer Night's Dream.* First of all, he is associated with the figure of the hobgoblin that plays tricks on the neighbors at night:

> TYRONE. [Harder] ... clings to his ice pond. And your pigpen is not far from his ice pond.
> HOGAN. A nice little stroll for the pigs that's all.
> TYRONE. And somehow Harder's fence in that vicinity has a habit of breaking down.
>   ...
> Simpson says he's had it repaired a dozen times, but each night on the following night it gets broken again.
> JOSIE. What a strange thing! It must be the bad fairies. I can't imagine who else could have done it. Can you, Father? [32].

Hogan is thus akin to Puck, who defines himself in Shakespeare's play as a trickster who waits for the night to fall to do some mischief:

> FAIRY. ... are you not he
>   That frights the maidens of the villagery;
>   Skim milk, and sometimes labour in the quern,
>   And bootless make the breathless housewife churn?
> PUCK. I am that merry wanderer of the night [II, 1].

If Puck appears as a comic character, his tricks can also be destructive, and he remains an inhabitant of the terrifying universe of the dark forest. Phil Hogan also appears as a morally ambiguous character, as is shown in the following stage direction: "*Hogan surveys* [Harder] *deliberately, his little pig eyes gleaming with malice*" (36–37). Indeed, the use of the word "malice" reveals the duplicity of a character who can be threatening despite a comic aspect and his bonhomie. Likewise, his pig eyes shed light on his two-fold nature, as he seems to belong to the world of wild creatures. The dual aspect of Hogan is also illustrated by the alternation of the words "trick" and "tick" throughout Act I. If "trick" is associated with mirth and humor, "tick" evokes a loss of blood and foreshadows Jim's pallor during the rest of the play. The use of the two words thus sheds light on the lethal potential of tricks, and on their possible connection to evil forces.

No matter how comic and clownish Hogan appears, he can sometimes be threatening and dishonest, as he is ready to use his daughter as bait to obtain Jim's land. In fact, he is like a stage director, turning Josie and Jim into actors in spite of themselves, and carefully planning a "bed trick"—another Shakespearean comic device that consists in attracting a man to a young woman's bed, so that the lady's father can accuse him of ruining her honesty and then force him to marry her. The setting in Act II illustrates Hogan's careful stagecraft, as the lighted kitchen appears as a stage, while Josie's bedroom is the backstage where Josie the actress gets herself ready for her performance:

> JOSIE. I'd better give a look at myself in the mirror. (*In a brazen tone*) Sure, those in my trade have to look their best! (*She hurries back across the room into her bedroom and closes the door*)
>
> ...
>
> (Josie's *door opens. She comes out, a fixed smile on her lips, her head high, her face set defiantly.*) [64].

Phil thus appears as a gifted manipulator, as a trickster staging his daughter's romantic life. Just as Oberon unites his wife Titania to Bottom in *Midsummer Night's Dream,* Hogan wishes to create a grotesque couple, using lies and tricks.[10] The love potion in Shakespeare's play is replaced here by whiskey, a beverage that is supposed to numb Jim. Likewise, the flower that Josie wears in her hair can be read as an echo of love-in-idleness, the plant that Oberon uses in *A Midsummer Night's Dream* to make Titania fall in love with Bottom. However, the two lovers finally turn into a tragic couple. The love story imagined by Hogan becomes a story of sleep and death, and the nocturnal interlude does not end happily, as opposed to festive comedy, which, according to Annabel Patterson, is supposed to end with a return to normality: "Both the archaic festivals and their Elizabethan echoes functioned to reaffirm, through reconciliatory symbolic action, the hierarchical structure of society" (181).

In *A Moon for the Misbegotten*, the father's plan fails and the play does not end with a wedding. The characters' metamorphosis only leads them to darkness and death, turning O'Neill's play into a convex mirror in which is reflected not the typical adventures of a young couple in a Shakespearean romance, but rather a tragic story of sleep and death similar to that of Pyramus and Thisby. *A Moon for the Misbegotten* turns thus into what Daniel Larner defines as "a tragicomedy of distant echoes": "O'Neill is not writing tragedy in these [last] plays, but an inverted kind of comedy in which we reenact the dying echoes of a long-forgotten, nameless catastrophe—a tragicomedy of distant echoes" (8). Further, the Shakespearean pastoral world is replaced by the rocky and barren soil of the Hogan farm. Indeed, the play takes place in autumn, which suggests that the characters' transformation can only result in an ephemeral renewal threatened by the arrival of winter—or death. The Shakespearean pastoral fertility disappears and gives way to dryness. The couple on stage has passed the age of reproduction. The apple tree in the background shows that the pleasures of the flesh are no longer accessible to Josie and Jim, and only reminds the audience of Tyrone's original sin. This season also announces melancholy brooding because, according to Robert Burton, "of seasons of the year, the autumn is the most melancholy" (172).

From the 17th century to the first half of the 20th century, melancholy has been defined in different ways.[11] However, the feeling of liberation of the characters at the end of *Moon for the Misbegotten* is redolent of the Romantic definition of melancholy as a mixture of pleasure and pain, as one finds it in John Keats's poetry:

> Keats's heart aches ... because the supreme happiness must end, but the fact of the inescapable end reveals and glorifies happiness. Keats is surprised by joy not because he has found it at the heart of pain, but because he has found mortality to be a catalyst of happiness [Baker 41–42].

According to E.C. Pettet, Keatsian melancholy encapsulates the oxymoronic notion of Romantic brooding:

> The Hamlet mood, and all the various shades of unhappy sentiment, are fundamental constituents of the Romantic temper. Most of the major poets of the period produced at least one important poem that can be grouped with the Ode on Melancholy, and this ode was written by one who ... had luxuriated in a "love of gloom" [qtd in Baker, 55].

In *A Moon for the Misbegotten*, melancholy is embodied by Jim Tyrone. The Keatsian influence is hinted at when Jim quotes from "Ode to a Nightingale" at the beginning of Act II, although the intrusion of the melancholy mood is announced as early as Act I, as the dialogues are peppered with expressions that evoke Eros and Thanatos, such as "The devil would die laughing" (12) or "It's like kissing a corpse" (33). Those lines reveal the ambiguous nature of comedy, which bears the seeds of death and tragedy. Indeed, they introduce the idea of decay and death within an otherwise very cheery and comic dialogue. Alcohol also belongs to both genres. It provokes comic situations, but it is also traditionally associated with the black bile, the bodily humor that causes melancholy.[12] Further, the melancholy mood is also conveyed by Hogan's Irish chant "Oh the praties" at the beginning of Act II:

> (*He only remembers one verse of the song and he has been repeating it.*)
> HOGAN. Oh the praties they grow small
> > Over here, over here,
> > Oh the praties they grow small
> > Over here.
> > Oh the praties they grow small
> > And we dig them in the fall
> > And we eat them skins and all
> > Over here, over here [47].

Albrecht Dürer, *Melencolia* [*sic*] (1514) (Courtesy the Trustees of the British Museum).

The assonance in /o/, the repetitions and the slow rhythm of the song set the tone for the rest of the play. The characters' movements and speeches become slower, and they are overwhelmed by torpor. The verb "mumble" appears more frequently in the stage directions and the pauses between sentences signal a collapse of language. The shorter sentences, the negative expressions and the use of aposiopesis contribute to the creation of a heavy and dense atmosphere.

The shift from the bombastic movements and speeches of Act I to the whispering and stuttering in the rest of the play also changes the mood toward melancholy. The clown of the first half of the play is finally replaced by the fool. Indeed, from Act II onward, the words "fool" and "loon" permeate the dialogues and reveal the negative effects of the moon on the characters. As opposed to the rustic clown who provokes unsubtle laughter, the fool entertains and reveals the failings of mankind at the same time. The laughter that he provokes is sarcastic and bitter, and signals a disturbing movement towards lunacy. Jim's sneers as he appears on stage mark the shift from comedy to sarcasm and irony. Tyrone is described by Hogan as a moody character who has fits of melancholy brooding: "He'll suddenly turn strange, and look sad, and stare at nothing as if he was mourning over some ghost inside him" (21). The mental and physical decrepitude of the character shows that he is a *typus melancholicus*, plagued by a bodily and psychological disease. This twofold nature of melancholy is described by Jean Clair:

> Melancholy is dual. It is an affection of the spirit and a bodily humor. Its name evokes the spleen, a smoke that darkens the thoughts and the face, a veil thrown on the world, sadness without a cause. But it is also physical; it is a visible matter, a material thing, a liquid with specific properties, black in color ... it is the black bile secreted by the spleen [82].

Jim's pose and look are in keeping with the traditional representation of melancholy: "*He sits hunched up on the steps, staring at nothing.... He continues to stare at nothing but becomes restless. His hands and mouth twitch*" (70–71). Jim's position is reminiscent of the famous engraving by Dürer, *Melencolia I*, which is often presented as the archetype of the melancholy figure (see fig.1).

The stasis of the characters also illustrates the physical and mental entrapment that characterizes the melancholy mood, as "*Tyrone starts pacing back and forth a few steps, as if in a cell of his own thoughts*" (72). This immobility contrasts with Josie's all-embracing movements in Act I, as she steps along the stage, thus marking her territory and staking claim to the farm. Her horizontal movement is then replaced by a vertical one, as the two characters fall under the influence of the moon and turn their gazes towards the skies. Jim's entrapment is reminiscent of Jean Starobinski's definition of melancholy as a distorted perception of space:

> Uncertain wandering; entrapment or closure; this is what a whole astrological tradition had in store for the melancholy man, for him who was born under the influence of Saturn.... In captivity and in disoriented wandering, consciousness does not fit in the space it occupies [27].

Josie and Jim also appear isolated. Their estrangement from the world is illustrated by the setting because the farm is not in keeping with its surroundings, and is described in the stage directions as an incongruous rocky spot amid the Connecticut landscape. The house is thus a metonymy of its inhabitants, the misbegotten who do not belong, except in the world of illusion:

> TYRONE. You and I belong to the same club. We can kid the world but we can't fool ourselves ... nor escape ourselves no matter where we run away [87].

The antics and the exaggerated movements and speeches of the first half of the play give way to the unveiling of the intimate space of the characters. The electric light in the kitchen, which is akin to the light of a theatre, is replaced by the *chiaroscuro* of the moonlight.

Because of its inherently changing nature, the moon symbolizes the characters' metamorphosis. As in *A Midsummer Night's Dream*, the moon successively stands for mutability, lunacy and otherworldliness (Suhamy 85). At the beginning of the play, it is used as a prop by Phil and Josie in order to seduce Jim. As a romantic cliché, the moon appears as the witness of Josie and Jim's love play. However, the moon turns into a symbol of sadness when Hogan says to his daughter: "I'd give a keen of sorrow or howl at the moon like an old mangy hound in his sadness, if I knew how, but I don't" (50). Finally, the moonlight defamiliarizes the setting and triggers the characters' confessions. The defamiliarization of the setting is signaled by the absence of temporal ellipsis between Act II and III. Time seems to be suspended and the realistic setting changes as it is bathed by the moonlight and as the characters become more and more inebriated. The moonlight conjures up the ghosts from the past and disturbs Jim's mind, so he utters a remembered quotation:

> TYRONE. "It is the very error of the moon: She comes more nearer earth than she was wont, And makes men mad" [9].

The quote is taken from Act IV in *Othello*, when Othello murders Desdemona. The moon thus has a lethal power and is linked to violence and death. It provokes hallucinations, and confuses Jim who tries to rape Josie, mistaking her for the prostitute he met on the train to the East Coast. His past trip in space from one end of America to another is superimposed on his mental journey towards forgiveness. However, instead of ending in guilt, the night spent with Josie will eventually lead to a form of rebirth. The dialogue between Jim and the personified moon allows him to evoke his mother's death, thus leading to his liberation. As in Keats's poetry, the moon turns the inanimate into the living and brings ghosts back to life.[13] In the following passage, it appears as a projection of Jim's memory, and his mother seems to turn into flesh again:

> TYRONE. She saw I was drunk. Then she closed her eyes so she couldn't see, and was glad to die! (*He opens his eyes and stares into the moonlight as if he saw this deathbed scene before him.*) [95].

However, Jim's terrible vision fades away, and the personified moon no longer appears as an accusing mirror, but as a benevolent face that washes the characters of their sins:

> JOSIE. (*She hugs him more tightly and speaks softly, staring into the moonlight*). She hears. I feel her in the moonlight, her soul wrapped in it like a silver mantle, and I know she understands and forgives me, too, and her blessing lies on me [99].

The moon thus participates in the shift from gloom to liberation as the ghosts from Jim's past and the usual grayness of mornings vanish into a specter of colorful light that bathes the two characters at the end of the play:

> JOSIE. You talked about how you'd watched too many dawns come creeping grayly over dirty windowpanes, with some tart snoring beside you...
> TYRONE. Have a heart. Don't remind me of that now, Josie. Don't spoil this dawn. (*He turns slowly to face the east, where the sky is now glowing with all the colors of an exceptionally beautiful sunrise. He stares, drawing a big breath.*) [110–11].

If melancholy is characterized by numbness and heaviness, it is also linked to the ethereal world and to elevation.[14] This contrast between heaviness and lightness is represented on stage in O'Neill's play by the rock around which the characters gather. This rock symbolizes the heaviness of the melancholy mood, while the bottle of whiskey that lays on it stands for lightness and evaporation. These two scenic elements can also be read as metonymies of the characters, as the rock stands for Josie's attachment and anchorage to her land, while the whiskey signals Jim's dissolute life and dissipation. The imagery of earth and air encapsulated in these two objects also foreshadows the characters' separation at the end of the play, because it sheds light on the impossibility to reconcile two different elements. The presence of the rock on stage thus foretells Josie's destiny. She is bound to her piece of land, while Jim is bound away, as his life, like the whiskey in the bottle, runs out. The elevation of the characters before the final separation is symbolized by the stairs they are sitting on, which show that Josie and Jim belong to an intermediary world, half-way between the earth and the sky. The characters' confessions lead them to a form of lyrical liberation, to the acceptance of death and to a revelation of the ephemeral beauty of the world. This shift is announced at the beginning of Act II, when Jim quotes the famous line from Keats's "Ode to a Nightingale," "Now more than ever seems it rich to die/To cease upon the midnight with no pain/ In such an ecstasy!" (68–69). In the Keatsian ode, the precariousness of the world and the poet's acceptance of his pain allow him to become aware of the beauty around him. Indeed, according to Wilson Knight in his analysis of Keats's poetry, "each image is enjoyed to the full, tasted, before it is let pass, fading with ... a sunset glory" (258). In *A Moon for the Misbegotten*, beauty is also associated with death. In spite of

Jim's terrible confession, the characters become aware of the uniqueness of the night and the lexical fields of beauty and death coalesce, as a faint echo of the poet's persona, "half in love with easeful Death," in the Keatsian ode.[15] The use of the pronoun "a" in the title of the play and the characters' referring to the uniqueness of the night pinpoint the ephemeral and yet eternal aspect of their moment of redemption. The melancholy mood of *A Moon for the Misbegotten* can thus be read as the Romantic experience of death and pain leading to the recognition of beauty. Denis Bonnecase sums up this definition of Keatsian melancholy:

> The subtle experience of melancholy lies in that rare moment when the discovery of beauty felt as permanent joy is coadunate with its opposite of inexorable loss, when the sense of plenitude incorporates that of impending death [84].

In *A Moon for the Misbegotten*, the melancholy mood is first expressed by a death wish on Jim's part, but is then replaced by a feeling of plenitude and peaceful rest. The suspension of time, the defamiliarization of space, and the stasis of the characters go hand in hand with their almost imperceptible but undeniable metamorphosis. The last two acts of the play are characterized by a tension between passion and passivity and by a discrepancy between immobility and movement. As in Keats's "Ode on a Grecian Urn," deathly stillness conceals action, passion and ecstasy:

> Ah, happy, happy boughs! that cannot shed
> Your leaves, nor ever bid the Spring adieu;
> And, happy melodist, unwearied,
> For ever piping songs for ever new;
> More happy love! more happy, happy love!
> For ever warm and still to be enjoy'd,
> For ever panting, and for ever young;
> All breathing human passion far above,
> That leaves a heart high-sorrowful and cloy'd,
> A burning forehead, and a parching tongue [219].

The stillness of the urn that is expressed by the repetition of "for ever" and by the two-fold meaning of "still" contrasts with the lively exclamations that are interspersed throughout the poem. In the same manner, *A Moon for the Misbegotten* oscillates between apparent death and inner passionate movements. Moreover, Jim's journey from guilt to liberation seems to stem from what Wilson Knight calls "a tiptoe effect" in his analysis of the ode:

> The ode concentrates and expands that recurring tendency in Keats to image a poised form, a stillness suggesting motion, what might be called a "tiptoe effect" [294–95].

The oxymoronic structure of Keats's odes seems to be reproduced in O'Neill's play, as it shifts between love and death, movement and stasis, and eternity and uniqueness. Borrowing from Shakespearean comedies of the green world, the American playwright then seems to turn the Connecticut farm into the locus of a "cold pastoral."[16] The multi-faceted moon mirrors the protean form of the play and the metamorphosis of the two main characters. Melancholy is first akin to sadness and pain but turns into a form of lyrical liberation. The explosion of colors at the end contrasts with the usual *chiaroscuro* that one finds in the rest of O'Neill's work. In this respect, the play illustrates Jean Starobinski's assumption that "the thickest darkness offers light a surface to reflect itself" (30).

Notes

1. "... *I mean it as a tribute to your love and tenderness which gave me the faith in love that enabled me to face my dead at last and write this — write it with deep pity and understanding and forgiveness for* all *the four haunted Tyrones*" (714).

2. "*His naturally fine physique has become soft and soggy from dissipation, but his face is still good-looking despite its unhealthy puffiness and the bags under the eyes.... His eyes are brown, the whites congested and yellowish*" (24).

3. "May you rest forever in forgiveness and peace" (115).

4. O'Neill conjures up elements from the New Comedy of Plautus, such as the *senex iratus*, a stock character embodied by Phil Hogan and that Northrop Frye defines as the "heavy father, who with his rages and threats, his obsessions and his gullibility, seems closely related to some of the demonic characters of romance..." (172). The influence of the carnival can also be evoked, as the grotesque appearance of Josie and the social reversal between the Hogans and Harder, the property owner, point at a world that is turned upside down. The farcical dimension of the play is briefly evoked later in this article.

5. Fade far away, dissolve, and quite forget
   What thou among the leaves hast never known,
   The weariness, the fever, and the fret
   Here, where men sit and hear each other groan;
   ...
   Away! away! for I will fly to thee,
   Not charioted by Bacchus and his pards,
   But on the viewless wings of Poesy (216–17).

6. "*He is still asleep, his head on her breast. His face has the same exhausted, deathlike repose. Josie's face is set in an expression of numbed, resigned sadness. Her body sags tiredly.... The two make a strangely tragic figure — the big sorrowful woman hugging a haggard-faced, middle-aged drunkard against her breast, as if he were a sick child*" (101).

7. Described as a good Catholic in the stage directions, Mick Hogan, Josie's brother, can be seen as a symbol of religion.

8. According to Wilson G. Knight, the starlit dome is the symbol of Romanticism (xii).

9. This and the following translations from Jean Clair, Jean Starobinski and Maxime Préaud are mine.

10. HOGAN — Sure, you're two of a kind, both great disgraces. That would help make a happy marriage because neither of you could look down on the other (15).

11. As early as the 17th century, Robert Burton emphasized the complex definition of melancholy. Described as a physical ailment by the Ancients, melancholy was then studied by Freud as a psychological illness stemming from the loss of an object and leading to suicidal tendencies. In the popular mind, melancholy is often described as sadness without a cause. In *A Moon for the Misbegotten*, melancholy is presented in these three ways, but this article will focus mainly on the Romantic definition of melancholy.

12. "To whom is sorrow ... to whom is woe, but to such a one as loves drink? It causeth

torture and bitterness of mind.... [I]t makes sound men sick and sad and wise men mad.... Drink causeth mirth, and drink causeth sorrow..." (Burton 291).

13. "Thou dost bless everywhere, with silver lip/Kissing dead things to life" (Keats, *Endymion*).

14. "It is his [the melancholy man's] primordial characteristic: this ability to stand at the frontier between the two realms, heavily and painfully bogged down in the material world on the one hand, and flying according to his fancy, wherever the spirit blows, on the other" (Préaud 229).

15. "Darkling, I listen; and, for many a time/I have been half in love with easeful Death" (Keats, "Ode to a Nightingale" 217). This line is also echoed in Act IV of *Long Day's Journey into Night*, as Edmund claims he will "always be a little in love with death!" (812)

16. "Oh Attic shape! Fair attitude! with brede
Of marble men and maidens overwrought
With forest branches and the trodden weed
Thou, silent form, dost tease us out of thought
As doth eternity; Cold Pastoral!" ["Ode on a Grecian Urn" 219].

Works Cited

Baker, Jeffrey. "Nightingale and Melancholy." *John Keats*. Ed. Harold Bloom. New York: Chelsea House, 2007. 37–65. Print.

Barber, C. L. *Shakespeare's Festive Comedy. A Study of Dramatic Form and its Relation to Social Custom*. Princeton: Princeton University Press, 1959. Print.

Bonnecase, Denis. "The Aesthetics of Keats: Intensity and Gusto, Beauty and Truth." *Keats ou le sortilège des mots*. Ed. Christian La Cassagnère. Lyon: Presses Universitaires de Lyon, 2003. 43–89. Print.

Bremel, Albert. *Farce: A History from Aristophanes to Woody Allen*. Carbondale: Southern Illinois University Press, 1990. Print.

Burton, Robert. *The Anatomy of Melancholy*. 1621. London and Toronto: J. M. Dent & Sons, 1973. Print.

Clair, Jean. "Un musée de la mélancolie." *Mélancolie. Génie et folie en Occident*. Ed. Jean Clair. Paris: Réunion des Musées Nationaux/ Gallimard, 2005. 82–88. Print.

Freud, Sigmund. "Deuil et mélancolie." 1917. *Métapsychologie*. Paris: Gallimard, 1968. 145–71. Print.

Frye, Northrop. *Anatomy of Criticism. Four Essays*. 1957. Princeton: Princeton University Press, 1973. Print.

Gelb, Arthur, and Barbara Gelb. *O'Neill*. 1962. New York: Harper & Row, 1973. Print.

Gelb, Barbara. "A Second Look, and a Second Chance to Forgive." *The New York Times*. March 19, 2000. eOneill.com. Web. 15 May 2011.

Keats, John. *Endymion*. 1818. Bartleby. Web. 15 July 2010.

_____. "Ode on a Grecian Urn." 1820. *English Romantic Poetry. An Anthology*. Ed. Stanley Appelbaum. New York: Dover, 1996. Print.

_____. "Ode to a Nightingale." 1820. *English Romantic Poetry. An Anthology*. Ed. Stanley Appelbaum. New York: Dover, 1996. Print.

Knight, R. Wilson. "The Priest-Like Task: An Essay on Keats." *The Starlit Dome. Studies in the Poetry of Vision*. 1941. Norwich: Methuen, 1968. 258–307. Print.

Larner, Daniel. "O'Neill's Endings: The Tragicomedy of Distant Echoes." *The Eugene O'Neill Review* 31(2009): 8–16. Print.

Laroque, François. *Shakespeare et la fête. Essai d'archéologie du spectacle dans l'Angleterre élis-abéthaine*. Paris: PUF, 1988. Print.

O'Neill, Eugene. *Long Day's Journey into Night*. 1941. *Complete Plays 1932–1943*. New York: The Library of America, 1988. 713–828. Print.

_____. *A Moon for the Misbegotten*. 1944. New York: Vintage, 1974. Print.

Patterson, Annabel. "Bottom's Up: Festive Theory." *A Midsummer Night's Dream*. Ed. Richard Dutton. London: New Casebooks, 1996. 172–97. Print.

Porter, Laurin. *The Banished Prince. Time, Memory, and Ritual in the Late Plays of Eugene O'Neill.* London: Ann Arbor/ UMI Research Press, 1988. Print.

Préaud, Maxime. "Et sur la tête un oiseau solitaire." *Mélancolie. Génie et folie en Occident.* Ed. Jean Clair. Paris: Réunion des Musées Nationaux/ Gallimard, 2005. 226–31. Print.

Shakespeare, William. *A Midsummer Night's Dream.* 1600. *The Complete Works.* New York: Random House, 1975. 153–73. Print.

Starobinski, Jean. "L'encre de la mélancolie." 1963. *Mélancolie. Génie et folie en Occident.* Ed. Jean Clair. Paris: Réunion des Musées Nationaux/ Gallimard, 2005. 24–30. Print.

Suhamy, Henri. *A Midsummer Night's Dream—William Shakespeare.* Paris: Ellipses/ Collection "Première leçon," 2002. Print.

Trailing Clouds of Glory

Glaspell, Romantic Ideology and Cultural
Conflict in Modern American Literature

Michael Winetsky

A soldier home from the war assaults one of his childhood friends, now a local fisherman. The story is a very strange one. The soldier pushes the fisherman off a great height when they are working together to remove an old willow tree damaged by a storm. Even more strangely, the soldier, lunging at his friend, cries out lines from William Wordsworth's *Ode on Intimations of Immortality from Recollections of Early Childhood*. This puzzling bit of intertextuality is not the only reference to Romantic literature in Susan Glaspell's 1945 novel, *Judd Rankin's Daughter*. In a curious final moment in the novel, there is an equally surprising and arbitrary comparison between a book of short stories written by the novel's fictional patriarch and the poems of Walt Whitman.

These puzzling references to Romantic texts and to the figures of British and American Romanticism become more comprehensible as we recognize them as part of a larger pattern of allusion in Glaspell's oeuvre — an extensive body of fiction and plays written between the approximate years 1900 and 1945. In looking at the larger pattern of Glaspell's career, I will focus on her early and late novels, which are seldom read or taught today, as well as a play from mid-career, *Inheritors* (1922). Glaspell's work that is best known today was written between 1915 and 1922. It was during this middle period that she was involved with the Provincetown Players and that she wrote the one-act play *Trifles* and the short story "A Jury of Her Peers." If Glaspell is known generally among scholars of American literature, it is often for these twin works. Scholars of the American theatre increasingly acknowledge Glaspell as one of its leading lights, but by taking into account a larger view of Glaspell's career, including some of the lesser known novels, we can deepen our understanding of not only Glaspell but what motivated what I identify as the cultural hierarchies of the modern era.

Romantic allusion for Glaspell is a way of negotiating these cultural hierarchies. Romantic allusion in Glaspell's oeuvre follows a pattern which could well be described as the reverse of Marx's famous remark about the repetition of history in the case of the Napoleons in France: Glaspell's echoes of Romanticism appear farcically initially, and then tragically. At first, this intertextuality reflects the wild hope that a religion of humanity might integrate the culture of the university seamlessly into popular American ethics. At last, this intertextuality reflects a sense of loss as literature and university culture become less involved in being the moral compass of American culture, and an intellectual elite pulls away from engagement with popular concerns. As such, Glaspell's references to Romanticism track the evolution of the concept of culture during the first half of the twentieth century in the United States.

Amid the cultural hierarchies of modern American literature, Glaspell is in a unique position: her plays for the Provincetown Players are often considered part of the high modern rebellion from the commercial theatre. Christopher Bigsby is an example of a critic who has evaluated Glaspell's plays according to this criterion. On the other hand, Glaspell's fiction, although seldom mentioned in the discourse on "the middlebrow," bear its distinct characteristics.[1] This unique doubleness has often left us with more questions than answers. For instance, J. Ellen Gainor once mused: "how high is Glaspell's brow?"[2] I argue in this article that Glaspell, with her unique position, shows us modern cultural hierarchies in the United States that are pervasive but have received little attention in the discourse that has sprung up since Huyssen's 1986 study *After the Great Divide*, including the privileging of certain regions of the United States over others and the privileging of an aesthetic discourse over an ethical one. The pattern of allusion to Romantic texts and figures in Glaspell's oeuvre provides a quick study of these hierarchies.

German, British, and American Romanticism are all frequently referenced in Glaspell's work. These references take many forms including direct quotation, allusive echo, use of Romantic tropes, and — perhaps most importantly for my purpose — reference to the figures of the Romantic writers themselves.[3] (For the sake of simplicity, my scope in this essay is limited to Glaspell's allusions to British and American Romantic authors. Glaspell regards Percy Shelley and Walt Whitman in much the same way as she would regard William Wordsworth or Ralph Waldo Emerson.) These references constitute some version of what Jerome McGann has called a "Romantic ideology." These references signify the "literature" of a higher purpose. For Glaspell, this higher purpose was usually aligned with philosophical idealism, as will be discussed below. Literature was a prophecy of the ethical ideas of the future.

We know that Romantic ideology was essential to the creation of our modern disciplines of literary studies, as well its canons of "Literature." Terry

Eagleton reminds us, "it was, in fact, only with what we now call the 'Romantic period' that our own definitions of literature began to develop" (16). Jerome McGann showed us that through most of the twentieth century, "the scholarship and criticism of Romanticism and its works are dominated by a Romantic ideology, by an uncritical absorption in Romanticism's own self-representations" (1). To Glaspell, as much as to her contemporary critics who were instituting "modernism" in literature, Romantic ideology offered the standard for what constituted imaginative literature. Since 1983, when Jerome McGann published *Romantic Ideology* and Terry Eagleton published *Literary Theory*, the rise of cultural studies and the increasing reception of the ideas of Bordieu into literary studies have made us rethink what constitutes literature worth studying. Glaspell's oeuvre gives us an opportunity to peer inside Romantic ideology and to understand in a new way what was at stake for a modern author actively negotiating her own place in literature. The new materialist critiques have tried to look beyond the exaltation of literature. However, in the process they have overlooked the place of religion in the structures of cultural capital. Romanticism, as M. H. Abrams observed, meant "the secularization of inherited theological ideas and ways of thinking" (12). This is particularly true of Glaspell whose relationship not only to literature and culture but also to faith and secularity are negotiated through Romantic tropes. By peering into Glaspell's Romantic ideology, we can also get a glimpse of the complete reevaluation in the first half of the twentieth century of the idea of a moral literature within the cultural hierarchies of the period.

Romanticism haunted the coterie of the high modernists, even while they sought to escape it. Edmund Wilson described this reaction in *Axel's Castle* (1931), when he wrote that modernism "thrives in [the] teeth" of Romanticism, that the later school is shaped by its rebellion against the earlier (10–11). Indeed, Glaspell's understanding of Romantic texts may have contributed to her exclusion from the list of writers who for Wilson, and for so many after him, constituted significant modernists.[4] However, like them, Glaspell was reacting to the claims for the imaginative artist that were established in the Romantic period.

Modern writers such as Glaspell could not escape the seriousness of these claims even while they rejected them as materially antiquated and as epistemologically suspect. Floyd Dell wrote in his "spiritual autobiography," entitled *Intellectual Vagabondage*:

> From the stormy mouthings of Byron to the sanctimonious solemnities of Tennyson, they were a bore.... We wanted a literature of our own — books produced by, for and out of the age in which we lived. But there were, quite literally, no such books.... It is true that the kind of Freedom which Thoreau and Emerson wrote about was a freedom far surpassing the Emancipation Proclamation. But we did

not know these things, and there was none to tell us... We had heard so much about the Civil War in those early years that we thought we never wanted to hear anything connected with it again. The fact that this part of American literature had something to do with Slavery was enough to scare us away from it ... [106; 108; 116].

This passage reveals the doubleness of the modern writer's relationship to Romanticism. On the one hand, we can note the modern writer's antipathy to the past. Dell could not appreciate Emerson on Thoreau, when he was younger, because American Romantics were too bound up in the history of the Civil War. We recall here the famous line from Joyce's *Ulysses*, in which Stephen Dedalus aphorizes that "history ... is a nightmare from which [he] is trying to awake," or Ezra Pound's famous injunction to "make it new" (Joyce 28). On the other hand, when Dell writes that Emerson and Thoreau "wrote about a freedom far surpassing the Emancipation Proclamation," he is suggesting that Emerson and Thoreau had a kind of prophetic vision, that the American Romantics were, in Shelley's words, "unacknowledged legislators of the world" (508). Emerson cultivates this notion of the poet, writing such words as "the birth of a poet is the principle event in chronology." Or, Emerson writes that Shakespeare "cast the standard of humanity some furlongs forward into Chaos"—"chaos" here referring to the future.[5] The idea is that the poet envisions the kinds of new ways of thinking and the kinds of ethical standards that then over the period of many years take on a wider cultural appreciation. The philosophical idealism of the Romantic writers was appealing to Dell as well as Glaspell and they were drawn to this idea of literature and its social role. However, they also knew that the time they lived in and the media of their writing were very different from the post–Civil War era. Romantic writing, if it successfully signifies "non-alienated labour," predates the mass market in which they found themselves operating (Eagleton 17).

For this reason, Romantic ideology is often figured in modern American writing comedically. For example, Wallace Stevens' "Comedian as the Letter C," transposes a Byronic hero of the sea, such as Childe Harold, with the hero of bourgeois domesticity that is Crispin with his "Nice Shady Home ... And Daughters with Curls" (Stevens 32 ; 35).[6] Seriously as these modern American writers might take the idea of the literary artist as visionary, they were living in a fully industrialized economy. Romantic literature with its ethereality, its solitude, its pre-industrial individualism no longer made sense. Still, the writing of visionary ideals was appealing, but its appeal was ironic: materialism was supposed to shut down the possibility of visionary idealism, but, contrary to expectation, this idealism was achievable precisely through accepting materialism as the precondition to the ideal — as we will see in Glaspell's case.

Glaspell's first novel, *The Glory of the Conquered* (1909) is full of this humor,

which reveals, even as it seeks to disguise, the seriousness of her vision. This
novel tells the story of a married couple: Karl Hubers and Ernestine Stanley.
Karl and Ernestine themselves are idealized figures. Karl is a medical researcher
at the University of Chicago who is expected to cure cancer; Ernestine is a promising painter who has just had her first successful showing of a painting in a Paris
salon. The subtitle of the novel is "the story of a great love." Their union is not
merely a union between individuals, but a kind of ideal union of science and
art that is the vision of the work. The novel's title chapter features the couple
setting up house. The couple is, to borrow a phrase from Walter Benjamin,
"unpacking the library." They are joined by some friends, Dr. Parkman, a
physician, and Georgia McCormick, a newspaper-writer. We see in this scene
an irreverence and a sense of play in how Glaspell regards Romantic texts. At
the same time, the scene clearly shows that Glaspell regarded her fiction,
although it was aimed at a mass market audience, as part of "Literature:"

> "Now here," said Dr. Hubers, picking up a thick, green book, "is Walt Whitman
> and that means trouble. No one is going to know whether he is prose or poetry."
> ...
> "When art weds science," observed Georgia, "the resulting library is difficult to
> manage. Mr. Haeckel and Mr. Maeternlinck may not like being bumped up here
> together..."
> "I think Browning and Keats are over there under the Encyclopedia Britannica,"
> said Ernestine....
> "This function," [Georgia] began [referring to the social gathering in the new
> home], "will make a nice little item for our society girl. Usually she disdains peo-
> ple who do not live on the Lake Shore Drive, but she will have to admit there is
> snap in this 'Dr. and Mrs. Karl Ludwig Hubers,'"—pounding it out on a copy of
> Walden as typewriter—"'but newly returned from foreign shores, entertained last
> night at a book dusting party. Those present were Dr. Murray Parkman, eminent
> surgeon, and Miss Georgia McCormick, well and unfavorably known in some
> parts of the city. Rug beating and other athletic games were indulged in. The host-
> ess wore a beautifully ruffled apron of white and kindly presented her guest with a
> kitchen apron of blue. Beer was served freely during the evening.'"
> ...
> "Is that last as close as your paper comes to the truth?" asked Ernestine, *piling
> up Emerson that he might not be walked upon* [41, emphasis added].

In this scene, the joke is that the physicality of the book should take on something of its meaning. The characters are playing with the books, experimenting
with which ones go together. I think we can easily see Glaspell, in her debut
novel, shelving her book among these works that, by the critical standards of
her day, commanded more respect. The image of Georgia McCormick pre-
tending that a copy of *Walden* is a typewriter is particularly significant. The
image recognizes that the production of literature is governed by material
forces; at the same time, it suggests the opportunity to reinvent the idealism
of Thoreau in a form suited to the age of mechanical reproduction. On the

one hand, the characters cannot escape the cultural hierarchy of high Literature and lowly society column. Ernestine must make sure that Emerson is not walked upon. On the other hand, this cultural hierarchy is undermined by the patent acceptance of Glaspell's own novel in its mass market commodification expressed in the transposition of *Walden* and the society column.[7] This scene projects the hope that Glaspell will be able to create a mass market fiction that embodies the hopes of Romantic idealism. The ideal of *The Glory of the Conquered* is a more whole culture; it envisions a unity of science and art. The University of Chicago, as it is set up in the novel, embodies this ideal, as it suggested to Glaspell the possibility of a new era in American culture — one in which the Midwest will be its own significant engine of cultural production. Ernestine and Karl are set up as heroes to the readers, passionately engaged in that work.

That hope is characteristic of Glaspell's early work. These humorous Romantic echoes continue to reverberate in Glaspell's writing, and remain humorous through her years with the Provincetown Players, the glory years of high modernism, roughly 1915 to 1922. In the drama *Chains of Dew*, Glaspell invokes Shelley, and makes a joke very similar to that of *Glory of the Conquered*. The play centers on Seymour Standish, a poet, who is also the president of a bank in a small Midwestern town. We can readily see how his character embodies the dichotomy of art and commerce that is central to Romantic ideology. In addition, his character represents a newly emerging cultural hierarchy that Glaspell was in a unique position to comment on — the elevation of the urban center above the small town, and of New York above the Midwest. In the opening act of *Chains of Dew*, Seymour Standish is a topic of conversation between Leon Whittaker, editor of *The New Nation* (an obvious pastiche of *The Nation* and *The New Republic*), and Nora Powers, Secretary of The Birth Control League. Whittaker reads from one of Standish's poems:

> LEON: We're using one of his poems in this number. I have it here. Listen, Nora. It's to Shelley.... "We need you, Shelley. / You whose vision had the power of light, / seeing that gave sight..."
> (NORA, though listening, turns to her machine and it squeaks;) [128].

Again we see the tropes of Romantic ideology such as vision and light, interrupted here by the sounds of the crude printing machine that Nora Powers is using to crank out her magazine. Here, mechanical reproduction is not in the service of the mass market, as it was in *Glory of the Conquered*, but of a political ideology. This was the very realpolitik that was opposed to highbrow literature. In fact, many of the practitioners of the burgeoning discipline of literary studies thought that the study of literature could mitigate the effects of realpolitik (Eagleton, 43). The joke about needing Shelley then negotiates a complex web of competing claims to cultural hegemony. It negotiates conflicts within the values of Greenwich Village. It expresses sympathy with the anti-commercialism of the highbrow literary establishment, represented here by *The Nation*, while it also indicts the political escapism and formal conservatism of this establishment.[8]

At the same time, this joke is an indicator of the larger cultural problem of social geography. Standish's poem is not modern. Whittaker likes it because he feels it is a "passionate cry for freedom," the kind of freedom that is envisioned in Greenwich Village but not practiced at large in the United States. When Standish is asked what his poetry lacks that keeps him from being a great poet, he replies, "perhaps America is the matter with me"(Glaspell, *Chains*, 130). The plot of *Chains of Dew* is driven by Powers' idea to liberate Standish from his midwestern domestic life by visiting him there and creating a scandal for him by revealing his Greenwich Village values. Standish resists this encroachment, trying to protect his wife and his mother from the sexual freedom of the Village. *Chains of Dew* parodies the ways the intellectual elite of Greenwich Village establishes itself as superior to the culture of the Midwestern heartland.[9] Glaspell is very suspicious of this cultural hierarchy, but more accepting expressions of this cultural hierarchy can be found in the work of many of her contemporaries. As Theodore Dreiser wrote in 1915, "What'll we do with the Middle West?" (240). This subject will become an increasing preoccupation of her work and will darken the comic cast of her Romantic reference, giving it an increasingly tragic aspect.

This begins to take shape almost immediately after *Chains of Dew* in another Provincetown Players drama, *Inheritors* (1921). *Inheritors*, which tells the story of three generations in the founding family of a small, Midwestern liberal arts college, directly confronts the cultural conflicts of modernism. The two middle acts of this four act play are set in the college library. There is even a scene in which undergraduates make fun of Matthew Arnold, saying, "old bones could sure spill the English" (125). Arnold's most famous line, "the best that has been thought and said in the world," actually cues the entrance of the dramatic heroine, Madeline Morton, who is described by her fellow undergraduates as "a highbrow in disguise" (126). In this scene, Romantic ideology is still treated with playful reverence. However, a newly grave aspect follows quickly upon it.

As with Standish's invocation of Shelley in *Chains of Dew*, we have in *Inheritors* a character, in this case Professor Holden, looking to Romantic texts for some salutary benefit. Romanticism represents freedom, as it did in *Chains of Dew* and also takes on some of the significance of the unitary view of culture that it expressed in *Glory of the Conquered*. Professor Holden has made public statements in support of a student who refused to fight in the Great War, and who was consequently expelled from Morton College and imprisoned by the federal government. Sadly, this has put him at odds with the President of the Board of Trustees of the college, Felix Fejevary, II, who is trying to obtain an appropriation from the State to expand the college. In this scene, Fejevary finds Holden in the library. Holden is hiding out from the ceremonies of the college's fortieth anniversary founder's day. On the table in front of Holden, Fejevary finds two books:

> FEJEVARY: (looking at the books) Emerson. Whitman. (with a smile) Have they anything new to say on economics?
> HOLDEN: Perhaps not; but I wanted to forget economics for a time. I came up here by myself to try and celebrate the fortieth anniversary of the founding of Morton College. (answering the other man's look) Yes, I confess I've been disappointed in the anniversary. As I left Memorial Hall after the exercises this morning, Emerson's words came into my mind — "Give me truth, / For I am tired of surfaces / And die of inanition." Well, then I went home — (stops, troubled) [204].

Holden is discouraged, and he reads Emerson and Whitman to try to recall the idealism that brought him to his profession. There is perhaps some inaccuracy in Holden's quotation; either Holden, or, more likely, Glaspell was quoting from memory. Emerson's poem, "Blight," reads: "Give me truths / For I am weary of the surfaces / And die of inanition" (139). This quotation from Emerson, and reference to Whitman, along with the reference to Matthew Arnold, are part of a serious confrontation in *Inheritors* with Romantic idealism. When Holden compares the play's fictional character of Silas Morton to Walt Whitman later in this same dialogue, it is neither ridiculous nor tragic. It is plausible not as an accurate reading of Whitman, but to the extent Whitman serves as an emblem of the very Romantic ideology that is confronted in Silas Morton's project of founding a college.

However, it is not at all plausible when Glaspell repeats this move some twenty-five years later in the novel *Judd Rankin's Daughter*, having Judson compare his grandfather's book of short stories, *The Swamp-Neck Jenkses*, depicting life in a small Midwestern town, to Walt Whitman. This comparison would seem absurd, as would Judson's cry of the *Intimations Ode* when he assaults his old friend. But neither of these references are exactly comic. The novel centers on the life of Frances Mitchell, who is the title character. Her father is the author of *The Swamp-Neck Jenkses*. Her husband is a literary critic, based in Provincetown and New York, who is at work on a book on modern poetry. Frances is alienated by her husband's intellectual circle, and she does not feel any greater sense of belonging in her father's world. She wishes both of them would take more interest in the condition of her son, Judson, who has returned from combat in World War II with a new personality. As she is trying to enlist her father's help, she relates the story of her son's unusual recitation of Wordsworth:

"Well, daughter, what are you talking about?"

"Judson. He went crazy. There's no other word you can use. When I came running out of the house there was Judson, high in the tree, arms out as if he were — charging, I thought he'd fall, and he was screaming lines from Wordsworth's ode on Intimations of Immortality, at that time screaming / And by the vision splendid / Is on his way attended. / ... I'll never forget it ... Johnny lying there — Judson up high, waving his arms, and all the time — over and over again — those horrible words."

[Judd Rankin] left his chair, pulled up a smaller one to sit near her. "Now there's some explanation for all this," he said quietly. Something that makes it not as crazy as it seems.... Those words themselves aren't horrible. They're a little highfalutin [sic] but I always kind of liked them" [206–7].

Rankin is correct. The explanation turns out to be that Judson witnessed the violent death of a friend and fellow soldier who was killed while reciting the *Intimations Ode*. Why the *Intimations Ode*? Is this supposed to be the prayer of a dying solider, whose early death meant that he was never separated by age and experience from an eternal divine? The words the soldier would next have spoken were, "At length the man perceives it [his vision] die away, / And fade into the light of common day" (Wordsworth, 359). The stanza that the soldier was reciting is this one:

> Our birth is but a sleep and a forgetting
> The Soul that rises with us, our life's Star,
> Hath elsewhere had its setting,
> And cometh from afar:
> Not in entire forgetfulness,
> And not in utter nakedness,
> But trailing clouds of glory do we come
> From God, who is our home:
> Heaven lies about us in our infancy!
> But shades of the prison-house begin to close
> Upon the growing Boy,
> But he beholds the light, and whence it flows,
> He sees it in his joy;
> The Youth, who daily farther from the east
> Must travel, still is Nature's priest,
> And by the vision splendid
> Is on his way attended;
> At length the man perceives it die away,
> And fade into the light of common day.

Is it Glaspell herself addressing the loss of her hope in the visionary?

The heroines of Glaspell's late novels offer stark contrast to the heroines of Glaspell's earlier work who are directly involved in the arts, in politics, and in the sciences. Like Norma Ashe, the eponymous central character of Glaspell's 1942 novel, who gave up on graduate study at the University of Chicago in order to get married, Frances is a woman just outside the work of cultural production. Glaspell herself never gave up on her work of producing culture. The gestures of that production are repeated even as the meaning of culture changes. This is not the poet beginning in gladness and ending in despondency and madness. Rather, it is the professional novelist and playwright who begins with an assertion of a whole and who ends with a recognition of cultural division.

Notes

1. Botshon and Goldsmith write: "not quite 'vulgar' enough to be deemed low culture, nor sophisticated or experimental enough to be deemed high culture, the middlebrow ostensibly offends the consumers and producers of both" (3). Writers such as Edna Ferber and Anita Loos are frequently discussed in this discourse.

2. The title of Gainor's unpublished paper delivered at the Association for Theatre in Higher Education Conference in 2004 is "How High Is Glaspell's Brow? Avant-Garde Drama, Popular Culture, and Twentieth-Century American Taste." The talk is cited in Demastes and Fischer, 118.

3. "Allusive Echo" might include direct quotation, but it also refers to a kind of looser quotation that might be accidental. It describes a mode of intertextuality in which authors incorporate words and phrases from other authors in ways that appear accidental or incomplete. See Hollander, 60–62.

4. Veronica Makowsky noted this as early as 1993 in her book, *Susan Glaspell's Century of American Women*, observing that "Glaspell's work was facilitated by [an] American literary tradition ... not prized by the pessimistic and elitist modernists, namely transcendentalism" (7).

5. This kind of Romantic ideology will later be recapitulated by Harold Bloom when he claims that Shakespeare "invented the human."

6. The "Comedian as the Letter C" is not always interpreted this way. Yet, clearly its relationship to Romantic ideology fits my description: "These bland excursions into time to come / Related in romance to backward flights.... Contained in their afflatus the reproach / That first drove Crispin to his wandering. / ... So Crispin hasped on the surviving form, / For him, of shall or ought to be in is" (31–32). The prolepsis of Romantic is vision already "backward" glancing. However, the Romantic notion of art cannot be completely abandoned, and remains in "surviving forms," but now instead of the visionary future we have the material present — "shall or ought to be in is."

7. *Walden* is a particularly savvy choice of books, reflecting the book's own materialistic idealism.

8. For more on this conflict, see Wertheim 3–5.

9. This hierarchy has been written about by Susan Hegeman, who establishes the connection between social geography of the United States and the evolution of what she calls "the culture concept" in her book *Patterns for America* (134–146). Hegeman does not mention Glaspell, but she might have. Her discussion of the connection between the Middle West and the Middlebrow would probably seem less labored if she had had reference to Glaspell.

Works Cited

Abrams, M.H. *Natural Supernaturalism*. New York: Norton, 1973. Print.

Botshon, Lisa, and Meredith Goldsmith, eds. *Middlebrow Moderns*. Boston: Northeastern University Press, 2003. Print.

Demastes, William W.. and Iris Smith Fischer. *Interrogating America Through Theatre and Performance*. New York: Palgrave Macmillan, 2009. Print.

Dreiser, Theodore. *A Hoosier Holiday*. Bloomington: Indiana University Press, 1998. Print.

Eagleton, Terry. *Literary Theory*. 1983. 2d ed. Minneapolis: University of Minnesota Press, 1998. Print.

Emerson, Ralph Waldo. *Poems*. Boston: Houghton Mifflin, 1904. Print.

Glaspell, Susan. *Chains of Dew*. 1920. *Susan Glaspell: The Complete Plays*. Eds. Linda Ben-Zvi and J. Ellen Gainor. Jefferson, NC: McFarland, 2010. Print.

_____. *The Glory of the Conquered*. New York: Frederick A. Stokes, 1909. Whitefish, MT: Kessinger, 2005. Print.

_____. *Inheritors*. 1921. *Susan Glaspell: The Complete Plays*. Ed. Christopher Bigsby. Cambridge: Cambridge University Press, 1987. Print.

_____. *Judd Rankin's Daughter*. New York: Lippincott, 1945. Print.

Hegeman, Susan. *Patterns for America: Modernism and the Concept of Culture*. Princeton: Princeton University Press, 1999. Print.

Hollander, John. *The Figure of Echo: A Mode of Allusion in Milton and After*. Berkeley: University of California Press, 1981. Print.

Joyce, James. *Ulysses*. 1923. Ed. Hans Walter Gabler. New York: Vintage, 1984. Print.

Makowsky, Veronica. *Susan Glaspell's Century of American Women*. New York: Oxford University Press, 1993. Print.

McGann, Jerome. *The Romantic Ideology*. Chicago: University of Chicago Press, 1983. Print.

Shelley, Percy Bysshe. "A Defense of Poetry." 1820. *Shelley's Poetry and Prose*. Ed. Donald Reiman and Sharon Powers. New York: Norton, 1977. Print.

Stevens, Wallace. "Comedian as the Letter C." 1923. *Wallace Stevens*. Ed. Joan Richardson and Frank Kermode. New York: Library of America, 1997. Print.

Wordsworth, William. *The Complete Poetical Works of William Wordsworth*. New York: Macmillan, 1899. Print.

On Closets and Graves

Intertextualities in Susan Glaspell's Alison's House *and Emily Dickinson's Poetry*

NOELIA HERNANDO-REAL

"Remember you are an individual and no fool. Nobody's fool," reads the note Harriet Parker, the protagonist of Glaspell's novel *Ambrose Holt and Family* (1931), receives with copies of two books: Virginia Woolf's *A Room of One's Own* and Genevieve Taggard's *The Life and Mind of Emily Dickinson* (*Ambrose* 240). Harriet, like most of Glaspell's protagonists, goes through a process of *anagnorisis*, from ignoring her subservience to her husband to realizing that she needs to have her own identity. As the narrator confirms,

> Harriet did just what was expected of her, as if all the affairs of her life, her own room, had been arranged by others, and the place where she was expected to move was the only place for her. What more could a girl have asked? But she had wanted something more, she could not have said what [62].

In the same manner that Susan Glaspell struggled to have a stage of her own, all her protagonists follow Woolf's dictum to have a room of their own where, furthermore, they can have an identity of their own. Mrs. Patrick confronts men and a very hostile environment to keep the abandoned old life saving station in *The Outside* (1917); Claire Archer retreats to the cellar and her thwarted tower to be left alone in *The Verge* (1921); and even lighter characters such as Dotty Standish in *Chains of Dew* (1920) and Henrietta Brewster in *Suppressed Desires* (1915), co-written with George Cram Cook, need their own places to develop their new identities. While Woolf's influence is felt in the continuum of Glaspell's work, Emily Dickinson's influence materializes very specifically in her three-act drama *Alison's House* (1930), where Dickinson not only serves as a model for one character but where the poet's words also reverberate quite overtly. The note Harriet is given in *Ambrose Holt and Family* summarizes perfectly well Glaspell's interest in Dickinson: for Glaspell, the Amherst poet encapsulated women's need to be considered individuals, one of the main themes in Glaspell's *oeuvre*.

As scholars have noted, the opening of *Alison's House* coincided with other centenary events of the poet's life, and it was assumed publicly from the very beginning, and indeed was used as a means of promotion, that Glaspell's play was a recreation of Emily Dickinson's life. Karen Laughlin affirms that for its first night at the Civic Repertory Theatre, "[Eva] Le Gallienne carefully promoted the play on the basis of the Alison-Dickinson link" (219). Going deeper into the first reviews the play received, J. Ellen Gainor claims that "almost every review of the play featured a comment about the drama being based on Dickinson's life" (223). Robert Littell's direct statement for the *World* exemplified this trend: "For the Alison Stanhope of Susan Glaspell's play read Emily Dickinson" (11).

However, it is also significant that, as Gainor has observed, "the connection between *Alison's House* and Emily Dickinson might not have been immediately obvious to all audiences were it not for the preponderance of early reviews and feature articles in which critics linked the two" (223). Interestingly enough, when the play was revived by the Orange Tree Theatre (Richmond, London) in 2009, the play was again advertised as a recreation of Dickinson's life, including a short biographical note on the poet and some of her poems in the program. In fact, there is no written record confirming that Susan Glaspell wanted to write a biographical Dickinson play. Indeed, the *New York Times* reported her saying that "the play was in no way founded on the life of Dickinson. It grew out of a feeling for her work and character" (qtd. in Ben-Zvi 335), and indeed the importance of the play relies on these influences of "work and character," that the poet exerted on Glaspell.[1]

Though still scarce, the critical studies examining *Alison's House* have discussed some of the parallels that can be found between Dickinson and her fictional Glaspellite counterpart. Katherine Rodier has focused on the similitude regarding Alison's and Dickinson's physical resemblances, their personalities, and the fact that both renounced an "illicit love" for the sake of their families' names. Rodier also mentions that poems 49, 61 and 258 reverberate in Glaspell's play. Ellen Gainor's brilliant analysis of *Alison's House* even provides a chart establishing parallels among the members of the Dickinson family and the Stanhopes. For Gainor, in *Alison's House* Glaspell "suggests more truthfully than does any Dickinson biography from the 1920s and 1930s the emotional and psychological foundations for what we now call dysfunctional family behavior" (222). The reason why Glaspell was able to advance some details of the Dickinson family, which were only made public in later biographies, is that Dickinson experienced what Glaspell herself was forced to endure. In Karen Laughlin's words, in *Alison's House* "a basic tension exists between what women, in Glaspell's view and experience, *are*— that is to say, sexual beings, desiring subjects, as well as creative artists — and what they *ought to be*" (220, emphasis added). Actually, many of Glaspell's plays, from *Suppressed Desires* to *Alison's House*, are built upon this anxiety and portray women who need to be agents but are reduced to subjects under patriarchal dominion.

This basic tension between what women are and what they ought to be reveals one of the most polemical parallels that can be established between Dickinson and Glaspell; this is their stance on the feminist movement. Both artists lived during times when women were challenging their subordination to patriarchal power. In Dickinson's time, at a women's rights convention in Seneca Falls, New York, in 1848, women issued the "Declaration of Sentiments," which asserted women's equality and their right to vote. During the 1850s and the 1860s, several "Women's Rights" conventions were held in Massachusetts, and Margaret Fuller published her *Women in the Nineteenth Century* in 1845, arguing that women should fulfill themselves not in relation to men, but as independent human beings. In Glaspell's era, women were still fighting to gain the vote, and once this was achieved in the United States with the passage of the 19th amendment in 1920, battles still had to be fought towards equality, such as the birth control campaign, or the Equal Rights Amendment, which has not been ratified yet.

Critics have usually had rather negative responses, however, as regards both Dickinson's and Glaspell's commitments to political campaigns for women's rights. Joan Kirkby has said that, given that Dickinson does not mention any of these ground-breaking events in women's history in any of her letters, she did not support them, and Kirkby even claims that Dickinson "did not sympathize with women in general" (166). Supporting this line of thinking, Juhasz and Miller also believe that "Dickinson was not a political feminist" (125). This sounds very similar to Glaspell's case. In a 1921 interview she was asked about her commitment, or rather lack thereof, to the feminist cause. Glaspell had a very straightforward response:

> "Of course I am interested in all progressive movements, whether feminist, social or economic." Again replied Miss Glaspell to a query, "but I can take no very active part other than through my writing. One can't work with too many things," said this most literary radical. "When one has limited strength one must use it for the things one feels most important" [qtd. in Rohe 18].

Emily Dickinson and Susan Glaspell both had their say on feminism in their own medium: their writings. As Helen McNeil has observed, Dickinson's "poems and letters constantly address specifically female problems of identity, fulfillment and freedom in relation to the conventions of her time" (31). Glaspell's works address similar issues; as noted above, Glaspell sought to portray women's need to have an identity of their own.

Interestingly, both women are also linked by their experimentation with form. Dickinson's poems have been praised for their dramatic value. Borrowing Fred White's words, Dickinson's poems are highly dramatic "in the way they construct a virtually Aristotelian problem/situation-crisis/climax-denouement progression" (93), and because they generate dialectical relationships among "purpose, setting, act, actor and agency" (92). Glaspell's plays, in turn, are marked by their poetic quality (Waterman, *Susan Glaspell* 536). Attempts to describe Dickinson's style are destined to be lost in a sea of juxtapositions — her famous dashes, digressions and capitalizations. Indeed, Thomas Wentworth Higginson advised Dickinson to revise her poems, by which he meant that she should adjust them to conventional literary taste. The poet trusted her innovative poetics and refused to do it. This rejection of traditional forms may explain why most of her poems were published posthumously, although even then some very imaginative editors "corrected" Dickinson's style, for instance finishing lines and changing punctuation in early editions of her poems.

The style that was once considered defective is now regarded as a departure from a patriarchal literary tradition and thus an act of rebellion in itself (Stonum 32). Many scholars consider Dickinson's writing an early example of *écriture féminine*, the unique female style of writing that French critics such as Hélène Cixous called for in the 1970s. Similarly, some early critics said that Glaspell was just learning to be a playwright, and that the open endings, the silences and dashes that crowd her plays merely showed her inability to find the right words (Waterman, *Susan Glaspell* 178). Many decades later, scholars have seen in Glaspell's style a forerunner of Beckett (Bigsby 14) and, as in Dickinson's case, an early example of *écriture féminine* (Noe, "*The Verge*" 133). Both Dickinson and Glaspell were moving beyond the margins, "creating something unprecedented" (Sarlós 254), and therefore they could not be judged using canonical (patriarchal) standards.

Glaspell's dramatic form in the case of *Alison's House* is maybe the most crucial issue, given that this play earned her the Pulitzer Prize for drama in spite of certain oppositions (Gainor 238–42). While in her previous plays Glaspell had surprised her audience with experimental forms, such as the symbolism of *The Outside* or the expressionism of *The Verge*, in *Alison's House* she made a sharp U-turn towards realism. According to Gainor, Glaspell "uses the form of the well-made play to depict the moment of its greatest popularity and theatrical strength, the end of the nineteenth century" (241), the time when *Alison's House* takes place. Besides seeking historical consistency, I believe Glaspell consciously made this formal choice to match, as she always does, theme and form. If, as feminist scholars have long warned, realism is "the prisonhouse" of the woman artist (Case 124), then shaping the story of a woman trapped in a house in this form is the most logical decision Glaspell could make.

The house is a highly charged place for Emily Dickinson, as charged as it is for the characters of *Alison's House*. In a letter to her close friend Elizabeth Holland, Dickinson wrote, "They say that 'home is where the heart is,' I think it is where the *house* is" (qtd. in Pollak and Noble 22, emphasis in original). By separating home from heart, the poet suggests that the house of her father, the Homestead, where she lived for most of her life, is "not a place of nourishment, not warm or a hearth, not a place of family love, society or celebration" (McNeil 113). As McNeil has analyzed in the imagery Dickinson creates to refer to the house of the father, this "offers little protection. It is easily invaded by death, objects of fear, or the gaze and acts of others" (113). The house in *Alison's House* follows this Dickinsonian pattern. Alison and Agatha Stanhope die on the premises, the family rejects Elsa, the woman who dared to elope with a married man and "disgraced" the family, and there is the constant fear that those outside the walls will learn the truth about the family: they are not the pious bearers of morality they claim to be. As Louise Stanhope says, "The trouble is, Father, the family has too many — on the outskirts, who like to snatch a little of the sensationalism" (315).

The figure of the house in Dickinson's and Glaspell's works has a correspondence in Freud's *Das Unheimliche*, the Uncanny. The Uncanny, as Freud defines it, "is the class of frightening which leads back to what is known and long familiar" (360). Freud identifies uncanny sensations in the experience of the dead inside the house and in the fear of being buried alive. As McNeil has observed, for Freud the "quintessential uncanny experience for men has been life in his first home, the womb, where he was both himself but not himself, both a whole and a part, inside his mother's body without being there sexually" (140). As the theory develops, men return to this imprisonment in the form of the tomb. For women writers such as Emily Dickinson and Susan Glaspell, the house may become their uncanny experience, the place of their own and not of their own, the place of entrapment where the rules of patriarchy confine women to domesticity.

Of the many poems in which Dickinson explores the gender conventions of the house, I have selected two which I think are constructed upon the same images that Glaspell elaborates in *Alison's House*. Dickinson's "The grave my little cottage is" and "They shut me up in Prose" reinforce the most persistent image of the poet, that of the "private woman who remained isolated" (Martin 1), the "helpless agoraphobic, trapped in a room in her father's house" (Gilbert and Gubar 583). While much has been written lately about the possibility that this isolation was a "positioning strategy that Dickinson herself deliberately adopted" (Bennet 217), the "private," "isolated" woman was the poet's image during Glaspell's lifetime and this is the image, accurate or not, that Glaspell employed to shape her Alison Stanhope.

"The grave my little cottage is" appeared in the 1896 edition of *Poems by Emily Dickinson: Third Series*, edited by her friends Mabel Loomis Todd and Thomas Wentworth Higginson, and "They shut me up in Prose" was published in 1930 in *The Poems of Emily Dickinson*, edited by Martha Dickinson Bianchi and Alfred Leete Hampson, shortly before the play's opening. As Glaspell's biographers tell us, Glaspell studied Dickinson very earnestly to write this play (Ben-Zvi 331–32, Ozieblo 240–41), and it is thus possible that Glaspell may have had the chance to get the latest book of Dickinson's poems, even in the manuscript form.[2] If Glaspell did not have these books in her hands, she could have known about the Dickinson poems in several ways. Mary Heaton Vorse, a friend and cofounder of the Provincetown Players, had grown up in Amherst and became one of Glaspell's main sources of information for *Alison's House*. As Vorse wrote, "Seeing Susan in those days when she was first plunging her mind into Emily Dickinson's story was seeing a creative force at work" (124). Vorse had known Martha Dickinson Bianchi and provided Glaspell with many details about the Dickinsons' family legend and the gossip from Amherst, as well as information about Emily Dickinson's poems (Gainor 223). Barbara Ozieblo also underlines the fact that Vorse was known to be knowledgeable enough to have been a subject of an interview by Genevieve Taggard, for her biography of Dickinson (241). Linda Ben-Zvi surmises that even though Taggard's book was published after Glaspell had completed the play, Glaspell might have read the manuscript or talked to Taggard herself, because Taggard was a well-known figure in Greenwich Village (332).[3]

Dickinson's and Glaspell's preference for the uncanny representation of home can be seen in unsettling images of fear and death associated with the environment that should be thought safe. The uncanny in Glaspell's *Alison's House* is evident when at the end of the first act Agatha sets the Stanhope house on fire and it becomes clear it is neither a safe haven nor a place for the living. The uncanny atmosphere of the place has been suggested in the opening scene; instead of showing the pleasant and comforting homestead it seemingly used to be, the audience sees a fading gray house in a state of disarray as the characters, packing for their upcoming move, throw away the things that once shaped their past. The house is also isolated; the closest city is "about ten miles up the river" (312), and in a description that resembles Eugene O'Neill's *Desire under the Elms* (1924), where the two big elms "appear to protect and at the same time subdue" with "a sinister maternity in their aspect, a crushing, jealous absorption" (28), nature also suffocates Alison's house: "Too many trees make a place gloomy.... And the lilac hedge — shuts the place in too much. What's the use of putting your money in a place nobody can see?" (328). The river, which is usually considered a source of life and a means of communication, here threatens the place: "And with the old Mississippi rising higher every year, seems like she'd wash this place away 'fore we could get dead and buried.... The place ain't healthy.... Seems like the river had something against this place. Right here on this bend's where she washes in more and more" (328–29).

Glaspell also verbalizes the connections between the Stanhope house and death; Alison's nephew, Eben, says, "When I got the first glimpse of the place through the trees I had a feeling of the whole century being piled on top of [Alison], that she couldn't get out from under" (321). From the very beginning of the play, the house is presented, metaphorically and literally, as Alison's grave. It is the place where she died eighteen years before, and this is also the place where she was secluded and buried alive. As in the Dickinson legend, Glaspell tells us that Alison had to renounce an illicit love in order to preserve the honor of the family. Alison obeyed the patriarch and stayed, never to abandon the house.[4]

In considering obedience, burials and departures, in Glaspell's play, it is difficult not to consider the influence of Emily Dickinson's poetry. As McNeil has suggested, "In Emily Dickinson's poetry there are houses from which no one emerges," instead "they are tombs and prisons, or combinations of the two in an uncanny, deathly womb" (122). For the poetic voice of the "The grave my little cottage is," the house is her grave, a tomb for the living, a case that parallels the life of Glaspell's Alison Stanhope. The house/grave marks very clearly the domain of geographical performativity and the gendered politics which operate behind them. I agree with Juhasz and Miller's observation that Judith Butler's concept of the performativity of gender identity clearly applies to Dickinson's poetry. As these scholars claim, "For Dickinson, gender and other attributes or categories of personal identity, such as class, race, and sexuality, may well be socially constructed, but they are constructed upon a core self that 'goes on being,' across time and experience" (126). The only activities that the poetic voice, the core self, performs in this poem are those of "keeping the house" and making the "parlor orderly," a patent acceptance of the geography of domesticity. Besides, the "I" indicates that she has submitted to the patriarchal rules that divided her from her lover, and as the poem concludes, the lovers' reunion will only take place in death, the "everlasting life" in the seventh line.

Dickinson's poem "The grave my little cottage is" can also be regarded as a reflection of Agatha Stanhope's life. Agatha, a minor character in Glaspell plays scholars have not paid much attention to, has been linked with Lavinia Dickinson, who "committed herself to the poet and to family honor" (Ben-Zvi 332). However, the way Glaspell shapes Agatha, she can also be regarded as Alison's double, a mirror character within the play who is also imprisoned by patriarchal strictures. Quite clearly, Alison lived imprisoned, but Agatha was also buried alive the moment she erected herself as Alison's guardian, a never-ending task. Eighteen years after her sister's demise, Agatha tirelessly claims, "I'll keep her from the world — I'll keep the world from getting her — if it kills me — and kills you all!" (318). So even after Alison's death, Agatha kept the house for her sister, the 'thee' of the poem, and Agatha will also meet Alison in the afterlife. The "marble tea" further connects Agatha to the "I" of the poem. When she appears onstage for the first time, she "is carrying a china tea-pot, and a sugar bowl" (316), a parallel image to the line in Dickinson: I "lay the marble tea." The imagery of both the dramatic and the poetic tea sets is also intertwined with death. In Dickinson's poem, the tea set is made of marble like a tombstone. Agatha's tea set is linked to death the moment she decides to burn the house down with everybody in it while packing it. Convinced that once she is forced to leave the house, everybody will "pry into — looking" (319), Agatha takes the straw she is using to pack and leaves the stage silently. It is not a coincidence that the place that Agatha chooses to start the fire also links *Alison's House* and Dickinson's poetry: the closet.

This closet establishes a powerful visual link between Glaspell's poet and Dickinson's poem "They shut me up in Prose," in which the notorious imprisoning closet visualizes the imagination of the neglected woman writer, and confirms closets as one of the main images within the female gothic of domestic terror. In *Alison's House* Glaspell provides the audience with an unprecedented privilege none of the famous absent protagonists from her oeuvre ever had; the audience sees onstage the protagonist's private space, the room of her own. From a purely dramatic point of view, showing this mysterious room and the closet onstage is an effective device. Throughout the play, many characters have referred to it and what it holds, highlighting its symbolic importance. Alison's closet shares something of the meaning of Dickinson's in "They shut me up in Prose." Referring to the geography of the poem, McNeil has said that that the poetic voice "is inside a box inside a box" (126), generating a multiplicity of images of entrapment. In her theatrical transposition, Glaspell also employs spaces to build several boxes, several forms of physical entrapment, for her protagonist: she places Alison inside a closet inside a room inside a house.

The main image of seclusion upon which Dickinson constructs the poem is the closet, and this is primarily used as a metaphor to denounce women writers' enclosure within the literary mode of prose. For centuries, women writers were relegated to prose, because theatre was too public, and poetry was too confessional, the form where the lyrical "I" can be most strongly heard. According to this poem, the speaker finds her creative wings thwarted by "They." "They" do not want her to write because "they" like her "still."

According to Wendy Baker, "They" stands for Dickinson's mother, father, the sermons she had to listen to and even God (78–80). In Glaspell's play, "They" can be seen as Alison's father, brother, sister, and all the constraining forces of society which prevented her from writing and doing what she wanted and from being herself. In a more feminist reading, "They" is the patriarchy, which considered that writing poetry was alien to female roles.[5] Alison Stanhope, as well as her real-life model, had most of her poems published posthumously. Moreover, the image of the closet and the fact that "They" want her "still" add to the other issue that brings Dickinson and the dramatic Alison together: both women's denial of love. Resisting their own will to join their lovers, Emily Dickinson and Alison Stanhope obeyed the rules, and kept "still," "in the closet."

In the second stanza of "They shut me up in Prose," Dickinson employs another metaphor of entrapment, the "bird" that is caged "for Treason," that is, for disobeying "their" rules. I agree with Mary E. Galvin's belief that "the charge of 'Treason' indicates [Dickinson's] awareness of the political implications of her resistance to this confinement" (13). These political implications, however, apply not only to women writers, but to the whole category of women. Glaspell would, like many other women writers, employ the image of the caged bird to stand for trapped women. Perhaps this is nowhere more evident than in Glaspell's best-known one-act *Trifles* (1916), where a bird with a broken neck leads Mrs. Peters and Mrs. Hale to the conclusion that Minnie Wright had killed her husband in retaliation for his having earlier killed the bird, a metaphor for Minnie's former liveliness. In Dickinson's poem, the beautiful image of the bird the poet constructs reveals her imaginative self as the means of overcoming physical entrapment. "They" are powerless to stop these women writers' minds, which take them to other places to end with their "Captivity." It is made clear that in Dickinson's bold assertion of freedom, this can only be achieved by separating mind from body (McNeil 126). Although Alison never left the house, the memories her relatives share about her now are all happy memories of the time when they saw Alison writing in her room. As has been said of Dickinson, Alison probably became an agoraphobic, or feigned this in order to challenge social ideologies that eclipse women's lives, inside the protective, yet imprisoning, space of her room.

Dickinson's and Alison's imaginations were reflected in their poems to escape their closet-prisons. One can then understand the symbolic connotation of Agatha's impulse to start the fire in Alison's closet. With her madwoman-in-the-attic's solution, Agatha wanted to put Alison, metonymically embodied in her poems, again in the closet. In spite of this seeming physical defeat, I also agree with Wendy Baker's affirmation that "They shut me up in Prose" "is not a bitter, resentful diatribe," but "a statement of victorious assertion"

(78). Taking a closer look at form regarding liberation, Galvin has insightfully observed that "The dash with which [Dickinson] 'ends' the poem is a poetic enactment of her resistance to confinement, by resisting closure" (13). As pointed out earlier, Glaspell favored open endings in most of her plays; in *Alison's House*, nevertheless, the process of resistance continues through a seemingly closed ending when Stanhope forgives Elsa, who had disgraced the family when she eloped with her married lover, and gives her the poems so that she makes them public.

Dickinson's and Alison's poems will never again be put in the closet. Alison, like Dickinson, "used her poetry as a force of liberation" (Martin 5), and it is through their poetry that both women are eventually liberated. In keeping with the gothic-like tension created around Alison's room, the content of the secret poems is only revealed in this place, where her closest relatives — her brother, her niece, and her nephew — gather in a ritualistic meeting to read them. While the whole family always thought that Alison was happy with the poems, after reading them they discover the true Alison, the tormented prisoner who only found some relief in writing:

> EBEN: (*slowly, as if trying to realize it*). And all of that — went on in this room.
> STANHOPE: If I had known it was as much as this — I would not have asked her to stay.... In this room I asked her to stay. He was below. He had come for her.... At once they seemed to recognize each other. He was for her. She was for him. That was — without question. But he was married. He had children. They parted. But — they were one. I know that now [349].

Alison's poems are the written proof of how the poet separated her mind from her body, the corporeal container that society could control: "It's here — the story she never told. She has written it, as it was never written before. The love that never died — loneliness that never died — anguish and beauty of her love!" (348).

Importantly, Glaspell provides Alison with the final liberation she did not find when she was alive. At the very end of the play, Alison's brother and her niece argue about what to do with her secret poems. While her brother wants to keep her in the closet, "What went on in this room — let it end in this room" (353), he says, Elsa will make him change his mind. In the final scene Glaspell employs one of her master techniques, her female characters' ability to use their bodies to communicate much more effectively than if they used the common language of words. Elsa draws on the same bird image from "They shut me up in Prose" to make herself understood. As Elsa's "*hands go out, as birds*" (353), she convinces her father that Alison will only be released if her words, the poems that tell of her loneliness and anguish, are given to the world; a lesson on women's entrapment that will also liberate the other characters, male or female, from their roles. As the family members agree that Alison's poems "are for the world," "a gift to all love" (351) that will outlive them all, and accept their publication, they open the door of the privacy that had controlled all their lives, fearful of what society could think of them. When they liberate Alison's poems, the Stanhopes release themselves from the chains that kept them in their own closets and graves. Interestingly, this final liberation is also enacted by making Alison's clock work, an intertextual link with Dickinson's poem "A clock stopped — not the mantel's." This poem, published in the 1896 third series of Dickinson's poems, presents the clock as a metaphorical figure that refers to the temporal nature of life. Alison's clock, as the stage direction tells us, is stopped when the characters gather in her room to read the secret poems. In Dickinson's poem, the clock cannot be repaired, not even by "Geneva's farthest skill," and the puppet does not come out anymore. This puppet, construed as a symbol of life that has come to an end, is also a trapped little figure inside a box — the clock. In its transposition to Glaspell's play, the puppet is, as seen, Alison herself. Elsa, the character who will take the lead in liberating her aunt, winds the clock, which becomes a bit obvious as a theatrical device, telling the hour at the end of the play, when the new century announces a new life for the Stanhopes.

To conclude, the present analysis of intertextualities has argued that Glaspell was particularly inspired by Dickinson when she used the images of the grave and the closet in *Alison's House*. These figures, as I have discussed, can be regarded as negative images of women's physical and metaphorical confinement. The house can be an uncanny place of entombment. There is, however, a more positive note. In the use Glaspell makes of these images one observes that women's liberation may start in the home, the room, or the closet, thereby construed as nurturing spaces. As Dickinson once wrote, "freedom *was* the ability to lock others out, *was* the privilege to be alone in her own room" (Bennet 225, author's emphasis). Read as a piece of literary history on the verge, in *Alison's House*, Dickinson and Glaspell suggest that women writers' only option may be spending some time buried in the closet, waiting for scholars and publishing houses to open the door and to keep it wide open.

Acknowledgments

The author is grateful to the Spanish Ministry of Education, research project FFI 2009-12221, for providing financial support for the writing of this essay.

Notes

1. Many scholars have debated why none of Alison's poems are read aloud in Glaspell's play. In his early work on Glaspell, Arthur Waterman stated that the Dickinson family obliged Glaspell

to change the locale and the name (*Susan Glaspell* 87). Since then, several scholars have followed Marcia Noe's belief that "the Dickinson family refused to allow Susan to use the family name or any of Emily Dickinson's poems in the play" (Voice 59). It has been noted that Emily Dickinson's biographers, Josephine Pollitt and Genevieve Taggard, were not allowed to quote from Dickinson's poems (Gainor 224), and this veto has been considered the main reason to support Noe's point. Barbara Ozieblo, nevertheless, affirms that although "literary history has insisted on interpreting the play as an account of Dickinson's life that the literary estate of the poet forced the author to modify ... no documents support the case" (239).

2. As Linda Ben-Zvi has argued, Glaspell had finished the play by February 1930, because she sent it to the Theatre Guild about that time (331), and wrote a letter to Barrett Clark confessing her disappointment at the rejection of *Alison's House* in April 1930 (Ozieblo 239). If Glaspell read the Dickinson poems that were published in 1930 it must have been in its manuscript form. It must also be noted that in 1924 Martha Dicksinson Bianchi had published *The Complete Poems of Emily Dickinson*, which included "The grave my little cottage is" and "A clock stopped-not the mantel's."

3. It should not be forgotten that Glaspell could have heard about these poems in the various clubs she joined in the Village. The Liberal Club and Heterodoxy combined debates about social and political issues with literary discussions. Therefore, given that Dickinson was such a radical and popular figure at that time, her work could have been the focus of some of these meetings.

4. At the time Glaspell was writing the play, Amherst gossip claimed that Dickinson had fallen in love with a married man, and unable to break the rules of respectability, she chose seclusion in her room. Though more contemporary approaches to Dickinson's life have seen in Dickinson's poetry evidence to claim that her "illicit love" was in fact for a woman (see Gainor 283, Galvin 11-12), and probably her sister-in-law, Glaspell built her play upon a heterosexual love affair.

5. In Charlotte Perkins Gilman's *The Yellow Wallpaper*, after the mental breakdown of the protagonist, the male characters attempt to turn her into a "proper" woman again by forbidding any kind of intellectual work, especially writing. As Gilbert and Gubar have pointed out, this was one of the main devices of woman's rest-cure, invented, obviously, by men (89- 90).

Works Cited

Baker, Wendy. "Emily Dickinson and Poetic Strategy." *Cambridge Companion to Emily Dickinson.* Ed. Wendy Martin. Cambridge: Cambridge University Press, 2002. 77-90. Print.

Bennet, Paula. "Emily Dickinson and her American Women Poet Peers." *Cambridge Companion to Emily Dickinson.* Ed. Wendy Martin. Cambridge: Cambridge University Press, 2002. 215-35. Print.

Ben-Zvi, Linda. *Susan Glaspell: Her Life and Times.* Oxford: and New York: Oxford University Press, 2005. Print.

Bigsby, C. W. E. "Introduction." *Plays by Susan Glaspell.* Cambridge: Cambridge University Press, 1987. 1-31. Print.

Case, Sue- Ellen. *Feminism and Theatre.* London: Macmillan, 1988. Print.

Dickinson, Emily. *Poems by Emily Dickinson: Third Series.* Ed. Mabel Loomis Todd and Thomas Wentworth Higginson. Boston: Robert Brothers, 1896. http://www.gutenberg.org/cache/epub/12241/pg12241.html. Web.

Dickinson, Emily. *The Poems of Emily Dickinson: Centenary Edition.* Ed. Martha Dickinson Bianchi and Alfred Leete Hampson. Boston: Little, Brown, 1930. Print.

Freud, Sigmund. "The Uncanny." *Sigmund Freud: Art and Literature.* Trans. James Strachey. London: Penguin, 1990. 335-76. Print.

Fuller, Margaret. *Women in the Nineteenth Century.* Mineola: Dover, 1999. Print.

Gainor, J. Ellen. *Susan Glaspell in Context: American Theatre, Culture, and Politics 1915-1948.* Ann Arbor: University of Michigan Press, 2001. Print.

Galvin, Mary E. *Queer Poetics: Five Modernist Women Writers.* Westport, CT: Greenwood Press, 1999. Print.

Gilbert, Sandra M., and Susan Gubar. *The Madwoman in the Attic. The Woman Writer and the Nineteenth-Century Literary Imagination.* New Haven and London: Yale University Press, 1979. Print.

Glaspell, Susan. *Alison's House.* New York: Samuel French, 1936. Reprinted in *Susan Glaspell: The Complete Plays.* Eds. Linda Ben-Zvi and J. Ellen Gainor. Jefferson, NC: McFarland, 2010. 310- 53. Print.

_____. *Ambrose Holt and Family.* London: Victor Gollancz, 1931. Print.

Kirkby, Joan. *Emily Dickinson.* London: Macmillan, 1991. Print.

Laughlin, Karen. "Conflict of Interest: The Ideology of Authorship in *Alison's House.*" *Susan Glaspell: Essays on Her Theater and Fiction.* Ed. Linda Ben-Zvi. Ann Arbor: University of Michigan Press, 1995. 219-35. Print.

Littell, Robert. "The New Play." *World,* 2 Dec. 1930, 11. Print.

Martin, Wendy. "Introduction." *Cambridge Companion to Emily Dickinson.* Ed. Wendy Martin. Cambridge: Cambridge University Press, 2002. 1-8. Print.

McNeil, Helen. *Emily Dickinson.* London: Virago, 1986. Print.

Noe, Marcia. *Susan Glaspell: Voice from the Heartland.* Western Illinois Monograph Series. Macomb: Western Illinois University Press, 1983. Print.

_____ "The Verge: L'Écriture Féminine at the Provincetown." *Susan Glaspell: Essays on Her Theater and Fiction.* Ed. Linda Ben-Zvi. Ann Arbor: University of Michigan Press, 1995. 129-42. Print.

O'Neill, Eugene. *Desire Under the Elms: 25 Best Plays of the Modern American Theatre. Early Series.* Ed. John Gassner. New York: Crown, 1967. 25- 56. Print.

Ozieblo, Barbara. *Susan Glaspell: A Critical Biography.* Chapel Hill: University of North Carolina Press, 2000. Print.

Pollak, Vivian R., and Marianne Noble. "Emily Dickinson, 1830-1886: A Brief Biography." *A Historical Guide to Emily Dickinson.* Ed. Vivian R. Pollak. Oxford: Oxford University Press, 2004. 13-63. Print.

Rodier, Katherine. "Glaspell and Dickinson: Surveying the Premises of Alison's House." *Susan Glaspell: Essays on Her Theater and Fiction.* Ed. Linda Ben-Zvi. Ann Arbor: University of Michigan Press, 1995. 195-217. Print.

Rohe, Alice. "The Story of Susan Glaspell." *New York Morning Telegraph,* 18 Dec. 1921: 18. Print.

Sarlós, Robert K. "Jig Cook and Susan Glaspell. Rule Makers and Rule Breakers." 1915. *The Cultural Moment. The New Politics, the New Woman, the New Psychology. The New Art and the New Theatre in America.* Eds. Adele Heller and Lois Rudnick. New Brunswick: Rutgers University Press, 1991. 250-59. Print.

Stonum, Gary Lee. *The Dickinson Sublime.* Madison: University of Wisconsin Press, 1990. Print.

"Susan Glaspell." *Theatre Arts Monthly* 11.7, sec. "Plays and Playwrights" (July 1927): 535-36. Print.

Vorse, Mary Heaton. *Time and the Town: A Provincetown Chronicle,* 1942. Ed. Adele Heller. New Brunswick, NJ: Rutgers University Press, 1991. Print.

Waterman, Arthur E. *Susan Glaspell.* New York: Twayne, 1966. Print.

_____. "Susan Glaspell and the Provincetown." *Modern Drama* (Sept. 1964): 174-84. Print.

White, Fred. "Emily Dickinson's Existential Dramas." *Cambridge Companion to Emily Dickinson.* Ed. Wendy Martin. Cambridge: Cambridge University Press, 2002. 91-106. Print.

UNIVERSITY OF WINCHESTER LIBRARY

Section Two: Playwrights and Performance Texts

The Tragic Heroine

An Intertextual Study of Thornton Wilder's Women in The Skin of Our Teeth, The Long Christmas Dinner, *and* Our Town

KRISTIN BENNETT

According to Ima Honaker Herron, the most prominent theme in Thornton Wilder's works is the "dignity of the human spirit" (49), which Wilder explored by "creat[ing] ... effective patterns of feelings and emotions [through] ... the aesthetic principles of repetition and variation" (51). Rather than portraying individuals as divided by social roles, Wilder was interested in highlighting their universal connectedness. Because Wilder saw the human condition as marked by cyclical behaviors founded in tradition, the characters in his plays live according to social standards set by the generations before them. In a world dominated by mechanical innovation, Wilder was interested rather in the patterns of human life.

Yet, Wilder's plays also reveal a darker side to this repetition, demonstrating a tendency in all individuals to ignore the significance of human universality. "Wilder ... invests living with value by forcing the attention of his characters and thus of his audience on the horror of its absence" (Haberman 27). Viewing Wilder's portrayal of death, his audience is awakened to the harsh reality of human mortality. Nancy Bunge consequently believes that although many critics interpret his plays as nostalgic for a time past, his works actually support the deconstruction of such ideal traditions. In Wilder's texts there "is certainly not [a] kind of nostalgia ... but an anti-nostalgia ... in favor of a plea for a universal, shared understanding that erases borders and barriers, physical or mental" (Bunge 7). Rather than promoting sentimental longing for a sheltered vision of the world, Wilder wishes to expand the human perspective. Bunge elaborates on her argument, explaining that unlike his characters in *Our Town*, reliant upon "the repetitive patterns of their community"

(360) for their understanding of the world, Wilder believed in the importance of experience. He stated, "You only know what you know by engaging yourself [in] the ... activity of life itself, by committing yourself" (as qtd. in Bunge 361). Representing the superficial nature of a life disengaged by blind adherence to tradition, Wilder's plays create not a sense of nostalgic longing, but one of individual loss.

One such loss portrayed in Wilder's works is that of the feminine self in light of socially constructed principles. His attentiveness to woman's potential may stem from his close relationship with his mother. "Considering [his] domineering father ... Thornton was something of a mama's boy. His mother provided the cheesecloth costumes of Thortie's dramatic projects" (Marshall 143). Given her artistic abilities, intellect, compassion, and active support for his theatrical endeavors, Wilder was able to relate to his mother in a way that was impossible with his father. "Isabel was unlike her husband in temperament ... [She] was artistic and refined.... She had had aspirations of attending college or becoming a teacher, but her father ... had definite restrictions for the education of his daughter.... Amos, too, showed a skepticism of Isabel's artistic inclinations" (Simon 6–7). Like the female characters in Wilder's plays, Isabel's personal growth was stifled by patriarchal restrictions.

Through her talent and intellect, Wilder's mother defied the nineteenth-century definitions and constraints that were believed to hinder women. Also like his mother, Wilder's intellectual sisters also challenged supposed feminine limitations. Charlotte, his older sister, was a poet and teacher at Smith College, while his other sister, Isabel, was a novelist (Simon 123). Made aware of woman's potential through his female family members' undeniable talents, Wilder "wanted wider recognition of women's strengths, outside as well as inside the home" (Harrison 175), and this understanding of gender constraints is reflected in his plays. Speaking of *The Woman of Andros,* Jennifer Haytock explains, "Wilder does not seem to have a clear idea ... of a 'clarified and released' femininity.... He does, however, recognize the signs and implications of a repressive gender system" (215). Thus, while not advocating a feminist doctrine, Wilder was aware of the unreasonable limitations imposed upon women by gender definitions. In his plays, he consequently presented femininity as a struggle between an untapped personal potential and a stifling, socially constructed, feminine ideal.

Ostensibly lacking a political agenda, Wilder's work has been believed by many to resist contemporary literary criticism. "In contemporary criticism ... the primacy of social construction or economic determinism [is] dialectically informed by cultural hegemony. Neither leaves much room for the idea of the individual as an independent and purposive agent concerned with the goals of his life" (Wheatley 26). However, many forms of contemporary criticism focus on deconstructing this "social construction" to reveal individual human identities amidst the remains. Wilder's characters are hidden beneath decades of tradition; rather than experiencing the world for themselves, they allow the rules and regulations established by their ancestors to shape their lives. Presenting individuals who unconsciously perform behaviors that have been rehearsed, or abided by, over time, Wilder's works consequently lend themselves to analysis through the lens of Judith Butler's theories of gender as performance. Both Wilder and Butler seek to enlighten us about the socialized repetition that inhibits humans from existing as unfettered agents within their own lives.

As do Thornton Wilder's plays, Judith Butler's theory of gender illustrates the constricting nature of historical tradition. She argues that "one is not simply a body, but ... one does one's body" ("Performative" 521) because "the body is always an embodying of possibilities both conditioned and circumscribed by historical convention" (521). Butler believes that gender consists of an externalized imitation of traditional and historical acts. Butler explains that gender is the outcome of these specific behaviors, abilities and experiences; it determines one's absolute being. "Discrete genders are part of what 'humanizes' individuals within contemporary culture ... [But] because gender is not a fact, the various acts of gender [create] the idea of gender, and without those acts, there would be no gender at all. Gender is thus a construction that regularly conceals its genesis" ("Performative" 522). Dependent upon this gendered dichotomy of socialized existence, individuals adhere to and uphold traditional patterns of behavior. Butler distinguishes such patterns as an effect of *performativity*, or "a compulsory repetition of prior and subjectivating norms ... which cannot be thrown off at will, but which work, animate, and constrain the gendered subject" ("Critically" 22). Wilder's plays likewise portray humanity's compulsive tendency to follow preconceived, traditional patterns of gender, rather than experiencing life spontaneously or authentically.

In his plays, Wilder presents a contrast between the boundless nature of female youth and the restricted existence of those women in socialized roles. He portrays feminine youth as not yet ensnared by habitual conventions. As Butler explains, "To be a woman is to ... compel the body to conform to a historical idea of 'woman'" ("Performative" 522). Young Emily of *Our Town* has not become a woman, for she has not yet integrated within herself the qualities and expectations deemed by society as "feminine." While the gendered dichotomy appropriates reason to the male, she still immerses herself in the intellectual. As she tells George, "I was ... ready to make a speech about the Monroe Doctrine, but ... Miss Corcoran made me talk about the Louisiana Purchase instead" (163). Likewise, she tells her mother, "I made a speech in class today.... It was like silk off a spool. I'm going to make speeches all of my life" (164). Refusing to abide by her "feminine limitations," Emily proves herself an intellectually motivated student. Contrarily, George is portrayed as academically lazy and rather slow, asking for Emily's help with his algebra homework. They provide a foil to the Gibbs and the Webbs, for in each older relationship women are limited to immediate and proximal concerns, like their families, while men situate themselves in the wider realm of historical and worldly matters, like the Civil War. "Gender norms operate by requiring the embodiment of certain ideals of femininity and masculinity, ones which are almost always related to the idealization of the heterosexual bond" (Butler, "Critically" 22). Therefore, rather than encouraging her daughter's intellectual endeavors, Mrs. Webb asks for help with "string[ing] ... beans for the winter" (164). Although not yet forced to portray femininity, Emily has begun struggling against it. While her mother pressures her with matters of the kitchen, Emily is more concerned with matters of the mind.

Like Emily, Gladys Antrobus of *The Skin of Our Teeth* is free to grow intellectually and longs to understand the nature of the world. However, her knowledge relies upon male validation. She continuously demonstrates her understanding to her father, begging him, "Ask me something. Ask me a question" (252). When her father asks her, "How big's the ocean" (252), she responds, "Papa, you're teasing me. It's — three-hundred and sixty million square-miles — and — it — covers — three-fourths — of— the — earth's — surface — and — its — deepest-place — is — five — and — a — half— miles — deep — and — its — average — depth — is — twelve-thousand — feet" (252). Gladys's intelligence exists purely on a superficial level. Instead of understanding the world through experience, she knows it through a series of disjointed facts and figures. Additionally, while she can cite those facts, her father is the one to verify them.

Sabina of *The Skin of Our Teeth* likewise reveals woman's dependence upon male authority. Socialization has taught her that man's desires determine not only woman's knowledge and behavior, but also who she is. Motivated by a need for social significance, she exists in a state of performance, portraying the idealized woman that men expect her to be. Consequently, Sabina's "personal [identity] has been expanded to include political structures" (Butler, "Performative" 525). As Sabina explains to Mrs. Antrobus, "You're going to study history and algebra — and so are Gladys and I — and philosophy.... You should hear him talk ... to hear him [Mr. Antrobus] talk, seems like he expects you to be a combination, Mrs. Antrobus, of a saint, a college professor, and a dancehall hostess" (272). While Gladys relies upon Mr. Antrobus to authorize her knowledge, Sabina relies upon his vision of femininity to determine her absolute actualization.

For the sake of her social survival, Sabina transforms her identity throughout the play, beginning as a maid and then becoming a beauty contestant in Act II. Through the external manipulation of her appearance, Sabina literally recreates herself in the form of "Miss Fairweather." Her name illustrates her personality, as she abandons herself and others in the face of struggle. Like a chameleon, Sabina transforms her identity in order to "fair" best in each particular situation. She proves that "the body is not merely matter, but a continual and incessant materializing of possibilities.... The 'I' that is its body, of necessity, a mode of embodying, and the 'what' that it embodies is possibilities" (Butler, "Performative" 521). Rather than representing anything inherently natural, Sabina's selfhood constitutes a perpetual act intended to gain social significance. Her personal power exists only in her ability to transform into different public identities. However, "the ascription of interiority is itself a publicly regulated and sanctioned form of essence fabrication" (528). Defined by a multitude of performances, Sabina surrenders her ability to simply "be." She is constituted and controlled by the very social malleability she thinks will provide her with power.

Wilder further reveals the shallow nature of such power through his comparisons of mothers and daughters in his plays. In Act II of *The Skin of Our Teeth*, Mr. Antrobus declares that he is leaving his family to marry Sabina. Hearing this, Mrs. Antrobus approaches her husband "composedly with lowered eyes" (259) and calmly states, "I didn't marry you because you were perfect. I didn't even marry you because I loved you. I married you because you gave me a promise" (259). She speaks stoically and submissively of their marriage as a "promise," similar to the way a businessman might speak of a contract. Rather than proving the means to power and influence that Sabina anticipates from it, the marriage contract has silenced Mrs. Antrobus. Contrastingly, Gladys tells her father, "I don't care a bit if you don't want to have anything to do with mama and me, because I'll never like you again and I hope nobody ever likes you again — so there!" (261). Reprimanding an older, socially prominent man, Gladys's emotions are raw, unrestrained, and honest. In nullifying her father's assumptions of male domination through her rebellious speech, Gladys challenges the dependency society claims she must have upon men:

> If the ground of gender identity is the stylized repetition of acts through time, and not a seemingly seamless identity, then the possibilities of gender transformation are to be found in the arbitrary relation between such acts, in the possibility of a different sort of repeating, in the breaking or subversive repetition of that style [Butler, "Performative" 520].

Because her speech does not correspond to the feminine role portrayed by her mother, Gladys reveals the artificially performative nature of the femininity that determines woman's personal expanse. Through this reading, Wilder's text aligns with Butler's assertion that "a performative 'works' to the extent that it draws on and covers over the constitutive conventions by which it is mobilized" ("Critically" 18). By uncovering the "constitutive conventions" of the feminine performative, Gladys challenges its authenticity. Because she proves that gender is not "seamless," but instead reliant upon repetitively submissive behaviors, she demonstrates that gender definitions can be disrupted, challenged and consequently overcome.

Wilder illustrates a similar generational gap between Emily and her mother. While Gladys exhibits an unrestrained connection to self, Emily represents an association with the natural world. One night, when her father tells her to go to bed, Emily responds, "I can't sleep yet, Papa. The moonlight's so wonderful. And the smell of Mrs. Gibbs' heliotrope. Can you smell it?" (172). Her father does not understand her reverence for the surrounding world. Instead of sharing in her serene enjoyment, he asks, "Haven't any troubles on your mind, have you, Emily?" (172). When she declaratively answers, "No" (172), he tells her, "Well, enjoy yourself, but don't let your mother catch you" (172). Emily's father views her dream-like reveries as socially aberrant and assumes there must be something wrong. As Nancy Bunge explains, "Undoubtedly with the best intentions and virtually no self-awareness, the parents of Grover's Corners repeatedly undermine the children's confidence and imagination" (359). Emily's parents, caught up in the social schema, cannot appreciate nature, which exists outside their realm of social responsibilities. However, for Emily, not yet bounded by these limitations, the world has "not cosmic value ... but human value" (Weales 94). Her surrounding environment is not merely a place in which she lives, but one that instead lives within her, actively affecting her identity.

Although similar to her daughter through her observations of nature, Mrs. Webb has fully surrendered to the social system. Viewing her surroundings one night, she sighs, "My, I hate to go to bed on a night like this — I better hurry. Those children'll be sitting up till all hours" (169). Though her speech parallels that of her daughter, Mrs. Webb lacks the time to appreciate the natural world, for her familial commitments are too consuming. She is likewise unable to relate to her children. When Emily seeks her mother's approval by telling her, "I'm the brightest girl at school for my age. I have a wonderful memory" (156), Mrs. Webb responds, "Eat your breakfast" (156). The two, existing in different spheres of socialization, have opposing responsibilities, thoughts and behaviors. "There is no subject who is 'free' to stand outside these norms or to negotiate them at a distance; on the contrary, the subject is retroactively produced by these norms in their repetition, precisely as their effect" (Butler, "Critically" 22). Neither Emily nor Mrs. Webb exists outside the social system; Mrs. Webb merely reflects a prolonged exposure to its regulations. Unlike Emily, Mrs. Webb no longer thinks of intellectual matters, or of her identity; she leaves these to the men of Grover's Corners. Subject to patriarchal reasoning, Mrs. Webb does not understand Emily's confident persona and imaginative view of the world; therefore, she discourages each. Butler explains that "Just as a script may be enacted in various ways, and just as the play requires both text and interpretation, so the gendered body acts its part in a culturally restricted corporeal space" ("Performative" 526). In different stages of rehearsal, the disparity between Emily and Mrs. Webb's interpretations of the social script is immense. While Emily is gradually adjusting to the socialized theater, Mrs. Webb has long rehearsed within it; by committing her lines to memory, Mrs. Webb has committed herself to social control.

Female generational gaps are likewise apparent in *The Long Christmas Dinner*. Although the women attempt to build familial connections between generations, the men keep the family strictly separated from the past. Lucia asks Mother Bayard, "What was ... [your mother's] name dear? ... You were a ... Genevieve Wainwright. Now your mother —" (62) to which Mother Bayard responds, "Yes, you must write it down somewhere. I was Genevieve Wainwright. My mother was Faith Morrison" (62). Lucia is genuinely interested in her family's past and longs to build a relationship with Mother Bayard. However, Roderick interrupts them, saying, "It's all down in a book somewhere upstairs.... All that kind of thing is very interesting" (62). To Roderick, the past belongs in books, disconnected from the present. Alienated by men from the historical legacies of their mothers, these women lack the foundation necessary for their personal development.

The effect of the socialized historical structure of gender is likewise seen in *The Long Christmas Dinner* through the treatment of youth. Lucia is in awe of her newborn child, saying, "O my wonderful new baby! ... Who ever saw such a child! ... What miraculous hands he has!" (64). She views her son as a "miraculous" gift, superior to all other children. However, Lucia's husband, Roderick, is concerned solely with naming him, that is, situating him within the patriarchal framework. As Butler argues, "The discursive condition of social recognition precedes and conditions the formation of the subject: recognition is not conferred on a subject, but forms that subject" ("Critically" 18). The manner in which one is "recognized" by others, or situated within social discourse, determines who one shall become. Roderick tells Lucia, "We'll call him Charles, after your father and grandfather" (64), and warns the nurse, "Don't drop him ... Brandon and I need him for the firm" (65). Rather than seeing his son's significance as an individual, as does Lucia, Roderick compares him to male figures of the past and values him according to his usefulness to society.

Hypocritically, Roderick responds to Lucia's assertion that she thinks her son "is destined for the ministry" (66) by saying, "Woman, he's only twelve. Let him have a free mind" (66). Yet, he continues, "We want him in the firm" (66). In calling her "woman," Roderick degrades Lucia's opinion as "female" and therefore illogical. Because men define the social framework, they likewise determine the logic governing it. Roderick wishes his son to have a mind "free" to follow existing paths, for, as a man, his vision of the social system is characterized by the power and possibility of discourse. As Butler maintains, "The power of discourse to produce that which it names is thus essentially linked with the question of performativity. The performative is thus one domain in which power acts as discourse" ("Critically" 17). Existing on the "superior," masculine side of the gender dichotomy, Roderick's own power and opinions about the world are dependent upon the same framework to which he binds his son. If the system upon which Roderick bases his strength collapses, he will lose both his reason and his identity. Because "performativity ... consists in a reiteration of norms which precede, constrain, and exceed the performer and ... cannot be taken as the fabrication of the performer's 'will' or 'choice'" (Butler, "Critically" 24), the very system upon which Roderick depends for his sense of power and influence is one which dictates his personal limitations, as well as those of his son.

Patriarchy's inconsistent and contradictory nature is likewise concealed by female submission within *Our Town*. In Grover's Corners, male voices speak for those of women. Mr. Webb tells the Stage Manager, "All males vote at the age of twenty-one. Women vote indirect" (160). As was the political situation at the time of the play's setting, the women in *Our Town* are denied the right to vote. By making a woman's political opinions contingent upon a man's, Grover's Corners secures all political power in the hands of men. This gendered division in politics suggests Butler's assertion that "primarily political interests ... create the social phenomena of gender itself" ("Performative" 529). Additionally, while the men of Grover's Corners are known by their family names and professions, the town's women merely reflect the names and thoughts of their husbands. Mrs. Webb says to Mrs. Gibbs, for example, "Well, Mr. Webb just admires the way Dr. Gibbs knows everything about the Civil War" (158). Similarly to the women in *The Long Christmas Dinner*, the women of *Our Town* are reliant upon men for a connection to the historical past and the political present.

Although limited by their immediate surroundings, the women in *Our Town* express dreams of life beyond the microcosm of Grover's Corners. Mrs. Gibbs says, "It's been the dream of my life to see Paris, France" (158), but laments that her husband refuses to go because "it might make him discontented with Grover's Corners" (158). Dr. Gibbs fears that which lies beyond

Grover's Corners, for the town's social order constitutes his entire existence. Should he become discontent with the town, he shall negate his identity and the power associated with it. As Butler explains, "The authors of gender become so entranced by their own fictions whereby the construction compels one's belief in its necessity and naturalness" ("Performative" 522). Genders and their corresponding identities are externally enforced fictions; reliant upon these fictions for a sense of self, individuals become convinced of their necessity. As Dr. Gibbs's wariness about leaving Grover's Corners represents, gendered identity proves unstable; if the setting is changed, the performance risks being altered and individual identities endangered.

As do the women of *Our Town*, Mrs. Antrobus of *The Skin of Our Teeth* has surrendered herself to a socially-defined identity. She, too, is known only by her married name, and continuously allows herself to be concealed by her husband's shadow. She discards her personal hopes and dreams in order to make room for those of her husband and to focus on her family's well being. However, while arguing with her husband, Mrs. Antrobus reveals the cost she has paid for her socialized feminization. Holding up a bottle, she tells Mr. Antrobus:

> In the bottle's a letter. And in the letter is written all the things that a woman knows. It's never been told to any man and its never been told to any woman, and if it finds its destination, a new time will come. We're not what books and plays say we are. We're not what advertisements say we are. We're not in the movies and we're not on the radio. We're not what you're all told and what you think we are: We're ourselves [260].

As Mrs. Antrobus explains, women are limited to performances directed by social ideals of "femininity." They play roles dictated by "books, plays, advertisements, movies, [and] radio." These women do not "know" themselves, for they have never been able to simply be; they are perpetually focused on how others perceive them. Although a personal reflection, Mrs. Antrobus's observations refer to all women, suggesting that "the life-world of gender relations is constituted ... through the concrete and historically mediated acts of individuals" (Butler, "Performative" 523). Both Wilder and Butler demonstrate that female identities are collectively constituted according to society's conceptions of women as performed in the media and their lives.

Through *Our Town*'s Emily Webb, Wilder demonstrates the manner in which socialized gendered roles are gradually acquired. In Act II, Emily has begun observing the world as strictly divided between male and female. She has likewise begun believing men's significance to be boundlessly superior to women's. As she tells George, "I always expect a man to be perfect, and I think he should be" (184). She expects perfection from men not because of their personal merit, but because of the definition of their gender. George then responds, "Oh ... I don't think it's possible to be perfect, Emily" (184). Emily consequently tells him, "Well, you might as well know right now that I'm not perfect. It's not easy for a girl to be as perfect as a man, because we girls are more — more — nervous" (184). Although continuing to act and speak for herself, Emily has begun seeing the world through society's lenses. Her vision of both herself and her life are no longer her own; they have been modified by social expectations. As Butler points out, "The personal is thus implicitly political inasmuch as it is conditioned by shared social structures, but the personal has also been immunized against political challenge to the extent that public/private distinctions endure" ("Performative" 523). Emily does not view George according to the same, equal terms under which she once did; instead, she has reshaped her mind's image of him according to society's expectations for men. Yet, by recognizing his own imperfections, George proves that there is little evidence upholding Emily's socially acquired beliefs.

Our Town further proves gender to be a performative process through Wilder's representation of marriage as tied to the repetition of gender patterns. Wilder himself recognized the pressures placed upon women to marry. He told his sister, Isabel, not yet married in 1937, "Don't overdo the notion ... that a woman has nothing to say or be or give unless she's a wife-mother-and-home-decorator. We're all people before we're anything else.... Don't insult 10 million women by saying a woman is null and void as a spinster" (as qtd. by Harrison 176). Wilder recognized that many women struggle between pursuing their own self-interests and fulfilling what society designates as their feminine duties. Seeking to satisfy social expectations, Wilder's female contemporaries often felt compelled to mold themselves according to such standards, sacrificing their personal identities for more public personas. As Butler notes, such personal transformation is a product of gradual, long-term repetition. "To the extent that this repetition creates an effect of gender uniformity, a stable effect of masculinity and femininity, it produces and destabilizes the notion of the subject as well, for the subject only comes into intelligibility through the matrix of gender" ("Critically" 21–22). The female subject is "known" only through her fulfillment of gendered expectations; she "is" to the extent that she satisfies what society claims she should be.

Not yet enveloped by the social framework, Emily Webb recognizes that she will experience vast change upon her marriage to George Gibbs and begs her father, "Papa — I don't want to get married.... Why can't I stay for a while just as I am?" (191). Emily knows that in becoming Mrs. Gibbs, she will lose her identity as Emily Webb. By struggling so hard against her social destiny, Emily illustrates that "there are acts in and of themselves that challenge the category of woman" (Butler, "Performative" 523).å By limiting women to particular "categories," society inevitably creates contradictions. Should marriage be her sole, natural propensity as a woman, Emily would not question it. However, by challenging the institution, Emily challenges society's definitions of women. As Nancy Bunge writes, both Emily and George are afraid of marriage "because with that sacrament, they bind themselves to the repetitive patterns of their community" (360). Enjoying their present freedom, both are scared to commit to the monotonous life to which their community has surrendered.

While Wilder's female characters are the products of the detrimental nature of gendered socialization, they also provide hope for future escape from such limiting forms. As Wilder stated during an interview with Jeanine Delpech, "I believe ... that woman inspires man to his noblest actions. She sees further. Man ... occupied with his little affairs, is more short-sighted" (as qtd. in Delpech 53). Wilder's female characters allow his audience members to see beyond their own limited perspectives. Genevieve of *The Long Christmas Dinner* does not initially recognize the limitations demarcated by life's cyclicality. She says to her mother, "I shall never marry ... I shall sit in this house beside you forever, as though life were one long happy Christmas dinner" (68). Genevieve does not wish to fulfill her feminine obligation to marry, for, like Emily, she recognizes that the institution requires a separation from those whom she loves. She longs to establish a connection with her mother, rather than with a man. However, far more socialized than Genevieve, Lucia responds, "O my child, you mustn't say such things! ... Forgive me. I'm just unpredictable, that's all" (68). Lucia realizes that unlike the society that governs it, life is chaotic and uncontrollable. She has lost her husband, Roderick, upon whom she relied for a connection to the surrounding world. Like Mrs. Webb, Lucia cannot relate to her daughter — without her husband — because she no longer knows herself.

Although Genevieve initially appears to exist beyond the realm of society's regulation and routine, her stability eventually proves false. Blind to life's temporality, Genevieve does not recognize her mother's significance until she has passed through the dark portal. She mourns, "I never told her how wonderful she was. We all treated her as though she were just a friend in the house. I thought she'd be here forever" (71). Exemplifying different roles in society, Genevieve and Lucia never truly know each other; each is caught up in her own individual presentation, and her vision is narrowed by the perimeters established by her mask.

While Genevieve is awakened to the importance of life, her family remains ignorant. When she and Ermengarde attempt to situate Charles within their family's history, he simply responds, "It's all in a book ... upstairs. All that kind of thing is awfully interesting" (73). Repeating Roderick's earlier statement, Charles illustrates the recurring nature of human ignorance; he is willing to keep his familial foundations confined to the pages of a misplaced family bible. However, Genevieve destroys this repressive cycle. She disrupts her family's security, stating, "There are no such books. I collect my notes off gravestones" (73). Genevieve realizes that rather than being appreciated while alive and honored upon death, family genealogy has been disregarded in light of more pressing social matters.

Therefore, in *The Long Christmas Dinner,* Genevieve serves as Wilder's tragic heroine, suffering upon her recognition of the socialized stigmas, structures, and limits forced upon individuals in the name of progress. Frustrated, she says, "I can stand everything but this terrible soot everywhere. We should have moved long ago.... It's not only the soot that comes through the very walls of this house; ... it's the thoughts of what might have been here. And the feeling about this house of the years grinding away" (77). Genevieve understands that in the name of progress, her family has come to an absolute standstill; unconsciously following social patterns, they are unable to achieve true progress for themselves. Genevieve sees that by offering a sense of control, gendered identities contribute to a charade that blinds individuals to life's actuality. She is left with thoughts of what "might have been" had she actually valued the world, rather than contributing to the mindless "grinding away" of years.

Similar recognition occurs through the voice of Emily Webb in *Our Town.* After her death, she chooses to relive her twelfth birthday. As she experiences the day again, she perceives unexpected significance in every detail. Focused on maintaining her individual performance while alive, Emily never saw the world beyond her role's specified stage directions; she saw others as an actor would see his or her company upon a stage, according to established cues. Now outside the social system, she states, "It goes so fast. We don't have time to look at one another.... I didn't realize. So all that was going on and we never noticed.... Oh, earth, you're too wonderful for anybody to realize you.... That's all human beings are. Just blind people" (207). Concentrated on enforcing a socialized representation of reality, those like Emily never fully "realize" the world; focused on satisfying the demands of the immediate present, most people consider neither the future, nor the past.

Ultimately, through *The Skin of Our Teeth,* Wilder provides hope for a future beyond such rehearsed performances. Despite time passing and social progress occurring, Gladys Antrobus maintains a strong connection to herself. Unlike the older generations of Wilder's women, Gladys establishes a connection and relationship with the child she acquires in Act III. When asked by Sabina, "Can it see? And can it cry and everything?" (270), Gladys responds "Yes, he can. He notices everything very well" (270). Gladys thus demonstrates a change in the life cycle similar to that represented by Genevieve in *The Long Christmas Dinner.* Refusing to promote blindness in her son by determining his life experience according to social norms and definitions, Gladys supports his ability to actively "see" the world through his own eyes.

As does Gladys for her baby, Wilder supports his audience's ability to truly see the world through his plays. By destroying the barriers separating stage from reality, as demonstrated by a lack of props, scenery, and curtain, his works encourage direct interaction from the viewers through their imaginations. Wilder did not intend to create a fantastical vision of the world outside reality, but to present and deconstruct a vision of reality familiar to all.

> A number of contemporary playwrights, of whom Brecht, Wilder, and Eliot are among the most accomplished, use the theater [for] their consciously worked-out moral or philosophical ideas.... They use the stage, the characters, and the story to demonstrate an ... undiscussable truth [Fergusson 61].

By presenting a world similar to, but different from that inhabited by the members of his audience, Wilder's plays allow the audience to relate to the action while remaining critically engaged in its presentation. By revealing the dissatisfying nature of unconsciously performed identities and creating a plot open to individual interpretation in the collective atmosphere of the theater, Wilder represents both the importance of the individual mind and the universality of the human experience.

In his plays, Wilder reveals the danger of lives unlived. Rather than forcing a particular vision of gender ideals upon his audience, Wilder provides them with material from which to draw their own conclusions. His works reflect an understanding that it is difficult "to articulate a ... feminist theory which ... emancipates an essence, a nature, or a shared cultural reality that cannot 'be found' ... It [is] ... important to represent women ... in a way that does not distort ... the ... collectivity the theory ... emancipate[s]" (Butler, "Performative" 529–530). Wilder instead presents women who challenge these normative definitions of gender in order to prove the possibility of an alternative and more complete human experience.

Thornton Wilder's *Our Town, The Skin of Our Teeth,* and *The Long Christmas Dinner* each explore the socialization of the gendered self in a manner that anticipates the gender theory of Judith Butler. Both Wilder and Butler show that by limiting individuals to strict definitions of gender, society narrows the expanse of human experience. Only by resisting these constraints as do Wilder's tragic heroines — Emily, Genevieve, and Gladys Antrobus — can people truly live as individuals.

Works Cited

Bunge, Nancy. "The Social Realism in *Our Town:* A Study in Misunderstanding." *Thornton Wilder: New Essays.* Ed. Martin Blank, Dalma Hunyadi Brunauer, David Garrett Izzo. West Cornwall, CT: Locust Hill Press, 1999. 349- 364. Print.

Butler, Judith. "Critically Queer." *GLQ*, 1 (1993): 17–32. Web.

_____. "Performative Acts and Gender Constitution: An Essay in Phenomenology and Feminist Theory." *Theatre Journal* 40.1. (1988): 519–531. Web.

Delpech, Jeanine. "Thornton Wilder: Author of *Our Town* and *The Ides of March* in Paris." *Conversations with Thornton Wilder*. Ed. Jackson R. Bryer. Jackson: University Press of Mississippi, 1992. 51–55. Print.

Fergusson, Francis. "Three Allegorists: Brecht, Wilder, and Eliot." *Critical Essays on Thornton Wilder*. Ed. Martin Blank. New York: G.K. Hall, 1996. 61–71. Print.

Haberman, Donald. *The Plays of Thornton Wilder: A Critical Study*. Middletown, CT: Wesleyan University Press, 1967. Print.

Harrison, Gilbert A. *The Enthusiast: A Life of Thornton Wilder*. New York: Ticknor & Fields, 1983. Print.

Haytock, Jennifer. "Women, Philosophy, and Culture: Wilder's Andrian Legacy." *Thornton Wilder: New Essays*. Ed. Martin Blank, Dalma Hunyadi Brunauer, and David Garrett Izzo. West Cornwall, CT: Locust Hill Press, 1999. 207–216. Print.

Herron, Ima Honnaker. "Wilder's Experimental Approach to Theater." *Readings on Our Town*. Ed. Thomas Seibold. San Diego: Greenhaven Press, 2000. 48–54. Print.

Marshall, Megan. "Review of American Characteristics and Other Essays." *Critical Essays on Thornton Wilder*. Ed. Martin Blank. New York: G.K. Hall, 1996. 141–144. Print.

Simon, Linda. *Thornton Wilder: His World*. New York: Doubleday, 1979. Print.

Weales, Gerald. "An Unfashionable Optimist." *Readings on Thornton Wilder*. Ed. Katie de Koster. San Diego: Greehaven Press, 1998. 92–97. Print.

Wilder, Thornton. *The Long Christmas Dinner*. *Thornton Wilder: Collected Plays and Writings on Theater*. New York: The Library of America, 2007. 61–79. Print.

_____. *Our Town*. *Thornton Wilder: Collected Plays and Writings on Theater*. New York: The Library of America, 2007. 145–209. Print.

Wilder, Thornton. *The Skin of Our Teeth*. *Thornton Wilder: Collected Plays and Writings on Theater*. New York: The Library of America, 2007. 211–284. Print.

"Cut out the town and you will cut out the poetry"

Thornton Wilder and Arthur Miller

STEPHEN MARINO

When Thornton Wilder died in December 1975, his drama and theatrical colleagues paid tribute to him, which underscored the significant impact of his artistry on twentieth century drama, theatre, and stagecraft. In an article in the *New York Times*, Garson Kanin called Wilder "the only survivor of that great breed — a man of letters"; Lee Strasberg judged that "as a playwright he had a very special quality of simplicity and humanity"; Tennessee Williams described him as "formidable; he was indeed a very fine, pure writer. He was an artist, an artist I admired" (40). Arthur Miller recalled that Wilder would often come by Miller's lodging from his nearby home in Hamden, Connecticut, for stimulating post mortems whenever a new Miller play would open in New Haven. He described Wilder as a "very generous man. He was magnanimous and wise and worth listening to" (*New York Times* 40).

Indeed, Arthur Miller listened. For Thornton Wilder's work — especially *Our Town* — had a strong influence on Miller, particularly during the 1930s, 40s, and 50s — the early part of Miller's seventy-year career — when his views about how form and structure, aesthetics, themes, poetry and poetic language operate in drama were evolving. Wilder's influence can be seen in Miller's first great hits *All My Sons* and *Death of a Salesman*, but both versions of *A View from the Bridge* show particularly strong evidence of Wilder's impact on Miller's theory of the poetic social drama. Although there are many theatrical connections between Miller and Wilder — Jed Harris had directed *Our Town* and *The Crucible*; Elia Kazan, the director of *All My Sons* and *Death of a Salesman*, had directed *The Skin of Our Teeth* — Wilder is not usually a playwright who is thought to have had a major influence on Miller's writing, mostly because Miller himself more consistently credited other playwrights.

Miller's undergraduate years at the University of Michigan from 1934 to 1938 are most notable as the start of his playwriting career. Miller had known little about the theatre before he arrived in Ann Arbor (although he had seen a production of *Ghosts* at the Brighton Beach Theatre at home in Brooklyn). However, during these formative years, he became aware of German Expressionism; he read Strindberg and Henrik Ibsen, whom he often acknowledged as major influences on him. He said in a conversation with Mel Gussow, "Ibsen was my inspiration for a long time" (117) and Miller also expressed a kinship with Strindberg: "He meant a hell of a lot to me" (Gussow 118). At Michigan, Miller also had read one-act protest plays about miners and stevedores and was markedly affected by the social protest work of Clifford Odets, the playwright about whom Miller most talked as an inspiration in this period. For example, in *Timebends*, Miller writes that in the 1930s Odets' plays *Waiting for Lefty, Awake and Sing,* and *Golden Boy* had "sprung forth a new phenomenon, a leftist challenge to the system, the poet suddenly leaping onto the stage and disposing of middle-class gentility, screaming and yelling and cursing like somebody off the Manhattan streets" (229). Most importantly for Miller, Odets brought to American drama a concern for language, an issue which would dominate Miller's stagecraft for his entire career. He wrote: "For the very first time in America, language itself had marked a playwright as unique" (*Timebends* 229). To Miller, Odets was "The only poet, I thought, not only in the social protest theatre, but in all of New York" (*Timebends* 212).

After Miller won his first Avery Hopwood playwrighting award at Michigan, he was sent to Professor Kenneth Roe, whose chief contribution to Miller's development was cultivating his interest in the dynamics of play construction. Miller said that from Rowe's playwrighting classes he "came to believe that if the dazzling glory of the masters was finally their poetry, the fundamental poem was the structure" ("The American Writer" 373). Thus, Odets and Rowe piqued Miller's concern with language, structure, and form — which Thornton Wilder would later do — to help Miller break out of what he termed the "dusty naturalistic habit of Broadway" (*Timebends* 228).

Indeed, Miller was ripe for concentrating on language and structure at the beginning of his career — especially when he graduated from Michigan and started his work with the Federal Theatre Project in 1938, coincidentally the same year as the premiere of *Our Town*, which Miller undoubtedly saw.[1] At this time he wrote *The Golden Years.*

> So when I got home from college and got on the project I thought it would be a hell of a tale. I also wanted to stretch the realistic theatre anyway; I was very impatient with it. I didn't know how to do that except by the use of language which always seemed to me terribly important in the theatre. The fact is we weren't using it, with the exception possibly of Clifford Odets who invented a kind of New York English which never existed in the streets. Apart from him, playwrights were using very crabbed and naturalistic language and this was a chance to get up off your feet

and use the language a little bit and that was attractive [Bigsby, *Miller and Company* 29].

From the very beginning of his career, Miller had obvious concerns with how poetics and poetic language, the staging of conflict, and the aesthetic illustration of theme worked in drama, and it seems Wilder's work, particularly *Our Town*, spoke to him. In fact, Miller's prodigious output of essays on theater and drama, his autobiography *Timebends*, and his frequent interviews include many musings about Thornton Wilder which clearly document Miller's indebtedness to him. For example, in *Timebends*, Miller acknowledged that *Our Town* was the nearest of any of the 1930s plays "reaching for lyricism" (229), and he recognized the impact of "the revolutionary idea of a setless play" (347).

From 1952 to 1957, Miller wrote a succession of highly significant articles, essays, and speeches, works such as "Many Writers: Few Plays," "On Social Plays," "The American Theatre," "1956 and All That," "The Family in Modern Drama," and the "Introduction" to the first volume of his *Collected Plays*, all of which probe the state of American theatre, examine the ways plays are made, and discuss the purpose of drama. In particular, Miller includes rather extensive commentary about Wilder and *Our Town* in "The Family in Modern Drama," completed in 1956. This essay, which appeared in *Atlantic Monthly* in April of that year, was a revision of a speech Miller had delivered earlier at Harvard. In "The Family in Modern Drama" Miller expanded on his original lecture remarks, which exist only in a radio broadcast.[2] In this essay, Miller discusses his observations about poetry, sentimentalism, realism, and the family and society in drama.

There is no doubt that Wilder and *Our Town* were much on Miller's mind when he was revising the lecture and writing both versions of *A View from the Bridge*. In 1955, he wrote the one-act version of "A View from the Bridge" which opened in New York with a companion one-act play "A Memory of Two Mondays" (Miller's dramatized recollection of the summer he spent working as a clerk in an auto parts factory before he attended the University of Michigan). The production had what Miller considered a disappointing run after *All My Sons* and *Death of a Salesman*, closing after 149 performances, though Miller won his third Drama Critics Circle Award. A year later in 1956, Miller revised and expanded *A View from the Bridge* to two acts and premiered it in London. Miller's concern with poetics and poetic language in drama and illustrating the conflict between family and society were particularly challenged in creating both versions, and it is no coincidence that "The Family in Modern Drama" contains analysis of these concerns.

Miller's commentary on Wilder and *Our Town* is striking when applied to his own work during this time. He acknowledges *Our Town*'s significance as a "progenitor of so many other works" (78). Miller foregrounds his discussion of *Our Town* with his analysis of what he calls the "poetic" drama as opposed to the "realistic" play. Miller best defined the poetic drama in his 1993 essay "About Theatre Language" as "the gradually revealed illuminating idea behind the whole thing" (84–85). For Miller, the poetic drama is differentiated from the strictly "verse" drama" that is, for a play to be poetic, it does not necessarily have to be written in verse/poetry — although Miller often did cite a connection between the two. In fact, Miller reported that he was "up to his neck" (*Arthur Miller: An Interview* 98) in writing many of his early full-length and radio plays in verse. Much of *Death of a Salesman* and all of *The Crucible* were written in verse. The one-act version of *A View from the Bridge* was written in a combination of verse and prose, and Christopher Bigsby relates that Miller regretted his failure to do this in *The American Clock* (*Critical Introduction* 136). For Miller, a "poetic" drama, as outlined in "The Family in Modern Drama," depends upon how the play presents itself primarily as a family relationship or primarily as a social relationship. For when a family and family relations are at the center, the play is drawn toward realism; when a play deals with men outside the home in society at large, away from the family context, the form of the play becomes openly and self-consciously symbolic and therefore, to Miller, "poetic"— and the characters heroic. He cites O'Neill's *The Hairy Ape* and *The Emperor Jones* as examples of plays which are poetic. He maintains that when a play deals with the question, "How may a man make of the outside world a home?" we have a clue to the inner life of the great plays ("Family" 73).

This idea reveals Miller's always great concern for the social implications of his plays:

> It is true to say, I think, that the language of the family is the language of the private life — prose. The language of society, the language of the public life, is verse. According to the degree to which the play partakes of either relationship, it achieves the right to move closer or further away from either pole ["Family" 76].

Miller offers Eliot's *The Cocktail Party* and *Murder in the Cathedral* as examples of this process. *The Cocktail Party*, Miller judges, is unpoetic in style because it is forced to keep the family situation as central, whereas *Murder in the Cathedral* does not mask its poetry because the situation is social, the conflict of a human being with the world.

In "The Family and Modern Drama" Miller discusses *Our Town* as exactly the kind of play which illustrates the complexities of tracing the influence of the family and social elements upon dramatic form. Miller declares that although it is a play that deals with

> the traditional family figures — mother, father, brother, sister — it uses the families as a prism with which is reflected Wilder's informing principle: the indestructibil-

ity, the everlastingness, of the family and the community, its rhythm of life, its rootedness in the essentially safe cosmos despite trouble, wracks, and seemingly disastrous, but essentially temporary dislocations [78].

Miller notes that the stage manager, as narrator, is there to remind the audience that the action is not so much real life as an abstraction of it. Miller judges that *Our Town* is a poetic play rather than a realistic play because the entire play is occupied with what the title implies: the town and the society, and not the family, is the larger context and the most significant aspect of the play. He proclaims: "Cut out the town and you will cut out the poetry" (79). Thus, Miller posits that Wilder sees his characters not primarily as personalities but rather as "forces." He individualizes them as characters only enough to emphasize their roles as forces to enliven and illuminate his symbolic vision and theme, which is that of the family as timeless, stable quantity (79). Miller declares: "It is a triumph in that it does open a way toward the dramatization of the larger truths of existence while using the larger materials of life: It is a truly poetic play" (81).

Miller's analysis of *Our Town* in "The Family in Modern Drama" shows how, while writing both versions of *A View from the Bridge*, he struggled to reconcile in dramatic form and poetic language the tale of the protagonist Eddie Carbone as a mythic tragedy, a psychological family drama, and a drama of family and society. Miller had, of course, tackled the subject of family and social drama before in his work, especially in his first Broadway hit, *All My Sons,* and his masterpiece *Death of a Salesman*. In the "The Family in Modern Drama" Miller also includes *Death of a Salesman* and Tennessee Williams's *A Streetcar Named Desire* as poetic plays because they extend outside of the family situations:

> If, for instance, the struggle in *Death of a Salesman* were simply between the father and son for recognition and forgiveness it would diminish in importance. But when it extends itself outside the family circle and into society, it broaches those questions of social status, social honor and recognition, which expand its vision and lift it out of the merely particular toward the fate of the generality of men.... The same is true of a play like *A Streetcar Named Desire* which could have easily been limited to a study of psychopathology.... Blanche DuBois and the sensitivity she represents has been crushed by her moving out of the shelter of the home and the family into the uncaring, anti-human world outside it. In a word, we begin to partake of the guilt for her destruction, and for Willy's, because the blow struck against them was struck outside the home rather than within it — which is to say that it affects us more because it is a social fact we are witnessing [73–74].

In *A View from the Bridge* Miller created the role of a narrator, Alfieri, similar to the Stage Manager in *Our Town*, who is crucial in showing to the audience the significance of the action on family and society. Miller's decision to use an outside narrator in *A View from the Bridge* was also undoubtedly influenced by Tennessee Williams's successful use of Tom Wingfield as the narrator to the same effect in *The Glass Menagerie* in 1945. Williams — who often cited his admiration for Wilder as an artist — is another playwright whom Miller frequently credited with influencing his art and craft.

Miller's commentary shows exactly how he struggled with both versions of *A View from the Bridge* in making the focus on society and the family simultaneously. The play exists in two forms: a one-act version was written in an intriguing mixture of verse and prose; an expanded two-act version eliminated the verse. Evaluation of the differences between these versions has focused almost exclusively on how Miller, in response to criticism of the sketchiness of the characters in the one-act play, enlarged the psychological motivations of the principal characters — Eddie Carbone, his wife Beatrice, and their niece Catherine — in order to emphasize the social consequences of the play's central action: Eddie's desire for his niece, Catherine. A bare bones synopsis of the plot of both versions[3] of *A View from the Bridge* shows how the family and social elements are in conflict in the action. Eddie Carbone, a Brooklyn longshoreman, and his wife, Beatrice, have raised her niece, Catherine, since she was a child. When the play begins, Catherine is seventeen and on the verge of becoming a woman. Eddie's affection as an uncle/step-father has changed into a physical and emotional attraction, which neither Eddie nor Catherine fully perceives, but of which Beatrice is aware. Eddie's emotion is transformed into jealousy when Catherine falls in love and wants to marry Rodolpho, one of two Italian illegal immigrants, the cousins of Beatrice living in the Carbone's Red Hook apartment. Eddie transfers his jealousy into an assault on Rodolpho's masculinity and tells Catherine that Rodolpho is only using her to obtain citizenship. After Eddie discovers Catherine and Rodolpho coming out of a bedroom, Eddie takes his jealousy outside his family. He informs to immigration authorities — a deed abhorrent to the social codes of the Sicilian-American community — who arrest Rodolpho and his brother, Marco, who publicly accuses Eddie of snitching. Out on bail, Rodolpho intends to marry Catherine, and Marco comes to vindicate his and his brother's honor. Eddie wants Marco to apologize in front of the neighborhood for his accusation because he wants his "name" back. When Marco strikes him, Eddie pulls a knife which Marco turns back on Eddie, killing him.

When the one-act "A View from the Bridge" was published in 1956, Miller wrote an introductory essay, "On Social Plays," which detailed his intention to have the one-act version illustrate much more than how Eddie's Carbone individual psychology results in confrontation with his society. Miller explains that when he first heard the tale in his Brooklyn neighborhood, he thought he had heard it before as "some re-enactment of a Greek myth." To Miller, it seemed the two "submarines," the illegal immigrants, set out from

Italy as if it were two thousand years ago; he was awed by the destiny of the characters, that "the weaving together of their lives seemed almost the work of fate." Moreover, he wanted to dramatize the story without embellishment, exactly in "its exposed skeleton" because he did not want to interfere with the "myth-like march of the tale" (17–8). The narrator, the lawyer Alfieri, functions as a Greek-like chorus as both a character and commentator. Alfieri's speeches to the audience directly connect Eddie to what Miller saw as the mythic level of the play: his destiny to enact the tragic action. The New York production used sparse staging — not unlike the bare stage in *Our Town*— to achieve the "skeletal" quality of the mythic story because as Miller wrote, "nothing existed but the purpose of the tale ("Introduction," *View* 2 Act, viii).

But Miller admitted that the meaning of Eddie's fate remained a mystery to him even after writing the play. In revising for the London production, Miller sought to place Eddie more in relation to his Sicilian-American society. Miller realized:

> The mind of Eddie Carbone is not comprehensible apart from its relation to his neighborhood, his fellow workers, his social situation. His self-esteem depends upon their estimate of him, and his value is created largely by his fidelity to the code of his culture [viii].

In this production, the set was more realistic; more actors played Eddie's neighbors. Miller ultimately judged that "once Eddie had been placed squarely in his social context, among his people, the mythlike feeling of the story emerged of itself, and he could be made more human and less a figure, a *force*" (ix). And of course, "force" is exactly the way Miller described the characters in *Our Town*. Thus, Miller realized how in the one-act play he indeed had cut out the town — Brooklyn as Grover's Corners — which effectively made it less poetic, but which he restored in the two-act drama to achieve the poetic social play as Wilder had done. Twenty years later in *Timebends*, Miller commented on how the new staging emphasized Eddie's universal destiny:

> The play began on a Red Hook street against the exterior brick wall of a tenement, which soon split open to show a basement apartment and above it a maze of fire escapes winding back and forth across the face of the building in the background. On those fire escapes the neighbors appeared at the end like a chorus, and Eddie could call up to them, to his society and his conscience for their support of his cause.

Donald P. Costello believes that the London production integrated all the circles — self, family, society, the universe — to which Eddie is responsible. Thus, the play moved "from private to mythic, from Eddie as psychological self to Eddie as participant in universal fate" (447) and thus a more poetic play.

Finally, it is notable that after writing *A View from the Bridge*, Miller did not have a new play on Broadway for nine years until the controversial *After the Fall*. In light of Miller's views of what constitutes a poetic play, it may be that in *After the Fall* he had tilted a bit too much towards emphasizing the family rather than social relationships. He failed to follow his and Wilder's prescription. For although the play clearly attempts to put the personal guilt of the main character Quentin in the context of the larger guilt of the Holocaust, critics, at least, thought the play too personal and autobiographical, reacting primarily to what they perceived as the close resemblance between the character Maggie and Miller's ex-wife Marilyn Monroe. Many critics ignored the play's social theme and implications, which has obscured the fact that *After the Fall* is a major drama in Miller's canon.

Wilder's continued influence on Miller is evidenced in other plays in the latter's long career. Late plays like *The Ride Down Mt. Morgan* (1991), *Broken Glass* (1994), *Mr. Peter's Connections* (1998), and *Resurrection Blues* (2002) show how Miller continued to tackle the complexity of illustrating family and social elements in the dramatic form — to continue to show Brooklyn and Grover's Corners.

Notes

1. Miller was back in New York in the spring of 1938 after his graduation from the University of Michigan and would have had the opportunity to see the original Broadway production at this time. In two conversations I had with Miller's sister, Joan Copeland, in March 2008 and January 2009, she assumed that he had seen the play. His commentary reflects familiarity with the text and performance.

2. The speech was originally broadcast over radio station WGBH, Boston, and is available on a sound reel tape at the Library of Congress.

3. A third version exists. Miller rewrote the end for the Paris production because he was advised that a French audience would not accept that Eddie and Catherine could not be unaware of the emotions between them. Ostracized by his society, Eddie kills himself. However, the form is two acts, the same as the London version (Carson 101).

Works Cited

Bigsby, Christopher. *Arthur Miller and Company*. London: Methuen Drama, 1990.

_____. *A Critical Introduction to Twentieth-Century American Drama, Vol. 2: Tennessee Williams, Arthur Miller, Edward Albee*. Cambridge: Cambridge University Press, 1984. Print.

Carlisle, Olga, and Rose Styron. "The Art of the Theatre II: Arthur Miller: An Interview." *The Paris Review* 10 (Summer 1966) 61–98. *Conversations with Arthur Miller*. Ed. Matthew C. Roudane. ed. Jackson: University of Mississippi Press, 1987. Print.

Carson, Neil. "*A View from the Bridge* and the Expansion of Vision." *Arthur Miller, Modern Critical Views*. Ed. Harold Bloom. New York: Chelsea House, 1988. Print.

Costello, Donald P. "Arthur Miller's Circles of Responsibility: *A View from the Bridge* and Beyond." *Modern Drama* 36.3 (1993): 443–53. Print.

"Colleagues Pay Tribute." *New York Times* 8 December 1975: A 40. Print.

Gussow, Mel. *Conversations with Miller*. New York: Applause Theatre and Cinema Books, 2002. Print.

Miller, Arthur. "About Theatre Language." *The Last Yankee*. New York: Penguin, 1993. Print.

_____. "The American Writer, The American Theater." *The Theatre Essays of Arthur Miller*, Rev. and expanded. ed. Ed. Robert A. Martin and Steven R. Centola. New York: Da Capo Press, 1996. Print.

_____. "Arthur Miller Delivering the Theodore D. Spencer at Harvard University, February 18, 1953." Archive of Recorded Poetry and Literature, Library of Congress. Audio recording.

_____. *Arthur Miller's Collected Plays*. New York: Viking, 1957. Print.

_____. "The Family in Modern Drama." *Atlantic Monthly* 197 (April 1956) 35–41; rpt in *The Theatre Essays of Arthur Miller*, revised and expanded. Ed. Robert A. Martin and Steven R. Centola. New York: Da Capo Press, 1996. Print.

_____. "Introduction" to *Collected Plays*. *The Theatre Essays of Arthur Miller*, Rev. and expanded ed. Ed. Robert A. Martin and Steven R. Centola. New York: Da Capo Press, 1996. Print.

_____. "On Social Plays." *The Theatre Essays of Arthur Miller*. Rev. and expanded ed. Ed. Robert A. Martin and Steven R. Centola. New York: Da Capo Press, 1996. Print.

_____. *Timebends: A Life*. New York: Grove Press, 1987. Print.

_____. "A View from the Bridge" (with "A Memory of Two Mondays"). New York: Viking Press, 1955. Print.

_____. *A View from the Bridge* (Two-Act Version) New York: Penguin, 1977. Print.

"And I am changed, too"
Irving's Rip Van Winkle *from Page to Stage*

JASON SHAFFER

In an era when ghost-written celebrity memoirs, fan fiction, and viral video have all contributed to a gradual erosion of the integrity of the relationship between a narrative and its putative creator, it offers some comfort to consider that even the most archetypal of stories have suffered from similar contingencies. Perhaps nowhere in the history of American literature or the American theatre is the vexed origin of all narrative more obvious than in the story of Rip Van Winkle. The cluster of literary and theatrical texts indicated by this title illustrates a complicated series of intertextual interactions that take place at the intersection of literature, theatre, and oral performance. Beginning in the pages of Washington Irving's *The Sketch-Book of Geoffrey Crayon* and gradually spreading into the theatre through the efforts of many different actors and playwrights, Rip's story seems to slip the bonds of both page and stage. This textual meandering culminates, perhaps, in the life of the American actor Joseph Jefferson III. Jefferson, who began portraying Rip onstage during the American Civil War and continued in the role for decades, long enough to be featured in a short silent film in 1896 and to be recorded speaking two of Rip's monologues on a gramophone in 1900 (Johnson 10; McArthur xiii).

At times since his first appearance in print in 1819, Rip, or at least an actor portraying him, has threatened to walk into entirely new and completely unattributable adventures. In his memoir of his long association with Joseph Jefferson, the actor Francis Wilson occasionally attempts to separate theatrical legend and fact. Jefferson's Rip spoke with a pronounced Dutch accent and shared with Irving's original a deep friendship with his dog, of whom he speaks frequently in the script. According to Wilson:

> I asked [Jefferson] if there were any truth in the story of his going into a bank to cash a check, and on being refused because of there being no one to identify him, he leaned up against the counter and, in the tones of Rip, exclaimed, "If my tog Schneider vas here he would recognize me!" and that instantly there were any number of people eager to identify him.

He laughed and said:

"No, it is not true, but it ought to be. It is too good to be disproved" [Wilson 31].

According to Wilson, Jefferson then goes on to wonder "who is it that rounds out all those stories [?]." Jefferson's willingness to acknowledge the truth value of an anecdote starring him not only as himself but also in a brief improvisation as his most famous character serves as a sharp reminder that seeking out the origins of a character with the popularity and staying power of Rip Van Winkle may be an exercise in futility.

Of course, origin stories, or at least creation myths, do abound for Rip. Washington Irving's composition of the story in 1818 is commonly depicted as having occurred in a burst of inspiration. Visiting his sister's family in England and passing a June evening swapping old tales of the Hudson Valley with his brother-in-law Henry Van Wart, so the story goes, Irving found himself shaking off a recent fit of melancholy, at which point he rushed to his room and began writing. When he emerged the following morning, he held in his hands a complete draft of his most famous work (Young 3). Several decades later, Joseph Jefferson would claim a similar moment of inspiration. Living in a rented farmhouse in Pennsylvania, Jefferson encountered a passage in Irving's *Life and Letters* where the author recounted having seen Jefferson perform and praised him, even comparing him favorably to his father, a favorite actor of Irving's. "I put down the book, and lay there thinking how proud I was," recalls Jefferson, who immediately began searching for ways to return the compliment (Jefferson 225). Suddenly, he had a revelation: "Rip Van Winkle! There was to me magic in the sound of the name as I repeated it. Why, was not this the very character that I wanted?" With that thought, Jefferson rushed to the bookshelves, pulled down a copy of *The Sketch-Book*, and set to work.

As is so often the case for historians of both literature and performance, the origins of the texts in question threaten to vanish under close scrutiny. While the story of Irving's drawing sudden inspiration from a night of tale-telling in the Hudson Valley seems quite believable, his interest in New York folklore is far less evident in "Rip Van Winkle" than is his interest in German folktales, and the story also touches on a much broader mythological motif (Rodes 10–13). In Jefferson's case, the actor readily acknowledges that several stage versions of Rip's story predate his own, including one by his step-brother Charles Daly Burke, in which he had already played a supporting role (Quinn, "Introduction" 461; Jefferson 225–6). Both stories feature a "Eureka!" moment that seems to defy the very nature of Irving's tale as it walks the fine line between myth and literature and between page and stage.

Irving's fictional account of Rip Van Winkle's twenty-year sojourn in the mountains of upstate New York is itself a cacophony of narrative voices.

The Sketch-Book is largely written in the voice of Geoffrey Crayon, a traveler whose cool demeanor and eye for detail recalls Joseph Addison and Richard Steele's Mister Spectator from their popular eighteenth-century essay series, but Rip's story was purportedly found among the papers of Diedrich Knicker-bocker, the addle-minded amateur historian in whose voice Irving wrote his first book, the satirical 1809 *A History of New York*. Irving, a great lover of both writing in personae and literary hoaxes more generally, both acknowl-edges the obvious debts that the story owes to German folktale traditions and at the same time jokingly demands that the reader give the same credence to this tall tale as to Crayon's various essays on his travels in England. "Knicker-bocker" appends a note to the tale declaring, "I have met with Rip Van Winkle myself, who when I last saw him was a very venerable old man and ... perfectly rational and consistent on every other point," and indicating that since a justice of the peace had deposed Rip, "the story therefore is beyond the pos-sibility of a doubt" (Irving 41). The rather less credulous Crayon backs up his source, declaring that Knickerbocker's note shows "that [the tale] is an absolute fact, narrated with his usual fidelity." In much the same way that Joseph Jefferson III's offstage life and the character of Rip meld in the fictional anecdote of his slipping into character as a paradoxical proof of his identity in a bank, Irving's Rip dwells in a multi-layered narrative that winkingly undercuts the purported truth of his story while insisting on its absolute veracity.

Irving's story is set in an unspecified village in the colonial Hudson Valley of upstate New York. The farmer Rip Van Winkle dwells in this village with his wife and two children, an unnamed daughter and a son also named Rip. Rip seems to be a parody of the virtuous yeoman farmer who served as the symbolic backbone of early American political culture, for he suffers from "an insuperable aversion to all forms of profitable labour," which while it leaves him civic-minded enough to be more than willing to assist his neighbors — "ready to attend to any body's business but his own" — also leads him to neglect his own family and farm (30). Perhaps unsurprisingly, Rip's wife, Dame Van Winkle, is the most notorious shrew in American literature. Rip, hunting in the Catskill Mountains with his dog, Wolf, to avoid a tongue-lashing from his wife, encounters a spirit dressed like a seventeenth-century Dutch settler and endeavoring to carry a heavy cask of liquor up the mountain on his back. Rip helps his new companion carry the keg into a clearing where a group of similar spirits awaits, drinking and bowling. Rip joins them in a few drinks and then falls asleep for twenty years. Upon awakening, he returns to his vil-lage, now part of the independent United States, where he goes unrecognized initially until he is inspected closely by an elderly neighbor. Rip, discovering that his wife has died during his absence, lives happily ever after, residing on the much better-maintained farm of his daughter and her husband and becoming something of a local celebrity, especially "among the rising generation" for whom he is an invaluable chronicle "of the old times 'before the war'" (40). Irving's Rip becomes a legend in, or perhaps out of, his own time.

Despite the obvious gender concerns raised for a contemporary reader by Irving's depiction of the termagant Dame Van Winkle, Rip's story features an appealingly happy ending. Easily lost in the story's conclusion, however, is the vertiginous experience of a loss of self that Rip experiences upon his return to the village. Part of Rip's displacement is political, for the world of the Hudson Valley has changed markedly after the Revolution, and indeed Rip narrowly escapes being lynched by a mob as a Tory when he declares himself a loyal subject of King George III. These changes are most readily visible in the reconstruction of Rip's beloved old village inn, where he was wont to escape Dame Van Winkle by drinking with his comrades, which has been replaced by a nationalist resort known as The Union Hotel and is surrounded upon Rip's return by crowds of Federalist and Democratic partisans on an election day. The sign of the old inn, featuring "the ruby face of King George III" has been "singularly metamorphosed," for the king's "red coat was changed for one of blue and buff; a sword was held in the hand instead of a scepter; the head was decorated with a cocked hat, and underneath was printed in large characters GENERAL WASHINGTON" (37).

Far more disturbing for Rip, whom Irving notes is less concerned with his new status as "a free citizen of the United States" than with his escape from the "petticoat government" of Dame Van Winkle (40), is his apparent displacement by his own son, which induces a moment of ontological crisis. When Rip inquires if no one in town knows Rip Van Winkle, he is directed toward the figure of his grown son, whom he does not recognize: "a precise counterpart of himself, as he went up the mountain: apparently as lazy and certainly as ragged!" (38). Rip's reaction to the sight of this apparent doppelganger is an outburst reminiscent of a theatrical mad scene:

> "God knows," exclaimed he, at his wit's end, "I'm not myself.— I'm else — that's me yonder — no — that's somebody else got into my shoes — I was myself last night; but I fell asleep on the mountain — and they've changed my gun — and everything's changed — and I'm changed — and I can't tell what's my name, or who I am!" [38–9].

Far more crucial for Irving's Rip than the emergence of Irving's namesake, General Washington, and the independent United States, is his being supplanted by a new Rip in the form of his son. Only when Rip's attention is caught by his daughter hushing her infant son, also named Rip, does the crisis pass as Rip quickly finds himself reintegrated into his family, and thus his community.

Irving's Rip serves as the namesake for both a son and a grandson, but his textual progeny, like his ancestors, are legion. Rip's most obvious antecedent is the German shepherd Peter Klaus, whose tale appears in Otmar Grimm's 1800 collection of *Volke-Sagen* (Young 7). Irving/Crayon also appends to Rip's story a misleading reference to the eternally slumbering emperor Frederick Barbarossa, although the Emperor is replaced in Irving's text by the chief of the mountain spirits, the Dutch explorer Hendrik Hudson, who was abandoned in the Hudson Valley by his crew after a mutiny in 1611 (13). Even more complex than the genealogy of folklore antecedents for Irving's Rip, however, is the family tree of theatrical Rips that sprang up as a result of Irving's authorial success.

In his introduction to one theatrical adaptation of Rip's story, Arthur Hobson Quinn observes in reference to the many dramatic versions of the tale and their interrelatedness that "Rip Van Winkle is a growth" (461). An astonishing total of ten dramatic versions of *Rip Van Winkle* from the nineteenth century have been identified (McArthur 218). The first, anonymous version was staged in Albany in 1828, starring Thomas Flynn, an English émigré who had debuted in Boston in 1827 (Quinn 461; Brown 129). The first attributed version, by another Englishman, John Kerr, debuted in Philadelphia in 1829 at the Chestnut Street Theater, where Burke and Jefferson would also play Rip (Quinn 461; Brown 206). In addition to Jefferson and Burke, the celebrated comedian James Henry Hackett — the most famous American Falstaff of his era and as well as a star fond of both "Yankee" and foreign dialect roles — also mounted a successful production, one which Hackett's son claimed had been praised by Irving himself (Quinn 461; Hodge 382; Hellman 338–9). While Irving's great success with Rip must certainly have intrigued theatrical entrepreneurs both onstage and in the manager's office, however, the story seems largely unsuited to theatrical adaptation, and certainly not likely to generate so many different versions. As Joseph Jefferson III realized after deciding to stage the story, nearly all of Irving's text "is descriptive": "The character of Rip does not speak ten lines. What could be done dramatically with so simple a sketch? How could it be turned into a play?" (225).

The question might well have intrigued Irving, a devotee of the theatre who had begun his writing career with a series of essays on the New York theatre under the moniker "Jonathan Oldstyle" and subsequently tinkered with playwriting before deciding that the drama was not remunerative enough for an author (Reichart 173). The answer to the adaptation question that most authors arrived at, however, was the same: melodrama. Most notably, Kerr, Burke, and Jefferson (with the assistance of the great melodramatist Dion Boucicault) made additions to Irving's original story that follow clearly the conventions of melodrama as laid out by historians of the genre such as David

Grimsted and Frank Rahill. Some elements of Irving's story, to be sure, made this task easy. Grimsted argues that the melodramatic hero is noble by nature regardless of class, a Jeffersonian notion aptly suited to the agrarian nostalgia for village life that ironically (given that Irving was a New Yorker by birth) pervades *The Sketch-Book* (Grimsted 209–10; Bowden 57–8). Then, too, Irving's tale answered Jefferson's desire to find an "American" character for himself as an American actor, but while patriotism is not lacking in most nineteenth-century melodramas, the genre's primary attachment is to domestic, not civic virtues (Grimsted 227). Here, of course, the shrewish Dame Van Winkle presents a stumbling block, since such depictions of domestic virtue depend on the moral heroism of the female lead (172). How might the family life of the Van Winkles be made presentable for the nineteenth-century stage?

One answer comes in the form of Rip's drinking. While he is a steady tippler in Irving's story and, as Rahill notes, drunkards were comic characters in most early dramas, by the late 1820s the drunkard had acquired legitimacy as a pseudo-tragic character (140). Rip's drinking, while it remains largely comic, becomes more pronounced and troublesome by the premiere of Jefferson's version, thus giving Rip's wife, Gretchen, a reason for her sharp tongue and temper. Moreover, in Jefferson's version the village burgomaster (and usually the Van Winkles' creditor), Derek Van Slaus (Jefferson changed the last name to Van Beekman), displays a lecherous interest in Gretchen, providing her with another opportunity to display her feminine virtue according to the generic rules of melodrama (Grimsted 177). In the Kerr and Burke versions, Rip's sister Alice lives with the family and adds a romance plot as she is courted by a schoolmaster turned clerk, Knickerbocker (an ironic choice of name to any student of Irving). Rip's son drops out of the play, but his daughter remains, and she acquires a childhood sweetheart. In each version, Rip's daughter is the central object of a scheme by Derek to acquire the Van Winkles' land by trapping her in a marriage contract that Rip has twenty years to revoke. Even Derek's profession—attorney—is pure melodrama, given the genre's penchant for villainous lawyers (Grimsted 201; Rahill 166). Amid all of this domestic intriguing, Rip is chased from the house by an angry Gretchen and encounters the spirits in the mountains before returning to the village on the very day when, unbeknownst to him, he must rescue his daughter from being forced into a loveless marriage to Derek's son or nephew and grant her hand to her sweetheart, who has just returned home from the sea. While Rip remains the title character of each play, the inflated plots of the adaptations allow for less vexed representations of virtue onstage, placing Rip firmly on the side of right against the play's villainous characters while also allowing his drinking and his irresponsible rambling in the woods to stand as a comic counterpoint to the scripts' dominant moral values (Grimsted 185).

(Examining these versions of his story, one can only imagine that Irving's Rip might declare himself once again to be changed!)

John Kerr, who starred in the 1829 *Rip*, was an English actor contracted by theatre manager Francis Wemyss to play as part of the company at the Chestnut Street Theatre in Philadelphia. Extant advertisements indicate that his *Rip* had been performed in London prior to Kerr's emigration to the United States and featured not only Kerr as Rip, but his children in the roles of Rip's daughter, Lowenna, and nephew, Gustaffe (Quinn 461). Given the script's frequent, and indeed at times somewhat strident, expressions of American patriotism, it seems fair to assume that the play underwent some alterations after its London performances and prior to its premiere in Philadelphia. These emendations should hardly be surprising. Philadelphia was the hometown of native-born theatre star Edwin Forrest, who would go on to make a living off expressions of broad-shouldered patriotism. Moreover, the Jacksonian movement in the Democratic Party took wing in Philadelphia, and in the wake of Andrew Jackson's victory in the election of 1828, the Chestnut Street Theatre produced a number of patriotic new plays. Notably, the years 1829 and 1830 also saw the premiere of two plays by Philadelphian Richard Penn Smith, *The Eighth of January* and *The Triumph at Plattsburg*, that recounted two American victories during the War of 1812 (Phillips; Smith).

The nationalist tone of Kerr's script is obvious in its sensational title: *Rip Van Winkle; Or, The Demons of the Catskills Mountains!!! A National Drama*. As with Forrest's vehicles, the script not only salutes the new country established during Rip's twenty-year slumber, but also the democratic leanings and economic interests of small property-holders that dominated Jacksonian politics, which Bruce A. McConachie refers to as "yeoman ideology" (104–5). The conflict over the marriage of Rip's daughter, Lowenna, unfolds alongside the resistance of the village's small property-holders and businessmen against the acquisitive impulses of Derrick Van Slous and, later, his son Herman. In the play's first scene at the village inn, the patrons sing a song recalling their lives in Europe, where "though we toil'd with patient care / But poor and scanty was our fare; / By petty despots reign'd" and celebrating their arrival in "Columbia," where "We saw no palace rear its head, / To shame the meanness of our humble shed" and the soil "Rewards us though we lightly toil" (3). Nor are American institutions neglected. During the course of the closing act, Knickerbocker, who has married Alice and succeeded Van Slous, is elected to Congress by voters who praise his public spirit, and Gustaffe returns from an apprenticeship at sea as a distinguished officer in the United States Navy. Contemporary politics even find their way into the play's patriotic discourse. Waking from his slumber, Rip discovers that the bush he fell asleep under has grown into a hickory tree, echoing Jackson's nickname, "Old Hickory" (Kerr 43). When Rip inquires as to the identity of "General Washington," whose name he sees on the sign at the inn, he is informed that the "shoot of that name" he remembers from the French and Indian War "has planted the tree of liberty in a soil which all the powers of the old world will never be able to uproot" (62). This paean suggests reverence not only for Washington himself, but also for Jackson, whose supporters regularly billed him as a second Washington (Ward 189). Rip has returned to a very strange new country, indeed.

Perhaps somewhat oddly, given the shock of his political alienation, Kerr's Rip is quite defiant about his identity. Informed that he has been dead for twenty years, Rip declares, "I'm not myself; but we'll not give up the ghost till a few more questions are asked and solved," even as he echoes Irving's Rip in declaring, rather more calmly than the original "I was myself last night, but I fell asleep on the mountains, and they've changed my gun,— and every thing's changed here, and I am changed too, for a cartinty [*sic*]" (Kerr 59–60). Kerr's Rip, more-over, is subjected to a variety of tests to prove his identity. Some members of his family recognize him on sight, but when he appears in court to revoke Herman Van Slous' marriage contract with Rowenna, he must force Herman to acknowledge his identity by revealing, Ulysses-like, a scar on his forehead acquired while saving Herman from a wolf when the latter was a child. Perhaps the most certain means by which Rip is identified, however, is his trademark toast: "[H]ere's your good health, and your families, and may you all live long and prosper!" (60, 76). He utters this line when handed a jug of liquor by his friend the innkeeper Nicholas Vedder, at which point Vedder suddenly recog-nizes him, and Rip also steps forward during the play's joyous conclusion to address it to the audience. Marked off as a comic figure for his tippling, Rip is brought back into the world, ironically, by indulging in his preferred vice.

The opening hymn to the freedom and plenty afforded by Columbian soil, like Rip's habit of tippling and much else from Kerr's play, survives into Charles Burke's 1849 rendition, *Rip Van Winkle: A Legend of the Catskills,* although the later play does bear some marked differences from its forebears. The alterations are obvious from Rip's first entrance. While Kerr's Rip speaks the same form of English as the rest of the dramatis personae, Burke's Rip speaks with a pronounced German accent and his dialogue is peppered with references to his *Frau* (wife). Burke, whose tall and spindly figure made him the physical opposite of the portly Hackett, nonetheless played a combination of low comic, Yankee, and foreign dialect roles not unlike Hackett's, and a comically foreign Rip must have offered Burke a chance to show off his skills with dialect (Winter 157–8). Burke's Rip, indeed, seems to be one of the ear-liest versions of the hard-drinking, superstitious, heavily accented "stage Ger-man" that would come to be familiar to American audiences during the 1850s as German immigration increased in the wake of the failed revolution of 1848

(Richardson 278). Likewise, while Rip's drinking and his wife's angry reactions to it remain largely unchanged from Kerr's version, where a tipsy Rip accidentally destroys his wife's fine china and spends money that the family needs for rent under the sign of King George, social attitudes toward drinking underwent a substantial change in the two decades between these plays. During the interim, the temperance movement cut the average hard liquor consumption in the United States by two-thirds, W.H. Smith's 1844 melodrama *The Drunkard; or, The Fallen Saved* became a major hit, and, as significant numbers of the urban middle and working classes who patronized the theatre began to turn away from alcohol, temperance plays gained popularity in a variety of theatrical genres (Bank 142–3; McConachie 177–80).

In Burke's text, then, Rip is marked off as an "other" to the audience both by his excessive drinking and his dialect. He is likewise treated as utterly alien by the villagers upon his return home, most notably because Burke chose to script a scene reenacting the moment in Irving's story when Rip is mistaken for a Tory and nearly assaulted by the townspeople. He is saved from violence only by the timely entrance of his freshly landed nephew Gustaffe, in this version reduced to the status of a common sailor but no less morally upright than his naval predecessor. Burke's version generally tones down the ferociously patriotic rhetoric of Kerr's script, channeling it primarily through Knickerbocker, who revels in his "dignified station as representative of an independent people" (67). It is, however, noteworthy that upon once again being informed of the new, independent status of his country, Burke's Teutonic Rip Americanizes himself by drinking his trademark toast, as does Kerr's version, to "General Washington's goot health" (62).

Rip's otherness is also made clear in Burke's text by the general lack of recognition afforded him by those closest to him. No old acquaintance knows him by his toast, and even Gustaffe, who saves him, believes Rip's identity only because he knows about the arranged marriage of his daughter, Lorrena. His identity is proven in court only by his producing his own copy of the marriage contract, and then he is recognized afterwards by Lorrena and Alice, who leave the stage before he arrives in court. These recognitions only occur, moreover, after Rip, asked by the presiding judge if anyone in town knows him, delivers this plaintive lament:

> No, no, I don't know dese peoples — dey don't know me neither, and yesterday dere was not a dog in the village but would have wagged his tail at me; now dey bark. Dere's not a child but would have scrambled on my knees — now dey run from me. Are we so soon forgot when we're gone? Already dere is no one wot knows poor Rip Van Winkle [70].

Although the play will once again end with Rip toasting the audience, the melodramatic tale told by Burke's script seems to alienate the earlier, jollier version of Rip from himself, as well as from the audience. Although the spectator cannot forget the man onstage in front of them, he seems nonetheless increasingly a stranger to the world around him with each revision of the story.

Charles Burke died in 1854, and Jefferson, who would become an institution in the role of Rip, drew inspiration from the memory of his performances (Winter 156; Wilson 29). When the inspiration to attempt Rip Van winkle onstage struck Jefferson, this influence was evident in not only his performance, but also his initial attempts to perform a modified version of Burke's play that he altered himself. The role fused low comedy, at which Jefferson excelled as a young performer, with melodrama, in which Jefferson also had experience (McArthur 93). Jefferson had, for a time, performed with the Warrens at the Boston Museum, the theater that premiered such melodramatic morality plays as *The Drunkard* and *The Gambler*, and he had originated the Yankee role of Salem Scudder in *The Octoroon*, perhaps the greatest work by Dion Boucicault, the great transatlantic melodramatist (121–2, 154).

However much interest Jefferson had in his script, American audiences initially had very little. Playing his modified version of the Burke script, Jefferson bombed in New York in 1860 (the year after Irving had died) and met with at best modest success in venues ranging from Washington, DC, to California (173–88). Only while embarked on a foreign tour that allowed him to spend the American Civil War abroad and which took him as far afield as Australia (where Rip was a hit) and London did Jefferson begin to achieve the success in the role that he would later find in the United States (194). While in London, Jefferson asked Boucicault to re-write his script, and their collaborative effort ran for one hundred and seventy nights in London (Wilson 37). By the time Jefferson returned to the United States in 1865 like Rip coming down from the mountain, and opened the new version of the play in New York on August 13, 1866, his version of Rip had evolved into a figure that would make both actor and role famous not just in a town in the Hudson Valley, but across the entire nation (Winter 190).

The Jefferson/Boucicault collaboration is, unsurprisingly, even more melodramatic than its progenitors written by Kerr and Burke. In this version, Rip has been reduced to his state of poverty by drink, having once been the largest landholder in the village but also having gradually mortgaged and consumed the value of all of his lands. In the play's first act, Gretchen prepares to sell the family's only bull, their last remaining asset, to the butcher, and even Rip shows an awareness of his folly, sadly telling his daughter, Meenie, that he has squandered her inheritance on drink. Nonetheless, Rip determinedly continues to drink throughout the play's first two acts, repeatedly swearing off liquor only to violate his oath a moment later — a device used for comic effect in Burke but done with great poignancy here. In the scene where Rip leaves the house for the mountain, fleeing like Lear into a storm, he has already threatened to wreck the house because Gretchen withholds liquor from him and leaves only because Gretchen finally forces him to face his own shame. During Rip's slumber, the impoverished Gretchen will be forced to marry Von Beekman and Rip will have to rescue his wife as well as his daughter and lands from the clutches of the villainous attorney.

Jefferson and Boucicault's script downplays the political changes that have taken place in the United States during Rip's twenty-year slumber while heightening the vertiginous quality of Rip's homecoming. Gone are the hymns to Columbian liberty, gone are the salutes to the heroism of George Washington, and gone is the angry mob of voters. The only reminder of American independence is the sign over the village inn, which both the script and contemporary photographic evidence indicate was switched from George III to George Washington during Rip's sleep (Jefferson and Boucicault 153; Johnson 7, 17). While it seems unlikely that Jefferson and Boucicault would have wished to stage loud declarations of American patriotism on the London stage, Hackett, Jefferson, and other Americans had played boisterously patriotic Americans onstage in Britain with success. The collaborators clearly made a decision to omit such displays of patriotism from the script, including, Jefferson claimed in his *Autobiography*, once rejecting a suggestion that he include "in the last act the Continental army with drums and fifes, a militia training, and the further introduction of patriotic speeches about American independence" (457). Indeed, Donald R. Anderson views the play as a text embodying the spirit of post-bellum reconciliationism, a story reflecting "the need of a divided and bewildered nation to move quickly beyond the reality of the last four years in order to draw the former combatants together" (14). Rip's struggle to remember and be remembered mirrors both Jefferson and Boucicault's struggles with the textual legacies of Kerr and Burke, and a national need to both remember and forget.

No version of Rip is more thoroughly forgotten upon his re-entry than Jefferson's. His nephew Gustaffe has been replaced by Henrick, the tavern keeper's son, but in any case his young champion does not recognize him. When Rip offers his trademark toast at the inn, nobody recognizes him. His own wife and daughter initially treat him as a mere indolent beggar. Questioning a villager about the fates of his old cronies, he finds that so many are dead that he wails "Is there anybody alive here at all?" (161). The play's heightened concern with memory and forgetting becomes particularly clear as the forgotten Rip pleads with Meenie for recognition in a speech that seems to be as much about reassuring himself of his own memories as trying to jog hers:

> This village here is the village of Falling Waters. Well, that was my home. I had here in this place my wife Gretchen, and my child Meenie — little Meenie — *A long pause, during which he strives to re-assemble his ideas and memories more accurately.*

and my dog Schneider. That's all the family what I've got. Try and remember dear, won't you?

Pleadingly.

I don't know when it was — This night there was a storm; and my wife drove me from my house; and I went away — I don't remember any more till I come back here now. And see, I get back now, and my wife is gone, and my home is gone, and my child — my child looks in my face, and don't know who I am! [188–9].

Only at this moment does Meenie recognize her father and begin a reconciliation process so complete that at the end Gretchen even grants Rip permission to get drunk as often as he likes, which he denies that he will do except to take up one final cup of liquor and drink the health of his audiences both on — and offstage. Rip's taking of the cup is "a reconciliationist moment in both the relief it provides and the forgetfulness it invites" (Anderson 27). Rip's own struggle to assemble his thoughts and memories in pleading with Meenie, so reminiscent of the stage drunk struggling to order his thoughts, concludes when he accepts the cup. The glass of liquor that consumes Rip's memory both before and after his flight into the mountains here becomes its own antidote, the social ritual that marks the prodigal Rip's reintegration into his community. By closing, as Kerr and Burke had done, with a toast, Jefferson and Boucicault mirror the conclusion of Irving's story, in which Rip becomes the center of his own historical spectacle. Joseph Jefferson, meanwhile, stepped into the national memory as the living embodiment of Rip, a figure whose very name conjures both distant historical memory and the collective amnesia of American society.

Washington Irving's story displays tensions between persistence and displacement, as well as between memory and forgetting, that echo in the dramatic adaptations of the tale that followed and the careers of the men who played Rip on stage. It is worth remembering that while the elder Rip is taken in by his daughter and her husband, his ragamuffin son and heir is never fully domesticated in the story once he usurps his father's place as the village idler. Jefferson, keenly aware of the mechanics of theatrical dynasties, likewise grew aware as he grew older that the part of Rip would not remain his forever. In 1897, he gave over his annual national tour as Rip and passed the role on to his son Tom (McArthur 345). Nor was Jefferson the only observer aware of the impermanence of even the most glorified theatrical role or career. In 1896, Jefferson's chronicler Francis Wilson proposed placing a memorial plaque at Jefferson's birthplace in Philadelphia. Jefferson rejected the idea, but Wilson and two friends erected the plaque anyway. The plaque commemorates Jefferson's birth at the site and addresses Rip's trademark toast to passersby. Irving's Rip is fated to pass from a local celebrity to a mere testimonial in a deposition whose identity and veracity are authenticated in writing by a justice of the peace, Diedrich Knickerbocker, and Geoffrey Crayon. Joseph Jefferson and his Rip eventually found themselves memorialized in print, even while still very much alive, in a testimonial designed to make sure that they would not soon be forgotten when they were gone.

Works Cited

Anderson, Donal R. "Renaming American Fault Lines in the Joseph Jefferson Version of *Rip Van Winkle.*" *Nineteenth-Century Theatre and Film* 30.2 (Winter 2003): 14–32. Print.

Bank, Rosemarie K. *Theatre Culture in America, 1825–1860.* New York: Cambridge University Press, 1997. Print.

Brown, T. Allston. *History of the American Stage.* 1870. New York: Benjamin Blom, 1969. Print.

Burke, Charles. *Rip Van Winkle: A Legend of the Catskills. Representative Plays by American Dramatists, 1856–1911.* Ed. Montrose J. Moses. 1921. New York: Benjamin Blom, 1964. 15–71. Print.

Grimsted, David. *Melodrama Unveiled: American Theater and Culture, 1800–1850.* Chicago: University of Chicago Press, 1968. Print.

Hellman, George S. *Washington Irving Esquire.* New York: Knopf, 1925. Print.

Irving, Washington. *The Sketch-Book of Geoffrey Crayon, Gent.* Ed. Haskell Springer. Boston: Twayne, 1978. Print.

Jefferson, Joseph. *The Autobiography of Joseph Jefferson.* New York: The Century Company, 1889. Print.

Jefferon, Joseph, and Dion Boucicault. *Rip Van Winkle.* New York: Dodd, 1896. Print.

Johnson, Stephen. "Joseph Jefferson's *Rip Van Winkle.*" *The Drama Review: TDR* 26.1 (Spring 1982): 3–20. Print.

Kerr, John. *Rip Van Winkle; Or, The Demons of the Catskill Mountains!!! A National Drama.* Philadelphia: R.H. Lenfestey, 1829. Print.

McArthur, Benjamin. *The Man Who Was Rip Van Winkle: Joseph Jefferson and Nineteenth-Century American Theatre.* New Haven: Yale University Press, 2007. Print.

McConachie, Bruce A. *Melodramatic Formations: American Theatre & Society, 1820–1870.* Iowa City: University of Iowa Press, 1992. Print.

Phillips, Kim T. "The Pennsylvanian Origins of the Jackson Movement." *Political Science Quarterly* 91.3 (Autumn 1976): 489–508. Print.

Quinn, Arthur Hobson. "Introduction." *Rip Van Winkle,* by Charles Daly Burke. *Representative American Plays, 1767–1923.* 3d ed. Ed. Arthur Hobson Quinn. New York: The Century Company, 1925. 461–3. Print.

Rahill, Frank. *The World of Melodrama.* University Park: Pennsylvania State University Press, 1967. Print.

Reichart, Walter. "Washington Irving and the Theatre." *Critical Essays on Washington Irving.* Ed. Ralph M. Aderman. Boston: G.K. Hall, 1990. 166–78. Print.

Richardson, Gary A. "Plays and Playwrights: 1800–1865." *The Cambridge History of American Theatre.* Volume 1 of 3. Ed. Don B. Wilmeth and Christopher Bigsby. New York: Cambridge University Press, 1998. 250–302. Print.

Rodes, Sara Puryear. "Washington Irving's Use of Traditional Folklore." *New York Folklore Quarterly* 13 (1957): 3–15. Print.

Smith, Richard Penn. *The Eighth of January.* Philadelphia: Neal and Mackenzie, 1829. Print.

_____. *The Triumph at Plattsburg. Representative American Plays 1799–1854.* Ed. Arthur Hobson Quinn. New York: The Century Company, 1917. 165–80. Print.

Ward, John William. *Andrew Jackson: Symbol for an Age.* Oxford: Oxford University Press, 1955. Print.

Wilson, Francis. *Joseph Jefferson: Reminiscences of a Fellow Player.* New York: Charles Scribner's Sons, 1906. Print.

Winter, William. *The Jeffersons.* 1881. New York: Benjamin Blom, 1969. Print.

Young, Philip. "Fallen From Time: Rip Van Winkle." *American Fiction, American Myth: Essays by Philip Young.* Ed. David Morrell and Sandra Whipple Spanier. University Park: Pennsylvania State University Press, 2000. 3–23. Print.

PART II
Cultural Intertextuality

Section Three: Cultural Texts

Looking for *Herland*

Embodying the Search for Utopia in *Susan Glaspell's* The Verge

FRANKLIN J. LASIK

When discussing feminist politics at the turn of the twentieth century, perhaps no two voices are more significant than those of Charlotte Perkins Gilman and Susan Glaspell; in this essay, I will discuss some hitherto unexplored connections between Gilman and Glaspell's presentation of the search for what should be termed a *female utopia*. Writing across several genres, Gilman spoke out on issues relevant to the role of women in American society, especially issues of work, education, and health care. Among these works are three novels dealing with feminist utopias: *Moving the Mountain*, *Herland*, and *With Her in Outland*. Each of these novels approaches utopia from a different perspective. In *Moving the Mountain*, Gilman employs a technique similar to that of Washington Irving's *Rip Van Winkle*, with explorer John Robertson returning to America in 1940 after having been missing for thirty years in Tibet, discovering society dominated by the "New Woman," who has found freedom through a reconstruction of American society. *Herland* tells the story of three male explorers who stumble upon a hidden land populated only by women, where they are educated in a way of life dominated by female values. The sequel to this novel, *With Her in Outland*, relates the experiences of Vandyck Jennings (one-third of the original expeditionary party), and his Herlander wife Ellador as they return to the outside world. There, Ellador notes the failings of contemporary Victorian society before ultimately abandoning Outland in favor of a return to Herland.

Of these three works, *Herland* continues to be the most relevant of Gilman's utopian novels, contrasting an ideal feminine society to a hegemonically masculinized civilization. Gilman reveals Herland through the eyes of outside intruders from the society of her contemporary readers, to whom the residents of Herland explain their feminist philosophies as standard and logical. By normativizing these feminine values as a guiding social principle, Gilman is able to present a clear, specific conception of a feminist utopia that exists outside of time rather than as a counterpoint to the dominant culture, thus freeing her from having to take on contemporary debates of feminist and anti-feminists alike. In essence, she is able to create a prescription for social improvement without necessarily concerning herself with its implementation within the context of an existing society. But the luxury of a depiction of a society outside of historical forces raises significant questions: what happens when the search for a feminine utopia is enacted in contemporary Western society? What struggles arise? How does a woman attempt to find an escape from hegemonic male dominance, and what obstacles stand in her way?

Susan Glaspell's 1921 expressionist play *The Verge* offers an excellent example of this embodied search for a female utopia. Ostensibly, Claire Archer is breeding plants in a greenhouse on her estate in search of a new form, a plant that is alien, unrecognizable, not better but "different" (Glaspell 76). This search, of course, represents more than botany; it is an attempt to discover life outside of the rigid definitions imposed upon Claire from all sides, from men and women, from the near and distant, all working in concert to limit the roles she may play in society. In many ways, Claire is less looking for a feminine utopia than she is creating one, metaphorically carrying out her search in the creation of the Breath of Life, a flower intended to be "alive in its otherness" (62). In this essay, I examine how *The Verge* serves as an embodied portrayal of the creation of utopia, and how the act of embodying utopia affects the way in which it is portrayed. I will begin with a brief discussion of how utopian literature functions as critical commentary, with emphasis placed on explicating *Herland* within this frame. I will then offer a description of the most significant elements of Gilman's image of utopia in this work, to be followed by an examination of whether, and if so how, *The Verge* addresses these issues. The final section of the paper will illustrate how the portrayal of utopia is complicated by the embodied nature of performance.

Utopian literature has a long history, beginning at least in ancient Greece and continuing to our own age. Most identify Thomas More's *Utopia* as the origin of the term, which is believed to be a combination of the Greek words *topos* (place) and *ou* (no), suggesting both a place that does not exist and a place existing outside the world as we know it. These ideal situations serve more as social commentary than as prescriptive recipes for creating a new society. Critic Elaine Hoffman Baruch suggests that "Utopias often reveal the times in which they were written more than the future" ("Visions" 204); by examining how a particular utopia is constructed in opposition to the existing social paradigms at the time of writing, a great deal can be gleaned about the environment in which the author created his vision. I consciously use the masculine pronoun here, as the vast majority of utopian writers have been male, and as such embrace a particular frame in their conception of the ideal society. Plato, More, Francis Bacon, and Aldous Huxley represent a small sampling of the writers who have produced utopian fiction. This preponderance of male viewpoints makes Gilman's *Herland* and other feminist utopian novels all the more important, providing an oppositional perspective to masculinized archetypes. Baruch believes that by being "deeply involved in personal relationships, in artistic processes, in the fusion of individual development and the cohesion of the group, women's utopias escape the statism and the cold rigidities of traditional male utopias at the same time that they avoid the glorification of the body to the exclusion of reason" ("Visions" 203). This understanding of female utopias reveals a more humanistic ideal, one focused on the nurturing and edification of people as relational, emotional beings, capable of reason but more interested in the interpersonal effects reason invokes. In Elaine Showalter's history of American women's writing, *A Jury of Her Peers*, a title incidentally taken from a Glaspell short story, the author calls Gilman "the leading American feminist theoretician and New Woman writer to come out of the 1890s," who put forth "the idea that writing itself could be a separate country for women" (221). This assertion, that the act of writing can create a utopic space, is fascinating, particularly in its focus on language. By using written language as a means of expression, Gilman is arguing a woman is in essence practicing active resistance through an act atypical to women at the turn of the twentieth century, particularly as a means of social criticism. Indeed, Baruch offers that "for women ... utopia is a way of arriving at freedom" (Introduction xii), an ideal society in an ideal situation, one that can be constructed and viewed from a wide variety of perspectives.

How, then, should we view Gilman's utopian vision in *Herland*? Several critics have weighed in on this subject. Libby Falk Jones suggests that "*Herland* may be described as a fiction organized to show what women can be and do when they are free to develop as persons, rather than as females in a patriarchal society" (117). This reading of the novel offers Gilman's utopia as a land in which the concept of gender is moot, and thus women are treated as people rather than "females." Carol Farley Kessler focuses on the intersection of societies, in which the potential of the utopian collide with the reality of the world in which the novel was written: "In Gilman's utopianism, a discourse of possibility (or realizability) collides with a discourse of realism, completely changing the latter" (*Charlotte* 8). Sally L. Kitch's understanding of *Herland* focuses primarily on the economic differences, noting that

> Charlotte Perkins Gilman identified women's economic self-sufficiency and support of children as essential to utopia ... public nurseries, communal kitchens, and woman-centered apartment houses replace the private home, and professionalized household services relieve the domestic drudgery of individual women. Gilman's other reforms include meaningful, paid work for women and the curtailment of men's prerogatives [65–6].

Thus, in Kitch's view, the social freedoms enjoyed by the women of Herland are the direct result of eliminating the distinction between public and private spheres. These various assessments of the utopian elements of *Herland* seem to point to a larger question, namely the ways utopian literature is meant to be used. Kessler, in another work entitled *Daring to Dream*, writes that "utopias, as apologues, foment speculation, offer alternative vicarious experience, spur us as readers to reevaluate and act upon our own world — create new consensus, establish new community" (xvii). In this view, utopia is less focused on the specific changes than the idea that change is possible, and that this type of literature provides opportunities for discussion and cooperation. Critic Erin McKenna seconds this view of utopian fiction's ability to effect change: "Common to definitions of utopia in terms of function is the idea that they are visions of optimism and hope that can inspire and help people to make changes. Utopian visions can be transformative" (8). Thus, for the purposes of this examination, the definition of the utopia presented in *Herland* is this: an idealized vision of a society constructed solely on feminist principles, with the intent of sparking discussion about the role of women in contemporary society without necessarily proposing direct implementation.

But how is this utopia actually presented in the text? As described above, the novel is the record of three male explorers who stumble upon an unnamed land inhabited only by women, which the men name Herland. Each explorer embodies a particular point of view: Terry O. Nicholson is a man's man, who struggles to accept that a land can exist without men (not just biologically, but socially as well); Jeff Margrave, the born romantic, who wants nothing but to take care of women, to remove any burden from them (whether real or perceived); and Vandyck Jennings (or simply Van), the narrator, a sociologist with perhaps the most flexible point of view. The three are eventually taken into the society and educated in the history of the land and the ways of Herland's culture. They learn that men were wiped out almost two thousand years ago, the result of war, revolt, and an "act of God" in the form of a volcanic eruption (Gilman 194). The resulting absence of men led to a societal sea change: "For five or ten years they worked together, growing stronger and wiser and more and more mutually attached, and then the miracle happened — one of these young women bore a child" (Gilman 195). Through parthenogenesis, the women were able to survive, replenishing the previously decimated population. In addition to their education, the explorers are each assigned a female companion, carefully chosen for their compatibility, with the intention that each woman would become a partner to her charge, although the concept of marriage is foreign to them. Thus, the dialogue becomes more personal than that between instructor and student, allowing for a more emotional discourse concerning the differences between the two societies. By the end of

Gilman's novel, each man has come to a different fate: Terry, charged with sexual assault, is expelled from Herland; Jeff, enamored with his new partner and Herland as a whole, decides to remain; and Van and his partner Ellador choose to leave Herland in order to allow Ellador to complete a report on Outland.

The Herlandian society differs from that of the outside world in several key ways. The first significant difference is a communal mode of thinking. Van, frustrated with Ellador's indifference toward sexuality, tells her that he "hadn't married the nation, and [he] told her so. But she only smiled at her own limitations, and explained that she had to 'think in we's'" (Gilman 255). Ellador's conception of society as a communal endeavor means that her personal desires are not in conflict with the community, nor are the community's expectations at odds with her. Rather, the two work in unison, and the decision to engage in sex, which might produce a child, runs counter to the needs of Herland. Indeed, population control is another significant element of the Herland society. However, rather than the stringent laws that exist in many parts of our own world, pregnancy is managed by the society as a whole, removing the hierarchical structure of power. Women will only become pregnant when they choose to do so, and this choice is made in concert with the rest of the village. As Van observes, "They were Mothers, not in our sense of helpless involuntary fecundity, forced to fill and overfill the land, every land, and then see their children suffer, sin, and die, fighting horribly with one another; but in the sense of Conscious Makers of People" (Gilman 205). The ability to control pregnancy also points to a degree of sexual control, which is a significant point for Showalter: "Among the more controversial elements of *Herland* is Gilman's insistence that their evolution depends on their acceptance of diminished and controlled sexual desire. For men to do well in Herland, they must learn to redirect their erotic feelings toward worship of women rather than domination..." (Showalter 251). This again points to the element of control possessed by women that is assumed to be unavailable in the world outside of Herland. Other elements of this society are: an absence of separation between public and private spheres, as evidenced by the women's confusion when one of the men mentions "the home" (Gilman 199); a lack of excessive pride in individual achievement, which is replaced by a gratefulness from those enjoying those accomplishments; and religion, which is described as a "Maternal Pantheism," devoid of deities related to war and strife (Gilman 198).

Perhaps the most important difference noted by the narrator is the importance placed on motherhood in this society. Quite early in his time in Herland, Van notes that "children were the — the *raison d'être* in this country" (Gilman 191). The focus on motherhood guides the vast majority of life in Herland.

The process of child-rearing involves the birth mother of the child, but her constant, direct interaction with her child lasts only a year or two. After this time, the child is taken into the care of women who are trained specifically to educate children, although the mother was "never far off, however, and her attitude toward the co-mothers whose proud child-service was direct and continuous, was lovely to see" (Gilman 234). The process of educating children is closely tied to the nurturing model of motherhood, as the children are not socialized to understand learning as a form of punishment. Rather, "they found themselves in an immediate environment which was agreeable and interesting, and before them stretched the years of learning and discovery, the fascinating, endless process of education" (Gilman 235). The central part of childhood education is that children are supported, that they will grow up in a society that seeks not to coddle them, but to provide for all their needs while allowing them to make mistakes, thus learning from their experience. This education is meant to encourage future generations to improve their state of being, always pushing toward a higher standard of living. In this sense, as Van notes, "their time-sense was not limited to the hopes and ambitions of an individual life" (Gilman 214). Critic Minna Doskow cites this maternal impulse as the organizing principle behind Herland: "On what foundation does she build her utopia, if not on formal systems? On one giant building block, and one only — motherhood, the relationship of mother and child" (56).

The utopian existence presented in *Herland* is appealing in many aspects. There is no war, no hunger, and no poverty. The community, working as a cohesive unit, strives for continual improvement of both the self and the society. However, it is important to note the limitations of the form in which Gilman chose to depict this society. By placing it within the static world of prose, Herland can exist in perpetuity, without the pressure to display the society as a functioning entity. Indeed, it seems the luxury of a motionless, changeless environment allows the utopian society to go largely unchallenged in any immediate sense, with responses delayed by the very act of reading and interpretation. Glaspell's *The Verge*, on the other hand, presents a character, Claire Archer, who is desperate to find utopia, to escape the masculine hegemony that surrounds her. By depicting her struggle on stage in dramatic form, which is played out in real time before an audience, the search for utopia is revealed to be a messy, difficult process, replete with obstacles. Glaspell's choice to embody the search for a feminist utopia in the theatre reveals feminist Utopian novels such as *Herland* as primarily theoretical in nature, a quality Kessler notes of Gilman: "In [*Herland*], she simply emulated scientific method: remove one variable to discover how another will function on its own, a veritable thought experiment" (*Charlotte* 69). We can thus read *The Verge* as an attempt to put this thought experiment into practice, with one important difference: here, it is Claire who wants to remove herself, as the ideal woman, from the dystopia in which she believes herself to be. Her utopia, unlike Herland, is to be a space large enough only for one, and defined largely by the possibility of escaping the rigid social codes laid down upon her by the masculinist society surrounding her.

From her first entrance, Claire Archer is clearly obsessed with the idea of change. Her plants represent an outlet for a desire to move beyond the established world and into the unknown; it quickly becomes clear, however, that these plants serve as a powerfully complex metaphor. C.W.E. Bigsby, in his introduction to *Plays by Susan Glaspell*, notes that Claire "breeds plants which will transcend their origins, make some leap beyond the norm. It soon becomes plain that she plans much the same for herself" (20); thus, the plants can be seen as a general allegory for Claire's own transformation. Other critics note more specific examples of the symbology of the plant-life in Claire's greenhouse. Monica Stufft connects Claire's botanical impulses to a reaction against paternalism: "Claire cultivates the flowers in resistance to a connection to her forefathers, but also as a means to refuse men's control over her activities and the resultant relegation to the domestic. The more successful Claire is with the flowers, the further she moves away from the social roles that bind her to the people in the play" (83). Barbara Ozieblo expands the reach of Claire's actions, noting the impact on her supposed sanity as constructed by the external society: "Throughout *The Verge*, Claire struggles to overcome the limitations of personal relationships, of family life, of science and nature and of all that holds human beings within bounds; she stands on the verge of society and therefore sanity" (73). In each of these readings, Claire's efforts reflect a vigorous resistance to attempts to define her identity as a woman, even, as Ozieblo hints at, redefining the concept of sanity.

Claire's attempts at escape are linked to two specific plants: the Edge Vine and the Breath of Life. The Edge Vine represents the as yet most successful experiment at the beginning of the play. Anthony, Claire's assistant, points to its uniqueness, contrasting it with Claire's husband Harry: "There's a million people like you — and like Mr. Archer. In all the world there is only one Edge Vine" (Glaspell 60). The vine is described in the stage directions as "arresting rather than beautiful. It creeps along the low wall, and one branch gets a little way up the glass.... The leaves of this vine are not the form that leaves have been. They are at once repellent and significant" (Glaspell 58). What is significant in this description is the way in which the vine is constructed as striking as opposed to attractive. By emphasizing this distinction, Glaspell points to the true character of the change Claire is seeking; in other words, Claire's efforts to devise new and unique life is driven by a desire for change divorced from the judgment of others, free from the stultifying influence of society as she knows it, particularly the masculine imperative that all women should strive for beauty over substance. This is made more clear when Claire rejects the Edge Vine, which she addresses directly, saying, "I thought you were out, but you're — going back home" (Glaspell 62). This implicit criticism of "home" calls forth a reminiscence of Gilman's rejection of the separation between the home and the public sphere, suggesting that the Edge Vine is therefore confined to the feminine home and should thus be considered a failure. Indeed, this rejection of the vine is brought to a climax at the end of Act I, when she pulls the plant out of the ground by its roots, an act that cements the failure of this particular experiment while simultaneously denouncing the subjection of women to the private sphere.

After the failure of the Edge Vine to continue over the edge, the Breath of Life stands as Claire's opportunity to achieve a botanical and resistive legacy. Claire's description of Breath of Life emphasizes the newness and fragility of the flower, a combination of past forms with the very air: "[d]istilled from the most fragile flowers there are. It's only air — pausing — playing; except for one stab of red, its quivering heart, that asks a question. But here's the trick — I bred the air — form to strength" (Glaspell 86). This depiction is less visual than thematic, both for Claire and the audience; rather than focusing on the aesthetic elements of this new breed of plant, she phrases her portrayal in terms of substance and implication. The flower is created from the very air, created from nothing, gaining strength from that very formlessness. And within that airy strength lies a "quivering heart," a red sliver remarkable for its starkness and apparent incongruity with the rest of the design. This juxtaposition between the solidity of the throbbing heart and the delicate transparency of the outer casing represents the new form Claire is seeking for herself, one that can embrace the delicate femininity without having to lose her heart, to give up her passion in order to fit within the constraints of the social order in which she lives. In Act III, it seems as though Claire's experiment is a success:

> CLAIRE: It has come through?
> ANTHONY: It has gone on.
> CLAIRE: Stronger?
> ANTHONY: Stronger, surer.
> CLAIRE: And more fragile?
> ANTHONY: And more fragile.
> CLAIRE: Look deep. No — turning back?
> ANTHONY: The form is set
> CLAIRE: Then it is — out [Glaspell 96].

And yet, despite this seeming victory, there is a sense that rather than finding escape, Claire has simply created a new form that has made no appreciable step forward. Bigsby notes this failure to achieve true escape, suggesting that "the Breath of Life has made its leap into a new existence only to become a new repressive form" (24). In this sense, then, Claire's second experiment is unsuccessful, and she must find some other means of escape.

The women of Herland have had two millennia to create social structures that encourage women to embrace their femininity free from the restraints of men. However, it was the initial catastrophe that allowed these women the opportunity to enact a nearly complete shift in their society, which has left them eminently content. In a sense, what Claire is seeking is her own cataclysm, a breaking of the societal norms that have largely determined the course of her life. Claire's botanical experiments can be seen as a metaphorical search for this catastrophic break with the deterministic social structures she is struggling to escape, a struggle opposed by both the men and the women surrounding her. Elizabeth and Adelaide, although women, represent for Claire the oppressive force of the masculine as imprinted on the feminine. Adelaide is an authority on normative behavior, several times castigating Claire for her refusal to accede to these cultural standards: "Come, come, Claire; you know quite well this is not the sort of thing one does" (Glaspell 84). This attitude is mirrored in Claire's daughter, which is unsurprising considering how much more time Elizabeth seems to have spent with her aunt than her mother. As Stufft notes, "Claire outright rejects her daughter, Elizabeth, because she upholds the traditional gender dichotomy Claire is trying to escape" (83). The same phrasing of behavior comes from Elizabeth, using the term "one" rather than the more assertive "I" or "you." Added to this is a flippancy about life, a leisure class-bred predilection toward idleness: "But you see I don't do anything interesting, so I have to have good manners" (Glaspell 74). Elizabeth's New England ethnic snobbery is reaffirmed in her view of her mother's botany, which reflects her teacher's assertion that "it is your splendid heritage gives you this impulse to do a beautiful thing for the race. She says you are doing in your way what the great teachers and preachers behind you did in theirs" (Glaspell 75). This inability to comprehend the world outside of patriarchal social constructions is what infuriates Claire, making her, in critic Mary E. Papke's words, "increasingly unable to connect to others and finally suffers an apartness the effects of which are ... disastrous" (27).

In addition to Claire's attempts to create a rupture with patriarchal social structures, other issues in *The Verge* seem tied to the idea of a female utopia as Gilman imagined it. The three primary male characters in Glaspell's play, Tom, Dick and Harry, share parallels with the three explorers from *Herland*. Harry matches closely with Terry, the man's man, set in his understanding of how the world works; Dick can be read as Jeff, who in many ways flows through life as it is handed to him; and Tom shares a great deal with Van, particularly in his efforts to understand Claire's attempts at escape, just as Van worked to comprehend his new wife and her society. In each case, these men stand as obstacles to Claire's work, either through direct opposition, as is the case with Harry, or as a seductive distraction, like Tom. Harry is clearly unsure of what Claire is really seeking, claiming that "you might know all there is to know about women and not know much about Claire" (Glaspell 66). Indeed, this particular phrasing carries a double meaning, that (1) Claire is so complex as to escape Harry's comprehension and (2) Claire is denied womanhood itself, at least as such a concept is constructed by Harry and, by extension, society at large. Thus, Harry's well-meaning attempts to "fix" Claire, to bring her within the acceptable margins of social norms echo, from Claire's perspective, the oppressive forces against which for so long she has been fighting.

Tom, on the other hand, seems to understand that Claire is different, noting that "Claire isn't hardened into one of those forms she talks about. She's too — aware. Always pulled toward what could be — tormented by the lost adventure" (Glaspell 71). In these terms, he seems to comprehend what Claire is saying: in order to escape, to find a way out, she must escape the formalistic patterns of existence that have been constructed around and for her. Tom also appears to recognize the restrictive effect his own presence has on Claire, that if a romantic relationship developed between them, it would give her a reason to remain in the world and not try to escape: "you've asked what you yourself could answer best. We'd only stop in the country where everyone stops" (Glaspell 86). Yet after seeing Claire's reaction to Breath of Life's return to a normal pattern, Tom reverses his decision to leave and begs her to stay with him. He entreats her in much more controlling language, exhibiting a masculinized dominance that was absent from his earlier speeches. He talks of owning Claire: "I love you, and I will keep you — from farther-ness — from harm. You are mine, and you will stay with me! You hear me? You will stay with me!" (Glaspell 99). This change in language coincides with Claire recognizing Breath of Life's failure, and thus, it becomes clear that Tom represents another change in patterns rather than an escape. The seeming violence of his language, centered on controlling Claire, means she only has one choice — she must physically destroy him before she can break free by symbolically destroy herself.

Much as Terry is ejected from Herland as a result of his inability to accept a feminist worldview, Harry is unable to comprehend Claire, both her actions and her motivations, and is essentially ejected from Claire's world. Dick, like Jeff, is willing to accept that there is something going on that is beyond his comprehension and is essentially a willing (if passive) participant in Claire's explorations. Tom, however, diverges from Van; whereas the latter is anxious to explore both Herland and Outland, Tom ultimately cannot relinquish his masculine power, and thus orders Claire to surrender herself to him. Ironically, it is because of Claire's act of resistance against Tom's demands that she is finally able to break through. Here is where the difference between the prose of *Herland* and the embodied struggle portrayed in *The Verge* is most concrete. In *Herland*, violence is unheard of— this makes Terry's act of violence against his partner all the more shocking. More importantly, it is the intruding male that instigates the violence, and as a result he is expelled from paradise. For Claire, it is only through the murder of Tom that she is able to escape the frames placed around her, to break out of her constrictive social roles once and for all. In this sense, her violence is constructive in its destruction. Veronica Makowsky reads the murder as Claire's "final and total alienation as she retreats into madness" (63); this alienation represents a complete break from the world, thus casting madness as a kind of rebellion against the traditional construction of sanity as acknowledgement and enactment of normalized behavior. Claire's strides toward utopia, then, are immersed in questions of madness and sanity, normal and abnormal, masculine and feminine. She is constantly struggling against pressure from all sides, and thus Glaspell shows us the difficulty in creating a utopian space within patriarchal society, a stark difference from the relative ease with which Gilman is able to explore Herland.

By using *Herland* as a frame for examining Claire's struggle against patriarchy in *The Verge*, several significant points are revealed. First, Gilman's novel is revealed to be a thought experiment, a hypothetical situation never intended to be literally enacted in real life. These kinds of work do have value, as a means of instigating debate and conjecture; however, they lack a good deal of practicality, as can be seen in Claire's situation. Rather than an arrival into a peaceful utopia, she is constantly at war with herself and others, fighting to make her point of view understood and heard, and she must ultimately construct her own utopia herself, out of the air, as it were. Second, the ideals espoused in *Herland*, such as motherhood, communal socialization, and a lack of gender division, become much more complex when resisted bodily. In particular, motherhood is complicated here by the socialization process Elizabeth has gone through, making her little more than a mouthpiece for the masculine ideals of femininity. While the Herlandian philosophy of life revolves around children, Claire is not given that luxury, as her child has ceased to become relevant to her. Finally, the acceptance of a feminine ideal of utopian existence is understood to be implicit at the end of *Herland*; while Terry refuses to accede to the Herlandian way of life, his exclusion is seen as a kind of poetic justice, a punishment for his inability to appreciate the ultimate egalitarian society. Claire's utopia, in contrast, is constructed as madness; the resolution of the play, in which Claire exits singing "Nearer My God To Thee," leaves the audience without a clear sense of resolution. Perhaps Claire is only able to get out by crossing over into insanity. It might also be that this mental breakdown reveals the world from which Claire is escaping as mad itself; thus, we might regard her transition as simply regained sanity in an otherwise insane world. The indeterminacy of Claire's "outside" is a necessary byproduct of the challenges in constructing a new utopia within an existing society. This embodied search is a productive counterpoint to Gilman's novel, revealing the difficulties attendant on such a large change in social structures. The question is whether one is willing to make those sacrifices.

Works Cited

Baruch, Elaine Hoffman. "Introduction: The Quest and the Questions, I." *Women in Search of Utopia: Mavericks and Mythmakers.* Ed. Ruby Rohrlich and Elaine Hoffman Baruch. New York: Schocken, 1984. xi–xv

_____. "Visions of Utopia: Introduction." *Women in Search of Utopia: Mavericks and Mythmakers.* Ed. Ruby Rohrlich and Elaine Hoffman Baruch. New York: Schocken, 1984. 203–8.

Bigsby, C.W.E, ed. "Introduction." *Plays by Susan Glaspell.* Ed. C.W.E. Bigsby. Cambridge: Cambridge University Press, 1987. 1–31.

Doskow, Minna. "*Herland*: Utopia in a Different Voice." *Politics, Gender, and the Arts: Women, the Arts, and Society.* Ed. Ronald Dotterer and Susan Bowers. Selinsgrove, PA: Susquehanna University Press, 1992. 52–63.

Gilman, Charlotte Perkins. *Herland. Charlotte Perkins Gilman's Utopian Novels:* Moving the Mountain, Herland, *and* With Her in Outland, Ed. Minna Doskow. Madison, NJ: Fairleigh Dickinson University Press, 1999. 150–269.

Glaspell, Susan. *The Verge. Plays by Susan Glaspell.* Ed. C.W.E. Bigsby. Cambridge: Cambridge University Press, 1987. 57–101.

Jones, Libby Falk. "Gilman, Bradley, Piercy, and the Evolving Rhetoric of Feminist Utopias." *Feminism, Utopia, and Narrative,* Ed. Libby Falk Jones and Sarah Webster Goodwin. Knoxville: University of Tennessee Press, 1990. 116–29.

Kessler, Carol Farley. *Charlotte Perkins Gilman: Her Progress Toward Utopia with Selected Writings.* Syracuse: Syracuse University Press, 1995.

_____, ed. *Daring to Dream: Utopian Fiction by United States Women Before 1950.* 2d ed. Syracuse, NY: Syracuse University Press, 1995.

Kitch, Sally L. *Higher Ground: From Utopianism to Realism in American Feminist Thought and Theory.* Chicago: University of Chicago Press, 2000.

Makowsky, Veronica. "Susan Glaspell and Modernism." *The Cambridge Companion to American Women Playwrights.* Ed. Brenda Murphy. Cambridge: Cambridge University Press, 1999. 49–65.

McKenna, Erin. *The Task of Utopia: A Pragmatist and Feminist Perspective.* Lanham, MD: Rowan & Littlefield, 2001.

Ozieblo, Barbara, and Jerry Dickey. *Susan Glaspell and Sophie Treadwell.* Routledge Modern and Contemporary Dramatists. London: Routledge, 2008.

Papke, Mary E. "Susan Glaspell's Naturalist Scenarios of Determinism and Blind Faith." *Disclosing Intertextualities: The Stories, Plays, and Novels of Susan Glaspell.* Ed. Martha C. Carpentier and Barbara Ozieblo. New York: Rodopi, 2006. 19–34.

Showalter, Elaine. *A Jury of Her Peers: American Women Writers from Anne Bradstreet to Annie Proulx.* New York: Knopf, 2009.

Stufft, Monica. "Flowers by Design: Susan Glaspell's Re-vision of Strindberg's *A Dream Play.*" In *Disclosing Intertextualities: The Stories, Plays, and Novels of Susan Glaspell.* Ed. Martha C. Carpentier and Barbara Ozieblo. New York: Rodopi, 2006. 79–92.

Intertextuality on the Frontier
in Susan Glaspell's *Inheritors*

SARAH WITHERS

All the new thinking is about loss.
In this it resembles all the old thinking.

— Robert Hass, "Meditations at Lagunitas"

It has become commonplace in the current thinking about theater and performance to write about loss. Peggy Phelan's well-known assertion of performance's ontology — that "performance's only life is in the present" and that performance "becomes itself through disappearance" (146) — established a dominant critical paradigm in performance studies over the last twenty years and scholars have since attended to the senses of performance as evanescent, ephemeral, disappearing, ghostly, haunting and haunted. Yet as William West and others have begun to trace, this new thinking about performance resembles much of the old thinking. West's essay on "Replaying Early Modern Performances" recounts how

> the melancholy of performance criticism is curiously predicted, or perhaps echoed in retrospect, by what English theater remembers about itself.... Early modern plays so often represent themselves to their audiences as moments that take place and then pass away, as unhappy vanishings that are imperfectly preserved in memory [31, 33].

Yet, even as it "imperfectly preserve[s]" performance, memory lingers as an integral component of performance and especially of the meaning-making that spectators themselves engage in as part of their experience of a theatrical event.[1]

In this essay, I would like to consider somewhat newer "old thinking" about the intersection of performance, loss, and cultural memory by looking at Susan Glaspell's 1921 play *Inheritors*, in which the ephemerality of history itself comes under examination. Like West, I am interested in the ways in which dramatists reflect on the centrality of an experience of loss to their theater practice as manifested in the dramas they produce. While West's early

126

modern dramatic examples are more explicit in their commentary on performance as loss, I argue that it is this ontological relationship to loss, as well as to memory, that makes the theater an apt medium for writers like Glaspell to contemplate both the actual and the ideal relationship of the past to the present.

The specific cultural experiences of loss that Glaspell explores are tied to her historical moment. Writing just after World War I, Glaspell's play is a critical response to an era marked by the first Red Scare and by heightened government scrutiny of its citizenry for any hint of "un–Americanism." Glaspell's play contends that it is precisely this culture of surveillance and censorship that is un–American, as it signals a loss of the freedom of expression that informed the founding of the nation and a loss of the openness to the Other, variously conceived, that likewise characterized the rhetoric of American national origins. As Glaspell asks, through her protagonist Madeline Fejevary Morton: is fighting "a great war for democracy ... any reason for not having it?" (140). But beyond simply responding to her specific historical moment, Glaspell's play also wrestles with a much more fundamental question, one that sits at the heart of American identity, namely, how does one inherit revolution? Put another way, how does one establish a radical break with the past as the basis for an identity that remains continuous through time? For if American national identity is rooted in pastlessness, in a revolutionary break with prior social, political, and economic patterns, the questions of how to perpetuate that identity and how to create ever-more ways to be new become pressing cultural concerns.

Like many in the American cultural tradition, Glaspell provisionally answers this question by turning to the American frontier as a site of perpetual renewal. More specifically, in *Inheritors* Glaspell figures the frontier as a space of revolutionary inheritance in which her main characters, the Morton family and their fellow pioneers, are able to exercise the rights to self-determination and self-patriation enjoyed by their American Revolutionary forbearers. Indeed, in Glaspell's vision of America as depicted throughout her oeuvre, it is the Midwestern pioneer, rather than the natural descendent of the New England revolutionary, who becomes the legitimate heir to the foundational principles of American democracy. Of course, Glaspell only temporarily circumvents the problem of inheriting revolution, and on one level her play simply yokes the past to the present more completely through her intertextual citations of significant historical events and texts of the predominantly (but not exclusively) American canon. Yet in the face of this seemingly irrevocable weight of the past, *Inheritors* offers performance, in its many valences, as a means to negotiate — though not to solve — the paradox of revolutionary inheritance.

Glaspell's Revolutionary Frontier

Glaspell makes the identification between the pioneer and the early American revolutionary figure clear throughout the first act in particular, where she relocates central myths of American national foundation from New England in the seventeenth and eighteenth centuries to the western frontier in the nineteenth. In so doing, Glaspell suggests that the spirit of revolution — of a break with the past and a desire for the new — belongs properly to the frontier rather than to a conservative East Coast that, according to Glaspell, has lost touch with its radical history and instead fetishizes an ossified version of the American revolutionary character.[2] While this figuration of the frontier as revolutionary space may not seem especially novel, what is significant about Glaspell's portrayal is that the frontier's intrinsic innovatory qualities are amplified by a citational link to America's radical past. This representation of the frontier as the site of a re-located revolutionary impulse amounts to a recapitulation theory of American history, in which the pattern of foundation and development that established the early nation is repeated along the western frontier. I am using "recapitulation" here in its sense understood by nineteenth-century evolutionary biologists, most notably the German zoologist Ernst Haeckel who proposed that "ontogeny recapitulates phylogeny," that is, that the embryonic development of an individual organism replicates and resembles the evolutionary development of its biological ancestors' adult forms — a theory that has since been discredited but that was widely (and not unproblematically) influential in the nineteenth and early twentieth centuries, not only in scientific circles but also in general understandings of social, cultural, and educational development.[3] For Glaspell, key events from America's early national past provide the adult ancestral pattern (a script, if you will) that embryonic social and cultural development on the frontier replicates (that is, performs). In this way, American history itself functions in *Inheritors* as an intertext, through which the past persists as a vital presence that both shapes and is shaped by the contemporary present.

That Glaspell is especially concerned with memory and with a desire to recapture a lost past is indicated by the temporal structure of the play, which spans forty years. The first act "was lived" (104) on July 4th 1879, while the remaining acts are set in Glaspell's contemporary moment — just after the end of World War I. J. Ellen Gainor argues that Glaspell's construction "was lived" "emphasizes the reality behind the action" (120); Glaspell thus frames Act I as a historical re-enactment or, perhaps more accurately, as a performed recollection. This performance of historical consciousness is echoed in the dialogue of Act I, much of which consists of characters' reminiscences of their personal past as it intersects with the history of the unnamed Midwestern town where the play is set (modeled, in part, on Glaspell's own hometown of Davenport, Iowa). Act I takes place in "the sitting-room of the Mortons' farmhouse in the Middle West — on the rolling prairie just back from the Mississippi" (104), and it introduces the audience to two pioneer families: the Mortons, the area's first white settlers, and the Fejevarys, Hungarian immigrants whose lives become intertwined with the Mortons' through bonds of friendship and, later, marriage. The first act is peppered with the at times caustic reminiscences of Grandmother Morton, who functions as the town's unofficial historian; she is, in the words of Felix Fejevary Sr., a "touch with the life behind us" (109). Her conversations with the land developer Smith, a stranger to the town, recount the history of the town's settlement for the audience as well. This civic history is inextricably tied to her personal family history insofar as the Mortons were the first to settle on what was then Native American land, a fact to which Smith responds with incredulity and awe:

SMITH: But one family! I should think the Indians would have wiped you out.
GRANDMOTHER: The way they wiped us out was to bring fish and corn. We'd have starved to death that first winter hadn't been for the Indians [105].

In Grandmother Morton's short speech, Glaspell rehearses and relocates a foundational national narrative, that of the fabled first contact between the Pilgrims and Native Americans at the Plymouth colony. The prototype for this mythic narrative can be traced to the collected journals of William Bradford, first governor of Plymouth Plantation. Regarding the Native American liaison Squanto's relationship to the Pilgrims, Bradford writes that

Squanto continued with them and was their interpreter and was a special instrument sent of God for their good beyond their expectation. He directed them how to set their corn, where to take fish, and to procure other commodities, and was also their pilot to bring them to unknown places for their profit, and never left them till he died [81].

Bradford's narrative has of course become the paradigm for popular perceptions of the early relationships between the Native Americans and English settlers, which reach their apotheosis in the perennially circulated parable of the First Thanksgiving. Grandmother Morton's specific citation of fish and corn, as well as the conviction that the early settlers would have perished without Indian cooperation are salient details from the originary myth that implicitly links the Morton family's pioneer endeavors to the prehistory of the American nation.

An arguably more significant invocation of a foundational narrative of American national identity occurs in Silas Morton's description of his vision for Morton College, the foundation of which is the central event of the first act:

It's a college in the cornfields — where the Indian maize once grew. And it's for the boys of the cornfields — and the girls. There's few that can go to Harvard College — but more can climb that hill. Harvard on a hill? A college should be on a hill. They can see it then from far around. See it as they go out to the barn in the morning; see it when they're shutting up at night. 'Twill make a difference — even to them that never go [113–114].

In his insistence that "a college should be on a hill," Silas calls to mind John Winthrop's famous image of the Massachusetts Bay Colony as "a city upon a hill," generally regarded as the inaugural instance of the doctrine of American exceptionalism. Glaspell's allusion to this iconic moment in Winthrop's sermon "A Model of Christian Charity," delivered on the ship carrying Puritan colonists to their future home in Massachusetts Bay, further yokes Silas's pioneer endeavors to the undertakings of the pre-national colonial project and thus to the very origins of American identity. In conjoining Morton College's foundation to the origins of the American nation, Glaspell thus establishes the college as a metonym for the nation as a whole — a symbolic identity that she exploits in the play's later acts to critique what she perceives as the betrayals of the principles upon which the nation was founded. These betrayals are actively interrogated in the play's contemporary acts, but Glaspell foreshadows this concern implicitly in the citation of Harvard (one of the nation's first educational institutions) as a model for Morton College. Even as Silas recognizes that his college can never be Harvard, he adds more significantly that "it needn't be" (113). For, though Harvard represents a paradigm for educational excellence, in its elitism and its restricted accessibility for women and other social minorities, the New England college is also a symbol of the failure of the democratic impulse to perpetuate itself in American social institutions.[4] Morton College seeks to rectify this failure through a more egalitarian openness to both the boys and the girls of the cornfields. This egalitarian spirit is further evinced by Silas's conviction that, in locating his college at a site of unrestricted visibility, he will be able to inspire even those who never attend the college, consequently making the hill an emblem not simply of American exceptionalism but also of the democratic virtue of radical hospitality.

Glaspell does more, however, than simply make Morton College the symbolic equivalent of the nascent American nation in order to investigate the decline of core American values. In re-placing key originary narratives from the Atlantic coast to the nation's heartland, Glaspell offers a specific vision of the role of the frontier in the formation of an American national identity, one that decenters the projects of the New England founding fathers — or, rather, displaces and literally centers that project in the heart of the American nation. In so doing, Glaspell is tapping into dominant cultural perceptions of the frontier famously crystallized by Frederick Jackson Turner in his pivotal 1896 essay "The Significance of the Frontier in American History." Turner's frontier thesis was part of the national zeitgeist in the first decades of the 20th century, finding its way into newspaper editorials, popular representations, and even national and foreign policy.[5] More specifically, the frontier anxiety that Turner articulated so famously — that is, the obsession with the disappearing or already disappeared frontier as a threat to American growth and, more to the point, as a threat to American national identity — was pervasive in Glaspell's time.[6] As such, Turner's work forms an implicit intertext for Glaspell's representation of the role of the (Mid)west in American history and, more pertinently, in the perceived crisis of American democracy in her contemporary moment, a crisis that is figured by Glaspell as a loss of a prior ideal state and is thus predicated on the memory of that idealized past.

In particular, there are clear formal resemblances between Turner's description of the expansion of the American West, which he posits is marked by a repetitive cycle of foundation and development along an ever-moving frontier, and Glaspell's representation of the history of her unnamed Midwestern "everytown" as a recapitulation of American revolutionary history. Turner posits that, in contrast to the gradual and continual development which marks the usual case for new nations, American national growth followed a unique pattern, explaining:

> [W]e have ... a recurrence of the process of evolution in each western area reached in the process of expansion. Thus American development has exhibited not merely advance along a single line, but a return to primitive conditions on a continually advancing frontier line, and a new development for that area. American social development has been continually beginning over again on the frontier [32].

In other words, according to Turner, every successive movement of the frontier line westward brought with it a repetition of the material conditions encountered by the early American colonialist, a phenomenon that historically ensured the preservation and continuity of the "American character" supposedly inculcated at the foundation of the nation. Turner continues: "this perennial rebirth, this fluidity of American life, this expansion westward with its new opportunities, its continuous touch with the simplicity of primitive society, furnish the forces dominating American character" (32). Turner's thesis is one of environmental determinism in which the characteristics of the frontier environment and lifestyle (in this instance, "fluid," "simple," and "primitive") are written onto the character of the American person and, by extension, the national culture. Furthermore, Turner explicitly connects this national character with political form, arguing that "frontier individualism has from the beginning promoted democracy," in that the expansion of the frontier both depended upon and produced in the pioneer a highly developed sense of autonomy that in turn encouraged "an antipathy to control, and particularly to any direct control" — an antipathy that undergirds liberal democracy and its resistance to aristocratic or authoritarian political orders (53). It is for this reason, in part, that the supposed closing of the frontier represented such a threat to American identity. As Turner laments in "Contributions of the West to American Democracy," "the great supply of free lands which year after year has served to reinforce the democratic influences in the United States is exhausted" (79).[7] In her depiction of the frontier as a repetition, and thus a safeguard, of America's revolutionary past, Glaspell complements Turner's theory of environmental determinism with one of discursive determinism, deploying history as an intertext to show that pioneer self-understanding was a product of prior narrative and textual patterns (again, a script) as well as of direct interaction with the American wilderness. Her staging of the recollection of the foundation and subsequent civic development of a frontier town as a means to explore the state of democracy in her own moment suggests that Glaspell agrees with Turner that "the true point of view in the history of this nation is not the Atlantic coast, it is the Great West" (Turner 32).

Yet while Glaspell shares with Turner a fundamentally similar understanding of the function of the frontier in the development and perpetuation of American democracy, as many scholars have noted, her play also offers several important correctives to Turner's idealization of the frontier as a free, democratic and masculine space dissociated from a bankrupt European influence. Both Gainor and Noelia Hernando-Real detail the myriad ways in which Glaspell "introduces ... meaningful change[s] in the traditionally male pioneer myth" (Hernando-Real 188), a myth that found its most influential champion in Turner. They explicate how Glaspell's play draws attention to the role that women played in the settlement of the frontier, a role exemplified by Grandmother Morton, who recounts her actions in the 1832 Blackhawk war in which she "threw an Indian in the cellar and stood on the door," further explaining, "We used to fight with anything we could lay hands on — dish water — whatever was handy" (104). Glaspell's de-romanticized depiction of the contest between natives and settlers, in which dish water becomes a weapon wielded in the hands of a female combatant, stands in marked contrast to Turner's aggrandizing prose with respect to the dignity and heroism of the male pioneer. Moreover, as Gainor observes, Glaspell's play "avoid[s] the traditional opposition of Indians and pioneers" (119) in the first place, and instead offers a more nuanced understanding of the relationship between white settlers and Native Americans, which Glaspell presents as marked by initially cooperative contact turned competitive contest for resources, particularly land. For his part, Turner is largely dismissive of the American Indian in his early thesis, noting simply that frontier settlement occurred after "a series of Indian wars" and apparently seeing no contradiction in characterizing "the Indian country" as "free land" (36, 33). Turner does remark that the American frontiersman initially took the Native American as a model of behavior, explaining that before long he [the frontiersman] has gone to planting Indian corn and plowing with a sharp stick; he shouts the war cry and takes the scalp in orthodox Indian fashion. In short, at the frontier the environment is at first too strong for the man. He must accept the conditions which it furnishes, or perish, and so he fits himself into the Indian clearings and follows the Indian trails [33].

This imitation of the American Indian is characterized as born of necessity, but Turner quickly points out that "little by little [the frontiersman] transforms the wilderness," making of it a uniquely American environment that is radically divorced both from the influence of "the Old Europe," which is obliterated precisely by this confrontation with the American wilderness, and from a "primitive Indian life" marked by rudimentary farming practices and savage violence (33–34, 40). Glaspell, in contrast, is vitally concerned with both the literal and moral debt owed to Native Americans by the white settlers and their descendents; she challenges Turner's notion that the American West was a repository of unlimited "free" land by narrating the history of war and unscrupulous financial transactions between the American government and the Native Americans whose land the pioneers often appropriated. Indeed, Grandmother Morton's invocation of the Thanksgiving paradigm is precisely an acknowledgement of that debt, which she elaborates on by noting that "for fifteen million acres of this Mississippi Valley land — best on this globe, we paid two thousand two hundred and thirty-four dollars and fifty cents, and promised to deliver annually goods to the value of one thousand dollars. Not a fancy price — even for them days" (106).

For my purposes, the most significant divergence between Glaspell and Turner is in their differing assessments of the social and political effects of the conscious and unconscious distancing from the past evidenced on the frontier. David Noble argues that Turner and his colleagues "wrote their histories from the paradigmatic assumption that Europe represented time" and thus corruption, while "America (the United States) represented timeless space" and thus innocence and purity (1). Accordingly, for Turner, American innovation of corrupt European time as effected by the frontier was an overwhelmingly positive event. Turner praises the influence of the frontier spirit on the origins of American institutions and their dissociation from a European past. As Wilbur Jacobs notes, Turner challenged the "worn out germ theory" of American history that preceded his work, which claimed that the seeds of American institutions originated amongst the ancient Teutonic tribes of the European forest, in order to "show that our inheritance was not at all dependent upon European germs of culture" (153). Glaspell is much more ambivalent about the veracity of this anti-inheritance as well as the positive valuation that Turner attributes to it. While Glaspell seems to participate in this characterization in her depiction of the origin of one specific institution — Morton College — as quintessentially American, she simultaneously questions the accuracy of understanding American institutions as radically removed from European influence. In fact, the earliest prototype for Silas's vision of Morton College stems from Felix Fejevary's reminiscences of his life at a Hungarian university, where he developed his own sense of revolutionary idealism. In defending his ambition for his college, Silas reminds Fejevary, "You told me what you studied in that fine old university you loved — the Vienna — and why you became a revolutionist.... Your face as you went on about the vision — you called it, vision of what life could be" (114). Silas's motivation for bequeathing his hill to the town is in part to bring to his fellow pioneers and their descendents this "vision of what life could be" — a vision first cultivated on European soil and then transposed to the American frontier through the interpersonal relationship of an American pioneer and a Hungarian immigrant whose memory of his former life has material effects on the development of his adopted town. In these ways, Glaspell complicates Turner's understanding of the frontier and of the American institutions it produced as completely removed from a European past, offering instead a more complex depiction of intercultural exchange between both settlers and natives and Americans and Europeans than Turner entertains.

Nevertheless, while Glaspell scholars are right to point out Glaspell's contentious relationship to the official history of her day, I would not go so far as Barbara Ozieblo in saying that Glaspell solely "mocks several male myths," including "the frontier myth" and the "learning myth" (68–69). Though Glaspell is indeed critical of the chauvinism of popular historical perceptions of the frontier (and of educational institutions), I am arguing that she nonetheless actively participates in an idealization of the frontier as a site for the preservation and perpetuation of a particularly American revolutionary and democratic heritage. She also upholds the university as a space for fostering revolution (literally, in the case of Fejevary's participation in the Hungarian Revolution) and for promoting a utopian "vision of what life could be." In other words, the "frontier myth" and the "learning myth" are ultimately sustained by Glaspell's play and what she mocks, then, are those individuals who hypocritically fail to embody their ideals while simultaneously paying lip service to them.

I mentioned earlier that Glaspell turns *provisionally* to the frontier in the first act as a solution to the paradox of ensuring the continuity of an American identity predicated on the rejection of older forms and institutions. However, as the rest of the play makes clear, this solution is only that: provisional, temporary. The play's contemporary acts contend that frontier society ultimately fails to uphold the promise of perpetual renewal as it tends towards ossification and sterility. As the play's protagonist, Madeline Fejevary Morton, bemoans: "I'd like to have been a pioneer! ... A whole big land to open up! A big new life to begin! Why did so much get shut out? Just a little way back — anything might have been. What happened?" The answer, given by Professor Holden, is that "It got — set too soon" (151). In this, as in other works by Glaspell, stasis — things becoming set too soon — is figured as the ultimate social ill. Madeline's vision of the pioneer past as limitless potential makes of her a kind of spokesperson for Walter Benjamin's notion of revolutionary nostalgia. As Frederic Jameson explains: "But if nostalgia as a political motivation is most frequently associated with fascism, there is no reason why a nostalgia conscious of itself, a lucid and remorseless dissatisfaction with the present on the grounds of some remembered plenitude, cannot furnish as adequate a revolutionary stimulus as any other" (575). In Madeline's case, the "remembered plenitude" is specifically the plenitude of revolutionary potential, so that revolutionary nostalgia becomes not simply a vision of the past that can be put to revolutionary purposes, as in Jameson's gloss on Benjamin, but precisely nostalgia for revolution. In her recapitulative representation of the frontier in Act I, Glaspell herself participates in this nostalgia for revolution and then stages that same longing in later acts through her mouthpiece, Madeline.

Yet, as should be evident by now, Glaspell's own dramaturgical project is implicated in this set-ness, this arrested motion that Holden and Madeline believe characterizes contemporary America. Indeed, Glaspell's re-location of American democratic origins on the frontier bespeaks a kind of principle of conservation, rather than revolutionary innovation. Glaspell's attempt to stage an inheritance of revolutionary content takes as its mode a citation of the national past, rather than pointing to the creation of new social or political forms. In her implicit critique of New England society for its failure to perpetuate revolutionary ideals, Glaspell advocates for the preservation and retention of those very principles through their transposition to the frontier. Glaspell calls upon these foundational moments from the national past to authorize the pioneer project, even as she implies that the frontier of the first act's present supersedes the Atlantic coast of the national past.

Moreover, Glaspell's modernist drive for the new and the revolutionary, in society and in art, is tempered by an equally sincere desire to preserve, in the words of another of her intertextual interlocutors, "the best that has been said and thought in the world." This phrase, taken from Matthew Arnold's 1869 work *Culture and Anarchy*, is introduced by Felix the 2nd to characterize his understanding of his neighbor's intentions for Morton College. Silas, for his part, approves of this characterization, exclaiming:

> "The best that has been thought and said in the world!" That's what that hill is for! Don't you see it? End of our trail, we climb a hill and plant a college. Plant a college, so's after we are gone that college says for us, says in people learning has made more: "That is why we took this land" [113].

The college is thus imagined as having the ability to speak for Silas and his pioneer compatriots after their deaths and to perpetually declare the motives of its own foundation — in short, to act as a conduit for the inheritance of its instituting principles. Furthermore, in envisioning his college as a repository for "the best that has been thought and said in the world," Silas conjoins a retentive impulse towards cultural conservatism to a vision of egalitarian access to education through the foundation of an educational institution that is itself the product of a democratic redistribution of material wealth. Matthew Arnold in fact becomes a cipher for this paradoxical mutual constitution of the revolutionary and retentive impulses in the foundation of the college and, by metonymic association, the American nation. Felix the 2nd, who is newly returned from Harvard and prone to showy displays of his elite education, describes Arnold as "the distinguished new English writer" — making of Arnold, in his "newness," a sort of symbol for innovative thought. Of course, the specific content of his work quoted in this act reflects a culturally conservative impulse, so much so that, in the later acts, Arnold can be cited approvingly by the contemptible and reactionary Senator Lewis as a "master of English!" (128) and disdained by the younger generation of Morton College students as dull and easily dismissed. Arnold's fate as a however unlikely avant-garde figure exemplifies what Paul Menzer, drawing on social critic Eric Hoffer, identifies as "the central irony of revolutionary impulses," namely that "[w]hen revolutions succeed ... they come to assume the dominance of the institutions they threw off" (101–102). It is this irony that Glaspell wrestles with as she looks for a revolutionary relationship to the past, a struggle that is compounded by a vision of the past as itself radical.

Performing Inheritance

Is there a way, then, out of the paradox of revolutionary inheritance? In a word, no. Yet, Glaspell does nonetheless posit the potential for small acts of individual revolution, especially if one is willing to go against "the spirit of [the] age" (Glaspell 134). In *Inheritors*, truly revolutionary and democratic behavior is ultimately to be found in the active, willful, and at times seemingly absurd conduct of the later generations. Fred Jordan, a former Morton College student and political prisoner who remains incarcerated for his conscientious objection to World War I, and Madeline Morton, who faces expulsion from her grandfather's college and impending imprisonment for her impassioned support of two Hindu students whose public protests of British rule in India have met with violent opposition from various town figures, both embody a radically democratic impulse that, in Madeline's case particularly, is directly fostered by a historical consciousness of a personal and national revolutionary past. Certainly, the parallels between India's fight for national independence and the America Revolutionary War are not lost on Glaspell, though they seem to be lost on the "one-hundred-per-cent American" Horace Fejevary, who leads the antagonism against the Hindu students. For Madeline, supporting the Hindu students is not only a specific defense of free speech but also a general defense of the nation's self-professed democratic idealism that attracted the foreign students to America in the first place.

Importantly, Madeline's actions are also explicitly linked to performance, variously understood, which I argue ultimately becomes the mechanism that enables revolutionary inheritance in the play. I opened this piece by considering "melancholic" and "elegiac" understandings of performance as loss, but alongside these (indeed, often in the same works) we can see conceptualizations of performance as a mode of preserving, however incompletely, some past material. That is, it is not just the case that memory is an imperfect record of performance, but rather that performance itself is an incomplete and partial manifestation of something prior to it. In a deft and concise overview of major theorists' endeavors to define performance, Joseph Roach explains that virtually all definitions of performance characterize it as "a substitute for something that preexists it," whether it is Victor Turner's etymological definition that a performance "carries out purposes thoroughly," Richard Bauman's contention that performance is located in "the actual execution of an action as opposed to its potential," Richard Schechner's notion of "restored" or "twice-behaved behavior," or Roach's own conceptualization of performance as surrogation (Roach 3). In all of these definitions, there is a temporal relationship between the past and the present that is activated in the moment of performance — a relationship characterized by the simultaneity of the two, as the past is made present through live performance. That is to say, performance is always an inheritance of a prior moment, text, or simply of performance's own potential. The temporality of the stage is, in perhaps counterintuitive ways, the temporality of inheritance, which is precisely why Glaspell turns to the seemingly conservative trope of inheritance in the first place as the umbrella concept she uses to consider the revolutionary potential of a selective yet lingering force of the past in the present.

It is this understanding of performance as inheritance that West is engaging when he asks us to consider performance not as an event (a "realized potential" that is "no longer kinetic," 30) but instead as a "replaying," which he describes as "the management of a rhythm of repetition — a practice of filling an ordinary gesture, word, or phrase with meaning through iteration, spacing, and change" (35). Importantly, for both West and Glaspell, "iteration [is] in the service of retention" (West 35), intertextuality being the specific mechanism of iteration that Glaspell deploys in this service of retention. In response to the hostile reactions that her nascent politically dissident activity garners from friends, family, and neighbors, Madeline observes that the Hindu students were drawn to America "by the things we say about ourselves" and proclaims that she is "going to pretend — just for fun — that the things we say about ourselves are true" (139). Glaspell's intertextual iteration of specific historical examples of "the things we say about ourselves" becomes a method for preserving that history in the play-text itself, though this preservation is not the end of these intertextual citations but rather a means of making the past available as a model for behavior in the present.

Madeline's self-proclaimed intention to "pretend," however sarcastically delivered, locates her in the realm of playacting and performance and explicitly ties this performance to political action. In defending the Hindu students, Madeline places herself in the midst of a violent confrontation with the local police and a group of jingoistic Morton College boys led by her cousin, Horace Fejevary. Madeline's uncle, Felix the 2nd, twice labels her altercations with the police a "performance," and a "disgraceful" one in his eyes (134, 137). Yet, Glaspell intends this to be an ironic characterization, for her own understanding of the role of performance in political life is far from that of disgrace.[8] Rather, it is through performance (in this instance, of a political protest) that Madeline is able to make manifest the revolutionary legacies of her grandfathers, Silas Morton and Felix Fejevary the 1st. Indeed, Professor Holden draws a parallel between Madeline's "disgraceful performance" and her Hungarian grandfather's exile from his native country for his own revolutionary activities, asking "wasn't [that] another disgrace?" — a characterization of his familial past that Felix the 2nd vehemently rejects, though that rejection does not correspond to a similar willingness to view his niece's "performance" of political dissidence in a favorable light (134–135).

Faced with the consequences of her actions, Madeline draws inspiration from the example of another student, Fred Jordan, who has been imprisoned for his conscientious objection to the war. In a moment of performative identification, Madeline inscribes with chalk the narrow dimensions of Jordan's prison cell on the floor of the Morton family farmhouse, and then figuratively imprisons herself within its borders: "*Slowly, at the end left unchalked, as for a door, she goes in. Her hand goes up as against a wall; looks at her other hand, sees it is out too far, brings it in, giving herself the width of the cell. Walks its length, halts, looks up*" (144). This sympathetic self-imprisonment is both a protest of Fred Jordan's inhumane living conditions and a foreshadowing — a dress rehearsal, if you will — of her own impending incarceration. Furthermore, Madeline's delineation of the prison cell's dimensions acts as a demarcation of ritual space in which Madeline is able to perform her American identity free from the corrupting influence of the mundane world. Madeline elaborates on this signification of her imminent actual imprisonment in a conversation with her neighbor Emil:

EMIL: ...You can't change the way things are.
MADELINE: (*quietly*) Why can't I?
EMIL: Well, say, who do you think you are?
MADELINE: I think I'm an American. And for that reason I think I have something to say about America.
EMIL: Huh! America'll lock you up for your pains.
MADELINE: All right. If it's come to that, maybe I'd rather be a locked-up American than a free American [145].

In this way, Madeline reinterprets prison as a quasi-sacred space that safeguards an idealism associated with America's revolutionary past (freedom of speech and of dissent), a place where ironically the "locked-up" individual is more American than the free.

Thus for Glaspell revolutionary inheritance is performative along multiple axes: it is an iteration of what has come before; it is something rehearsed; it occurs in a ritual space; it is bodily and behavioral; it is "pretend"—though, potentially, doing makes it so. The frontier, Glaspell's site of revolutionary inheritance, is similarly theatrical; it is both evanescent and permeated by loss and, like a play, it is "not something that happens for the first time" (Menzer 102). The impossibility of preserving something dynamic is ultimately not a paradox to be got around but rather is precisely the point for Glaspell. In *Inheritors*, valor is found in the struggle to embody a revolutionary and innovatory spirit that is nonetheless informed by and indebted to the past. In her own struggle to perform a radical relationship to the past, Madeline herself becomes a revolutionary legacy, that is, as a model upon which the audience can pattern their own interrogation of their national and personal past in the service of defending democratic idealism on the domestic front.

Notes

1. See, for example, Aleksandra Wolska's account of the meaningful afterlife of a contemporary performance in "Rabbits, Machines, and the Ontology of Performance," in which she argues that "a performance does not stop with the fall of the curtain, but continues in the body and mind of the viewer" (88).

2. This critique of a calcified East Coast society remains implicit in *Inheritors*, but is rendered much more overt in *The Verge*, which was first staged in the same year and can be read as a development of the themes of the earlier play. *The Verge*'s Harry Archer, husband to protagonist Claire Archer, believes himself to be praising his wife when he calls her "the flower of New England," descendent of "the men who made the laws that made New England"—"those gentlemen of culture" who (in another character's words) "moulded the American mind" (64). Claire, however, is horrified by such an attempt to delimit her as either a literal or figurative Daughter of the American Revolution, proclaiming, "I want to get away from them!" (64). Claire later renounces her "hymn-singing ancestors" (77), whose association with the past and with what has "already been" make them a metonym for the conservative and normalizing impulses of society that she actively resists throughout the play.

3. For a thorough account of the theory of recapitulation, see Stephen Jay Gould's *Ontogeny and Phylogeny*, especially chapter 5, "Pervasive Influence." In addition to his work on recapitulation, Haeckel was a "great popularizer of a monist conception of the universe," which "drew together energy and matter, life and nonlife, man and animals into a great, mysterious unity" (qtd. Murphy 28). Haeckel's work greatly influenced the members of the Davenport Monist Society, amongst them Glaspell and Cook who first got to know one another through the Society's meetings.

4. Gainor notes that Glaspell makes frequent reference to Harvard in her collected works and suggests that Cook's experience there made a strong impression on Glaspell as well. Gainor goes on to argue, however, that "the sense of elitism associated with the college must also have affected Glaspell, for she often contrasts it with other institutions of greater accessibility, particularly for women" (121).

5. Of note is the fact that Turner enjoyed a close friendship with President Woodrow Wilson, whose "New Freedom" legislation was, according to Wilbur Jacobs, "based on the recognition of the end of a frontier era" as described by Turner (112).

6. David Wrobel's *The End of American Exceptionalism: Frontier Anxiety from the Old West to the New Deal* offers an extensive study of the origins, development, and significance of this frontier anxiety in American public life. Wrobel explains that "Turner's writings were symptomatic of a wider frontier anxiety that emerged in embryonic form in the 1870s and became more pronounced in the succeeding decades" (3) — an anxiety that, as the scope of Wrobel's study suggests, persisted well into the early twentieth century. It is not coincidental, I think, that Glaspell's first act takes place in 1879, in the initial years of this emergent frontier anxiety, which then receives explicit expression in the subsequent contemporary acts.

7. Tuner based his thesis in part on an 1890 Census bulletin, which reported that the American frontier line was now broken by isolated settlement and "can not, therefore, any longer have a place in the census reports" (qtd. Turner 31). Yet to some extent Turner's conclusions drawn from this account were predicated on a faulty premise, as John Mack Faragher explains in his introduction to Turner's work. Faragher observes that the West was far from settled by the time Turner wrote his paper, arguing that "the cartography that so inspired Turner, it turns out, was less a work of science than of the imagination. A century later, the West has yet to fill up" (6).

8. In a 1921 interview, Glaspell remarked, "I am interested in all progressive movements, whether feminist, social, or economic, but I can take no very active part other than through my writing" (qtd. Ozieblo 67). Though meant as an explanation for her lack of "active" participation in political life (a lack attributed to her poor health), this quote reveals Glaspell's self-understanding of her writing, including her theatrical work, as a form of political contribution.

Works Cited

Bradford, William. *Of Plymouth Plantation, 1620–1647*. Ed. Samuel Eliot Morison. New York: Knopf, 1952. Print.

Gainor, J. Ellen. *Susan Glaspell in Context: American Theater, Culture, and Politics, 1915–48*. Ann Arbor: University of Michigan Press, 2001. Print.

Glaspell, Susan. *Plays*. Ed. C.W.E. Bigsby. Cambridge: Cambridge University Press, 1987. Print.

Gould, Stephen Jay. *Ontogeny and Phylogeny*. Cambridge, MA: Belknap Press of Harvard University Press, 1977. Print.

Hass, Robert. *Praise*. New York: Ecco Press, 1979. Print.

Hernando-Real, Noelia. "*E Pluribus, Plurum*: From a Unifying National Identity to Plural Identities in Susan Glaspell's *Inheritors*." *Codifying the National Self: Spectators, Actors and the American Dramatic Text*. Ed. Barbara Ozieblo and María Dolores Narbona-Carrión. Brussels: P.I.E.-Peter Lang, 2006. 185–200. Print.

Jacobs, Wilbur R. *On Turner's Trail: 100 Years of Writing Western History*. Lawrence: University Press of Kansas, 1994. Print.

Jameson, Frederic. "Walter Benjamin, or Nostalgia." *The Salmagundi Reader*. Ed. Robert Boyers and Peggy Boyers. Bloomington: Indiana University Press, 1983. 561–576. Print.

Menzer, Paul. "The Spirit of '76: Original Practices and Revolutionary Nostalgia." *New Direc-

tions in Renaissance Drama and Performance Studies. Ed. Sarah Werner. London: Palgrave Macmillan, 2010. 94–108. Print.

Murphy, Brenda. *The Provincetown Players and the Culture of Modernity*. Cambridge: Cambridge University Press, 2005. Print.

Noble, David W. *Death of a Nation: American Culture and the End of Exceptionalism*. Minneapolis: University of Minnesota Press, 2002. Print.

Ozieblo, Barbara. "Rebellion and Rejection: The Plays of Susan Glaspell." *Modern American Drama: The Female Canon*. Ed. June Schlueter. Rutherford, NJ: Fairleigh Dickinson University Press, 1990. 66–76. Print.

Phelan, Peggy. *Unmarked: The Politics of Performance*. London; New York: Routledge, 1993. Print.

Turner, Frederick Jackson. *Rereading Frederick Jackson Turner: The Significance of the Frontier and Other Essays*. Ed. John Mack Faragher. New York: Henry Holt, 1994. Print.

West, William N. "Replaying Early Modern Performances." *New Directions in Renaissance Drama and Performance Studies*. Ed. Sarah Werner. London: Palgrave Macmillan, 2010. 30–50. Print.

Wolska, Aleksandra. "Rabbits, Machines, and the Ontology of Performance." *Theatre Journal* 57.1 (March 2005): 83–95. Print.

Wrobel, David M. *The End of American Exceptionalism: Frontier Anxiety from the Old West to the New Deal*. Lawrence: University Press of Kansas, 1993. Print.

Fighting Archangels

The Deus Absconditus in Eugene O'Neill's Dialogue with the Bible, Nietzsche and Jung

ANNALISA BRUGNOLI

This essay explores the issue of "divine hiddenness," namely the *deus absconditus* leitmotiv, as it appears as a recurring intertextual reference in Eugene O'Neill's published, unpublished, fictional and non-fictional work. Originally worded in Isaiah 45:15 "vere tu es Deus absconditus Deus Israhel salvator/ Verily thou *art* a God that hidest thyself, O God of Israel, the saviour," the idea of God's deliberate absence or unbridgeable distance from the human world subtends a wide and comprehensive transcultural tradition. This involves Greek and Jewish antecedents, medieval philosophy, Catholic and Protestant theology, and addresses soul-compelling issues, such as the problem of evil, the freedom of the will, and the necessity of pain, grief, and loss. I regard this theme, together with its far-reaching ramifications and transliterary implications, as central to an understanding of O'Neill's biographic and artistic personality, and of the way these two elements interconnect in the playwright's life and work. On the one hand, O'Neill's reference to the *deus absconditus* theme effectively epitomizes his own faltering faith halfway between his frustrated need to believe and his lifelong quarrel with God. On the other hand, O'Neill's rejection of his faith stands as a reaction both to his Irish Catholic upbringing and to his family's religious attitude, and, therefore, deserves attention as an important element of criticism. Like all shadows, those elements one deliberately chooses not to include in one's life, O'Neill's discarded religious feelings exerted upon him an influence that is no less powerful than the tug of ideas and beliefs he openly endorsed.

In the first part of this paper, I will briefly review the phenomenology of the *deus absconditus* theme in O'Neill's life and work. The cross-references that lie behind it will then be the object of the second section, where I also focus on the subtle but significant differences that exist between the narrative of God's hiddenness as an exile and the narrative of the divine silence as a trial of the soul. Finally, I will introduce a lesser-known book by Carl Jung, *Answer to Job*. The book was translated into English in 1954, which of course excludes any direct influence upon O'Neill. Yet, the analogous cultural conditions into which Jung's and O'Neill's works came into being, the biographic affinity that can be observed between the two authors, as well as O'Neill's overt interest in the Swiss psychoanalyst's work (*Letters* 386) may lie behind the fact that, at the end of their respective lives, O'Neill and Jung came to similar conclusions as to the reasons and effects of God's hiddenness. On account of this, I will regard Jung's *Answer to Job* as an ideal element of unity in O'Neill's rendering of the *deus absconditus* leitmotiv in connection with an issue of boundary-crossing, the latter inevitably mediated by the influence of Nietzsche's philosophy in O'Neill's work. The purpose of this paper is, thus, to highlight the significance of Eugene O'Neill's positions on divine hiddenness in the frame of an ongoing historical discourse that, having started before history can record, lasts to the present.

The Deus Absconditus and the God-Forsaken

O'Neill's resentment of God's judgmental remoteness can be found throughout his works. Admittedly originating from a personal trauma, namely the discovery of his mother's morphine addiction at fifteen (Gelbs 174), O'Neill's desertion of God was the consequence of his keen feeling of having been abandoned by God first. As we know from his biographers, O'Neill abhorred abandonment. As the playwright himself subsequently rationalized, this experience marks "the spiritual turning point in his life" (Gelbs 174). Scarred in the spirit just like John Loving in *Days Without End* (3:151), O'Neill came to incarnate the Black Irishman stereotype. According to a friend of O'Neill's, this is "one who had believed in the Catholic religion and then lost his faith and spends the rest of his days searching for life's meaning in a world without God" (qtd. in Diggins 185). Thenceforth, this struggle for meaning in the name of godlessness informed O'Neill's life and work to a point the playwright himself makes clear in an oft-quoted 1931 letter to Brook Atkinson:

> If we had Gods or a God, if we had a Faith, if we had some healing subterfuge by which to conquer Death, then the Aristotelian criterion might apply in part to our Tragedy. But our tragedy is just that we have only ourselves, that there is nothing to be purged into except a belief in the guts of man, good or evil, who faces unflinchingly the black mystery of his own soul! [*Letters* 390].

Accordingly, in O'Neill plays, this idea of man's "tragic" loneliness due to God's neglect provides a pivotal theme that the author addressed through various rendering devices, ranging from the symbolism and massive use of objective correlatives in early works, where the *deus absconditus* is visually personified as a remote and yet judgmental figure in the sun (*Thirst*) the sea (*Anna Christie*) or the light and candlelight symbolism (*Mourning Becomes Electra*), to the characters' explicit admission of godlessness in later plays.

In *Thirst*, O'Neill's second published play, an early embodiment of the *deus absconditus* as an intentionally distant divine figure is found, as "The sun glares down from straight overhead like a great angry eye of God" (1:31), remotely enjoying the castaways' dance of death. According to Egil Törnquist, "[t]he sun ... is masculine — like God" (80) in O'Neill, whose use of lightning would invariably "suggest a relationship between men and some external fate" (77). Lightning is a telling theme in *Mourning Becomes Electra*, too. Here, the light *versus* darkness imagery recurs almost obsessively, with the "[t]he white columns" of the Mannons' mansion "cast[ing] black bars of shadow on the gray wall behind them" (2:893); Ezra Mannon, Seth Beckwith and Christine all moving in and out of the shadow; and the symbolism in the contrast between sunlight and candlelight in Part Three. We see this last culminating in Orin's suicide and Lavinia's self-entombment:

> ORIN — (*harshly*) I hate the daylight. It's like an accusing eye! ... And I find artificial light more appropriate for my work — man's light, not God's — man's feeble striving to understand himself, to exist for himself in the darkness! It's a symbol of his life — a lamp burning out in a room of waiting shadows! [1027].

As the playwright's style developed from his early expressionism to what Törnquist defined as O'Neill's "supernaturalism," i.e., O'Neill's "ability of transcending naturalism without losing touch with recognizable reality" (32), the *deus absconditus* came to be rendered no longer as a distant and indifferent supernatural figure but rather as the imagery of a spiritual wasteland engendered by the divine absence and inhabited by the God-Forsaken. In order to cope with the *horror vacui* of a godless dimension where, in Nietzsche's words, there is no "up or down," and man is left "straying as through an infinite nothing" (*Science* 125), O'Neill's people — insightfully grouped by Doris Falk as "The Searchers," "The Extremists," "The Finders," "The Trapped" — are thus seen to develop an "insatiable, unscrupulous greed for substitutes to fill the emptiness, the loss of love" (*Mansions* 3:534). Captain Keeney in *Ile*, Bartlett in *Gold*, Robert and Andrew in *Beyond the Horizon*, Emma Crosby in *Diff'rent*, Yank in *The Hairy Ape*, Ponce de León in *The Fountain*, the Polos in *Marco Millions*, Jim and Ella in *All God's Chillun Got Wings*, Reuben Light in *Dynamo* and Simon in *More Stately Mansions*, among others, all display elements of what would subsequently be called a self-defeating behavior, which condemns them to be baffled in the end. Traumatized by past events or simply victims of their restless and somber nature, these characters come to replace their quest for meaning with an equally intense search for material possessions, success and recognition, which of course drives them to a dead-end. Ensnared in a game they can no longer control, these characters realize they have failed, usually when it is too late. This is very much the case of Robert and Andrew Mayo and Reuben Light in, respectively, *Beyond the Horizon* and *Dynamo*, as in both works the protagonists' tragic ending comes as retribution for their misplaced quests. Moreover, even in plays where the sinful protagonist is finally saved through his belated atonement, as in *Days Without End* and *More Stately Mansions*, this final plot twist is perceived as defective and inappropriate both by the author and by his critics (see, among others, Voglino 59–65). As a matter of fact, O'Neill disavowed both plays and left uncompleted the cycles to which they were to belong (i.e., respectively, "Myth Plays for the God-Forsaken" and "A Tale of Possessors Self-Dispossessed"). However abandoned by God, O'Neill's people may still be inclined to pray, namely to recover their original religious feeling and language — both of which, as Thomas Porter has shown, are still massively present in O'Neill texts — but only to discover that their prayers remain unheeded. Jim Harris' pleas ("Forgive me God, for blaspheming You!" 2:315) and Brutus Jones' invocations ("Oh Lawd! Mercy! Mercy on dis po' sinner.... Mercy, Lawd, Mercy! ... Lawd, save me! Lawd Jesus, heah my prayer!" 1:1058–1059) find no answer, and Dion Anthony's and John Loving's final conversion appears equally ambiguous to say the least. As to the reason for God's persistent hiddenness, it remains largely unexplained in the early plays, whereas in the later works it is implied that God's absence comes as a consequence of His death. In *The Fountain*, Nano provides a picturesque account of this divine murder:

> NANO — (*contemptuously*) [The White Man's] Medicine Men tell of a God who came to them long ago in the form of a man. He taught them to scorn things. He taught them to look for the spirit behind things. In revenge, they killed him. They tortured him as a sacrifice to their Gold Devil. They crossed two big sticks. They drove little sticks through his hand and feet and pinned him on the others — thus (*He illustrates. A murmur of horror and indignation goes up among them*) [2:214].

Quite dissimilar in form, but analogous in content, is Edmund's claim in *A Long Days' Journey into Night* that "Nietzsche must be right" when he maintains that "God is dead: of His pity for man hath God died" (3:759).

The Hidden God of Intertextuality

The references to divine hiddenness quoted so far brim with intertextual allusions. While the wasteland leitmotiv clearly draws on James Frazer's *The Golden Bough*, the theme of God's Death is explicitly taken from Nietzsche's *Thus Spake Zarathustra*, the book that, as O'Neill admitted, "influenced [him] more than any book [he] ever read" (*Letters* 246). Here the idea of God's murder, which appears in slightly different versions also in *Human, All Too Human* and *The Gay Science*, is complemented by the Ugliest Man avowal of the divine assassination on account of God's exceeding pity:

> But he — had to die: he looked with eyes which beheld everything, — he beheld men's depths and dregs, all his hidden ignominy and ugliness. His pity knew no modesty: he crept into my dirtiest corners. This most prying, over-intrusive, over-pitiful one had to die.... Thus spake the ugliest man [300–301].

But the *deus absconditus* theme can also be traced back to religious texts of a much earlier origin than Nietzsche's and Frazer's. These involve the Greek and Jewish views concerning divine hiddenness. As I will try to show, in the Greek world God's disappearance becomes a refined metaphor of man's development of civilization. In Jewish culture the recurring episodes of God's absence stand instead as exemplary moments of punishment or as tests for the soul, while this condition is not irredeemable as in the coeval Greek texts. I argue that these two different and yet complementary visions are simultaneously present in those O'Neill plays that address the *deus abscounditus* theme, thereby constituting a cross-cultural influence upon which O'Neill massively and yet reticently built. As for the reasons for this effacement, they have to do with the playwright's personal life, and in specific with the anxiety of influence that O'Neill ostensibly felt towards the classics — which he always felt the need to mediate through psychoanalysis, as in *Mourning Becomes Electra* and *Desire Under the Elms*, and Nietzscheanism, as in *Lazarus Laughed*— while the Jewish antecedent was inextricably intertwined with the playwright's Catholic background. However unacknowledged, these references provide the subtextual foundations of O'Neill's work; all the more so, since they are connected with subsequent intertextual influences, such as Frazer's, Nietzsche's or Jung's, through a multilayered network of cross-cultural interplay.

In the Western world, the idea of God's hiddenness or disappearance develops almost simultaneously in the Greek and Jewish cultures, in texts written between the 7th and the 6th centuries B.C.E., i.e., in what Karl Jaspers called the Axial Age, drawing on oral traditions of antiquity. Indeed, Hesiod's twin works *Theogony* and *Works and Days* as well as the Bible make reference to the *deus absconditus*. In *Works and Days*, Hesiod provides the first recorded account of the Ages of Man, representing the passage of humans from a golden age when men "lived like gods" (89) and often intermingled with them, through the age of "hero-men," also portrayed in Homer's works, to the degraded age of iron, when eventually

> Aidos and Nemesis with their sweet forms wrapped in white robes, will go from the wide-pathed earth and forsake mankind to join the company of the deathless gods: and bitter sorrows will be left for mortal men, and there will be no help against evil [69].

As Roberto Calasso argues, the Greek myth of the marriage of Cadmus and Harmony figuratively portrays the final merging of gods and men before the two dimensions came apart forever. In Greek culture the separation is, indeed, irreversible. When the gods abandon the earth, it is for good. This very development from a God-oriented perception of the world to a nontheistic and markedly rational attitude also informs the subsequent development of Greek philosophy. Here the change from pre–Socratic expressions to the later Classical and Hellenistic periods is impressive. According to Friedrich Nietzsche, the responsibility for this secularization would lie in Socrates' lifelong commitment to "creat[ing] a tyrant out of reason" (*Twilight* 15). Be it as it may, an abyss stands between Parmenides (5th century B.C.E.) achieving the Truth through the revelation of a goddess and Epicurus' man-centered philosophy (4th-3rd century B.C.E.), whereby the gods would lead their separate lives in *intermundia*, perpetually happy and supremely indifferent to human matters.

As to the Jewish idea of God's hiddenness, this stands as a recurring theme in the Bible, aimed either at punishing mankind, or at testing its faith. Adam's expulsion from Eden, Cain's banishment ("from thy face shall I be hid" [Genesis 4:14]), the Hebrews' exiles in the desert of Sinai and in Babylonia ("Wherefore hidest thou thy face, and forgettest our affliction and our oppression?" [Psalms 44:24]), the destructions of the temple of Jerusalem, among others, are all occurrences in which God turns away in exercise of divine wrath. Even more remarkable, at least to the purpose of this paper, are those episodes in which God's silence stands not as a punishment but rather as a trial of faith. Abandoned by the Lord for no apparent reason, the believer suddenly finds himself exposed to the machinations of the Great Tempter. Indeed, both in the Old and in the New Testament, the theme of divine hiddenness as a trial is almost invariably associated with Satan's appearance. In the Book of Job, God lets himself be persuaded by Satan to test Job, "a perfect and an upright man, one that feareth God, and escheweth evil" (Job 1:8), by depriving him of his possessions and eventually of his health. Again, in the Gospel, another *agnus dei*, Christ himself, undergoes a similar trial in the Temptation and in the Passion ("My God, my God, why have you forsaken me?" [Matthew 27:46 and Mark 15:34]). Over the centuries, an extensive theological debate called theodicy has developed in order to answer the questions left open by the deeply problematic issue of God's silence as a test to the soul. In both the Catholic and Protestant world, the *deus absconditus* illustrates how the problem of evil and free will interconnect, as the evidence of universal suffering inevitably questions God's omnipotence.

All themes mentioned above, from the Greek myth of the Ages of Man to the biblical lessons and implications, are explicitly echoed in O'Neill plays involving the *deus absconditus*. On the one hand, the playwright's lifelong struggle to "pursue ... the unattainable" (qtd. in Törnquist 14) is declaredly heroic, "in as near the Greek sense as one can grasp it" (*Letters* 195). On the other hand, the environment of wasteland and defeat where his "Myths Plays for the God-Forsaken" take place clearly pertains to the age of man. Forever abandoned by the Gods and compelled to live in a secular dimension that, just as in Hesiod's work, is but a pale and degraded version of a pristine golden age, O'Neill's God-Forsaken characters — most noticeably Dion Anthony, Reuben Light, John Loving and Simon Hartford — turn into living specimens of a logical paradox that the tradition significantly attributes to Epicurus:

> Is God willing to prevent evil, but not able? Then he is not omnipotent.
> Is he able, but not willing? Then he is malevolent.
> Is he both able and willing? Then whence cometh evil?
> Is he neither able nor willing? Then why call him God? [qtd. in Mabry 160].

I believe that such "Epicurean" intertextual references broaden significantly the understanding of the influence of the Greek element upon O'Neill. Far from being the paradise of primeval social and personal harmony for which the Provincetown Players repined, the Greek civilization becomes in O'Neill not only the place of the Nietzschean antithesis Apollonian/Dionysian, but also a wasteland of people irreversibly abandoned by their temperamental gods.

As to the biblical rendering of the *deus absconditus*, this is taken up again and again in O'Neill's texts, most noticeably in his unpublished or uncompleted works. In this sense, it can be argued that the playwright's unanswered spiritual questions acted as "intruder[s] from the shadows" (Watt 24) in his art, thereby undermining the success of his "religious" plays in the end. This is the case not only of the unfinished trilogy "Myths Plays for the God-Forsaken" but also of the gigantic saga "A Tale of Possessors Self-Dispossessed," both of which focus on the destabilizing effects of God's hiddenness upon the modern mind. In the latter cycle of plays, *More Stately Mansions* deserves special attention, as here O'Neill juxtaposes the biblical theme of God's abandonment as an exile with the issue of the divine silence as a test for the soul. As to the exile theme, it stands out in the tale of the banished prince Simon painfully recalls (3:442–444), which Laurin Porter thoroughly analyzed in *The Banished Prince: Time, Memory and Ritual in the Late Plays of Eugene O'Neill*. According to Porter,

> Deborah's garden becomes for [Simon] the Garden of Eden where he once walked in prelapsarian bliss. When forced out of paradise into the world of adulthood with its attendant ills, Simon lost a peace that he could not replace. He says to Deborah in religiously laden language, "I have waited ever since I was a little boy. All my life since I have stood outside that door in my mind, begging you to let me re-enter that lost life of peace and trustful faith and happiness! You once drove me out, and all that has happened since began. Now you must either choose to repu-

diate that old choice and give me back the faith you stole from me, or I will choose her!" His Mother becomes the angel barring the gate to heaven [44].

Simon's narrative of his fall also recalls Hesiod's description of the way the golden age was scattered by Pandora's opening the jar of evils, which in turn bears marked resemblances to the main theme of the Original Sin. No less explicit is, in *More Stately Mansions*, the reference to the theme of God's hiddenness as a trial of the soul as it appears in the Book of Job. At the end of the play Sara cries, "We've nothing in the world except this farm. We're as poor as Job's turkey. You're free as you always wanted to be in your heart. We're back where it started with only our love for riches!" (3:555). Thus, in the Epilogue, O'Neill's final twist inverts the relationship between fiction and reality, as the plays' circular ending implies that the Hartfords' changing fortunes have been but a parable of the spirit, aimed at a moral rather than material improvement. However explicitly compared to Job, neither Simon nor his family is the champion of perfection, uprightness and disinterestedness Job is. Far from that, it is O'Neill's interest in *More Stately Mansions* to point out and criticize the rapacious and acquisitive drives that take possession of the soul as a consequence of God's desertion. This brings about a double paradox. No one is ever innocent in this or any other O'Neill plays, which instead massively focus on the devastating consequences of guilt. Yet hardly anyone takes the full responsibility of his or her own faults. This is because, as O'Neill has William Brown declare in *The Great God Brown*, "Man *is born* broken" (2:258, italics mine). As evil is regarded as partially independent from the human will, O'Neill's characters come to embody the double status of recipients of God's retribution (divine hiddennes as well-deserved punishment) and victims of a temperamental and unpredictable God (divinie hiddennes as a trial). Accordingly, tragedy is engendered by the awareness of the immense hiatus that exists between the origin of the punishment and the atrocity and inexpiabilty of it. This is what brought Dorothy Day to maintain that "If ever a man had the tragic sense of life it was Eugene O'Neill" (qtd. in Shaughnessy 31). In this sense, O'Neill voices a tragic attitude that is intrinsic to the Western religious sensibility, and whose origin lies in the perception of the *deus absconditus* and of the issues this divine absence encompasses.

The richness and complexity of the biblical attributions mentioned so far is further enhanced by the fact that in O'Neill the boundary between good and evil is not as clear-cut as in the Bible. On the contrary, both forces are simultaneously present in the God-Forsaken soul of modern man, often as interchangeable doubles. This is the Faust-Mephistopheles leitmotiv, of course, a landmark in O'Neill's artistic development, as the playwright himself also emphasizes in his "Memoranda on Masks." This very issue of the interchangeability between good and evil was to be the main theme of "The Last Conquest," a work of temptation and greed in a New Testament environment O'Neill left uncompleted. Together with *Lazarus Laughed*, this would have been O'Neill's most explicitly bible-inspired play, focusing once again on the "duality of Man ... Good-Evil, Christ-Devil" (qtd. in Floyd 317). Before he eventually abandoned the play in 1948, O'Neill worked on it from 1940 to 1943, and even considered including a Dictator figure clearly modeled on Hitler. Initially set in "The Hall of Black Mirrors in the Savior's Palace on a night in the Future" (328), "The Last Conquest" recounts Christ's Passion from the standpoint of "The 13th Disciple" (321), Satan, whose last temptation was to be accomplished through the "parable of the Siamese Twins," Man and the Devil, recounted by Satan to his dying "Brother... on the Cross" during the final Calvary scene (326–327).

Despite the foundational religious imagery, "The Last Conquest" would never have existed without the influence of Nietzsche's philosophy, which had already pervaded the other O'Neill biblical play, *Lazarus Laughed*. Indeed, while Lazarus clearly stands as an early example of Nietzsche's *ja-sagend* Superman, a markedly Nietzschean issue of boundary-crossing and transvaluation of values is at stake in "The Last Conquest," too. The influence of Nietzsche's work upon O'Neill has been studied in detail,[1] and, therefore I will not linger on it, but only mention that perhaps not only *Thus Spake Zarathustra*, but also Nietzsche's *Letters of Insanity* may have been a major inter-textual influence on O'Neill's treatment of the mask-person duality. In *The Great God Brown, Days Without End* and "The Last Conquest" the protagonist's personality shatters from its initial Dionysian unity into the two opposing doubles Saint/Satan. Similarly, O'Neill's "literary idol" had signed his *Letters of Insanity* alternately as "The Crucified One," "Dionysus," and "The Antichrist," thereby implying that the path to transvaluation not only crosses the limit between man and superman, but, in its most radical statements, it also blurs the thin line that stands between sanity and madness.

On Jung, O'Neill and Boundary-Crossing

An issue of boundary-crossing is also at the core of Carl Jung's meditation on God's hiddennes as it appears in his late book *Answer to Job*, first published in 1952 in German, and in 1954 in English, which of course makes it a text O'Neill could not have read. Nevertheless, I regard Jung's book as an appropriate *trait d'union* to the inter-textual references to the *deus absconditus* quoted so far, not only on account of the cultural milieu it shares with O'Neill's work, but also because it provides the missing connection between the issue of divine hiddenness as a trial, together with the problem of evil that ensues, and the typically O'Neillian leitmotiv of the opposing doubles "Good-Evil,

Christ-Devil." In *Answer to Job*, Jung addresses the *deus absconditus* theme from a psychological point of view by arguing that Job's story is the inevitable condition for God's human Incarnation in Christ. According to Jung, "Job is no more than the outward occasion for an inward process of dialectic in God" (18). By questioning Job's integrity, God "raises himself above his earlier primitive level of consciousness by indirectly acknowledging that the man Job is morally superior to him and that therefore he has to catch up and become human himself" (52). The ultimate goal in Job's trial would thus be "the differentiation of Yahweh's consciousness," i.e., His becoming aware of the inner antinomy that constitutes the divine being. According to Jung, this "unconscious split in the divine nature" (40) is of primary importance, both to the understanding of Job's parable, hence, of the *deus absconditus* theme, and in order to parse the dual nature of those made after His likeness.

> Because the *imago Dei* pervades the whole human sphere and makes mankind its involuntary representative, it is just possible that the four-hundred-year-old schism in the Church and the present division of the political world into two hostile camps both express the unrecognized polarity of the dominant archetype [70].

Luigi Aversa, a Jungian scholar, resumes and completes Jung's point in his insightful essay "Il Male e la coscienza." There Aversa argues that the dualism within God is indeed made of a dialectic contraposition between the intelligence that pushes over the limit and the conscience that brings one back to it (134). The fight between God's two favorite archangels and perpetual competitors, Lucifer and Michael, would figuratively incarnate the warfare between the two poles of this antinomy. As their names suggest, Lucifer (*lux-fero*, "Light-Bearer") and Michael (*mi-ka-El?*, "Who is like God?"), both of whom are "spiritual embodiments" (133)[2] of their creator, stand indeed for the drive to pursue unlimited knowledge (also the theme of the Original Sin) as opposed to the awareness of the limit. Hence the problem of evil. For in Aversa's view, "evil is closely connected to the antinomy knowledge/conscience" (134), or rather "to the risk of knowledge without conscience" (135). As soon as the unity of the antinomic symbol (*syn-ballein*, "to keep together") is shattered, Lucifer becomes, indeed, the devil (*dia-ballein*, "to divide").

> Just as in the story of Job and God the antinomic nature of existence is revealed, in the confrontation with the unconscious the conscience discovers the possibility to lose its symbolic capacity in the diabolic (dia-ballein) experience of dividedness ... [137].

In conclusion, according to Jung, and to Aversa's reading of his book, a soul-compelling question of boundary-crossing in terms of symbolic dialectic between equal competitors — or mirror-images — would be at stake in the *deus absconditus* leitmotiv. This very issue runs through O'Neill's work, itself pervaded by the perception of God's hiddenness and by the tragic sense this divine remoteness engenders. Forsaken by God, possibly forever as in Greek myths, O'Neill and his characters find themselves exiled in a spiritual wasteland with no way out. Torn as they are between longing and despair, they hardly ever realize that God's hiddenness may be a test for the soul, and thus they fail it. As a consequence, they physically turn into the inner contradiction they suffer, which in Aversa's definition is by itself a "diabolic experience." Such treatment of the *deus absconditus* in connection with a matter of boundary-crossing and antinomic duality, together with the classical, biblical, Nietzschean and Jungian echoes it encompasses, is clearly a major issue in O'Neill's art. To deal with it meant for the playwright to keep pursuing his lifelong wish to

> develop a tragic expression in terms of transfigured modern values and symbols in the theatre which may to some degree bring home to members of a modern audience their ennobling identity with the tragic figures on the stage [*Letters* 195].

In this sense, I believe, O'Neill's "dream in tragedy is the noblest ever."

Notes

1. A detailed list of existing scholarship on the influence of Nietzsche in O'Neill's work is provided at http://www.eoneill.com/library/playbyplay/nietzsche.htm

2. This and the following translations of Aversa are my own.

Works Cited

Aversa, Luigi, "Il male e la coscienza." *Il male*. Ed. Pier Francesco Pieri. Milano: Raffaello Cortina, 2000. Print.

Bisutti, Francesca. "Arcangeli a duello: educazione e mito nelle rappresentazioni del West." *America Today. Highways and Labyrinths*. Siracusa: Grafià Editrice, 2003. 322–334. Print.

Calasso, Roberto. *Le nozze di Cadmo e Armonia*. Milano: Adelphi, 2004. Print.

Diggins, John Patrick. *Eugene O'Neill's America: Desire Under Democracy*. Chicago: University of Chicago Press, 2007. Print.

Falk, Doris. *Eugene O'Neill and the Tragic Tension. An Interpretative Study*. New Brunswick, NJ: Rutgers University Press, 1958. Print.

Gelb, Arthur, and Barbara Gelb. *O'Neill: Life With Monte Cristo*. New York: Applause, 2000. Print.

Frazer, James G. *Il ramo d'oro. Studio sulla magia e la religione*. 2 vols. Torino: Boringhieri, 1973. Print.

Hesiod. *Theogony. Works and Days. Shield*. 2d ed. Ed. and trans. Apostolos Athanassakis. Baltimore: The Johns Hopkins University Press, 2004. Internet Sacred Text Archive. Web. 10 June 2011

Howard-Snyder, Daniel, and Paul K. Moser. *Divine Hiddenness: New Essays*. Cambridge : Cambridge University Press, 2002. Print.

Jung, Carl Gustav. *Answer to Job*. London and New York: Routledge, 1954. Print.

Mabry, Hohn R. *Noticing the Divine. An Introduction to Interfaith Spiritual Guidance*. Harrisburg: Morehouse, 2007. Print.

Nietzsche, Friedrich. *The Gay Science*. Trans. Walter Kaufmann. Web. 10 June 2011. http://www.bilkent.edu.tr/~thurston/nietzsche.pdf

____. "Letters of Insanity." *Scribd*. Web. 10 June 2011.

____. *Thus Spake Zarathustra*. Trans. Thomas Common. Charleston: Forgotten Books, 2008.

Print.

____. *Twilight of the Idols. With the Antichrist and Ecce Homo*. Trans. Anthony Ludovici. London: Wordsworth, 2007. Print.

O'Neill, Eugene. *Complete Plays 1913–1920*. New York: The Library of America, 1988. Print.

____. *Complete Plays 1920–1931*. New York: The Library of America, 1988. Print.

____. *Complete Plays 1932–1943*. New York: The Library of America, 1988. Print.

____. *Selected Letters*. Ed. Travis Bogard and Jackson R. Bryer. New Haven: Yale University Press, 1988. Print.

Porter, Laurin. *The Banished Prince: Time, Memory, and Ritual in the Late Plays of Eugene O'Neill*. Ann Arbor: UMI Research Press, 1988. Print.

Porter, Thomas E. "Jansenism and O'Neill's 'Black Mystery of the Soul.'" *The Eugene O'Neill Review 26* (2004). Web. 10 June 2011.

Shaughnessy, Edward L. *Down the Nights and Down the Days: Eugene O'Neill's Catholic Sensibility*. Notre Dame: University of Notre Dame Press, 2000. Print.

Törnquist, Egil. *A Drama of Souls: Studies in O'Neill's Super-Naturalistic Technique*. New Haven: Yale University Press, 1969. Print.

Voglino, Barbara. *"Perverse Mind": Eugene O'Neill's Struggle with Closure*. Cranbury: Associated University Press, 1999. Print.

Watt, Stephen. "O'Neill and Otto Rank: Doubles, 'Death Instincts,' and the Trauma of Birth." *Critical Approaches to O'Neill*. Ed. John H. Stroupe. New York: AMS Press, 1988. Print.

Intertextual Insanities in Susan Glaspell's *The Verge*

EMELINE JOUVE

A sound novel, a real beautiful book, should make us understand better the people around us, help us in understanding ourselves.
— Susan Glaspell, "On the Subject of Writing."

In an unpublished essay in which Susan Glaspell expounds her view "on the subject of writing," the playwright praises Evelyn Waugh's work for its capacity to take the reader "a little farther into understanding, into tolerance, to a keener amusement and to warmer sympathies":

> Evelyn Waugh could do that in his earlier books; and in making things extravagant, preposterous, perfectly crazy, he has jostled you out of a too fixed state and in giving you a life standing on its head he has somehow given you a new way of seeing what life is about. It's a craziness that is like a new dimension in sanity [Glaspell typescript].

This seemingly paradoxical correlation between "craziness" and "sanity" on which Glaspell insists in her essay resonates with a previous text by the author, a drama written in 1921 on the subject of women's emancipation, *The Verge*.[1] In this play, Glaspell has her heroine, Claire Archer, declare that "madness ... is the only chance for sanity" (251). This (conscious or unintended) textual echo opens the way to a reflection on both the relative opposition between reason and insanity and the notion of intertextuality: Glaspell recommends novice writers to consider a book as a "weaving pattern," where "the different elements ... must not be detached things, but thread held together, as a weaving pattern" (Glaspell typescript). Not only does Susan Glaspell stitch the different constitutive elements of her plots together, but she also weaves into her texts earlier textual or cultural references to present her readers and spectators with a dramatic embroidery to interpret. The audience who attended the original productions of *The Verge* at the Playwright's Theatre on MacDougal Street, New York City, was encouraged to decode Glaspell's textual weaving, to make sense of her use of intertextuality to interpret the issue of madness in the play. Claire, who departs from the traditional image of the Victorian wife and mother, is believed to be on the verge of insanity by the conventional members of her household who are eager to help her back to "normality." In his 1931 chronicle of American literature, *Expression in America*, Ludwig Lewisohn defines *The Verge* as a landmark in the history of American theatre. Victim of its originality in both content and form, the play, Lewisohn notes, has been criticized as abstruse by some contemporary reviewers. "There is nothing didactic or polemical about 'The Verge,'" Lewisohn states, "had there been it would have seemed more penetrable to many when they first heard it" (395–396). One may also suggest that, had these dramatic critics who condemned Glaspell's work as sibylline paid attention to the intertextual references present in the play, they would have judged *The Verge* differently. Intertextuality, I argue, opens doors to Glaspell's fictional world by providing keys to penetrate the work and make sense of Claire's alleged madness.

The concept of intertextuality was first coined in the work of Mikhaïl Bakhtin but the word was redeployed by Julia Kristeva to describe the idea that "any text is constructed as a mosaic of quotations; any text is the absorption and transformation of another" (66). In *Palimpsest: Literature in the Second Degree*, Gérard Genette defines intertextuality "as a relationship of coresponence between two texts or among several texts" (Samoyault 9–10). He distinguishes three types of intertextuality: quoting, plagiarism and allusion. Allusion, the "less explicit" and "less literal" kind of intertextual reference, is "an enunciation whose full meaning presupposes the perception of a relationship between it and another text, to which it necessarily refers by some inflections that would otherwise remain unintelligible." For Michael Riffaterre, "the intertext is the perception, by the reader, of a relationship between a work and others that have either preceded or followed it" (qtd. in Genette 1–2). In "Compulsory Reader Response: the Intertextual Drive," Riffaterre refers to the reader's "urge to understand" a text that compels him or her to "look to the intertext to fill out the text's gap" (qtd. in Genette, 2). Riffaterre, like Kristeva and Genette, all relate intertextuality to the act of reading, but their analyses are still pertinent when considering plays and the act of watching. Drawing on Riffaterre's reflection about the reader's responses to intertextual references, I will analyze the relevance and significance of the intertexts which can be traced in *The Verge* in relation to the theme of insanity dramatized in Glaspell's play. I thus consider intertextuality, helping the audience to "fill out" the play's gap on the issue of mental derangement, as a method of interpretation, a hermeneutic of madness. This article will untangle some of the social, artistic or philosophical allusions woven into *The Verge* and decipher in what ways they "produce significance" (Worton and Still 70). I focus on three specific cultural references which Glaspell brings together in dialogic confrontation: Sigmund Freud's "Fragment of an Analysis of a Case of Hysteria," Robert Wiene's 1920 movie *The Cabinet of Dr. Caligari* and Plato's Allegory of the Cave.

In *Freud on Broadway: A History of Psychoanalysis and the American Drama*, W. David Sievers introduces Susan Glaspell and her husband, George Cram Cook, as the authors of one of the "first Freudian plays."[2] In *Suppressed Desires: A Comedy in Two Scenes* (1915), Glaspell and Cook satirize "the effects of amateur psychoanalysis in the hands of a giddy faddist" (52–53). If Glaspell and Cook mocked the people who were absurdly uncritical about psychoanalysis and turned it into a craze, they were, however, not deriding psychoanalysis itself. On the contrary, the two playwrights took Freudian theory seriously as Glaspell indicates in a 1920 letter to the *New York Times* protesting a review of *Suppressed Desires*. Glaspell specifies to the dramatic critic that she and Cook "have been students of psychoanalysis for a number of years" (qtd. in Carpentier 2007, 154). We could thus logically conclude from this statement that Glaspell was certainly well-versed in Freud's theories, notably his analyses of neuroses.

Popular interest in psychoanalysis in the United States was aroused in 1909 when the Austrian neurologist was invited to Clark University in Worcester, Massachussetts, to give a series of lectures presenting his discoveries to the United States. It then gathered considerable impetus during World War I when, according to Nathan J. Hale, Jr., "in the colossal human laboratory of the Great War some of Freud's theories seemed strikingly confirmed." The war gave birth to a new syndrome which was called "shell shock," a psychiatric illness resulting from injury to the nerves during combat (13–24), now known as post traumatic stress disorder. As J. Ellen Gainor points out, Glaspell demonstrates in *The Verge* "her clear understanding of the latest trends and theories in psychoanalysis" because "her depiction of Claire and her symptoms, as well as Dr. Emmons and his diagnosis, closely mirrors the descriptions of traumatic disorders brought on by the war, documented in both the medical literature and memoirs from the era" (151). Worried about his wife's unconventional attitude, Harry wants Claire to see Dr. Emmons, arguing that the neurologist has "fixed up a lot of people shot to pieces in the war" (236). For Harry, Claire exhibits the same symptoms as the shell-shocked soldiers. Her search for intellectual stimulation, for Harry, is symptomatic of an unhealthy retreat within "her mind" and is thought to be the evidence that Claire has turned "hysterical" (241). To prove his point to Dick, Claire's lover, Harry reveals to the young man that he caught Claire "reading Latin": "What do you think I caught her doing the other day? Reading Latin. Well — a woman that reads Latin needn't worry a husband much" (237). This remark tinged with dramatic irony betrays Harry's selfish anxiety that he might lose his wife rather than a sincere concern for Claire's well-being. If the explicit references to the shell-shocked soldiers lead us to believe that Glaspell has indeed drawn on the medical literature of war, the striking similarities between Claire and Freud's patient, Ida Bauer alias Dora, lead us to assume that Freud's seminal "Fragment of an Analysis of a Case of Hysteria" (1905) could also be considered as an intertext of *The Verge*. Whether Glaspell consciously or not alluded to Freud, the numerous parallelisms between Claire and Dora justify a first reading of the heroine's alleged hysterical state through the prism of Freud's work.[3]

In his study, the psychoanalyst enumerates a series of symptoms from which his patient suffers. Some of Dora's symptoms coincide with Claire's attitudes in the play. Freud explains that Dora is affected by "low spirits and an alteration in her character" (16) and so is Claire, according to her husband who tells Tom that "she used to be the best sport a man ever played around with" — the phrase "used to" emphasizes the rupture between the past and the present and the alteration in Claire's personality (241). Freud also specifies that Dora was "clearly satisfied neither with herself nor with her family" (16). In her conversation with her sister Adelaide, Claire exclaims: "I'm tired of what you do — you and all of you. Life — experience — values — calm — sensitive words which raise their heads as indications" (251). Claire's spasmodic enumeration shows that she is dissatisfied not only with her family but also with what they represent, that is conventional rationality as the personification of the "words" underscores. Feeling estranged from her family and friends, Claire isolates herself in her "tower" where she does not like to be disturbed, as her sister is made to realize at the opening of Act II (248). Likewise, Dora "tried to avoid social intercourse" (16). Finally, both Dora and Claire pretend to want to kill themselves while, in Freud's words, they actually have "no serious suicidal intentions" (17). This aspect is illustrated in the play when, in Act III, Claire points a revolver at herself:

> TOM. Claire! (*now sees the revolver in her hand that is turned from him. Going to her*) Claire!
> CLAIRE. ... you think I mustn't shoot anybody — even myself.... I shall never shoot myself [261–262].

Glaspell seems thus to have fashioned Claire upon Dora whose hysterical symptoms were caused by forbidden sexual desires — triggered by the advances made to her by Herr K. Glaspell does not deal explicitly with Claire's sexual life but the presence of her lovers, Tom and Dick, in her house suggests that sexuality is not taboo for her. Sexual frustrations, therefore, cannot be seen as the cause of her disturbed state. The reason for her dissatisfaction with life is consequently to be looked for elsewhere, in her general aversion to conventionality itself. Her activity with plants reminds us of the concept of "sublimation" that Freud introduced to his American audience in his Fifth Lecture delivered at the Clark conference. Sublimation is a process by which sexual impulses are transformed into "higher," "socially more valuable goals" such as artistic or scientific accomplishments. Claire has turned the family greenhouse into a laboratory where she grows new breeds of plants. Paradoxically, this act of creation which should enable her to channel her forbidden desires into socially acceptable achievements is also the symbol of her rebellion. Geographically, the greenhouse stands on the margins of the house. This transformation of the established function of the greenhouse and its liminal position are emblematic of Claire's rejection of norms and conventions. The greenhouse is where she creates "otherness":

> CLAIRE. These plants —(*beginning flounderingly*) Perhaps they are less beautiful — less sound — than the plants from which they diverged. But they have found — otherness (*laughs a little shrilly*). If you know — what I mean [246].

The plants symbolize Claire. They do not conform to the norm as the comparative structure suggests, but "diverge" from it. The last sentence hints at Elizabeth's and the rest of her family's lack of understanding of her scientific experimentation. Like her plants, Claire wants to be different. Discussing her experiments, she explains: "We need not be held in forms moulded for us. There is outness — and otherness" (235). The use of the pronoun "we" while the conversation deals with plants is significant. The mould obviously stands for the norms. At the end of the play, Claire destroys "Breath of Life," the plant she has created, and kills Tom, the one she loves. The process of sublimation gives way to destruction.

As if Glaspell had anticipated Freud's "death drive," theorized in *Beyond the Pleasure Principle* (1920) and first published in English in 1922, she dramatizes the enactment of Claire's primitive impulse to destruction not of herself but of those around her. At the end of the play, the heroine seems to embrace hysteria as if it were the only way to free herself from the frustrations of life in society, as if, as Claire argues at the beginning of Act II, "madness [was indeed] the only chance for sanity" (251). Thus Glaspell uses Freud's figure of the hysterical woman but gives it a different spin. In *The Verge*, hysteria is not a pathology but a form of rebellion against social constraints. The dramatist seems to go further than the psychoanalysis by throwing light on the alienating nature of conventions. Freud believed that Dora could be cured; Glaspell demonstrates that Claire cannot, not in a patriarchal system which controls and restrains women's lives. Interestingly, however, after only eleven weeks of treatment, Ida Bauer decided to break off her therapy to Freud's dismay. Freud himself admitted that his treatment was a failure but did not recognize that, as second wave feminist scholars have pointed out, his analysis failed "because of its inherent sexism." "Freud," Toril Moi writes, has proved himself "authoritarian, a willing participant in the male power game conducted between Dora's father and Herr K., and at no time turns to consider Dora's experience of the events" (182). If, as Michel Foucault argues, Freud demystified the "asylum structures" and delivered "the patient from the asylum within which his 'liberators' had alienated him" he, however, transferred all the powers in the practitioner's hands turning the doctor into "an alienating figure." Foucault asserts that "it is perhaps because it did not suppress this ultimate structure, and because it referred all the others to it, that psychoanalysis has not been able, will not be able to hear the voices of unreason, not to decipher in themselves the signs of the madman" (277–278). Agreeing to be cured by Dr. Emmons would have come down to conforming to patriarchal gender roles which Claire strongly denies.[4] Unable to penetrate Claire's expressions, of what they consider as "unreason," the alienating Dr. Emmons and his proponents like Harry and Adelaide have failed to understand Claire's need to break away from any form of alienation, they have failed to realize that Claire's "otherness" was the expression of her rebellion.

Claire's hysteria is thus to be taken metaphorically as symptomatic of the ills of patriarchal society which alienates female individuals by trapping them within convention at the expense of personal freedom. Such a symbolical reading of the play is encouraged by Susan Glaspell's recourse to expressionism. In his study of expressionism in the American drama of the 1920s, Mardi Valgemae notes that *The Verge* was the first American play to be qualified as "expressionistic" (25). The expressionist movement that emerged in Europe at the turn of the century reached American shores in the 1920s. American dramatic expressionism, Valgemae argues, is much indebted to "one single work of Continental expressionism," *The Cabinet of Dr. Caligari* by German director Robert Wiene (9). Premiered before American audiences in April 1921, this silent is said to have been deeply influential in opening new dramaturgical horizons and believed to have influence Glaspell's herself. Struggling to put into words "what appeared to be so different from the usual realistic fare on the stage," two 1921 reviews in New York newspapers, "the *New York Globe and Commercial Advertiser* and the *Greenwich Villager*, both described *The Verge* as reminiscent of the film *The Cabinet of Dr. Caligari*:

> In 1921 the *Greenwich Villager* reviewer, discussing the play's mixture of realism and symbolism, described how the "mythical tower room in the [second] act suggests Caligari." Similarly, Kenneth Macgowan's *New York Globe and Commercial Advertiser Review* noted that the "second act has an expressionistic setting by Cleon Throckmorton. A tower room with lantern-flecked walls seen through a crazily latticed window, almost out of 'Caligari'" [Frank, 119–120].

The reviewers are referring to Glaspell's setting of Act II with its entanglement of disrupted and distorted lines and its play on light and shadow characteristic of the expressionist nightmarish atmosphere created in *The Cabinet of Dr. Caligari*. The opening stage direction of this second act reads:

> Late afternoon of the following day. CLAIRE is alone in the tower — a tower which is thought to be round but does not complete the circle. The back is curved, then jagged lines break from that, and the front is a queer bulging window — in a curve that leans. The whole structure is as if given a twist by some terrific force — like something wrong. It is lighted by an old-fashioned watchman's lantern hanging from the ceiling; the innumerable pricks and slits in the metal throw a marvelous pattern on the curved wall — like some masonry that hasn't been [247].

Although there is no direct evidence — let us here recall that Susan Glaspell has bequeathed scholars very little information about her creative process — it is quite plausible that Susan Glaspell was among the spectators who attended the projection of *Caligari* in the spring of 1921.[5] Eugene O'Neill, a friend of Glaspell's and prominent member of the Provincetown Players, wrote on June 10th in a letter to movie producer Ralph Block that seeing Wiene's film opened his mind to "wonderful possibilities" he had never "dreamed of before" (156). This biographical element about one of Glaspell's closest acquaintances, with whom she actually spent a lot of time during the summer 1921, the similarities between the German director's and the American dramatist's settings as well as the dramatization of the patient-physician couple in both pieces make of *The Cabinet of Dr. Caligari* a cogent intertextual allusion in *The Verge*.[6] The eponymous hero of Wiene is first believed to be a malevolent hypnotist exploiting his faithful spleepwalking Cesare to perpetrate a series of murders. The end of the movie reveals, however, that the flashback about the deranged doctor and his hypnotized slave was in fact a mere fantasy of Francis, the narrator of the embedding story. The viewers discover that Francis is, in fact, an inmate of an insane asylum and that the man he says is the crazy Caligari is the director of the asylum. This inversion of the insane/sane figures calls up the reversal taking place in *The Verge* when Claire ironically thanks Dr. Emmons for "helping people go insane":

> CLAIRE. (*to EMMONS*) It must be very interesting — helping people go insane.
> ...
> EMMONS. (*easily*) I hope that's not precisely what we do.
> ...
> CLAIRE. ... I think it is very kind of you — helping people go insane. I suppose that they have all sorts of reasons for having to do it — reasons why they can't stay sane any longer. But tell me, how do they do it? It's not easy to — get out. How do so many manage it?
> EMMONS. I'd like immensely to have a talk with you about all this some day [258].

In this exchange with the neurologist who has been invited by Harry to restore Claire to health, the female protagonist strategically upends the traditional medical discourse by arguing that doctors assist people to escape their problems, that is society and its crippling customs, through insanity. The prosodic pauses underscore the power of Claire's seemingly paradoxical point. Claire slyly plays with her family's expectations by inducing that she is not "insane" as her use of the pronoun "they," setting distance between her and "the people," shows. Claire's rhetorical reversal, nevertheless, reinforces her relatives' intuitions that she is "sick": "HARRY: (*brokenly*) You're sick, Claire. There's no denying it. (*looks at EMMONS who nods.*)" (259). The professional practitioner's paraverbal avowal confirms the family's diagnosis: Claire suffers from deviance; her rebellion against conventions is perceived by the right-thinking characters as pathological. Yet, as Steven Frank demonstrates, siding with the family members and taking for granted that Claire is indeed crazy would obliterate the symbolical scope of the play and thus lead to a faulty interpretation of Glaspell's work.

Alexander Woollcott, who reviewed the play for the *New York Times* in November 1921, gives us a relevant illustration of the dangers of analyzing the play as a realistic piece. For Woollcott, "'The Verge' is a play which can be intelligently reviewed only by a neurologist or by some woman who has journeyed near to the verge of which Miss Glaspell writes." The view that one must be either a neurologist or neurotic to make sense of the play is, in itself, spurious: the flaw in this reasoning may be due to the fact that he interprets *The Verge* as a realistic play and thus takes the play as a confusing representation of a woman's descent into insanity. According to Frank, a realistic reading of *The Verge* tends to "devalue the experimental aspects of the play and/or view them as manifestations of the protagonist's disturbed mind-set" (120). The expressionist form, which plunged the audience into a world of subjectivity, of symbolic representations of "inner truths" and thus broke with the objectivity of realism, encourages the spectators to surpass the literal interpretation of the plot (Valgemae 12).

Ideologically, J.L. Styan reminds us, expressionism was originally a "drama of protest, reacting against the pre-war authority of the family and community, the rigid lines of the social order" (3). Expressionism can consequently be considered as a "counterdiscourse" and such is Richard Murphy's opinion in *Theorizing Avant-Garde Theatre*. For Murphy, expressionism functions as a mode of "counterdiscourse making visible those meanings and values which remained repressed and unarticulated by the socially legitimized discourses and by conventional modes of representation such as realism" (143–144). The *Caligari*-like atmosphere of *The Verge* should thus be interpreted as a counterdiscourse. Glaspell raises the curtain on this symbolical violence which individuals have to endure in conventional society and magnifies its dangers by staging the drastic rebellion of a Nietzschean female *Übermensch*. Contrary to Michael Cotsell who equates Dr. Emmons with Dr. Caligari in *The Theater of Trauma*, Frank casts Claire in the part of the Wiene's fictional doctor (Cotsell 143):

Claire is less like Francis, the film's insane narrator, and more akin to the film's namesake, Dr. Caligari. Even their names — "C-L-A-I-R-E" and "C-A-L-I-G-A-R-I" — suggest a strong affinity. Both Caligari and Claire are scientists who express an intense passion for and commitment to their work. Just as Caligari pronounces, "I must know everything," Claire announces her Promethean goals: "I want to give fragrance to Breath of Life — the flower I have created that is outside what flowers have been." Like Caligari, whose work is not condoned by authorities, Claire hopes, in the process of creating something new, to undo old forms, proclaiming, "But it can be done! We need not be held in forms moulded for us ... I want to break it up!" And just as the mad scientist, as represented by Caligari, works outside the realm of conventional scientific inquiry and is therefore exiled, even hunted down, by the community at large, so too is the Woman Artist, in her attempt to subvert patriarchal artistic forms, ostracized and labeled "mad" [Frank 126].

This comparison between Claire and Dr. Caligari raises several questions. In the movie, the director exploits the technique of the embedded structure to dramatize the seeming double-identity of the physician, and therefore the confusion between illusion and reality. On the other hand, at the end of the movie, the doctor of the framed story declares that he knows how to cure his patient. As in the film, the dichotomy between appearance and reality is central in *The Verge*. Glaspell's handling of this philosophical issue evokes Plato's Allegory of the Cave, an intertext which enables the spectators to understand why, contrary to Caligary, Claire does not manage to eventually cure her patient, that is society.

In *The Theory and Analysis of Drama*, Manfred Pfister distinguishes between the traditional expository scene, which he defines as the "transmission of the information to do with the events and situations from the past that determine the dramatic present," and the "dramatic introduction" or "what E.T. Sehrt describes metaphorically as the 'dramatic upbeat'" (86). *The Verge*, which immerses, from the outset, the audience into the dramatic present of the play, without hinting at any preliminary information about the "what," "who" and "why" of the plot, thus starts with a "dramatic introduction." Not only is the emphasis laid on the "atmosphere of the fictional world," in Pfister's words, but it also "stimulate[s] the audience's attention" by giving them keys to interpret what follows (86). As the curtain rises at the opening of the play, the spectators discover an enigmatic setting:

> *The Curtain lifts on a place that is dark, save for a shaft of light from below which comes up through an open trap-door in the floor. This slants up and strikes the long leaves and the huge brilliant blossom of a strange plant .... A moment later a buzzer ... Then from below — his shadow blocking the light, comes ANTHONY ... — He goes back down the stairs, closing the trap-door upon himself, and the curtain is drawn upon darkness and wind. It opens a moment later on the greenhouse in the sunshine of a snowy morning ... The frost has made patterns on the glass as if — as Plato would have it — the patterns inherent in abstract nature and behind all life had to come out, not only in the creative heat within, but in the creative cold on the other side of the glass...*

At the back grows a strange vine. It is arresting rather than beautiful. It creeps along the low wall, and one branch gets a little way up the glass. You might see the form of a cross in it, if you happened to think it that way. The leaves of this vine are not the form that leaves have been. They are at once repellent and significant [230].

The explicit mention of Plato by the playwright, who studied philosophy and Greek in her college years, prompts the readers to take into consideration the reach of Glaspell's reference to the Philosopher. I would argue that Plato's Cave Allegory introduced in *The Republic*, George Cram Cook's bedside book, can be read as an intertext of these introductory stage directions.[7] This parable, related to Plato's theory of Forms, is an invitation not to mistake appearances, the material world of changes known to us through sensation, with reality grasped not by the senses but by the intellect (Plato *The Republic*, 177–251).

The chiaroscuro effect reminiscent of Plato's shadows, the underground room from which Anthony emerges as a prisoner from the cave and the reference to the "pattern inherent in abstract nature" recalling the Forms theory are some of many elements which legitimate a platonic reading of Glaspell's dramatic introduction which conditions the receptors' interpretation of the whole play. From the start, Glaspell's audience is enjoined to pay attention to the issue of appearances versus truth. The final specification that the leaves "*are at once repellent and significant*" implies that Glaspell departs from the Aristotelian tradition, according to which art and theatre should aim at beautifying and improving reality. Glaspell is not interested in beauty ("repellent") but in intelligibility ("significant"). It is worth remembering that Plato denies that poetry can imitate ideas. As he has Socrates explain to his interlocutor in the last book of *The Republic*, poets are "only imitators" who "copy images of virtue and the like, but the truth they never reach" (257). Glaspell seems to play with these assumptions by staging the very act of representation and foregrounding the presence of the theatrical curtain ("*The Curtain lifts on a place that is dark ... the curtain is drawn upon darkness and wind*"). With this metatheatrical strategy, Glaspell makes clear that what the members of the audience are about to witness is an illusion. As the address to the readers/spectators "*you might see the form of a cross in it, if you happened to think it that way*" suggests, the playwright warns her audience against mistaking appearance and form or idea, in Platonic thinking: what has the appearance of a plant is in fact the idea of a cross. With this direct address, Glaspell sets out a reading method which the spectators are invited to adopt throughout the play. Consequently, the members of the audience, who enjoy the privileged standpoint of omniscient receptors, are encouraged to systematically go beyond the material world, into the realm of "forms," the world of knowledge. As we have already seen, Act II takes places in Claire's expressionist tower. The second paragraph of the location didascalia indicates that the spectators see Claire *"through the huge ominous window"* (248). The Fourth Wall is thus materialized on stage. The window through which the spectators can observe the course of Act II can be considered as the literalization of the point of view of the spectators who witness what is going on without taking part in the action. Not only do the members of the audience see the external aspects of things but they also have the power to reach what remains invisible to the protagonists' eyes.

At the opening of the second act, the stage directions inform the readers that the tower back wall is spattered with light: *"the innumerable pricks and slits in the metal throw a marvelous pattern on the curved wall."* The word "pricks" appears a few pages later in the play when Claire accuses the members of her family of never having "once — looked with [her] through the little pricks the gaiety made," never " — once, looked with [her] at the queer light that came in through the pricks" (250–251). By enabling the spectators to see the strange patterns of light which Claire's relatives have decided to ignore, the playwright dramatizes the family's unwillingness to reach Claire by looking beyond appearances and the screen of conventions. Claire's initial aim was to break away from those stifling traditions, those "forms moulded for us," which alienate the individuals from their inner truths (235). Yet, her use of the term "forms" proves that she confuses what Plato also names the ideas and the material shapes of reality. In fact, Claire mistakes feeling and knowing: "To know — to feel, / And do nothing with what I feel and know — / That's being good. That's nearer God" (256). The structural repetition ("To know — to feel") and the parataxis ("what I feel and know") stylistically highlight Claire's confusion between the world of senses and "the world of knowledge." "Nearer to God" is an anaphoric intertextual hint at "Nearer, My God, to Thee," the song on which the play ends. The divine world of God may be viewed as a Christian version of the realm of Ideas which, according to Plato, paves the way to the power of "reason and truth," a power Claire is deprived of as the hymn sung by the heroine at the closing of Act III testifies (179):

> CLAIRE. Out. (*as if feeling her way*)
> Nearer,
> (*Her voice is now feeling the way to it.*)
> Nearer —
> (*Voice almost upon it.*)
> — my God,
> (*Falling upon it with surprise.*)
> to Thee,
> (*Breathing it.*)
> Nearer — to Thee,
> E'en though it be —

(*A slight turn of the head toward the dead man she loves — a mechanical turn just as
    far the other way.*)
a cross
That
(*Her head going down.*)
raises me;
(*Her head slowly coming up — singing it.*)
Still all my song shall be;
Nearer, my —
(*Slowly the curtain begins to shut her out. The last word heard is the final Nearer — a
    faint breath from far* [266–267].

The silencing of the last word, "God," is emblematic of Claire's failure to raise
herself above materiality. The intratextual reference of the "cross" brings us
back to the introductory stage directions of the play and to the description
of the "strange vine." This plant creeping along the wall is Claire's creation
which she has baptized "Edge Vine." She destroys it at the end of Act I, just
as she kills the "man she loves," Tom Edgeworthy — the onomastics is obviously meaningful — when he eventually agrees to stay with her. Claire uproots
Edge Vine when she realizes that "it's turning back," that despite her effort
to create a plant different from the others it now looks like any other normal
plants (233). Similarly, when Tom eventually agrees to live with her a normal
couple's life, she murders him because she does not want to be held back by
the traditions from which she has been trying to escape.

Not only does the cross at the beginning of the play set out a reading method
but it also foreshadows Claire's failure. The concluding intertextual reference of
the play, the song "Nearer, My God, to Thee," popularly believed to be as the
last song the band on the Titanic played before the ship sank,[8] symbolically
confirms the heroine's downfall (Howells, 120). Like her family enmeshed with
the patterns of Victorian traditions, Claire is trapped by shapes and moulds.
Her mistake is to believe that she can change life, the reality of life, by reforming
the material world around her when, according to Plato, she should be dealing
with Ideals. Contrary to the director of the asylum in *The Cabinet of Dr. Caligari*, Claire has thus paradoxically not found the solutions to cure her patient,
to cure society from the tyranny of appearances and the illusion of conventional respectability. In enticing her audience to adopt a Platonic reading of
The Verge, Susan Glaspell encourages them to take on the position of the
philosopher, to apprehend truth through the channel of the soul. The spec-
tator-philosopher-interpreter will be able to draw, if not lessons, at least some
conclusions from Claire's failure. Hence, the heroine's alleged craziness opens
the way to "a new dimension in sanity" for, as Socrates demonstrates in Plato's
Phaedrus, "prophecy is a madness": in performing her prophecy in front of
the audience, Claire takes them "a little farther into understanding, into tolerance, to a keener amusement and to warmer sympathies."[9]

Notes

1. Glaspell's essay "On the Subject of Writing," archived in the Berg Collection of the New York Public Library, is undated. Because Evelyn Waugh's first novel, *Decline and Fall*, was published by Chapman & Hall in 1928, we are thus logically led to conclude that Glaspell's reflection on the subject of writing dates from after 1928 and the production of *The Verge*.

2. Sievers calls *Suppressed Desires* the second play to dramatize Freud's theories on stage in America; Alice Gerstenberg's *Overtones* (written 1913, performed spring 1915) earlier employed the concept of the id and ego (58). However, Gerstenberg mentions neither Freud and his theories of the unconscious nor therapy in the form of psychoanalysis. Drew Eisenhauer has added that Floyd Dell's *St. George in Greenwich Village* (1913) may be he earliest mention of psychoanalysis in an American play, but Dell does not focus on or dramatize the concept, and this play received only a private performance by the Greenwich Village Liberal Club before being published in *The Masses* (*n* 349–350).

3. For Roland Barthes and Michaël Riffaterre, references to external textual sources do not have to be conscious to be considered as allusions: "L'intertextualité ne se réduit pas évidemment à un problème de sources ou d'influences; l'intertexte est un champ général de formules anonymes, dont l'origine est rarement repérable, de citations inconscientes ou automatiques, données sans guillemets" (qtd. in Samoyault, 15).

4. I am grateful to Martha C. Carpentier for her invaluable insight on psychoanalysis.

5. As J. Ellen Gainor, author of *Susan Glaspell in Context*, reminds us, "Glaspell rarely spoke of the direct influences on her work": "She gave few interviews, kept only the sketchiest of diaries, and left behind almost no evidence of creative process. In trying to determine what informed her writing, scholars have had to speculate on potential influences and dig deeply in historical records to uncover events that may have sparked her imagination" (Gainor *Susan Glaspell in Context*, 70).

6. Following our analysis of the Freudian intertext, it is worth noting that the character of Dr. Caligari was thought, when the film went out, to have been modeled after Sigmund Freud (Packer 32).

7. For different interpretations of the platonic reference in *The Verge*, consult Monica Stufft and Julia Galbus. In "Glaspell's Re-vision of Stringberg's *A Dream Play*," Stufft proposes a brief analysis of Glaspell's reference to Plato by focusing on the dichotomy between heat and cold, interior and exterior. She writes: "Both heat and cold are taken as productive, as being useful, just as Plato specifies that you cannot have one without the other. The patterns are created not only by the heat generated inside of the greenhouse, but also the cold produced by the storm outside. The freezing environment outside of the greenhouse could have been configured as purely a place of destruction, instead, Glaspell says that the frost — and the 'truth,' to use Plato's terms, which the pattern suggest — results from the combination of both. Glaspell gestures towards dichotomies between inside and outside, hot and cold, low and high, in order to draw attention to the fact that each dichotomy is at least partially collapsed. In *The Verge*, both hot and cold can be creative, and illumination can come from 'low places'" (88). In "Susan Glaspell's *The Verge*: a Socratic Quest to Reinvent Form and Escape Plato's Cave," Galbus argues that the playwright "foreshadows late-twentieth-century criticism of Plato and depicts clearly why forms can hinder creativity language, and societal roles." Her analysis is based on "Judith Butler's work on gender as a constructed social category and her work on the implicit gendered role of matter in Platonic metaphysics" (82).

8. Recent scholarship suggests the band on the titanic was actually playing a popular song called "Autumn" or "August" but for obvious reasons survivors preferred to remember it as "Nearer My God to Thee" and Glaspell would probably have believed this was true.

9. For another interpretation of Claire's recitation of "Nearer my God to Thee" at the end of the play, consult Martha C. Carpentier's 2006 essay "Apollonian Form and Dionysian Excess in Susan Glaspell's Drama and Fiction" (48).

Works Cited

Ben-Zvi, Linda. *Susan Glaspell: Her Life and Times*. New York: Oxford University Press, 2005. Print.

Carpentier, Martha C. "Apollonian Form and Dionysian Excess in Susan Glaspell's Drama and Fiction." *Disclosing Intertextualities: The Stories, Plays, and Novels of Susan Glaspell.* Eds. Martha C. Carpentier and Barbara Ozieblo. Amsterdam: Rodopi, 2006. 35–50. Print.

_____. "The Deracinated Self: Immigrants, Orphans, and the 'Migratory Consciousness' of Willa Cather and Susan Glaspell." *Studies in American Fiction* 35.2 (Autumn 2007): 131–158. Print.

Cotsell, Michael. *The Theater of Trauma: American Modernist Drama and the Psychological Struggle for the American Mind, 1900–1930.* New York: Peter Lang, 2005. Print.

Eisenhauer, Drew. *"Something Sweetly Personal And Sweetly Social": Modernism, Metadrama, And The Avant Garde In The Plays Of The Provincetown Players.* Ph.D. diss. University of Maryland, College Park. 2009. Print.

Foucault, Michel. *Madness and Civilization.* Trans. Richard Howard. New York: Vintage, 1988. Print.

Frank, Steven. "On 'The Verge' of a New Form: The Cabinet of Dr. Caligari and Susan Glaspell's Experiments in *The Verge.*" *Experimenters, Rebels, and Disparate Voices: The Theatre of the 1920s Celebrates American Diversity.* Ed. Arthur Gewirtz and James J. Kolb. Westport, CT: Praeger, 2003. 119–129. Print.

Freud, Sigmund. *Dora: an Analysis of a Case of Hysteria.* Ed. Philip Rieff. New York: Collier Books, 1973. Print.

Gainor, Ellen J. *Susan Glaspell in Context: American Theater, Culture, and Politics, 1915–48.* Ann Arbor: University of Michigan Press, 2001. Print.

_____. "Woman's Honor and the Critique of Slander *Per Se.*" *Susan Glaspell: New Directions in Critical Inquiry.* Ed. Martha C. Carpentier. Newcastle: Cambridge Scholars Press, 2006. 66–79. Print.

Galbus, Julia. "Susan Glaspell's *The Verge*: A Socratic Quest to Reinvent Form and Escape Plato's Cave." *Journal of Dramatic Theory and Criticism* 15.1 (Fall 2000): 81–95. Print.

Gebauer, Gunter, and Christoph Wulf. *Mimesis: Culture, Art, Society.* Berkeley: University of California Press, 1995. Print.

Genette, Gerard. *Palimpsests: Literature in the Second Degree.* Trans. Channa Newman, Claude Doubinsky, and Gerald Prince. Lincoln: University of Nebraska Press, 1997.

Glaspell, Susan. "The Verge." *Susan Glaspell: The Complete Plays.* Ed. Linda Ben-Zvi and J. Ellen Gainor. Jefferson, NC: McFarland, 2010. 229–267. Print.

_____. "On the Subject of Writing." Susan Glaspell Papers, The Henry W. and Albert A. Berg Collection of English and American Literature, The New York Public Library, Astor, Lenox and Tilden Foundations. Undated Typescript.

Hale, Nathan G. *The Rise and Crisis of Psychoanalysis in the United States: Freud and the Americans, 1917–1985.* New York: Oxford University Press, 1995. Print.

Howells, Richard P. *The Myth of the Titanic.* New York: St. Martin's Press, 1999. Print.

Kristeva, Julia. *Desire in Language: A Semiotic Approach to Literature and Art.* Trans. Thomas Gora, Alice Jardine and Leon S. Roudiez. New York: Columbia University Press, 1980. Print.

Lewisohn, Ludwig. *Expression in America.* New York: Harper & Brothers, 1932. Print.

Moi, Toril. "Representation of Patriarchy: Sexuality and Epistemology in Freud's Dora." Ed. Charles Bernheimer and Claire Kahane. *In Dora's Case: Freud — hysteria — feminism.* Gender and Culture. New York: Columbia University Press, 1985. 181–199. Print.

Murphy, Richard. *Theorizing the Avant-Garde: Modernism, Expressionism, and the Problem of Postmodernity.* Cambridge: Cambridge University Press, 1999. Print.

Packer, Sharon. *Movies and the Modern Psyche.* Westport, CT: Praeger, 2007. Print.

Papke, Mary E. *Susan Glaspell: A Research and Production Sourcebook.* Westport, CT: Greenwood Press, 1993. Print.

Pfister, Manfred, and John Halliday. *The Theory and Analysis of Drama.* Cambridge: Cambridge University Press, 1993. Print.

Plato. *Phaedrus.* Trans. Bejamin Jowett. The Internet Classics Archive. Web. 12 July 2010. http://classics.mit.edu/Plato/phaedrus.html

_____. *The Republic.* Trans. Benjamin Jowett. New York: Cosimo Classics, 2008. Print.

Samoyault, Tiphaine. *L'intertextualite: Memoire De La Litterature.* Paris: A. Colin, 2005. Print.

Sievers, W. David. *Freud on Broadway: A History of Psychoanalysis and the American Drama.* New York: Hermitage House, 1955. Print.

Stufft, Monica. "Flowers by Design: Susan Glaspell's Re-vision of Stringberg's *A Dream Play*." *Disclosing Intertextualities: The Stories, Plays, and Novels of Susan Glaspell*. Ed. Martha C. Carpentier and Barbara Ozieblo. Amsterdam: Rodopi, 2006. 79–91. Print.

Styan, John L. *Expressionism and Epic Theatre*. Modern Drama in Theory and Practice, 3. Cambridge: Cambridge University Press, 1983. Print.

Valgemae, Mardi. *Accelerated Grimace: Expressionism in the American Drama of the 1920s*. Carbondale: Southern Illinois University Press, 1972. Print.

Woollcott, Alexander "The Play." *New York Times* 15 Nov. 1921: 27. Print.

Worton, Michael, and Judith Still. *Intertextuality: Theories and Practices*. Manchester: Manchester University Press, 1990. Print.

Female Playwrights, Female Killers

*Intersecting Texts of Crime and Gender
in Glaspell, Watkins and Treadwell*

LISA HALL HAGEN

Between 1926 and 1928, three American women parlayed their experiences as journalists into dramatic texts about notorious female murderers. Although Susan Glaspell, Maurine Dallas Watkins and Sophie Treadwell also wrote in other forms and other plays, they are often defined and anthologized by their plays *Trifles, Chicago* and *Machinal*. Glaspell, Treadwell and Watkins wrote about female murderers in plays that were culturally subversive in that they offer space for a nuanced critique of gender and society, an intertextual space. The power of these subversive narratives is especially clear because the three writers were also journalists who created newspaper stories about women murderers. In the 1920s, mainstream journalism was conservative in form because it often reinforced cultural norms. Jessie Ramey writes, for example, that tabloids "reproduce cultural norms (such as gender roles), encouraging people to feel comfortable in their place in society" (Ramey 629). Thus these playwrights could offer a more critical view of murderesses and their crimes within the play form than from within their journalism. I will argue that Watkins, Glaspell and Treadwell created destabilizing and investigative narratives out of a potentially conservative form, the mainstream press, including the norm-enforcing discourse concerning the punishment of female criminals.

In the final section, I will argue that we have defined each of these writers by these particular plays. For Glaspell and Treadwell, that means these plays often represent them in the canon of American theatre, inasmuch as "the canon" represents "the serious substance of university curricula ... if not also ... the objects of emulation and possible contestation for new writers who aspire to a place in the pantheon" (Hulbert 20). For Watkins, it means she has been defined and remembered in the popular theatre almost exclusively by *Chicago*. Additionally, "the inclusion of a text in the canon also implies for most of us that some claim is made for its excellence, importance, or influence" (Hulbert 120). A play's inclusion in this impalpable and contested grouping is important because the literary canon, although often redefined, represents "legitimized" and "authenticated" literary or popular masterpieces.

Plays like *Trifles, Machinal* and *Chicago* that re-create a crime for the stage "revel in the telling of the lineaments of the society that spawned the crime" (Ben-Zvi 142). Glaspell, Watkins and Treadwell each situate a female murderer in the socio-cultural context that "created" the offense. By doing so, each writer exposes the hidden mechanics of that context, potentially implicating society in the crime eventually committed. Furthermore, each play delves into the cultural, social and gender implications of these three famous murders, demonstrating how crime and legal punishment can illuminate a society's deep-seated fears, hopes and expectations during particular historical moments.

The U.S. of the first three decades of the 20th century can be thought of in terms of several important areas of change. The era was a time of great economic growth as a reliance on agriculture shifted to a reliance on the manufacturing industry. Consequently, there was a movement of the mass of the population from rural to urban livelihoods. In fact, "by the 1920s the urban population had passed the rural population in numbers" (Hodgson 35). The country had also experienced great population growth, resulting in part from increased immigration. In 1920, the ratification of the Nineteenth Amendment gave women the right to vote, and the ensuing decade saw increased independence for American women. These areas of change, however, created a backlash of fear against the social advancement of women and immigrants.

In *Trifles, Chicago* and *Machinal* the playwrights re-create the gendered cultural discourse on crime contemporary to their plays, which they had already helped to establish in their original newspaper articles about the cases. The ways that they re-imagined the stories for the stage bring to light the broader conversation on gender taking place in the media and in society in the early 20th century. At the time of each play's composition, women's narratives and experiences were submerged beneath a cultural discourse that sensationalized the "modern" or "new" woman. The "modern" woman of the early 20th century was a rapidly changing role that allowed women new aspirations. The image of the modern woman was a confident and often sexualized woman out in the public eye. This identity wasn't rooted in life at home as a wife and mother, and thus was often seen as a challenge to patriarchal centers of power. Kleinberg writes that "the New Woman ... turned toward pleasure and a freer lifestyle. These women discarded their long skirts and corsets.... They smoked cigarettes, went to nightclubs, and drank alcohol.... They engaged in increased levels of premarital sexuality, and divorced unsatisfactory spouses more readily than previous generations" (Kleinberg 200). June Sochen further defines the New Woman of the early 20th century as a woman who has traded in the role of homemaker for "the factory, a career, and the marketplace" (Sochen ix). Both definitions imply that the choice to leave the home (whether for work or play) was a radical shift in cultural expectations for women.

In the crimes and trials that Glaspell, Watkins and Treadwell covered, the journalistic and legal discourses also rejected the accused women's authentic narratives in favor of often negative generalizations. These plays then "stage the *process* through which event becomes representation, and a woman's experience is obscured, as legal and journalistic forces transform it to [a culturally sanctioned] narrative" (Strand 163, emphasis added). By staging the stories of the crimes, Treadwell, Glaspell and Watkins critique the U.S. legal system, gender norms and even their own, at times, sensationalistic journalism by exposing the translation of the murder event and accused women's lives through the parlance of the media, law and social codes.

The plays tell a version of the women's stories disallowed in the press and the courtroom, so it is no surprise that these crime narratives serve as a fulcrum between society and the gendered experience of the era's social norms. Writing about *Trifles*, Linda Ben-Zvi notes, "Women who kill evoke fear because they challenge society's constructs of femininity — passivity, restraint, and nurture; thus the rush to isolate and label the female offender, to cauterize the act" (Ben-Zvi 141). Dramatizing these stories is one way to synthesize society's response to women who kill through the examination of the submersion of their narratives, but perhaps it is also a way to "cauterize" the act in time, space and our collective psyche. If the social impulse is to seal off and sterilize the acts of women who kill, then the playwright's function in cauterizing the act is more akin to burning it into our collective memory, to fix it in time and space by representing it on stage, and continually bringing us back to that cultural moment to examine its elements. If creative writing is "one respectable means to challenge the dominant patterns of [a] culture" (Sochen *Enduring Values* 11), then the playwrights in these cases are not only fixing these events in our cultural memory, but interrogating those events in a subversive way.

An obvious anxiety throughout the journalistic coverage of the women murderers expressed society's fraught relationship with women's modern identities. However, if "the news accounts offer what the society will bear" (Ben-Zvi 160), then the coverage of these murders reinforced new gender norms and condemned the women for breaching those norms. This is especially true because the murders depicted in these three plays are all the murder of a husband or male figure by their wife or female lover. The women all disrupt social concepts of passive femininity and restraint in the act of violently freeing themselves from the relationship that binds them. Translating the stories for the stage was a creative way to explore these gender norms and consequences for rejecting them on a more nuanced and critical level than the news reports had allowed, or risked. This essay examines how the interpretation of female criminals by female playwrights created an intersected space where social and artistic texts on gender in the early 20th century met, defining it further as an intertextual space.

For the purpose of this analysis, I will define text as either the material content or an area of socio-cultural thought/discourse that presents a "coherent set of symbols" (Cantrell 4). This idea embraces both the concept of a material, authored text (as thought of in the field of theatre and literature) and the concept of a text as a specific cultural or social discourse (as thought of in the field of cultural studies and performance studies). An intersected space is the figurative overlap of these cultural and material texts. This figurative overlap contains the historical events of the murders, the public discourse of journalism about the murders, the cultural perception of women's changing identities, and the plays that contain and examine all of those elements. This intertextual space implies that something new and distinct about each cultural and material text is revealed within the intersection.

The Development of the Plays

First, it's helpful to look at the circumstances surrounding each play's development, as well as each author's personal context. Susan Glaspell wrote prolifically in multiple genres, an output that includes the Pulitzer-Prize-winning *Alison's House* in 1931. Her work earned her a lauded and influential place in American drama. *Trifles*, however, is the work of her oeuvre most widely anthologized and examined. Glaspell wrote this short play in 1916 about the 1900 murder of John Hossack and the subsequent trial of his wife Margaret. The play was based on Glaspell's experience as a journalist with the *Des Moines Daily News*, where she was employed after her college graduation in 1899, and where she was assigned to the Hossack case.

Seeing the home of the accused murderess and gaining insight into the lonely circumstances in which Hossack lived became the inspiration later for both *Trifles* and its incarnation as the short story "A Jury of Her Peers." Ben-Zvi deems Glaspell's journalism an act of creating a "revisionary image" of Hossack, as her writing about the Hossack case "borrow[ed] devices from popular detective fiction of the time," a way of writing that "dangles tantalizing questions" (Ben-Zvi 147). Her embodied, visceral writing may have indicated

Glaspell's interest in the more complex aspects of the events than the journalistic mode normally allowed.

Margaret Hossack claimed to have woken in the night to find that an intruder had killed her husband with an axe to the head. Although she maintained her innocence until the end of her trial, the public thought Hossack was guilty: her chemise was stained with blood, and the murder weapon, covered in brain matter and hair, belonged to the family. Furthermore, Mrs. Hossack had complained to neighbors about marital trouble and had once left her husband; both actions were considered "questionable female behavior" (Ben-Zvi 152) at the time. However, Margaret Hossack's story was as compelling for her contemporaries as it is for the audiences of Glaspell's play because it presents powerful commentary on the lived experiences of women in less-than-ideal marriages. Glaspell's journalistic work on the story only hints at the social implications of Hossack's "un-womanly" behavior; her play, however, is able to dig much deeper.

Trifles is a deceptively simple play that contains many layers of social critique and meaning. In the play, a rural farmer, John Wright, has been murdered, and his wife, Minnie Wright, has been arrested after being found quietly sitting in her rocking chair, pleating her apron in her hands as her husband lay dead, strangled in the other room. The local Sheriff and County Attorney go to the home of Mr. Wright, with his neighbor as a guide, to collect evidence that might support the prosecution of his wife for the murder.

Mrs. Peters, the Sheriff's wife, and Mrs. Hale, the neighbor's wife, have accompanied the men to the farmhouse to collect some personal items to bring to Mrs. Wright in jail. The characters enter Minnie's empty, cold kitchen and the men begin looking for evidence. After a cursory judgment on the messiness of Minnie's kitchen, the men's search quickly takes them into the bedroom. Mrs. Peters and Mrs. Hale are left alone in the kitchen. They discover the evidence of Minnie's unhappy home life in every detail of her home as they read the domestic codes and clues invisible to the men, such as the uneven stitching in her quilt or a half-cleared kitchen table. They lament their past failure to reach out to the isolated Minnie, and discuss the men's attempt to find a motive for the murder.

They discover an empty birdcage, and as they are collecting Minnie's sewing items, they find the corpse of a tiny bird in her sewing box, its neck wrung. Certain that John Wright has done this, and knowing that for an isolated, abused woman the death of something dear could be devastating, Mrs. Peters and Mrs. Hale eventually decide to conceal the evidence of the bird (as well as the other things they've noticed) from the men, despite their concerns over the morality of such a decision. The play ends quietly with this moment, only implying the consequences of the women's clear obscuration of the evidence, and never answering the question of whether Mrs. Peters and Mrs. Hale have actually changed Minnie's fate.

Glaspell can be considered a visionary playwright of her time, who "dealt almost exclusively with the dilemma of the modern woman" (Sochen 8). However, she was not necessarily the most lauded. Veronica Makowsky notes that the American modernist literature movement, which depicted early 20th century life in a new light, "stimulated [Glaspell's] best work, and then scorned her aesthetic. It incorporated her theatrical innovations, and proceeded to ignore their creator. It made her reputation, but only to repudiate it" (Makowsky 49). Makowsky emphasizes that the modernist movement caused male writers to be praised by the public and especially the academy over their female counterparts, and suggests that the imagery of suppression in *Trifles* reflects the position of Glaspell in the modernist writing community.

A decade later in 1926, Maurine Dallas Watkins wrote the non-musical play *Chicago*, which follows the trials of glamorous Chicago murderesses Roxy Hart and Velma Kelly. Although it later gained most of its popularity as a musical, the play was first based on Watkins' experience as a journalist for the *Chicago Tribune* covering the case of two 1924 murders by Belva Gaertner and Beulah Sheriff Annan. Unlike Glaspell and Treadwell, Watkins had no success in the theatre beyond this play. It enjoyed a prosperous run when it opened, and was turned into the musical and several films. Watkins became popular with the play-going public after the play's success, but she couldn't maintain that popularity in her subsequent works. The original play was only published once, and was never as prominent as its adaptations, notably the 1975 musical by John Kander, Fred Ebb and Bob Fosse. Similarly to Glaspell's, it was Watkins' journalistic coverage of the Annan and Gaertner cases that lead to this remarkable play.

Belva Gaertner was a married cabaret performer with a reputation for infidelity. In March of 1924 her lover, Walter Law, was found behind the wheel of her car, shot in the head by her gun. Gaertner denied involvement at first, but later simply said, "I don't know. I was drunk" (Pauly xiii). It's easy to see how Watkins interpreted this woman for the stage — turning her into the sultry and irreverent Velma Kelly — because Gaertner's flippant comments about her involvement in a murder are a fundamental part of Kelly's character. Beulah Sheriff Annan was the inspiration for Roxie Hart. Watkins got newspaper readers hooked on the story of a beautiful young woman who shot her lover in the back and then listened to the record "Hula Lou" before calling her husband for help. Annan told several conflicting stories in the days immediately following the crime; it became a case where the press (Watkins) defined both her story and her defense, which eventually resulted in her acquittal. Watkins was writing to sell headlines and create a vivid character of Annan for the readers, but Watkins also selected a particular version of the murder events to portray: she emphasized Gaertner's story about not remembering what happened, and defined Annan's plea of self-defense (Pauly 125). As a result, Annan's previously disparate stories became solidified and defined, making as good a legal defense as they did a news story.

Watkins is credited with sensationalizing the coverage of these crimes, making them front page news. She discovered the cases when she was working on the police reports for the *Tribune*. She effectively created a public persona for the two murderesses, making their statements famous even before immortalizing them in her play. Gaertner, for example, is quoted as saying, "Gin and guns — either one is bad enough, but together they get you in a dickens of a mess" (Watkins xv). Watkins had great success at the paper using quotes like this to convert "a murderess into a zany character who entertained readers" (Watkins xv). She continued writing in this vein throughout both trials. Watkins focused on Gaertner and Annan, but she also wrote about some of the other, less well-known women who were also in jail for killing men.

Although she clearly played by the rules of the media (as a conservative form) in order to stay on the front page, Watkins' writing hints at her larger interest in and concern for the jailed women and the justice system that processed them. Pauly attributes this to her "precocious understanding of jailhouse theater" (xviii), or the theatrical aspects of the justice system, especially of women caught up in the justice system. Shortly after the media coverage of the Annan and Gaertner cases died down, Watkins relocated to New York and took classes in playwriting at Yale University in order to turn the Annan and Gaertner cases into a play.

Chicago begins with the story of Roxy Hart, a young woman cheating on her reliable husband with a traveling salesman. When her lover threatens to leave, she kills him in her home. When the police arrive she quickly maneuvers her husband into claiming he shot an intruder. However, Roxy's attempts to hide her deed don't last long, and she is soon taken to jail. The jail's Matron explains to Roxy that her time in jail should be spent getting ready for a spectacular, highly staged murder trial: she must find the best lawyers, nice clothes and a good story. Roxy procures Billy Flint to defend her and then meets his other star client: Velma Kelly, in jail for murdering her husband and sister. The play follows Roxy's trial as well as the other women in jail, who all exhibit varying degrees of guilt. In the final act Roxy wins her coveted "not guilty" verdict after a highly theatrical turn on the stand, in which she claims pregnancy by her estranged husband. She wins over the jury and her husband too. At the end of the play, another murderess is brought into the jail, which quickly eclipses Roxy's triumph.

In 1928, Sophie Treadwell wrote her most famous play, *Machinal*. Tread-

UNIVERSITY OF WINCHESTER
LIBRARY

well's background as a reporter also influenced her use of the 1927 trial and execution of Ruth Snyder for the murder of her husband as the subject of her play. Although Treadwell did not report directly on the case, she was a regular spectator at the sensational trial proceedings. She worked as a journalist between about 1916 and 1918, and although she wrote many more plays, *Machinal* has become her legacy. The case began when Ruth Snyder reported that an intruder had murdered her husband and had also tied her up and robbed the home of some jewelry. Snyder was deemed a suspect in the murder when she neglected to show what investigators deemed a "proper" concern for her husband. Later, when the missing jewelry was found beneath her mattress, their suspicions were confirmed. They also discovered that Snyder was having an affair with corset salesman Judd Gray.

Gray had actually been the one to deal the death blow to Mr. Snyder, striking him with a sash weight, which was a heavy object used as a counterweight to a vertically opening window. The case blew open and the public became obsessed with the story. Over 1,500 people were spectators at the trial and about 180 reporters were assigned to cover the case (Jones, *Medea's Daughters* 2). It was the first trial to electrically amplify the testimony for all in the room to hear. Tickets were sold and scalped, and spectators were famously described by the *New York Times* as "a typical Broadway audience, sophisticated and cynical" (Jones, *Medea's Daughters* 2). Even the producers of the musical *Chicago* were among the audience (Ramey 626). In many ways, the case exemplified social anxieties over gender and identity, because if Ruth was an "ordinary" woman and wife, then any woman/wife could kill.

Treadwell had covered other sensational murder trials in her work as a journalist. "In each of these instances, Treadwell's reportage suggests that the truth in the cases remained far more elusive and complicated than the official court testimony and traditional media coverage would indicate" (Dickey 72). Writing *Machinal* provided her the opportunity to delve into that elusive and complicated truth. The play uses expressionism as a model to explore the consciousness of the female murderer: it looks at the motivations of the murderess in the context of women's lives at the time, as well as at contemporary legal and social norms regarding gender roles.

Machinal follows a young woman named Helen: at the outset of the play she works in an office and lives with her mother, and is only referred to as "Young Woman" in the script. She is suffocated by life and seemingly terrified by the trap of her existence. Her wealthy boss proposes marriage, and although Helen does not love him, her mother pressures her into the union. After they are married, scenes show her growing discontentment and disconnection: after she gives birth to their child, she cannot bear to see the baby. Then, Helen meets an intoxicating and exciting man who becomes her lover. She opens up to him and shows a verve and passion for life as a result of their relationship.

He impresses her with tales of killing a man, and woos her with a gift of a small vase filled with stones. Helen is enamored with the excitement her life could hold if she were with this man, so she kills her husband by smashing him over the head with the heavy vase. At first she claims innocence, but during the trial a letter arrives from her former lover that reveals he gave her the vase that killed her husband, and she is prompted to confess. In the final scene she is led to the electric chair and executed, finally subdued by the machine of life and the society that surrounds her.

Reconstructing the Jury, Critiquing the Media and Legal Systems

In each of these plays, a female playwright translated a crime story for the stage (a material text) in a way that delved further than the news stories into the cultural texts on gender, society and even the role of female playwrights at the time. The social critique in the translation of crime story to stage is most apparent in three areas: first, the playwrights' treatment of the jury; second, their embedded critique of both journalism and the trial process; and finally, their inclusion of the female murderers' lives in the story, including the personal reasons for the murders they committed.

The playwrights' treatment of the jury is one way to look at how the translation between trial and stage reveals an intersected space — a space where the text of the trial is embedded in the text written for the stage. In each play, the jury is redefined, primarily in terms of gender. In the real-life cases, the juries were entirely male. The inequity of this system was not lost on Ruth Snyder, who remarked, "I'm sorry. I believe that women would understand this case better than men, and that women have a better sense of justice" (Strand 168). Submitting to legal judgment by an all-male jury reflects the broader social situation in which Hossack, Snyder, Annan and Gaertner found themselves. The real juries assigned characters and fates to these women, just as women of that era were characterized and controlled by public perceptions of gender roles.

When Treadwell, Glaspell and Watkins staged these stories, they replaced the courtroom juries with audience-juries, who observe the women's stories over the course of the plays, before reaching a judgment. These audience-juries differ from the real juries in one important aspect: they are made up of both men and women. In *Trifles*, Glaspell presents the nuanced narrative that legal analysts and journalists are often unable to explore. She includes a jury, first replacing men with women (the characters Mrs. Hale and Mrs. Peters), but ultimately those characters with the audience, both men and women. As Ben-Zvi explains, "With her deft parody, Glaspell undercuts the authority the men wielded in the original case, and throws into question their sanctioned preserve of power" (Ben-Zvi 155). In *Chicago* too, the male jury is replaced by an audience that contains women. In the case of *Machinal*, Jones states she "believe[s] *Machinal* is the testimony, disallowed by the court of law" (Jones, *Medea's Daughters* 2). By taking an alternate view of the story, focusing on the circumstances of the Young Woman/Helen's life, the new audience-jury has the chance to seriously consider the same evidence that, during the staged trial, was briskly dismissed as "irrelevant [and] immaterial" (Treadwell 393).

The way that these three journalists developed murder stories into narratives through newspaper stories and then plays results in a sometimes comic, sometimes biting critique of both the media and legal systems, *especially* the ways these systems treated women in the early 20th century. The intersecting texts of media and law highlight potentially difficult issues of gender within society, crime and eventually theatre. The dramatic texts, therefore, contain two other critical conversations: a social text about gender roles as originally told through the media, and a larger historical text about women in American theatre. Because each play challenges the public perception of a female killer by the audience and in the world of the play, the dramatic text focuses on the often sensational performance of the female criminal in the media and the courtroom. By analyzing the transition of both the trials and the reporting from the real life events to the staged events, we can see how Treadwell, Glaspell and Watkins provided a social commentary through the intersected space of the plays, referencing both the world of crime and the world of women in the early 20th century.

The discourse displayed in newspaper articles about these murder stories revealed this intersected space, as it referenced both the crimes themselves and the role of women in society at the time. News reporting had changed dramatically around the turn of the century. It had become very visual and sensational, and it was widely circulated. Dynamic typeface was used to emphasize outrageous headlines, or "screamers" (Biers 239). This change brought the public into intimate contact with the crimes of their society. In the cases presented here, the newspapers provided a running commentary on the events of the trials and allowed the public to become judge and jury to the criminals. The murderesses discussed here, therefore, had to provide "interesting copy": "This discovery leads to a realization that newspapers are simply one aspect of an entrenched urban conspiracy that demands that she be eye-catching if she is to get noticed" (Watkins xxiv). A critique of the media can be found in the focus of the newspaper articles produced about these three cases. In other words, the interest in only the most shallow and sensational aspects of the accused women can be evidence of the media's inability to provide overtly challenging discussions of normative gender politics.

In her articles about the Hossack case, Glaspell sets forth the facts of the event and trial clearly, but she also uses some of the sensational language that will become so dominant in Watkins's journalism. Describing Hossack, Glaspell wrote: "Though past 50 years of age, she is tall and powerful and looks like she would be dangerous if aroused to a point of hatred" (Glaspell, "She Prepares to Fight"). Interestingly, Glaspell provides a character for Hossack, thus defining her for the public by describing her physical appearance and observing the moments in the trial that affect her. Her reports are not as sympathetic to Hossack as is *Trifles*, which points to the ways Glaspell's creative output is more critical of dominant gender ideals (through its display of sympathy) than her journalism was allowed to be. In other words, the reports about the Hossack trial, while illuminating Hossack's character for the public, ultimately steer clear of a commentary on the situation that spawned the crime — I would argue that to do so would alienate the newspaper-reading public, who perhaps simply wanted to hear of Hossack's punishment.

The play *Trifles*, on the other hand, is freed from the burden of the limitations of journalism in that it presents a very sympathetic image of Hossack. Glaspell could more deeply explore the gender inequalities that produced a crime like Hossack's in the play than was appropriate for a string of newspaper articles reporting on the proceedings of a trial. The final run of headlines on the case shows how Glaspell captured her readers' imaginations: she painted a picture of the forlorn Mrs. Hossack wasting away in a prison cell as the birds sang outside on Easter day (Glaspell, "Her Dreary Easter Day"). Glaspell's growing sympathy is clear, but it is not until she wrote *Trifles* that she fully explored this sympathy.

Maureen Dallas Watkins likewise first used her articles about the Annan and Gaertner trials to explore the gendered implications of the trials. It is easy to see the roots of the play *Chicago* in the articles; Watkins even generated many punch lines eventually used in the play's dialogue. She also creates dramatic structure in her reports, creating dramatic characters out of the individuals in the trial and feeding the public information on what the murderesses wore, ate and said. The way that Watkins participated in, shaped and even changed Annan and Gaertner's public narratives is apparent in the progression of her articles. At the end of one news report, she describes the way Annan "powdered her nose" while she "await[ed] developments" (Watkins 128), but the next headline proclaims, "Beulah Annan Sobs Regret For Life She Took."

After she has been covering the Annan and Gaertner cases for some time, Watkins begins to write about the other women in the jail and how juries are influenced. She writes in one article that the most powerful influence on whether a jury will issue the death sentence is gender and looks (Watkins 134). The suggestion the articles make is that in a jury's eyes, a woman who closely adheres to dominant ideals of beauty (or even better, submission) may be "forgiven." However, Watkins also critiques the image-creation in which she participates, by painting Annan as a vulnerable, feminine victim, but with one sarcastic turn of phrase she reveals Annan's pensiveness and passivity: "Early in the trial she leaned wearily on one white hand—with Raphaelite profile turned toward the jury—and pensively sighed now and then. But she revived sufficiently to powder her nose and pose for some pictures while she chatted of her recent illness" (Watkins 137).

Watkins then critiques the system by comparing Annan's taking the stand with a "debut as an actress" (Watkins 144); in other words, she recognizes the performativity of the victim in court and the ways that these women's testimonies were in some ways a performed fiction designed to win the jury's favor. She humorously points out salient points to her reader: "Cabaret dancer and twice divorcee, Mrs. Gaertner was as demure as any convent girl—yesterday!—with brown eyes dreamily cast downward" (Watkins 149). As such Watkins perpetuates the entertaining and sensational journalistic style of the day, but she also brings forth more pointed concerns, such as the fates of the other, less-publicly-recognized women in jail.

Treadwell did not directly report on the Snyder case, which became the basis of *Machinal*, although she did work as a journalist and sit in the "audience" of that trial. At the time, newspapers concerned themselves with minutia—Treadwell would have observed that the ways Snyder talked, ate and dressed became front-page news : articles covered the trial every day, reviewing Snyder's performance on the stand, and noting the "audience's" reaction (Jones, *Medea's Daughters* 2). The theatrical metaphor continued throughout the coverage; in fact, the final headline read, "The End of the Show" (Jones, *Medea's Daughters* 4). Within the coverage, Ruth was portrayed in one of two ways: as "Bloody Blonde" or "Marble Woman." The idea of the "Bloody Blonde"—a sexualized, hyper-feminine and immoral woman—was juxtaposed with the "Marble Woman"—an unfeeling serpent capable of a cold-blooded murder. Both of these characterizations convicted Snyder of transgression against the normative roles for women as sensitive, caring and nurturing and may have led to her death sentence despite her not having struck the fatal blow in the murder.

The coverage was acutely concerned with the ways that Ruth represented the negative aspects of women's role in modern society in the 1920s, which many viewed as "threatening patriarchal centers of power, namely the family and state" (Ramey 627). Tabloids became a fixture of public discourse about this time, rapidly disseminating a particular kind of information to many people. Ramey quotes anthropologist Elizabeth Bird when she asserts that "tabloids convey a quite conservative message, aimed at reinforcing the status quo" (Ramey 628). Treadwell would have seen the ways that the tabloid coverage of the Snyder case reinforced, rather than critiqued, gender norms.

A critique of the media and legal systems was mirrored in the creative works produced about the cases. In all of the plays, the work of journalists writing about crimes is highlighted and often mocked — which is all the more interesting given that the playwrights were involved in the production of the news reports of the cases. In a sense, the playwrights were mocking the roles they performed as journalists at the same time as they were re-creating these roles as playwrights. Through this seemingly contradictory process, a writer becomes involved after an event has taken place and attempts to recapture and synthesize that event. Journalists do this under the auspices of assumed objectivity, while playwrights do so under an assumption of creative license. It's possible that for the writers who wrote their plays well after writing newspaper stories about the cases (especially Glaspell), coming back to re-synthesize the story in the critical, nuanced theme of a dramatic work was a purposeful feminist act. This could potentially be related to their personal journey in the years after writing the news stories.

In *Chicago*, Watkins provides perhaps the best example of critiquing how the system of journalism deals with female murderers. She acknowledges the realities of the system by repeating the idea that "yuh've got to play ball" (Watkins 8) with the press in order to be successfully acquitted. The press, however, in the form of Jake, is portrayed as bloodthirsty and heartless. Jake says to Roxie: "*Want* you to go free! How d'yuh get that way! Say, I'd give my last dollar — all three of 'em — and ever' night when I kneel down by my little bed I'll ask God to put a hemp rope around your nice white neck! *O baby*, that would mean headlines six inches high — the story of the year!" (Watkins 14). Watkins mocks the sensationalism of the press and its disregard for the women it effectively consumes in the name of profit.

Furthermore, Watkins mocks the assumed objectivity of journalism as when she has the Matron say, "Now listen, dearie, if you're goin' to believe what the papers say, you'll be suspicious of ever'body here — includin' yourself" (Watkins 30). The character Mary Sunshine paints journalists as sentimental fools, ready to create any reality for a subject if it fits in with the ideas they want to put forth. The idea that women are best situated to present stories about women in an entertaining and sympathetic way explains why Watkins was called upon to cover women's crimes. Sunshine helps Roxie shape her narrative for consumption by the public. They feed each other's needs in a symbiotic, intersected performance.

Similarly, Treadwell creates a memorable trial scene in her play, in which the journalists are directly involved in the legal act of sentencing the Young

Woman. In a way, there is a relationship between *Machinal*'s structural style and journalism: the single set that is transformed through the actions/episodes reflects the way that articles take a single story through changing sentiments and developments. Indeed "the play's episodes are located within 'interlocking social and political discourses...'" (Glaspell, *Trifles* 363). Of the trial scene, Strand notes, "The presence of reporters at the scene makes it clear that even though it is not directly witnessed by the populace, this execution, like Ruth Snyder's, is destined to be experienced by great numbers of people through press mediation" (Strand 173). Reporters translate the events of the trial to the public; their selective description of events displays the journalistic interpretation that shapes the trial for the vast "audience" of readers.

Reporters provide conflicting representations of the same trial: while one reports coolly that the Young Woman is put on the stand by her lawyers in a confident and "daring defense strategy" (Treadwell 392), another reports that she is "trembling and scarcely able to stand" (Treadwell 392). It's not hard to imagine Treadwell witnessing this kind of selective interpretation while attending the Snyder trial. The evidence suggests that Treadwell noticed that the content of the story is not ever as important as the media's judgment of the performance. Throughout the trial scene, the reporters break in with blurbs from their notes as they take them, every time contradicting one another. Portraying these repeated conflicting and incorrect assessments on the event allows Treadwell to criticize the absurdity of journalistic "objectivity," and the idea that mere facts are being disseminated. The arduous trial jars the Young Woman into a confession, and finally the Reporters' headlines align: "Murderess confesses;" "Paramour brings confession;" "I did it! Woman cries!" (Treadwell 399). Only here do they actually get her words right. However, in the final moments of the play, it is the Reporters who note how little the Young Woman's words actually matter:

> 1ST REPORTER: Her lips are moving — what is she saying?
> 2ND REPORTER: Nothing [Treadwell 402].

All three writers also critique the trial and legal system in their translation of the events of the crime to the stage. Because Glaspell herself played Mrs. Hale, it's possible that through Mrs. Hale's dialogue, Glaspell critiques the larger social systems that isolate and oppress women. In a way, this also critiques the trial system that exposes a woman's life to the public and to a jury, who then search for the parts of that life that they can "turn against" the woman, just as *Trifles* shows how a woman's kitchen can be a source of clues to aid in her conviction. Watkins offers insight on the trial system by presenting a highly sensational and theatrical trial. As the Matron in *Chicago* states, "Never skimp on a funeral or a trial — especially a murder trial. Do it *right*" (Watkins 27).

Treadwell provides the clearest commentary on the legal system within her play. The real-life defense portrayed Snyder as the ideal wife and mother as a way of gaining sympathy for her from the jury. Treadwell presents in her play what the trial could not and would not: a critique of the marriage machine. The legal system and media in 1920s America were still too mired and invested in gender norms to criticize oppressive marriages, but that is exactly what Treadwell does in *Machinal*. Treadwell's ultimate critique is her realization that the Young Woman had finally escaped the marriage machine only to be promptly re-deposited into a different machine: the legal system. The mechanics of the trial are portrayed as brutal, without even the glittering facade shown in Watkins' *Chicago*: the judge and lawyers deliver a face-paced dialogue, nearly drowning out the Young Woman's words, and the Lawyer for the Prosecution bullies and mocks her throughout her testimony. All three plays, however, share the same critique of the legal mechanics that sometimes operate without regard to their own compromises and hypocrisies.

Finally, the most subversive aspect of the way the authors translated the stories for the stage was the re-examination of the crimes within the context of the women's lived experiences. Strand notes that the trial system notoriously constructs its narrative "on the suppression of female experience" (Strand 172). In each of their plays, Treadwell, Watkins and Glaspell subvert this imperative by presenting the aspects of *circumstance* and the women's *lives* that were omitted from the trial. Through this, they imply exoneration of the murderesses and a condemnation of the society in which the women lived.

Glaspell concentrates on the daily crime of loneliness and abandonment, as well as the moral/ethical obligations women have *to each other*— certainly a radical statement in the pre-suffrage era in which the play was written. She relocates the story to the home, rather than the courtroom, and places a tight focus on the ways that the home itself, as the place of living, reveals a justification for Margaret Hossack's crime. Certainly, justifiable homicide in a marriage was a long way from what the press, including Glaspell in her own articles, was capable of discussing:

> [I]t becomes clear that acquittal is not Glaspell's intention, not why she wrote the play. Whether Margaret Hossack or Minnie Wright committed murder is moot; what is incontrovertible is the brutality of their lives, the lack of options they had to redress grievances or to escape abusive husbands, and the complete disregard of their plight by the courts and by society. Instead of arguing their innocence, Glaspell concretizes the conditions under which these women live and the circumstances that might cause them to kill. She thus presents the subtext that was excised from the original trial ... men's fears of women who might kill, and women's fears of the murder they might be forced to commit [Ben-Zvi 157].

Treadwell's use of expressionism is perhaps the most pointed attempt to reveal the psychological circumstances underlying the murder committed. She also takes the most time of the three plays to set up the woman's life before the murder, which doesn't take place until episode 7. In effect, all of the plays deal with the circumstances of a female killer's existence that lead her to kill. While the press at the time used these circumstances to condemn the women (Hossack was immoral, Annan and Gaertner were floozies and Snyder was unfeeling), the plays cast the very same details of their lives as oppressive and use them to justify or explain the women's actions. In this way, Treadwell, Watkins and Glaspell — especially as female writers — play a critical role in the dissemination of these women's stories: they captured part of what the press and trial had "excised," and they exposed how the media and the law worked to reinforce gender norms.

Canonizing and Defining Watkins, Treadwell and Glaspell

Each of these plays illuminates a larger historical conversation concerning the role of women in American playwriting and suggests several questions: Why did these playwrights' journalistic experience receive such positive response from the American reading public? How did their depiction of female killers in their plays "qualify" them for the American theatre and literary canon? Although I largely discuss canonization here, I do so with the recognition that Watkins is not a part of the literary canon. However, the process by which we define, recognize or even anthologize her by *Chicago* is process of selection that mimics or parallels literary canonization. In other words, *Chicago* is here called "canonized" because the play *represents* Watkins in our world of known plays.

It's possible that these writers were lauded for their plays because the plays were composed with stories legitimized by journalistic "truth." It is generally assumed that journalism is not literature — that news stories are not invented by their authors. Reporters are expected to simply translate events for the public, as objectivity is supposed to be one of journalism's major tenets. Although the possibility of pure objectivity has been undermined in contemporary theory, it was still the normal expectation of early 20th century readers of newspapers stories. It should be noted that although I explore this possible reasoning for the recognition of these writers, Glaspell particularly was not always included in the canon. It was only with the attention and argument of feminist scholars that she was included.

This suggests that, in some ways, female playwrights require authentication, and that the "truth" of the stories told in their plays can provide that. In other words, the women's act of "translating" events from real life rather than "creating" fictional stories removed them as sole creative agents. But in fact, the playwrights criticize the notion of journalistic objectivity and therefore the "truth" of journalistic output. The literary and theatrical community may have indeed canonized or defined these women based on their journalistic background and the legitimizing "truth" of the real-life murders, but these playwrights subvert this recognition by presenting deeper, more subversive narratives of the women's stories.

The inclusion of these ultimately subversive plays within the canon in some ways negates the possibly negative process of their inclusion. Indeed, we "live and read and write in a world shaped by literary canon. The canon itself is constantly undergoing redefinition and ... exists in multiple versions at any one time; moreover, we ourselves may play a role in canon formation each time we speak or fail to speak of specific texts" (Hulbert 120). By recognizing, analyzing and "speaking" of these plays, even within this chapter, their position is reinforced, and therefore also the inclusion of subversive narratives is reinforced. This may not be unusual for the canon. Inasmuch as it is thought of as a normative force, the "great" writers included within it can be considered "subversive of all values, both ours and their own" (Bloom 29).

Furthermore, each of these plays is subversive despite addressing a topic, the punishment of female criminals, which is a discourse that often reinforces norms. In her work on "female offenders and offensive females," Jones writes, "the retelling or reenacting of crime stories reinforces existing power relations and maintains the status quo" (Jones *Medea's Daughters* xii). She further states that surges of drama about female offenders, like the plays discussed here, come at times of women's increased visibility, as a way of putting "in their place" women who offend against gender norms of passivity and peace. This superficial view of femininity "deflect[s] attention away from the systematic repression of women" (Jones *Medea's Daughters* xiii). However, Glaspell, Treadwell and Watkins all subvert this system. Dramatic images of women being punished for their crimes could serve, as the journalistic images do, to "calm" a nervous public that the institutions these women subverted (marriage, morality) are safe. However, plays like *Machinal, Chicago* and *Trifles* undermine the comfortable lesson of punishing offending women because they explain the psychology and sociology of the offenders' actions, thereby creating a justification for those actions.

Theatre reveals conversations that integrate social, political and creative threads. In the case of these three authors and three plays, the reader and audience are presented with dramas about gender and society that reach far beyond the bounds of the playhouse. These plays by women, about women who kill, paint an intricate portrait of the culture that produced them at the turn of the 20th century — a time of change when women's complex social and cultural experiences were still being stereotyped but also exposed and examined. These dramatic texts tap into the social conversations that were playing out in the media, revealing the overlap of the dramatic performance of women murderers and the performance expected of them within the public eye and the courtroom.

When Glaspell, Watkins and Treadwell used their own journalistic eyes to bring these controversial stories to the stage space, we can see within the text not only an echo of the authors' own place in the history of theatre, but also an effort to illuminate the socio-cultural perceptions of women living within the "man's world" of early 20th century America. Ben-Zvi asserts that Glaspell's "writing acts as a palimpsest for the shifting roles of women in the early twentieth century, and for her own shifting attitudes toward the possibilities for women and for herself" (Ben-Zvi 161). Indeed, each of these plays reflects a layered perspective in which the role of women in society, the role of women in crime and the role of women in playwriting are explored. The relationship between these concurrent barometers of social change is significant because it captures an intersected space wherein each text reveals something distinct about the other.

The plays I have discussed capture within material texts the cultural contexts of women's changing roles, both in society and within the world of theatre. This is unique because the three women who wrote the plays were involved in the creation of the original material text of the news stories, and thus helped to reinforce the cultural discourse around the modern woman. It was through their plays, however, that they were able to dismantle and comment on that discourse through their depictions of the juries, critiques of the legal and media systems and inclusion of the murderesses' life circumstances and motives.

Glaspell, Watkins and Treadwell link potentially disparate texts in a revolutionary way, as evidenced by their inclusion in the canon or recognition by the literary and theatre communities. Although they may originally have been lauded for these plays in part because the creation of the stories was legitimized by the perceived objective "truth" of their journalism, the intertextual space of the plays also reveals deeply subversive commentary, which has *kept* them visible and relevant. As Bloom posits, "All strong literary originality becomes canonical" (25); thus we can consider these three plays examples of works that have survived and become representative of their playwrights because they combine powerful cultural and material texts in a unique and revealing way.

Works Cited

Ben-Zvi, Linda. "Murder, She Wrote: The Genesis of Susan Glaspell's Trifles." *Theatre Journal* 44.2 (1992): 141–162. Print.

Biers, Katherine. "Djuna Barnes Makes a Specialty of Crime: Violence and the Visual in Her Early Journalism." *Women's Experience of Modernity 1875–1945.* Ed. Ann L. Ardis and Leslie W. Lewis. Baltimore: Johns Hopkins University Press, 2003. 237–253. Print.

Bloom, Harold. *The Western Canon: The Books and School of the Ages.* New York: Harcourt Brace, 1994. Print.

Cantrell, Tania Heather. "How Do News Issues Help Frame Telenovela Plots? A Framing Analysis of Brazilian Print National Press and TV Globo's 8 P.M. Telenovela *Duas Caras* [*Two Faced/s*]." Diss. University of Texas, Austin, 2009.

Dickey, Jerry. "The expressionist moment: Sophie Treadwell." *The Cambridge Companion to American Women Playwrights.* Ed. Brenda Murphy. Cambridge: Cambridge University Press, 1999. 66–81. Print.

Glaspell, Susan. "Her Dreary Easter Day." 6 Dec. 1900. Patricia Bryan and Thomas Wolf. *Midnight Assassin.* University of Iowa Press, n.d. Web. 15 Feb. 2011.

_____. "She Prepares to Fight." 9 April 1901. Patricia Bryan and Thomas Wolf. *Midnight Assassin.* University of Iowa Press, n.d. Web. 15 Feb. 2011.

_____. *Trifles. American Drama: Colonial to Contemporary.* Eds. Stephen Watt and Gary A. Richardson. Heinle & Heinle Publishing Company, 2003. Print.

Hodgson, Godfrey. "The American Century." *The Cambridge Companion to Modern American Culture.* Ed. Christopher Bigsby. Cambridge: Cambridge University Press, 2006. 33–52. Print.

Hulbert, James. "The Problems of Canon Formation and the 'Example' of Sade: Orthodox Exclusion and Orthodox Inclusion." *Modern Language Studies* 18.1 (1988): 120–133. Print.

Jones, Jennifer. "In Defense of the Woman: Sophie Treadwell's *Machinal.*" *Modern Drama* 37 (1994): 485–496. Print.

_____. *Medea's Daughters: Forming and Performing the Woman Who Kills.* Columbus: Ohio State University Press, 2003. Print.

Kleinberg, S.J. "Women in the Twentieth Century." *The Cambridge Companion to Modern American Culture.* Ed. Christopher Bigsby. Cambridge: Cambridge University Press, 2006. 194–214. Print.

Makowsky, Veronica. "Susan Glaspell and Modernism." *The Cambridge Companion to American Women Playwrights.* Ed. Brenda Murphy. Cambridge: Cambridge University Press, 1999. 49–65. Print.

Ozieblo, Barbara, and Jerry Dickey. "Introduction." *Susan Glaspell and Sophie Treadwell.* London: Routledge, 2008. 1–13. Print.

Procock, Stephanie J. "The Judicial and the Melodramatic Stage: Trial Scenes in Boucicault's *Arrah-na-Pogue* and *The Octoroon.*" *Theatre Journal* 60.4 (2008): 545–561. Print.

Ramey, Jessie. "The Bloody Blonde and the Marble Woman: Gender and Power in the Case of Ruth Snyder." *Journal of Social History* 37.3 (2004): 625–650. Print.

Sochen, June. *Enduring Values: Women in Popular Culture.* New York: Praeger, 1987. Print.

_____. *The New Woman: Feminism in Greenwich Village, 1910–1920.* New York: Quadrangle Books, 1972. Print.

Strand, Ginger. "Treadwell's Neologism: *Machinal.*" *Theatre Journal* 44.2 (1992): 163–175. Print.

Treadwell, Sophie. *Machinal. American Drama: Colonial to Contemporary.* Ed. Stephen Watt and Gary A. Richardson. London: Heinle & Heinle, 2003. Print.

Watkins, Maurine. *Chicago.* Ed. Thomas H. Pauly. Carbondale: Southern Illinois University Press, 1997. Print.

A "Psalm" for Its Time

*History, Memory and Nostalgia in
Thornton Wilder's* Our Town

Jeffrey Eric Jenkins

The Unhappy Journey

After seeing the 1938 New York premiere of Thornton Wilder's *Our Town*, Alexander Woollcott is purported to have sat on a curbstone, weeping at the emotional profundity of the playwright's work. There appear to be three versions of the tale told with only slight variations in the wording. None of these, unfortunately, comes with what one might call completely reliable sourcing, although one was included in Wilder's *New York Times* obituary. In the *Times*'s telling, Woollcott, the professional gadfly, is asked by a publicity man if he will "endorse" the play. Woollcott supposedly replied: "I'd rather comment on the Twenty-Third Psalm than *Our Town*" — implying that it was not his place to pass judgment upon holy text. In each of the versions, the details and phrasing are slightly different, but the consistent element is the scriptural allusion (Whitman 1).

For Woollcott, perhaps, *Our Town* was sacred, but its forty-year-old playwright — by then a prestigious author and world traveler — constructed consciousness onstage in ways that reminded its characters (and audiences) of the fragility of the human condition in 1938. As the play unfolds, Wilder's narrator prods audience members to consider the patterns of their intimate histories even as he encourages them to recall a simpler time in their own lives. By the play's end, however, the reader or listener is unsettled when the playwright brings to mind the anxiety provoked by the unknowable when juxtaposed with the comfort of the known. Written in an era when cultural upheaval seemed the new normal, when the drums of war again sounded in Europe, and economic turbulence seemed a constant, *Our Town* transported its audience to a time when cultural disturbance was a drunken Polish immigrant asleep in a snowdrift. Through the course of this essay, it may become

188

clear that Wilder's play draws its 1938 contemporary context into sharp relief even as it lulls its audience into a nostalgic stroll — a stroll that might well have taken place by the "still waters" of the psalm invoked by Woollcott. Wilder's letters to friends detail his own anxieties about his work and demonstrate his concern that *Our Town* be seen not as simplistic nostalgia nor as what he calls "abject truth."

It is significant to note here that by the time of *Our Town*'s opening, the vagaries of dramatic criticism were in Woollcott's past. He was no longer a drama critic but was the so-called "Town Crier" broadcasting *bons mots* over the radio waves. It is also worth mentioning that Woollcott was by 1938 a close friend to whom Thornton Wilder had confided his misgivings about the Boston tryout of *Our Town*. (Wilder later dedicated the published version of the play to Woollcott.[1]) In his letter dated 27 January 1938, Wilder's anxiety is palpable as he frets over producer-director Jed Harris's "lost courage about my central intention" and the production's shift to a "different set of emphases." He goes on to deplore the casting of Frank Craven, as the Stage Manager, and Tommy Ross, as Editor Webb — even referring to Ross as a "garrulous Irish mugger." Wilder also records his disturbance at the "storms of nose-blowings and sobs" by the play's end, which indicate to him that the third act's cemetery scene is too "abrupt a change of tone," signaling to the playwright "the strength of the earlier acts has been devitalized" (*Selected Letters* 333–38).

Are these merely the panicked words of an award-winning writer en route to a Broadway production? Did the evoked emotional response make Wilder fear another attack by the likes of radical critic Mike Gold?[2] Christopher Bigsby quotes a broadside launched in 1930, when Gold referred to Wilder as "the poet of a small sophisticated class ... our genteel bourgeoisie ... Wilder is the perfect flower of the new prosperity" — this, as the economic calamity of the Great Depression gained momentum — "This Emily Post of culture will never remind [the parvenu class] of Pittsburgh or the breadlines" (Bigsby 256).

Wilder himself, however, seemed to recognize his elitist *bona fides* when, two years before Gold's attack, he told André Maurois:

> My weakness is that I am too bookish. I know little of life. I made the characters of *The Bridge* out of the heroes of books. My Marquesa is the Marquise de Sévigné. In my first novel, *The Cabala*, the hero was Keats. The method has served me well, but I don't want to use it again. I shall not write again before I have actually observed men better [Maurois 13].

It is no small irony, perhaps, that Gold's condemnation of rarified Wilderian prose came in response to *The Woman of Andros* (1930). Bruce Bawer notes that Gold referred to *Andros* as "a daydream of homosexual figures in graceful gowns moving archaically among the lilies" (Bawer 506). Wilder, it appeared, had not held to his commitment to become less "bookish."

In a 1938 letter to designer Sibyl Colefax, sent three weeks before the Woollcott letter, Wilder works through some of his concerns about *Our Town*, noting at one point that he had come near to "withdrawing my play from the producer's hands" (*Selected* 328). He goes on, however, to commend producer Harris's changes to the script:

> Jed had made some admirable alterations in the order of the scenes, and some dele-
> tions that I would have arrived at anyway, and proposed the writing of a transi-
> tional episode that seems quite right. He has inserted a number of tasteless little
> jokes into the web, but they don't do much harm and they give him that sensation
> of having written the play which is so important to him. The main tendency of his
> treatment is to make the play "smoother" and more civilized, and the edge of bold-
> ness is being worn down, that character of a "primitive" with its disdain of lesser
> verisimilitude; but I guess the play remains bold enough still [328].

Wilder is ambivalent about the development process, but he can hardly have been surprised by the weeping that Act III induced in Boston theatregoers. As he reported to Colefax, the first reading of the script caused the actors to weep so much during the third act that "pauses had to be made so that they could collect themselves" (328). He even lauded, in the letter to Colefax, Frank Craven's portrayal of the Stage Manager though he would denounce the casting to Woollcott a little more than three weeks later.

Wilder's letter to Woollcott arises in the wake of early reviews that the playwright interpreted as dismissive. "Our reviewers say," he writes, "that it is a nostalgic, unpretentious play with charm." His concern over Harris's "lost courage" led him to argue that the "vestiges of my central attention that remain stick out as timid and awkward excrescences." As for "unpretentious," Wilder was having none of that: "What I wrote was damned pretentious" (333).

> The subject of the play I *wrote* is: the trivial details of human life in reference to a
> vast perspective of time, of social history and of religious ideas. It's too late to
> change it into a genre play. The succession of brief scenes can only be justified
> against the larger frame [of time, history, philosophy]; if it had been written as a
> picture of rural manners it would have been written differently [333, emphasis
> added].

But Wilder believes that Harris and Craven have shifted the play in ways that run counter to his intent:

> The subject of the play I wrote *now* is: homely, humorous, touching aspects of a
> village life; of a wedding there; on to which is added a sad and all but harrowing
> last act [334, emphasis added].

The shredding of the fourth wall and the Stage Manager's commentary on "our living and our doctoring and our marrying and our dying," were resisted by Harris, who argued, in Wilder's telling, that:

those things interrupt the affectionate interest in the family lives before us. Frank Craven is embarrassed by [the interruptions]. But that's the central intention of the play. And it is picked up everywhere.... Yes, Alec it's a great play. And all good people are deeply rejoiced by it. But from what's there now they have to guess and grope for that side of it [335].

What is missing for Wilder is "that deep New England stoic irony that's grasped the iron of life and shares it with the house." Writing from Boston, eight days before the Broadway opening, Wilder clings to his ideal: "I'm all right. I fight for the restoration of lines and for the removal of Jed's happy interpolations of New Jersey-New Hampshire.... I'd rather have it die on the road than come into New York as an aimless series of little jokes, with a painful last act" (336).

It is unclear from these letters if Wilder had the "aimless little jokes" removed by the Broadway opening, or if Harris's directorial "smoothing" in effect smothered the play's boldness. But the question of what Wilder expected — or desired — his audience to experience remains. Burns Mantle noted in his *Best Plays* seasonal overview that when the play opened:

Broadway was a bit awed.... A majority of the reviews were mildly ecstatic. A few were modestly doubtful of the complete impressiveness of Mr. Wilder's statement. One or two questioned the effectiveness of the sceneryless stage.... Audience response was also divided, but generally favorable [67].

Mantle's seeming lack of enthusiasm may be attributed to his temporary absence among the first-night critics. The *Daily News* critic was scheduled to give a talk to the Chicago Drama League 9 February 1938 (Cass 13). He was thus forced to miss the opening due to his travels and relied on "correspondents" sending "daily dispatches from the front." His "chief spy," presumably John Chapman whom Mantle quotes by name later in his report, told Mantle, "It is a brand new form ... and everybody raved about it" ("Critic Covers" E2).

The raving of the critics (except Mantle) and the weeping of the audiences (including Woollcott) may have soothed whatever birth pains Wilder suffered in the weeks before the Broadway opening. By 13 February, nine days after the opening, Wilder published a preface to the play in *The New York Times*. The piece discusses how the play came into being, drawing parallels between his play and the work of archaeology. In unfolding his process, Wilder states the "central theme" of *Our Town*:

What is the relation between the countless "unimportant" details of our daily life, on the one hand, and the great perspectives of time, social history and current religious ideas on the other? ["Preface" 1].

Beyond shining light on the playwright's process and central intention, however, the preface also serves as an apologia of sorts for Wilder's choices in scenic representation — or lack thereof. Wilder writes that the "theatre longs to represent the symbols of things, not the things themselves" and he frets over the limits of realism that he credits William James with noting as "abject truth": "Most works in realism tell a succession of such abject truths; they are deeply in earnest, every detail is true, and yet the whole finally tumbles to the ground — true but without significance" ("Preface" 1).

By eliminating scenic realism, Wilder tries to "restore significance to the small details of life.... The spectator, through lending his imagination to the action restages it inside his own head" ("Preface" 1).[3] In 1938, flush with success, Wilder argues for his audience to engage memory: for what is imagination if not a reconstruction of images recalled? Winfield Townley Scott argued from a similar perspective fifteen years later in an essay on *Our Town*, "Again and again we do not construct ... an invented scene: as [the writer] constructs it he *reminds* us ... of something we know — and, hardly conscious of the process, we adapt our memory to his text at once " (Scott 104).

In a 27 March 1938 letter to the widow of renowned playwriting professor George Pierce Baker, Wilder said he did not mind critical charges of "immaturity, confusion, and even pretentiousness":

> It's a first play; it's a first sally into deep waters. I hope to do many more — and better — and even more pretentious. I write as I choose; and I learn as I go; and I'm very happy when the public pays the bills [*Selected* 341–42].

A few months later, and with the Pulitzer Prize in Drama for *Our Town* recently to his credit, Wilder's sanguinity had deepened as he told Lucius Beebe of the *New York Herald Tribune*:

> *Our Town* evades every possible requirement of the legitimate stage. It is pure description, entirely devoid of anything even resembling conflict, expectation or action, which are usually considered the component parts of any play. The only other drama in all literature that I know of that is as static as *Our Town* is *The Trojan Women*.... Any other play I write will have to be more active [qtd. in Beebe 19–20].

Troubling the Waters

The 23rd Psalm is a poem of comfort and reassurance, which reminds the faithful that they are protected by God's calming, restorative powers; that all is well, that all shall be well. When Woollcott drew the hyperbolic parallel between this scripture and his friend's play, he employed imagery more patently religious than Wilder himself appeared comfortable expounding in the public square. A decade earlier, in his 1928 foreword to "*The Angel That Troubled the Waters*" and Other Plays, Wilder writes of that collection of religious plays:

Almost all the plays in this book are religious, but religious in that dilute fashion
that is a believer's concession to a contemporary standard of good manners.... It is
the kind of work that I would most like to do well, in spite of the fact that there
has seldom been an age in literature when such a vein was less welcome and less
understood. I hope, through many mistakes, to discover the spirit that is not
unequal to the elevation of the great religious themes, yet which does not fall into
a repellent didacticism [*Collected Plays* 653–54].

Christopher Bigsby argues from this foreword that, for Wilder, "the failure
of religion to engage the modern mind stemmed from a failure of language"
(257). It is also possible, however, that the playwright locates this "didacticism"
in what he calls the "intermittent sincerity of generations of clergymen and
teachers" who have "rendered embarrassing and even ridiculous all the terms
of spiritual life" (653–54). Although Wilder declares that the "revival of religion is almost a matter of rhetoric" and wonders if all religions die "with the
exhaustion of the language," one suspects that the impact of 1928 American
culture also informs his concern (653–54).

Wilder is, after all, writing these religious plays from a perspective that
reflects his own spiritual "aspirations," to employ a word that recurs in the
foreword. But only a year earlier, in 1927, Sinclair Lewis published *Elmer
Gantry*, which became a bestseller, roiled midwestern clerics, and was adapted
into a (failed) Broadway play by Patrick Kearney. Such diverse personalities
as the Kansas editor William Allen White and Yale professor William Lyon
Phelps decried Lewis's depiction of men of the cloth.[4] This satire of religion,
in which belief is manufactured just as surely as consumerist desire is created,
showed, as *Chicago Daily Tribune* book critic Fanny Butcher noted, "how easy
it is for a thoroughly worthless, selfish pig to get ahead if he just puts his
mind to it" (13). The mainstream success of cynicism toward religion — as
displayed in *Elmer Gantry*— may be part of what drove Wilder to despair of
religious writing being welcomed or understood in American culture.

Just two weeks after Butcher proclaimed *Elmer Gantry*'s literary merit —
while noting repeatedly that it was sure to offend many of the faithful — in
the *Chicago Daily Tribune*, Winfred E. Garrison wrote in the same newspaper
that during the present "period which is sometimes spoken of cynically as the
age of irreligion, there has been a notable increase both in the number of religious titles and in the total number of religious volumes sold." Garrison, a
dean at the University of Chicago and literary editor of *Christian Century*,
goes on to argue persuasively that readers are "perennially interested in the
problems which ... old theologies undertook to solve, for they represent the
most vital and universal concerns of men" (10).

Although Wilder may have felt somewhat isolated in an arid landscape
of religious rhetoric, Preston William Slosson notes in a 1930 social history
of life in America that in spite of "interpretations of religious history in the

terms of modern American commercial life," which arose in certain veins of literature, "popular interest in the problems of religion and the church was still active." Slosson's research — which relied on government surveys, periodicals, newspapers, and scholarly works — found that although the "impression widely prevailed that the increasing pressure of secular interests was crowding religion out of American life," there was a "large increase in church membership" (427).

In this age of supposed irreligion, Slosson also found that "church organizations and associations were never so active in projects of social welfare and civic reform, and many complaints were heard, especially in connection with the prohibition question, that the United States was politically ruled by the churches" (427). Citing U.S. Department of Commerce statistics, Slosson marks an almost twenty-five percent increase in church membership in the decade of 1916 to 1926, though he also notes trenchantly, "In what other country would the collection of religious data be done by the Department of Commerce?" (428).

It is ten years after Wilder's foreword to his religious plays that the preface to *Our Town* first appears in the *New York Times*. As that preface draws to a close, it includes an elision from a monologue by the Stage Manager, which the author apparently could not quite let go. This deleted text crosses from the quasi-ecumenical construct of much of the rest of the play into a recognition of Christianity's primacy in American culture. In the removed text, the Stage Manager speculates about a projected civilization, a thousand years into the future, that might recover the play *Our Town* from a time capsule.

The Stage Manager was to have said, "The religion at that time was Christianity; but I guess you have other records about Christianity" ("Preface" 1).[5] Is this a Wilderian fantasy of Christianity's future doom, based on his concern for the decay of language as noted in the *Angels* foreword? Is it a supposition of Christianity's continued ubiquity? The Stage Manager goes on to describe marriage as a "binding relation" between "a man and one woman" — a definition certainly expanding in the twenty-first century. As the deleted text draws to a close, the Stage Manager adds, almost as an afterthought, that after death people were "buried in the ground just as they were" — as if it might seem a novel idea ("Preface" 1).

Does Wilder imply (or fear) that Christianity might disappear in another millennium? Why comment on the marital paradigm? Why the offhand comment on the handling of the dead? One suspects from Wilder's 1928 foreword to his religious plays that he — or, more likely, his producer — may have sought to vitiate somewhat *Our Town*'s religious overtones. Despite these deletions from the text, changes that appear to subtly distance from a dominant religious model, Brooks Atkinson wrote on just this topic in the *New York Times* — in answer to Eleanor Roosevelt's published complaint that *Our Town* had depressed her "beyond words":

> When I went to see *Our Town*, I was moved and depressed beyond words. It is more interesting and more original and I am glad I saw it, but I did not have a pleasant evening. Sometimes we need a pleasant evening, so why must we have all our plays in the same vein? What can't the critics have standards for different types of plays and give us an idea of the kind of an evening we may have if we go to this play or that? Usually I want to be amused, then again, I want to be stirred. But it is rather rare that you can find out what kind of a play you are going to see by reading any of the criticisms [14].

After gently chiding the president's wife, Atkinson wrote, "In the deepest sense of the word, *Our Town* is a religious play" ("Standards" 1).

Wilder continued to wrestle with the religious thematics in *Our Town* for years to come. In a letter to Esther W. Bates, in which Wilder responded to Scott's 1953 essay on the play, the playwright noted that "committed Christians are severe with me that I indicated without pressing their eschatology" (*Selected* 507).[6] He went on to point to "literary borrowings" — which he often acknowledged — such as the inspiration he took from the "muted hope of Dante's Purgatory" (*Selected* 507). He noted as well to journalist Heinrich Walter, and to Bates, that the litany of Emily's goodbyes to her material life — "Good-by to clocks ticking ... and Mama's sunflowers. And food and coffee. And new-ironed dresses and hot baths" (*Our Town* 108) — were an echo of Achilles's "praise of the things he had valued in life," (*Selected* 477, 508) where the ancient hero's "'fresh raiment' becomes 'new-ironed dresses'; his wine — naturally — becomes coffee" (*Selected* 508).

In the *Virginia Quarterly* essay, Scott particularly noted the contradistinction of the universal and the particular, those poetic (and historical) elements with which Aristotle was concerned:

> This is the great thing that *Our Town* accomplishes; simultaneously we are made aware of what is momentary and what is eternal.... [W]e are doubly spectators, having a double vision.... And indeed we are not taken out of ourselves, we are driven deeper into ourselves. This, we say, is life: apparently monotonous, interminable, safe; really all mutable, brief, and in danger [109].

Scott remains with the notion of doubled experience when he discusses Emily's return to her twelfth birthday. The Stage Manager says, "You not only live it, but you watch yourself living it" (*Our Town* 99). From this moment, Scott conjures an emotional vision,

> Now Emily ... will achieve that double vision we have had all along; and now we shall be burdened also with her self-involvement.... Now *we* are taken back with Emily's double-awareness accenting our own. Though the then-living are unaware as always, now the golden veil [of nostalgia] shines everywhere, even all around us ourselves.... Here if the play is to get its proper and merited response there is nothing further to say of it: one simply weeps [116–17].

Wilder's grateful response to Scott demonstrated his persistent concern that *Our Town* was not taken seriously enough, even as it continued to grow in the American canon: "There is a Pompeii aspect to Grover's Corners.... The theme words of *Our Town* are: hundred, thousand, million. I have no other subject; but now it is the one soul in the billion souls" (*Selected* 333). Wilder felt as though Scott's appraisal had "made the play respectable" at a time when the playwright believed *Our Town* "embarrasses 'professionals' — professors and critics" (*Selected* 508).

History or Poetry?

By invoking influences such as Homer and Dante, and declaring his interest in universals, Wilder leads us to Part IX of the *Poetics* where Aristotle discusses the difference between history and poetry: "The true difference is that [history] relates what has happened, [poetry] what may happen. Poetry, therefore, is a more philosophical and a higher thing than history: for poetry tends to express the universal, history the particular" (68). This is not to suggest that Wilder's work in *Our Town* is Aristotelian, but one overlooks such a dominant construct at one's peril. Wilder, however, accomplishes in *Our Town* what appears to be a conflation of history and poetry. By demonstrating what has happened in this mythical Grover's Corners, and disrupting that narrative with commentary, with flashes forward and back, Wilder allows his audience to imagine a wider range of possibilities than might be experienced with a more linear narrative.

It is very nearly Brechtian: the fourth wall is shredded; the stage space filled only by a few utility items and whatever we are able to conjure in our imaginations; the Stage Manager describes what we are about to see (or imagine, in the case of scenic elements), which allows the audience to analyze what happens; the Stage Manager destabilizes the narrative by interrupting scenes before audiences can be lulled into the spiritual somnolence that often attends theatrical realism. *Our Town* opens with a stage image akin to that of the beginning in Luigi Pirandello's *Six Characters in Search of an Author* where an unadorned proscenium stage with its curtain raised and rehearsal furniture are "scattered about as during rehearsals" (524–25). Wilder had written to his mother about Pirandello — "whose plays I adore" — in April 1921. He had seen an early performance of *Six Characters*, though it was not mentioned in the letter to Wilder's mother (*Selected* 145).

Wilder's 1957 comments in the Preface to *Three Plays*, also give clues to certain affinities he shared with Bertolt Brecht. Wilder describes his dissatisfaction with the theatre: "It was on the stage," he wrote, "that imaginative narration became false.... I found the word for it: it aimed to be *soothing*."

These are words that might not be out of place in Brecht's 1948 theoretical work "A Short Organum for the Theatre," and Wilder was definitely concerned, as noted above, over Jed Harris's "smoothing" of *Our Town*.[7]

Wilder points to the rise of the middle class as the turning point for "where the theatre had run off the track" and shied away from "heat," from "bite," from "social criticism" because the bourgeoisie "chose to ignore wide tracts of injustice" that represented "precarious positions" where "abysses yawned on either side. The air was loud with questions that must not be asked. These audiences fashioned a theatre which could not disturb them" (*Collected* 682–84). Wilder registers the early annoyance with theatre, which may have awakened his antirealist approach:

> Toward the end of the 'twenties I began to lose pleasure in going to the theatre. I ceased to believe in the stories I saw presented there.... Finally my dissatisfaction passed into resentment. I began to feel that the theatre was not only inadequate, it was evasive; it did not wish to draw upon its deeper potentialities [*Collected* 682–84].

In the first moments of *Our Town* Wilder disseminates a great deal of dramatic information, which is not unlike the narrative captioning that Brecht employs at the beginning of scenes in works such as *Mother Courage and Her Children*. Before Doc Gibbs even enters the stage, we know he will die in 1930; we also learn that his wife, who busies herself before us in an imagined kitchen, will die many years before him. A few minutes later the newsboy, Joe Crowell, hands a paper to Doc Gibbs, they exchange pleasantries and Joe exits. The Stage Manager stops the action, with a comment:

> Want to tell you something about that boy Joe Crowell there. Joe was awful bright—graduated from high school here, head of his class. So he got a scholarship to Massachusetts Tech. Graduated head of his class there, too. It was all wrote up in the Boston paper at the time. Goin' to be a great engineer, Joe was. But the war broke out and he died in France.—All that education for nothing [9].

It is a poignant moment of audience recognition not unlike the one that comes at the end of *Mother Courage*, when the title character — beaten, impoverished, and alone — goes in search of Eilif, the son Courage believes to be alive but whom the audience knows has been executed for looting (86–88). Less than five minutes into *Our Town*, the Stage Manager has already collapsed what is actual and what is possible, where we are and where we will be, lifting the dramatic moment to a plane where the particular meets the universal, history encounters poetry. No wonder Brooks Atkinson, and so many others, have seen religion inscribed across this text.

When one continues to consider the cultural moment in which the play premiered, certain elements come into sharper focus. From the perspective of popular media of the day, the *Times*'s Atkinson wrote three prominent and favorable pieces about the play within six weeks of its premiere, calling it a "hauntingly beautiful play" in the opening night review ("Frank" 18); Stirling Bowen of the *Wall Street Journal* called it "heart-warming," "heart-lifting," "witty and touching," and "wise" (9); Joseph Wood Krutch wrote in the *Nation* that Wilder had "succeeded in communicating a mood as rich and tranquil and satisfying as it is hard to define" (224).

Although Mantle does not name those who were "modestly doubtful of Mr. Wilder's statement" (*Best Plays* 67), he might have included John W. Gassner who wrote:

> It is a mistake to consider Grover's Corners real except in our dreams, for the idyllic nature of Mr. Wilder's town is open to suspicion. Our history tells a different story — one of social stratification, greed, corrupt business practices and politics, and even crass intolerance [218].

Mantle correctly notes, however, that the Pulitzer Prize in Drama helped to develop new interest "that carried the play" well into the next season (*Best Plays* 67). By the time of the end-of-season awards, the *Times* characterized *Our Town's* business as "doing comfortably" though not a "smash hit" before the Pulitzer, which became a "potent lure at the box office" ("Rialto Gossip" 1).[8]

Memory and Nostalgia

The 1937–1938 theatre season had, as Mantle recorded it, "statistically ... fallen somewhat behind the two previous [economic] recovery seasons, which is in keeping with the record, there having been a recession noted in the commercial world" (*Best Plays* 3). The so-called "Roosevelt Recession," which roughly paralleled the 1937–38 season saw nearly a five percent increase in general unemployment between 1937 and 1938 — this after five years of declining unemployment. Indeed, between 1935 and 1938, a nearly six percent decline in unemployment was reversed by the steep rise of 1937–38, and it was beginning to feel like 1931 again to many Americans (*Statistical* 135). On the day that the *New York Times* reported the impact of the Pulitzer Prize on *Our Town's* box office receipts, the margin-to-margin banner headline on the first page of the arts section read: THE BROADWAY THEATRE: NO NEW PLAYS DUE THIS WEEK ("Rialto Gossip" 1). In an odd turn, there is no article discussing the dearth of new production to accompany the headline. Brooks Atkinson assesses the Theatre Guild's "private depression" of the past two seasons, which is more about artistic achievement than financial woes, and other pieces discuss theatre gossip, the relationship between Hollywood and Broadway, and a new Shylock by John Gielgud in London.

During this same season, the embattled Federal Theatre Project was far from immune to theatrical vicissitudes as it saw significant new productions limited in 1937–38 to the new Living Newspaper production *One Third of a Nation* and a revival of the prior season's *Power*. After the budgetary debacle at the FTP in 1937, which resulted in Orson Welles and John Houseman's *The Cradle Will Rock* publicity stunt that Barry B. Witham calls a "romanticized" account, much of the creative energy of the government-funded FTP in New York seemed to have been drained (84). The 1937–38 FTP season also saw short runs of plays such as O'Neill's decidedly lesser play *Diff'rent*, Shaw's *Pygmalion*, Fitch's *Captain Jinks of the Horse Marines*, Toller's *No More Peace*, and Shakespeare's *Coriolanus*. Mantle looked askance at those who referred to the season as "exciting," presuming that these assessments meant the season had been "punctuated with novelties" and had "exceeded expectations in the matter of the quality of the plays produced." Mantle also suggested that there had not been much in the way of "artistic advance" in that season (Mantle, *Best Plays* 3).

For the purposes of this study, however, Mantle's observations on the pre-Pulitzer size of the audiences are interesting, especially when taken into consideration with Wilder's concerns about excessive weeping at performances of his play. One key is to consider what theorist Jill Dolan might call the "presumed spectator." Although women have long been the backbone that keeps theatre standing, it is the theatre critics whose identities and ages one may note most easily. While spectators today might see *Our Town* as old-fashioned, in its reconstruction of a time before the automobile was omnipresent, to its first audiences it was a construct with which they almost certainly were quite familiar. Indeed, if one figures that Emily was twenty-six when she died in 1913, she would have been fifty-one in 1938 — precisely the age of the weeping Woollcott, and within a decade of such critics as Atkinson (44), Krutch (45), Clayton Hamilton (57), Walter Prichard Eaton (60), George Jean Nathan (56), Stark Young (57), and Gilbert Seldes (45). The skeptical Mantle, at 65, perhaps was inured to certain nostalgic parallels that might be drawn to that earlier twentieth century era.

When it comes to the 1938 audience for *Our Town*, however, the bulk of that group would certainly have had strong memories of the era that comprised Emily's life. This is the strength of Wilder's narratorial construct: it exists almost entirely before the dawn of the modern era in America. It is before World War I, before the influenza pandemic, before the cultural contradictions of loosened morals and straitened drinking laws, before the Wall Street crash, before the rise of Fascism, before the privations of economic calamity. It is, to re-purpose the words of a former speechwriter, "a kinder, gentler" era. And yet, Wilder tacitly uses the impact of war and pestilence — as he would do more overtly in *The Skin of Our Teeth* — to puncture the comfort of his audience's reverie, to shake them awake, to remind them how quickly sand flows through the hourglass, how unceasing is the ticking clock.

This is Wilder's vision of the theatre described in his 1941 essay, "Some Thoughts on Playwriting," where he notes that "Novels are written in the past tense.... The novel is a past reported in the present. On the stage it is always now" (124–25). These thoughts of Wilder's and his stated fascination with theatrical art of the Elizabethan era, put one in mind of Shakespeare's Scottish usurper intoning "tomorrow, and tomorrow, and tomorrow," eternally reminding his audience that in the theatre there is only now, and now, and now — before the performed moment recedes into the corridors of memory.

After bathing in the glow of an early twentieth-century town in New Hampshire, Wilder's audience is exhorted to live fully in the moment because now forever becomes then. This point is driven home when Emily is allowed, after her death, to return to an earlier moment in her life. Upon arriving in her own past, she is immediately and repeatedly stung by the knowledge of how the future will unfold; and of how unaware we all are of our own presence in our own present. After a few torturous minutes she returns to the town graveyard, where she joins the community of the dead.

Despite its apparent nostalgia here and there, the final scenes of *Our Town* force the audience to confront the modern dilemma: it is a thorny existential question, filtered through a premodern lens. The Stage Manager unsettles the audience when he asks, "And what's left when your memory's gone, and your identity, Mrs. Smith?" (88). It is, one suspects, a question with such broad and deep implications that it may be what led Winfield Townley Scott to write of the final effect: "one simply weeps" (116–17).

Director David Cromer apparently disagrees with Scott's assessment of this ultimate impact. In Cromer's Off Broadway production — which originated in Chicago, collected critical accolades and awards, and ran in New York for eighteen months — the director added his own twist to Wilder's structure of presence and absence. Although Scott argues that as the writer "constructs it he *reminds* us... of something we know ... [and] we adapt our memory to his text at once" (Scott 104), Cromer's conception of Grover's Corners was contemporized in order to shake his audience from its twenty-first century torpor. Cromer's rethinking — in which he also played the omniscient role of the Stage Manager — shifted the audience's attention away from existential questions and onto the delicious smell of bacon frying in a pan. Ignoring Wilder's instruction, repeated time and again during his life, that "when Emily 'returns' there is not even the table and two chairs [in her parents' kitchen]: all, all is in our minds" (*Selected* 508), Cromer elected to heighten the impact of Emily's own nostalgic experience by creating an idealized image of her early life.

In Cromer's vision, Emily's return is marked by a scenic shift to a hyper-real setting where none had existed before. The colors were vivid and the aroma overpowering; but the directorial *coup de théâtre* in the play's penultimate moments drew attention from the question Wilder asks of his audience and shifted focus onto a theatrical parlor trick — to "oohs," "aahs," and "yums" from the audience, it must be noted. This was not the gauzy, soft-focus imagery of nostalgia's gentle embrace, which makes Emily's recognition of reality more powerful. Cromer's concept was not unlike a "laugh track" employed by television producers concerned that audiences will not get the joke. To turn Wilder's phrase: nothing, nothing was in our minds. Cromer chose to ignore that the *Our Town* characters represent the stout middle class of Grover's Corners — a virtual ruling class, in fact — and made them into members of a postindustrial working class. This shift may make the play more contemporary, but it vitiates key thematics in the play. The director's vision also undermined the power of the text with an arena staging, which, perhaps unintentionally, emphasized the pantomimic dramatization of mothers preparing their families for the day — as opposed to focusing on Wilder's "countless 'unimportant' details of our daily life" ("Preface" 1). Wilder might have told Cromer, as he wrote in "Some Suggestions for the Director,"

> that Mrs. Gibbs and Mrs. Webb in the preparation of breakfast perform much of their business with their back to the audience, and do not distract and provoke its attention with too distinct and perhaps puzzling a picture of the many operations of coffee-grinding, porridge-stirring, etc. [*Collected* 661].

Indeed, Wilder vigorously opposed stagings that did not employ "that homely even ugly 'rehearsal stage'" offered by an empty proscenium theatre with its "steampipes and back stage ladders" because the "audience's imagination has to fight doubly hard to overcome and transcend those concrete facts" (*Selected* 652).[9] Frying bacon in the theatre requires no construction of imaginative audience memory — one simply triggers the salivary glands and hopes for a long run.

One might argue that Wilder's original vision — which we know the playwright struggled to see enacted from its earliest rehearsals — may continue to languish in a netherworld at the nexus of text, memory, and nostalgia. After *Our Town*'s initial success, as noted above, Wilder used the "preface" published in the *New York Times* to explain what might seem scenically strange to potential audience members. From that 1938 perspective, the smell of frying bacon in 2009 carries with it the aroma of Wilder's despised "abject truth." As Wilder evolved into the avuncular national writer of the 1930s and after, an author who also played the Stage Manager role in productions from time to time, perhaps the "abject truth" of success eventually obscured his early impulses and anxieties about the play, perhaps he got his wish, or perhaps there is a version yet to be done.

It is tempting to ascribe Cromer's decision to make *Our Town* "relevant" and "theatrical" to the same cultural ennui some theatregoers experience when they think of seeing the play. The eminent playwright Robert Anderson — he of the aphorism "you can't make a living in the theatre, but you can make a killing"— spoke for some when he said:

> I have seen *Our Town* many times under many different circumstances, and, as with Beethoven's Fifth, my tendency is to ask, "Do I have to see it again?" But I do see it, and its deceptively simple magic always moves me deeply [qtd. in Bryer, "Thornton" 15].

Consider also Donald Margulies's take on *Our Town*, prior to seeing a 1988 landmark production at Lincoln Center Theatre (ironically, the theatre roundly rejected by Wilder when approached in 1967 for a thirtieth anniversary production). Margulies spoke at a 1997 Yale symposium regarding Wilder's legacy and, as Jackson R. Bryer notes, admitted that he was "prejudiced against Thornton Wilder" because his first exposure had been a "hackneyed reading" of the play. His experience of the Lincoln Center production, however, gave him a "truly thunderous experience in the theatre." He told the symposium:

> Rereading it just days ago I was struck again by its poetry and its lack of sentimentality — which is something that high school productions simply do not convey [qtd. in Bryer, "Thornton" 17–18].

From the comments of these playwrights a picture continues to emerge of the adapted memory about which Scott writes. Anderson celebrates the play's "deceptively simple magic," even as he admits resisting its charms. Margulies is entranced by *Our Town*'s "poetry" and "lack of sentimentality," while implying there is a need for virtuosity in performance. Is there something about memory and its softer-focused sibling, nostalgia, that may have caused Cromer to overdetermine the emotional experience of Emily's return? Did Wilder's quiet simplicity in a time of hypermediated culture, rising irony quotients, and shortened attention spans, make the director feel a need to compensate for raw, quiet emotion?

Emily has her moment of clarity. It comes when memory, nostalgia, and "reality" conflate to show her what we who live cannot see: how it all will end. We know generally how it will end, of course, but if we focus on it we might become paralyzed with anxiety. Emily knows the loss of being unable to be "present" in one's own present. Director Cromer, perhaps with good reason, does not trust his audience to have the doubled experience of Emily's recognition, as Scott refers to it, so he gives us something else to think about.

A stroll through the Broadway theatre district of today provides a possible entrance point to this construct — although "stroll" is not what one does among the jostling throngs that pack Times Square. Everywhere one glances there are cellphones, cameras, and video recorders capturing digital images that create mediated experience through lenses that are neither figurative nor theoretical. Observing the effort expended on the electronic capture of the Broadway or New York "experience" leads one to the conclusion that these mediated encounters provide fodder for future nostalgia.

There, in that most public of squares, we see experience disappear down the rabbithole of two-inch by three-inch color screens. Was one really present if there is no image? Or, more to the point: Can one truly be present if the focus of the experience is the capture of images? One might well amend Wilder's question: "What's left when your camera's gone, Mrs. Smith?"

Notes

1. Woollcott's last name is misspelled in the dedication to *Our Town* as "Woolcott" (v).

2. Christopher Bigsby has noted the presence of a Mike Gold-like character in *Our Town*: the Belligerent Man at Back of Auditorium who asks simplistic questions about "social injustice and industrial inequality" (Bigsby 260). See also Wilder, *Our Town* 25.

3. Those few words about "inside his own head," makes one wonder if Arthur Miller might have taken them as inspiration for his tragedy of the "small details of life," *Death of a Salesman*, which was first titled *The Inside of His Head*.

4. See Butcher; Atkinson, "The Play: *Elmer Gantry* Reaches the Stage"; "Lewis's Novel on Religion Branded Punch and Judy"; and "Elmer Gantry Not Real."

5. Despite Wilder's seeming assertion in the *New York Times* "preface" that these and adjacent lines have been deleted from the text, virtually all of the purported deletions appear in the *Best Plays* excerpt of *Our Town* (Mantle, *Best Plays* 73–74). In the 1998 edition of the play, the references to Christianity's primacy, marriage between men and women, and burial of the dead are the only "deletions" that do not appear (Wilder, *Our Town* 32–34).

6. The letter to Bates was in appreciation of Winfield Townley Scott's essay, *"Our Town* and the Golden Veil" in the Winter 1953 number of the *Virginia Quarterly Review*.

7. Brecht writes that the "stage's inaccurate representations of our social life, including those classed as so-called Naturalism, led it to call for scientifically exact representations; the tasteless rehashing of empty visual or spiritual palliatives, for the noble logic of the multiplication table." Brecht's strident call is unlike Wilder's in his focus on the political, but his reference to theatres as "having degenerated into branches of the bourgeois narcotics business" might well have induced a sympathetic nod from the American playwright. See Brecht, "A Short Organum for the Theatre" 179.

8. The article also suggests that the Pulitzer Prize has stronger drawing power than the New York Drama Critics' Circle Award.

9. Wilder also refers to Pirandello's *Six Characters in Search of an Author* in this letter to Schuyler Chapin, which explains why the *Our Town* author is unwilling in 1967 to allow a production at Lincoln Center Theater's Vivian Beaumont Theater due to its deep thrust stage.

Works Cited

Aristotle. *Poetics*. Trans. S.H. Butcher. New York: Hill and Wang, 1961. Print.

Atkinson, J. Brooks. "The Play: *Elmer Gantry* Reaches the Stage." *New York Times* 10 Aug. 1928: 14. Web.

_____. "The Play: Frank Craven in Thornton Wilder's *Our Town*, Which Is the Anatomy of a Community." *New York Times* 5 Feb. 1938: 18. Web.

_____. "Standards in Drama Criticism." *New York Times* 13 Mar. 1938, sec. 11: 1. Web.

Bawer, Bruce. "'An Impersonal Passion': Thornton Wilder." *Hudson Review* 61.3 (2008): 506. Web.

Beebe, Lucius. "Stage Aside: From Thornton Wilder." *Conversations with Thornton Wilder*. Ed. Jackson R. Bryer. Jackson: University Press Mississippi, 1992. 19–20. Print.

Bigsby, Christopher. *A Critical Introduction to Twentieth-Century American Drama: Volume I, 1900–40*. Cambridge: Cambridge University Press, 1982.

Blank, Martin, Dalma Hunyadi Brunauer, and David Garrett Izzo, eds. *Thornton Wilder: New Essays*. West Cornwall, CT: Locust Hill Press, 1999. Print.

Bowen, Stirling. "The Theatre: Village Anthology." *Wall Street Journal* 7 Feb. 1938: 9. Web.

Brecht, Bertolt. *Mother Courage and Her Children*. Trans. John Willett. Eds. Willett and Ralph Manheim. New York: Arcade, 1994. Print.

_____. "A Short Organum for the Theatre." *Brecht on Theatre: The Development of an Aesthetic*. Ed. and trans. John Willett. New York: Hill and Wang, 1997. Print.

Bryer, Jackson R., ed. *Conversations With Thornton Wilder*. Jackson: University Press Mississippi, 1992. Print.

_____. "Thornton Wilder at 100: His Achievement and His Legacy." *Thornton Wilder: New Essays*. Eds. Martin Blank, Dalma Hunyadi Brunauer, and David Garrett Izzo. West Cornwall, CT: Locust Hill Press, 1999. Print.

Butcher, Fanny. "*Elmer Gantry* Is Proclaimed Best by Sinclair Lewis." *Chicago Daily Tribune* 12 Mar. 1927: 13. Web.

Cass, Judith. "Chicago Girls Will Attend Cornell Prom." *Chicago Daily Tribune* 10 Feb. 1938: 13. Web.

"Elmer Gantry Not Real." *New York Times* 20 Mar. 1927: 19. Web.

Garrison, Winfred Ernest. "What Is a Religious Book — and Why?" *Chicago Daily Tribune* 27 Mar. 1927: 10. Web.

Gassner, John W. "The Theatre Forum." *Forum and Century*, Apr. 1938: 218. Web.

Krutch, Joseph Wood. "Drama: *Our Town*." *Nation* 19 Feb. 1938: 224–25. Web.

"Lewis's Novel on Religion Branded Punch and Judy." *Washington Post* 11 Mar. 1927: 3. Web.

Mantle, Burns. *The Best Plays of 1937–1938*. New York: Dodd, Mead, 1938. Print.

_____. "Critic Covers Broadway by 'Remote Control.'" *Chicago Daily Tribune* 20 Feb. 1938: E2. Web.

Maurois, André. "A Holiday Diary, 1928." *Conversations With Thornton Wilder*. Ed. Jackson R. Bryer. Jackson: University Press Mississippi, 1992. 13. Print.

Pirandello, Luigi. *Six Characters in Search of an Author. The Drama: Traditional and Modern*. Eds. Mark Goldman and Isadore Traschen. Boston: Allyn and Bacon, 1968. 524–25. Print.

"Rialto Gossip." *New York Times* 15 May 1938, sec. 10: 1. Web.

Roosevelt, Eleanor. "My Day." *Atlanta Constitution* 3 Mar. 1938: 14. Web.

Scott, Winfield Townley. "*Our Town* and the Golden Veil." *Virginia Quarterly Review* 29.1 (1953): 104. Print.

Slosson, Preston William. *The Great Crusade and After: 1914–1928*. New York: Macmillan, 1930. 427. Print.

The Statistical History of the United States: From Colonial Times to the Present. New York: Basic Books, 1976. Print.

Whitman, Alden. "Thornton Wilder Is Dead at 78." *New York Times* 8 Dec. 1975: 1. Web.

Witham, Barry B. *The Federal Theatre Project: A Case Study*. Cambridge: Cambridge University Press, 2003.

Wilder, Thornton. *Our Town*. New York: Perennial Classics, 1998. Print.

_____. "A Preface for *Our Town*." *New York Times* 13 Feb. 1938, sec. 10: 1. Web.

_____. *The Selected Letters of Thornton Wilder*. Ed. Robin G. Wilder and Jackson R. Bryer. New York: Harper, 2008. Print.

_____. "Some Thoughts on Playwriting." *American Characteristics and Other Essays*. Ed. Donald Gallup. New York: Harper and Row, 1979. Print.

_____. *Thornton Wilder: Collected Plays and Writing on Theatre*. Comp. J.D. McClatchy. New York: Library of American, 2007. Print

Rain in an Actually Strange City

Translating and Re-Situating the Universality of Arthur Miller's Death of a Salesman

RAMÓN ESPEJO ROMERO

Although Arthur Miller is best known as the playwright responsible for some of the most outstanding of the world's 20th century plays, he was also a consummate essay and fiction writer. While he was always given credit for his dramas, rarely are his non-dramatic pieces the object of much scholarly attention. However, aside from their intrinsic values, they often shed surprising and unexpected light on his dramatic oeuvre and his agenda as a writer and intellectual. In 1974, Miller wrote the short meditation "Rain in a Strange City." It is a rare non-fiction work, which opens as follows:

> A rainy day out there does it. Paris in rain, Budapest, London. Also Leningrad, Stockholm and Vienna. And Rome, Rome, yes. Oh, and Amsterdam. Yes, Amsterdam especially. Yes, and New York, come to think of it, or Mexico City. And of course Dublin. Oh definitely Dublin, and almost any suburb in this chill but not freezing late morning. Even Moscow [155].

After constructing the particular microcosm evoked by such different cities, we are let in on what all these cities have in common, as Miller, in Whitmanesque fashion, points out the "heads-down people, indrawn and all thinking of shelter, everywhere alive below the incoherent languages, alive to the drizzle and the gray, the plans that must be changed are everywhere the same plans" (155). In "Crossing Brooklyn Ferry," the 19th century American poet had also referred to the way in which, when it comes to human events and feelings, "distance avails not, and place avails not" (l.56). Shifting to Thoreauvian Transcendentalist exultation, Miller then affirms that the "oneness of all countrysides is the same, the dank short grass is always making the same remark" (155).[1] The next sentences are devoted to describing how all cities look alike under a rain that seems to round up all mankind, cleansing as it were the differences among men and uniting them under a universal mantle.

In such views, Miller shows himself as an inheritor of the American humanist tradition, traceable as far back as the Bill of Rights and the Declaration of Independence, the latter declaring that "all men are created equal." Like Miller, either the Founding Fathers or the more restless Transcendentalists assumed a set of traits which underlay men and women, and posited that these were (for their own humanist projects) far more important than whatever differences existed between them, which tended to be slighted, regarded as merely superficial accidents.[2] Referring specifically to his *Death of a Salesman*, Miller derided the opinion of those American critics who in 1949 believed that "the Salesman, and the story itself, were so American as to be quite strange if not incomprehensible to people of other nations" ("1956" 93). In his essay "1956 And All This, " Miller allowed himself to disagree with them:

> In Catholic Spain, where feudalism is still not a closed era; among fishermen in Norway at the edge of the Arctic Circle; in Rome, Athens, Tokyo — there has been an almost disappointing similarity of reaction to this and other plays of mine in one respect at least. They all seem to feel the anxieties we do [93].

It is not the only time we have heard or read Miller uphold such a view. There was practically not a single interview with the playwright in which he failed to mention this would-be homogeneous reaction to his plays, especially *Death of a Salesman*, no matter where or when they were played, as though, going back to Whitman, indeed "distance avails not, and place avails not." The "universal" nature of the plays would apparently always triumph over anything specifically American, or Jewish, or Brooklynese, or temporal, in them.

Before moving on, and giving some more thought to the central idea in "Rain in a Strange City," we might wonder: How is Miller so sure that there exists only "one" rain, and that the rain falling on Ethiopia is the same which falls on Philadelphia, or that it is experienced in the same way, or that it has the same effects, or that it possesses the same quality and intensity, or that people relate to it in an identical fashion? Probably the destitute who are left without a shelter after the storm will not feel as transcendentally invigorated by it as the Philadelphians who spy it from the windows of their high-rise condos (with gas fireplace on!). Even if it were truly the same rain, it would undoubtedly always fall on an indeed *strange* city, and the circumstances of its occurrence would inevitably make it always a different rain.

In his celebrated 1999 piece "Salesman at Fifty," Miller explains that the language of *Death of a Salesman* was not as bluntly faithful to real Jewish speech as people used to claim. He argues that "[t]he Lomans, like their models in life, are not content with who and what they are, but want to be other, wealthier, more cultivated perhaps, closer to power" (272). This is the reason why Biff Loman says that he has been "remiss" in taking proper care of his father, hardly a word a Brooklyn young man of the age would use. Biff's conscious rejection of his own disorderly, unruly past is evoked by the very use of a word that falls outside his lexical scope but sounds to him as an appropriate starting point for that new life he plans to pursue. Similarly, Willy's famous dictum "be liked and you will never want," and its different versions, try to carry the weight of a sort of "Victorian authority to back him up"; Miller concludes that "[t]hese folk are the innocent receivers of what they imagine as a more elegant past, a time 'finer' than theirs" (272). Yet, is the word "remiss" supposed to mean as much to a contemporary American as it did to a New Yorker from the late 1940s? Miller depends on the magic of choosing some words over others and then hoping the audience is going to be aware of such nuances. Is that something we may realistically hope for? What kind of an audience do we (did he) have in mind? Is there such a thing as a universal, timeless audience for *Death of a Salesman* (or any other play, for that matter)? What about a foreign audience, from whom the play is screened by a translation, carried out, most times, by a translator who is unlikely to perceive the subtleties surrounding the use of the word "remiss"?

Miller goes on to say that his play

> seems to have shown that most of the world shares something similar to that condition. Having seen it in five or six countries, and directed it in China and Sweden, neither of whose languages I know, it was both mystifying and gratifying to note that people everywhere react pretty much the same in the same places of the play [272–273].

Is that really so? Such an assertion would seem to imply that a universal audience does indeed exist. How did those foreign translators cope with a word like "remiss" and all its nuances? Of course, it is true that, as Miller says, there is a bedrock foundation to the play,

> namely that being human — a father, mother, son — is something most of us fail at most of the time, and a little mercy is eminently in order given the societies we live in, which purport to be stable and sound as mountains when in fact they are all trembling in a fast wind blowing mindlessly around the earth [273].

Nice words indeed, but they threaten to neglect two important facts: (1) that a play, or a literary work, is always more than its central message; (2) that the different languages in which a play is reaching audiences and the people responsible for making that happen are, all the time, turning out different plays, hopefully similar in their contours but different in their nuances and subtleties, masterpieces being masterpieces just because every nuance in them does indeed matter.

In preparing a critical edition of Arthur Miller's *Death of a Salesman* for the leading publishing house of annotated literary works in Spain, Cátedra, which involved introducing the theatrical context of the play, its location within Miller's career and an extended analysis of the text itself, as well as its translation, I went through the experience of re-discovering this "universal" text. After months of working very closely with Miller's exact words and sentences, allusions, references, different nuances, I found myself wondering why it was generally believed (even by me) that the text was endowed with such great universality and could be transferred from one culture to another without anything really significant being lost. The more I delved into the text, the more convinced I became of its take on a given time and place. Be it clear from the start that my purpose in this essay is not to argue that Miller's masterpiece is not sufficiently relevant for people from all over the world or that its interest is confined to one time and place. What I do intend to prove is that there are very specific traits in Miller's piece, which, far from being universally understood, are, as it were, dark spots under which a part of his message is concealed to more and more people as the play moves farther across cultures and leaves behind the moment for which it was written and the audience which it originally targeted at *its* audience.

As anyone acquainted, even superficially, with Miller's career well knows, *Death of a Salesman* was not yet the work of a famous or acclaimed playwright. It is true that his previous play, *All My Sons*, which premiered two years before *Salesman*, in 1947, had been a moderate hit. A New York run of over 300 performances was not long enough to make Miller a consummate or internationally famous playwright, but it at least guaranteed that the 32-year-old author was not going to have as hard a time exhibiting his next play on Broadway as he had had for almost a decade before for *All My Sons*. However, the budding playwright who sat down to write what was to become a seminal play of the American theatre could not imagine that he *was* writing a seminal play of the American theatre, that audiences worldwide were going to react to it so strongly, so quickly and for such a long time. In no way could he realistically guess that the play he was writing was rapidly going to make its way into the canon and that over sixty years after it was written we would still think of it as among the best that the American theatre has produced and hail it as a modern classic. Though Miller may have had his ambitions and was certainly aspiring to write as universal a play as possible, it would be unrealistic to conclude that his "implied reader" was humanity at large. If that had been the case, he would not have included such a large number of references to things which only a Broadway theatergoer of the late 1940s, at most an American citizen of the same epoch, could know. Certainly, Miller was not telling his story, to borrow from Emily Dickinson's well-known poem, "to the ages" (272).

As a consequence of the above, Miller speaks (why shouldn't he?) to people who were familiar with the same things he was familiar with, and therefore includes place names he knew they would immediately recognize, as well as popular brand names of the decade, terms taken from American sports, cultural allusions, catchphrases, popular figures of the time, stores, clothes...It is curious to realize how, in the plays that would follow *Death of a Salesman*, the number of culturally specific references of the kind mentioned above would greatly shrink. Thinking of *A View from the Bridge*, for instance, also set in New York at about the same time, it is astonishing to see how disembodied from specific marks of the culture the play is and how much easier it is for anyone from a different part of the world to understand. Miller's refusal of realism in the original American production of *A View from the Bridge*, written in verse, devoid of a set and only employing two Greek columns, could be interpreted as an attempt to reach the universality which he appreciated in Greek theater. The character Alfieri tries to reinforce such a connection by insisting at the outset of the play that

> every few years there is still a case, and as the parties tell me what the trouble is, the flat air in my office suddenly washes in with the green scent of the sea, the dust in this air is blown away and the thought comes that in some Caesar's year, in Calabria perhaps or on the cliff at Syracuse, another lawyer, quite differently dressed, heard the same complaint and sat there as powerless as I, and watched it run its bloody course [12].

The play may be set in Red Hook in Brooklyn, New York, but Miller does not lose any chance to point out the fact that its scope is undeniably universal and timeless. Even *The Crucible*, set in late 17th century New England, tries to concentrate on that which anyone from any country might understand (and those things which to Miller were likely to be less understandable were addressed from within the text in the form of interpolations). Though this would probably merit further discussion elsewhere, it is important, in order to make my point clearer, to establish that in these and other plays, Miller is aware that his audience are not only his neighbors any longer, or those who tread the same streets he does, or buy the same brands of cars, or admire the same sports heroes.[3]

When faced with the (unexpected) difficulties involved in translating *Death of a Salesman* into the language of my own culture, I did not want to follow the path that some previous translators had followed, discarding most of the references that did not make ready sense to a Spanish audience as useless or irrelevant to foreground the play's central message.[4] Provided there was indeed such a "central" message, the play was for me that as much as the different details surrounding it. In a previous well-known Spanish translation by José López Rubio, endless passages had been re-written or cut and even characters had been eliminated (or had their names changed, Uncle Ben inexplicably becoming "Fred" in Spanish). For López Rubio, these were "elementos innecesarios bien porque alargaban la duración del espectáculo, bien porque habían de resultar incomprensibles para nuestro público" (23).[5] One critic, Alberto Vilá San-Juán, applauded this mutilated version, considering that it preserved "el mensaje de Miller, dando a sus pensamientos el cauce exacto para que pudieran desembocar en el Mediterráneo" (15),[6] and many other critics followed suit. Though I was determined to preserve the integrity of the play, which to me included preserving everything which had been so far deemed unnecessary, I soon discovered that most of the time it was simply impossible to do this from within the text, and my only chance was to use footnotes. Mine being an annotated edition, I could count on having as many notes as I needed. The introduction also contributed to providing the necessary background to clarify the references and other details I felt necessary.

Annotated editions, however, tend to be tools for the scholar and/or the student of literature and drama, but fall outside the scope of ordinary theatergoers, whose acquaintance is only with the work as produced on a stage or, at the most, with an "acting edition," a term coined by Spanish scholar Raquel Merino to refer to editions of plays practically devoid of any additional material other than the play itself (original or in translation); at the most, they may include one or two pages on which the biography of the playwright and typically the list of his plays are given.[7] I may as well add that there had never been an annotated edition of Miller's *Death of a Salesman* in my country, so, in the case of this particular work, Spanish readers had not had much choice other than to use "acting" editions, in which translators did not have specific tools for conveying Miller's meaning (or American references) other than the translated texts themselves.

What ensues is a brief overview of some of the material which, in my opinion, most foreign readers or spectators of *Death of a Salesman* would need to understand in order to grasp its full import. I will begin by distinguishing between non-meaningful and meaningful references. The former do not convey any specific meaning and are therefore less problematic. A few examples follow: Biff and Happy tease each other about a girl they both knew who lived on Bushwick Avenue (in Brooklyn); Willy Loman says he has visited Albany; Ben mentions he has an appointment at Ketchikan, Alaska; car brands are brought up; a reference to Ebbets Field is introduced; or a string of stores in Boston, where Willy Loman maintains he is exceptionally well-liked, is encountered. One may have never been to Albany, Ketchikan or Bushwick Avenue, and yet they are merely place names, which a translator would probably preserve and which would not mean much for a foreign spectator or reader. The foreign spectator or reader would not be missing anything on account of his never having heard such words. Something similar happens with Al Smith or Jack Benny. Probably a member of the original audience of *Salesman* would know them better than, for instance, a Spanish person today does (or an American person today?), and yet one is a politician, the other a popular radio and TV comedian (Miller makes clear in the text, however, who they are), but there is nothing pivotal in the play which hinges upon such an understanding.

Among the references I call meaningful, I identified three major groups: those understandable across cultures; those that are self-explanatory; and those that are somewhat inaccessible. Thus, a limited number of references will not necessitate further explanations, since most people would understand them. To say that Willy has been sent to Florida probably does not require the explanation that it is a place associated with sun, warmth and rest, particularly for aging citizens. To hear someone recite places like Nebraska, Dakota or Colorado and think of the American West, the pioneers and the westward marches in the 19th century can safely be trusted to any reader's basic familiarity with the idea of America. There is a second group, which we might call self-explanatory. By hearing in the second act that Biff has run off to Grand Central Station, we are expected to guess that he intends to take a train to Boston. Probably Miller thinks that a non–New York audience would not make that connection so instantaneously, and after Bernard says that Biff "went to Grand Central" to talk to his father, Miller has Linda utter: "Grand — You mean he went to Boston" (87). Similarly, even if we do not know where Hackensack is, Stanley makes clear what he means: that Happy is a classy young man, with proper manners and sophistication. Probably not that many people in the 1940s had the slightest idea what J. P. Morgan looked like. Thus, Charley has to mention that his money made him well-liked (Willy Loman's unattainable dream), but "in a Turkish bath he'd look like a butcher" (77), to signify that good looks and charm are not indispensable for success.

A third group of references is made up by those which are not so accessible, indeed the ones causing most trouble to a translator. When Willy Loman mentions he has never been able to go past Yonkers, how is one supposed to realize the sad plight in which the salesman has fallen unless one knows that Yonkers is just a few miles from New York? When Willy boasts of his acquaintanceship with the mayor of Providence, he is speaking of the second largest city in New England, a fact that helps us see where he tries to be in the eyes of his sons. Unless we know that Boston is indeed the cradle of the Revolution and Waterbury has a famous clock, we will never understand that together with the flawed lessons Willy is passing down to his offspring, he earnestly tries to teach them something real, hopefully useful (meaning that Willy Loman is not invariably proud, or arrogant, or obsessed with finding shortcuts to success), albeit less useful than Howard Wagner's having his son recite the names of all the American states in alphabetical order. By the way, unless one knows that Cincinnati is not the capital of Ohio, one will never see that Wagner's son is not perfect, however, and also makes mistakes. On the other hand, if we are not familiar with the brand names of American appliances, we will never realize how superior a status for Charley is signaled by his General Electric refrigerator (vs. Loman's Hastings one). How important it is for Biff to impress his father is shown by his insistence on making a touchdown for him, even if doing so might be too showy probably. Nevertheless, how is one to see that unless one is familiar with the rules of American football (almost nobody in Spain is)? Similarly, Charley teases Biff about his playing baseball or "knocking" a homer, further showing what to Willy Loman must have been clearer, that sports are not everything. His feigned ignorance of what sport Biff plays will be completely lost on Spaniards, though, since they can not often tell American football from baseball and are even less likely to know what a homer is (there is not even an equivalent word in Spanish). When Miss Forsythe at the restaurant asks Happy about the team Biff is supposed to be with, he replies that he is with the Giants. Probably American audiences in the 1940s would realize that he is playing it safe in bringing up a team that was a little eclipsed at that time, thus minimizing the risk that Miss Forsythe would "discover" the lie. Happy is thus posited as a good liar and a superb candidate to be the next Willy Loman, but is a Spanish audience supposed to see all this? (Let me add here that I reckon this would be valid for audiences outside Spain as well, maybe even American ones.)

At one point in the play Willy Loman mentions that his clothes are a little drab and he is not "dressing to advantage." Linda replies that he is "the handsomest man in the world" (29). We never find out whether Willy is actually in need of an enhanced wardrobe or not, or perhaps we do. When Charley enters in knickers, Willy makes fun of him. Actually, the scene where this happens is supposed to take place in the 1920s, when knickers were a sensation (students were so fond of them that Oxford University had to forbid its students to wear them on campus). That Willy Loman finds the latest fashion in clothes ridiculous signals his old-fashioned tastes. Again, this is very difficult to understand if simply enacted on a stage, except for the most dogged connoisseur of old fashions. In Willy's characterization, on the other hand, there is an insistence on his talking about things he does not know well. At one point he mentions B. F. Goodrich and Thomas Alva Edison as examples of late achievers (hoping Biff can "join" them). In truth they were not; both succeeded at an early age. In Willy's inflated expectations about his son, he compares the success he is sure Biff will meet with in selling sporting goods with Albert Spalding's, and his performance as a football player with that of Red Grange. That Albert Spalding was a successful sportsman turned business tycoon, one of the most successful ever, or Red Grange one of the greatest players in the history of college football (according to a survey by the ESPN network in 2008),[8] are facts beyond the knowledge of many people today. Yet, unlike Bushwick Avenue, they flesh out the characters and make them less universal, figures from a time and place, situated within a given class and members of a particular culture.

Dealing with the play more from a literary than a strictly dramatic point of view, there are a couple of instances worth mentioning. First is the reference to Hartford, Connecticut. After mentioning how badly sales are going, Willy points out, as a kind of solution, that he is going to visit Hartford, where people like him well. Ironically, Hartford is known as the city where most worldwide insurance companies have their headquarters, Willy's insurance being the final "solution" to all of his problems. Such a dramatic irony will be lost on any Spanish audience completely, just as much as the fact that some areas of New England are quite far from New York (Bangor and New York, for example, are almost 450 miles apart), as great a distance as exists at a psychological level between Willy Loman and customers who no longer take to him as much as they used to.[9] How is that to be seen unless one is familiar with such distances? For most people, at least in Spain, New England is just a name, devoid moreover of the echoes of America's early days, which Willy Loman would like to revisit, but which are fast receding from him and taking with them the promise that the salesman still tries desperately to believe in.

Some cases are peculiar and will be more or less understandable according to the culture to which the play is transposed. For instance, the importance of passing a Regents exam needs to be realized in order to absorb how much Biff spoiled by flunking it. There happens to be an almost identical exam in Spain called "Selectividad," which any translator or director would probably employ to replace the original term, with no loss of meaning. Arguing a case before the Supreme Court is similarly as much a matter of pride to an American attorney as it is to a Spanish one to do so before our Tribunal Constitucional (almost having the same functions), so the latter could be used to translate the reference satisfactorily. We do have traveling salesmen in Spain (my father was one), so knowing what a salesman is will cause no problem. However, in other cultures it can. As noted by John T. Dorsey, Japanese audiences for Miller's play have systematically encountered trouble with the very notion of "salesman," an alien concept in their country. In *Salesman in Beijing,* Miller explains that he had to work hard to convince the Chinese actors in his famed Beijing production of *Death of a Salesman* that the WOMAN in his play was not a prostitute, as any such woman in China would be. In many countries (including mine), the American system of higher education is not easy to understand. The importance of sports, or how some students make it to the "big" universities just because they excel in them, have no equivalent whatsoever in Spain. The competition between universities is also non-existent in countries where higher education has always been the domain of governments (even if in Spain private universities have been around for a while now, they are still far less prestigious).

The question remains: Aside from the fact that an annotated translation may explain the arcane references and fill readers in on the cultural substratum, how is a theatre director to carry all of the above to his production, or a translator to his acting edition? Though an exhaustive analysis would be probably too tedious, I thought it was necessary at least, for the sake of my argument, to take a look at the only available translations of Miller in Spain before mine came along (I will not deal with Latin American ones, especially Argentinian, because, in spite of deploying the same language, they belong in a radically different cultural context). In the 1952 translation by José López Rubio (reprinted many times, in 1958, 1962, 1969, 1983 and 1985), used in almost every Spanish production so far, only half the references I mentioned throughout this chapter were kept. Those which he dropped included Ebbets Field, Filene's, Slattery's and the other Boston stores, Al Smith, Jack Benny, Grand Central Station, Hackensack, the Regents exam, the General Electric fridge, the New York Giants, Charley's knickers, B. F. Goodrich, Albert Spalding and Red Grange. Conversely, the 2000 translator, Jordi Fibla, kept all these and the rest mentioned throughout the paper, with two exceptions: Hackensack and, curiously, the Regents exam. The latter is a very faithful translation, which follows closely a text that López Rubio had negotiated much more carelessly. Yet, even if Fibla's acting edition preserves so much which had been removed before, it seems certain that a Spanish reader or actor or spectator is not, in 2010, discovering the same play that a Broadway spectator of the late 1940s did. Even if he is using an annotated edition, the Spanish spectator is not before the same play, because that Broadway spectator of the late 1940s did not have to be told about things he would recognize immediately, references that were woven into the very texture of the play (they still are, even if we may no longer recognize the fabric).

It seems obvious that such gaps as emerge in any contemporary approach to the play are a consequence of the fact that it was written more than 60 years ago and it has aged already. Judging by how productions of *Death of a Salesman* tend to be successful everywhere, it is aging well. That is, unlike other plays, it preserves enough which does not need explication to make sense to audiences, but we should avoid the temptation of concluding that this is due to its universality, because such a trait is one which, far from emanating from the play, we rather impose upon it. Of course, the play makes sense even if most of the references discussed (and others) are not understood, but it is, to be sure, not exactly the same play. Some directors will even do without such references, confident that the play will yet make sense. Even if they are kept, in a translation or production which stakes out a claim to utmost fidelity to the original, a reader/spectator who does not know who or what those things are will simply ignore them and will go on to concentrate on everything else which the play has to offer. That is, if they are not obliterated on the page or the stage, they will be in the reader's process of reception. They will be lost nonetheless. Thus, whether it is the reader, the spectator, the director, or the translator, universality and timelessness will be enforced on a play which does not have them to the degree that is generally assumed. I think it is important to take into account such considerations if Arthur Miller's *Death of a Salesman* is to be understood fully by the community of Miller scholars and critics.

The purpose of this essay was, then, not so much to deal with translation problems involved in intertextual exchanges, but rather, through such problems, to suggest new possibilities for looking at Miller's masterpiece, using its problematic transference to another culture as the way to open up fresh insights into Miller's original. Goethe said long ago that "a national literature has little left to say, the age of world literature has dawned and each of us must contribute to hastening its arrival" (qtd. in Fischer-Lichte 173). However, there is surely a price to be paid for hastening the arrival of such a global kind of literature, or drama, and every time *Death of a Salesman* goes up on a stage, such a price is being paid in the form of little patches of meaning that keep eluding us. How long will it take for such patches to be more conspicuous than the still bright sparks of light with which they coexist?

Notes

1. In his masterpiece, *Walden* (1854), Thoreau had affirmed that the remark being made by the grass nourished and invigorated by the rain was to the effect that we should "take advantage of every accident that befell us, like the grass which confesses the influence of the slightest dew that falls on it; and did not spend our time in atoning for the neglect of past opportunities" (213).

2. Recent Miller criticism, while admitting these views, insists that they are really unfair and dated. For David Savran, "Miller produces false universals," essentially by "dissolving the concreteness and specificity" of individuals "into a set of imprecise and quasi-mystical universals" (28). Savran is especially critical of the way Miller understands *one* kind of masculine experience as *the* universal experience of mankind. Most contemporary critical thinking denounces the humanist, essentializing agenda of people like Miller as responsible for the long history of invisibility of so many subjugated, neglected identities, whether determined by class, gender, ethnicity, or sexual preference. Savran complains that "although attempts have been made in recent years to historicize their work [he refers to both Miller and Tennessee Williams], most notably by C.W.E. Bigsby, theatrical and critical fashions continue to champion the ostensibly 'universal' qualities of plays such as *Death of a Salesman*" (6).

3. It seems as if after learning of the successful reaction to his plays all over the world, Miller started to broaden his focus and cater to this new audience which was no longer American. By the time he sat down to write *The Crucible*, such an awareness was already in Miller's mind. Would he have explained who the Puritans were, for instance, as he does in the published version, if he was still writing only for the sake of American people?

4. I was well aware of the nature of previous Spanish translations. See my *España y el teatro de Arthur Miller* (2010) and, particularly about the translations, "Traducciones al español de Arthur Miller, 1950–1952" (2003). See also John London, *Reception and Renewal*.

5. "unnecessary elements since they made the play last for too long and were also to prove arcane to our audience" (this and subsequent are my translations).

6. "Miller's message, channelling his thought in such a way as to allow it to reach Mediterranean people."

7. See Merino's *Traducción, tradición y manipulación. Teatro inglés en España 1950–1990* (1994). The (largely austere) editions of the Dramatists Play Service in the United States might serve as an example of what Merino means by an "acting edition."

8. Red Grange (1903–1991) was known by his 75 touchdowns in only four seasons during the 1920s. In 1925 he appeared on the cover of *Time* magazine.

9. I am indebted to the editors of this volume for bringing to my attention the fact that the salesman's itinerary — Providence, Waterbury, Boston, Portland, Bangor and straight home — actually makes no sense geographically, since it involves backtracking. See Brenda Murphy, "Willy Loman: Icon of Business Culture."

Works Cited

Dickinson, Emily. *The Complete Poems.* Ed. Thomas H. Johnson. Boston: Little, Brown, 1960. Print.

Dorsey, John T. "Miller, Mingei, and Japan." *Arthur Miller's Global Theater.* Ed. Enoch Brater. Ann Arbor: University of Michigan Press, 2007. 107–113. Print.

Espejo, Ramón. *España y el teatro de Arthur Miller.* Alcalá de Henares: Instituto Franklin, 2010. Print.

_____. "Traducciones al español de Arthur Miller, 1950–1952." *Trans. Revista de traductología* 7 (2003): 21–32. Print.

Fischer-Lichte, Erika. "Intercultural Aspects in Post-Modern Theatre: A Japanese Version of Chekhov's *Three Sisters.*" *The Play Out of Context: Transferring Plays from Culture to Culture.* Ed. Hanna Scolnicov and Peter Holland. Cambridge: Cambridge University Press, 1989. 173–185. Print.

London, John. *Reception and Renewal in Modern Spanish Theatre: 1939–1963.* London: Modern Humanities Research Association, 1997. Print.

López Rubio, José. "Autocrítica." *Abc* 10 Jan. 1952: 23. Print.

Merino Álvarez, Raquel. *Traducción, tradición y manipulación. Teatro inglés en España 1950– 1990.* León: Universidad de León / Universidad del País Vasco, 1994. Print.

Miller, Arthur. *A View from the Bridge. All My Sons.* Harmondsworth: Penguin, 1961. Print.

_____. *Death of a Salesman. Certain Private Conversations in Two Acts and a Requiem.* 1949. Harmondsworth: Penguin, 1961. Print.

_____. *La muerte de un viajante.* Trans. and ed. Ramón Espejo. Madrid: Cátedra, 2010. Print.

_____. *La muerte de un viajante.* 1952. Trans. José López Rubio. Madrid: Mk, 1983. Print.

_____. *La muerte de un viajante.* Trans. Jordi Fibla. Barcelona: Tusquets, 2000. Print.

_____. "1956 and All This." 1956. *The Theater Essays of Arthur Miller.* Ed. Robert A. Martin. New York: Viking, 1978. 86–109. Print.

_____. "Rain in a Strange City." 1974. *Echoes Down the Corridor. Collected Essays, 1944–2000.* Ed. Steven R. Centola. New York: Viking Penguin, 2000. 155–156. Print.

_____. "Salesman at Fifty." 1999. *Echoes Down the Corridor. Collected Essays, 1944–2000.* Ed. Steven R. Centola. New York: Viking Penguin, 2000. 270–273. Print.

_____. *Salesman in Beijing.* New York: Viking, 1983. Print.

Murphy, Brenda. "Willy Loman: Icon of Business Culture." *Michigan Quarterly Review* 37 (Fall 1998): 755–66. Print.

Savran, David. *Communists, Cowboys and Queers. The Politics of Masculinity in the Work of Arthur Miller and Tennessee Williams.* Minneapolis: University of Minnesota Press, 1992. Print.

Thoreau, Henry David. *Walden.* 1854. Ware: Wordsworth Editions, 1995.

Vila Sanjuán, Alberto. "COMEDIA. 'La muerte de un viajante,' de Arthur Miller." *La Vanguardia* 10 Jan. 1953: 15. Print.

Whitman, Walt. *Leaves of Grass. Authoritative Texts. Prefaces. Whitman on His Art. Criticism.* Ed. Sculley Bradley and Harold W. Blodgett. New York: W. W. Norton, 1973. Print.

"Doorways" and "Blank Spaces"

Intertextual Connection in John Guare's
Six Degrees of Separation

GRAHAM WOLFE

Ouisa Kittredge, in John Guare's *Six Degrees of Separation*, connects the play's famous titular phrase to an anonymous text: "I read somewhere that everybody on this planet is separated by only six other people. Six degrees of separation. Between us and everybody else on the planet" (81). Internet resources such as Wikipedia are more specific, linking the concept to a 1929 Hungarian short-story entitled "Chain-links" by Frigyes Karinthy, yet they generally credit Guare with coining the phrase itself.[1] Today, some twenty years after the play's premiere, "six degrees of separation" has almost achieved the status of a critical idiom, used to describe a dynamic found in recent movies such as *Crash* and *Babel*, and TV shows such as *Lost*, with their focus on unexpected connections and complex interrelations between seemingly disparate lives. *Lost* involves a particularly intriguing link, since the show's creator, J. J. Abrams, was himself a cast member of the film-version of Guare's play, and he also went on to create a TV show entitled *Six Degrees*, set (like the play) in New York and exploring the notion of interrelations beneath apparent disconnection. The play's "six degree" motif is thus compellingly redoubled through this array of intertextual linkages.

In what consists the peculiar attraction of this motif? Popular engagements with "six degrees" often play upon the romantic mysteriousness of unperceived connections and possibilities. As the teaser for Abrams's show asserts, "In New York City, they say you walk by the person you're going to marry three times before you ever meet them." Otherwise meaningless encounters begin to resonate with potential significance because, as Ouisa puts it, "every person is a new door, opening up into other worlds" (81). Stories constructed around this motif may also satisfy our desire for unification and completeness, bringing diverse strands together and gradually filling in the gaps that separate characters. Yet simultaneously, the motif's force may derive from the tragic irony of connections that characters *fail* to recognize, their inability to discover the links. And if the idea of intimate interconnection is inspiring, it can also be daunting and disturbing, reminding us (in Ouisa's words) that we're "bound to everyone on this planet" (81), and that the Other may be much closer than we'd like to think. As David A. Zimmerman writes, "if all people on the planet are connected by six degrees of separation, it is clearly at their peril" (116). In the era of AIDS, "connection has come to signify contagion and the impossibility of resistance."

Yet perhaps what is ultimately "comforting" (Guare 81) about the notion of six degrees is the implication that gaps between people are *contingent* rather than fundamental. Finding the points of contact can be difficult, but it's possible — the doorways aren't always easy to open, but they're *there*. In Mark McPhail's terms, the experience of "implicature" can move us toward "coherence"— a "recognition of similarities in difference" (141). This, for many critics, constitutes the central idea of Guare's play — the insistence that, "despite differences, there is a fundamental humanity shared by all people" (Román 198). "The president of the United States. A gondolier in Venice.... A native in a rain forest. A Tierra del Fuegan"— if we open the right doors we can establish a connection with *"anyone"* (Guare 81).

The fact that this play, through the increasing popularization of its central motif, has entered into such a complex web of connections with other texts, seems triply appropriate given the fascinating role of intertextual "doorways" within the play itself. Toward its conclusion, a character quotes Donald Barthelme's statement (as quoted in his own *New York Times* obituary) that "collage was the art form of the twentieth century" (107)— a self-referential statement in the context of Guare's play, whose characters repeatedly make reference to well-known playwrights (Beckett, Chekhov, Shakespeare), novels (*Catcher in the Rye, Lord of the Rings*), films (*Star Wars, Star Trek*), and Broadway musicals (*Cats, The Fantasticks*). Discussions revolve around famous artworks and artists (Cézanne, Kandinsky, Warhol), psychoanalytic writings (Freud and Jung), as well as contemporary news stories (from South African oppression to "the joke page of things around New York" [13]). The play's events are themselves framed as a series of anecdotes — Ouisa and her husband Flan eagerly share with us the astonishing tale of their encounter with Paul, a young black man who arrived one evening at their Fifth Avenue apartment, bleeding from an apparent stab wound and claiming to be the son of movie-star Sidney Poitier. Paul is eventually revealed as a type of con-man, performing a role that he has himself constructed from a collection of news stories, biographies, speeches, literary quotations, and snippets of second-hand information about other people's lives.

Crucially, Guare's play-text does not merely establish connections with other texts, opening into their worlds, but simultaneously explores the complex nature of our connection *to* texts, as well as the role of texts in connecting people to each other. Through the doorways it opens, it encourages us to explore both our desire for connections and the complex ways in which connections evoke desire. In this manner the motif of six-degree interconnection enters a fascinating interplay with the dynamics of intertextuality, and I suggest that it is amidst the complexities of this interplay that some of the play's profoundest insights emerge. Drawing upon the work of Slavoj Žižek and the Lacanian psychoanalysis that inspires it, I aim to show how an intertextual approach to *Six Degrees of Separation* enables and encourages us to complicate existing assessments of its engagement with social unity, interconnection, and love in a fractured world. Given the proliferation of "six-degree" thinking in popular contemporary artworks, it becomes especially important to examine the complexities of the motif's treatment in the text which coins the phrase.

Toward the end of Paul's initial visit with the Kittredges, the discussion turns to his undergraduate thesis which, he claims, was stolen from him by muggers. The lengthy monologue in which Paul explains his work, which had focused on Salinger's *Catcher in the Rye*, is for many of us a memorable part of the play, tapping into our own sense of connection with this iconic text. Paul's analysis, complete with precise quotations and page references, is itself an attempt to explain connections. Mark David Chapman, who killed John Lennon, "said he did it because he wanted to draw the attention of the world to *Catcher in the Rye*" (31). John Hinckley, who shot Ronald Reagan, had likewise made of the novel a central piece of his defense. Alarmed to discover the book's association with these and other apparently unconnected killers, Paul had sought to discover "why this touching, beautiful, sensitive story" had turned into a "manifesto of hate" (32). His approach involves probing the text for unsuspected points of contact and hidden links, things the story of Holden Caulfield and the stories of the killers might share. The "six degree" motif is here extended to the analysis of a text.

As a con-man seeking to seduce his audience, what Paul seems intuitively to grasp is the paradoxical fascination of these connections. The traumatic act of assassination, so out of place in the context of Salinger's "touching, beautiful, sensitive" story, operates like what psychoanalysis might call the "phallic" detail, "the detail that 'does not fit,' that 'sticks out' from the [familiar] surface scene and denatures it, renders it uncanny" (Žižek, *Looking* 90). When we contemplate *Catcher* in light of this detail, its familiar elements become suddenly suspicious — everything is to be interpreted anew; Holden's most casual remarks become loaded with terrifying undertones, imbued with potential depth (*I wonder what they — the killers — saw in this passage?!*). Paul's exploration of this connection introduces an *unheimlich* self-difference into the text, initiating a search for hidden messages and meanings which went unnoticed in previous readings. If paradoxical, our fascination with such connections would come as no surprise to Lacan, for whom this dynamic is fundamental to the force of *desire*. Desire for Lacan is correlative to the evocation of an enigmatic, inaccessible dimension beyond the surface of a thing — in Žižek's terms, "something in it more than itself" (*Sublime Object* xiv).

This dynamic appears in a different guise apropos the musical *Cats*. Paul's assertion that Sidney Poitier (his "father") is directing a movie of this show brings two incommensurable textual worlds into collision for the Kittredges. The name of Poitier, synonymous for them with cultural achievement and "barrier-breaking" films (25), simply does not fit within the context of *Cats* as they know it: "an all-time low in a lifetime of theatre-going ... a bunch of chorus kids wondering which of them will go to Kitty Kat Heaven" (72). This unaccountable connection has the effect of introducing a mysterious depth that ignites desire: what has Poitier, this legendary figure, discerned beyond the familiar surface of this commercial show? At stake in their sudden attraction to *Cats* is something more than vacuous liberal chic (Plunka 365) or a "desire to bask in the glow of the rich and famous" (Rich) — there is important truth in Ouisa's assertion that she and Flan are not simply "star fuckers" (30). The deeper dimensions of her desire are affirmed in her dream of Poitier, whose enigmatic defence of *Cats* alludes to the entire mystery of human existence — birth, death, and everything "between those two inexorable bookends" (45).

Accepting Guare's invitation to wander through these intertextual doorways, we might consider the disturbing ways in which "six degrees" operates within the stories of the *Catcher* assassins themselves. The fact that Lennon was murdered while returning to the Dakota Hotel — the setting for Roman Polanski's *Rosemary's Baby* — has struck many as impossibly coincidental, given that the infamous murder of Polanski's wife was apparently inspired by a Beatles song ("Helter Skelter"). From another angle, Abrams's notion that New Yorkers unknowingly pass their future spouse several times before meeting them takes a horrifying twist when we recall that Lennon himself had earlier met Chapman face-to-face, autographing his *Double Fantasy* album and never realizing, in that moment, that he was staring into the eyes of his own killer. Such associations reflect the "dark side" of the six-degree motif, yet perhaps they also bring into relief the paradoxical duality on which our attraction to this motif hinges. On one hand, six-degree thinking has the effect of rendering the *strange familiar*. The stranger beside me is revealed in his or her connectedness to me; the two of us have unsuspected points of contact, our isolation from each other is a mere appearance. Conversely, six degrees also renders the *familiar strange*, introducing an uncanny self-difference into my most casual encounters — people who would otherwise form an unremarkable backdrop to my daily reality are suddenly infused with unfathomable significance.

Yet most important is how this link with *Catcher* functions to complicate the very idea of "connection" as it emerges in the play, subjecting this central theme to a type of speculative twist. If Guare is seeking to explore "doorways" between human beings, he could hardly have chosen an intertextual link that introduces a more troubling blot into the picture of human interconnectedness, foregrounding the (traumatic) impossibility of definitively filling in the gaps and finding the points of contact between people. James R. Gaines's famous 1987 articles in *People Magazine* accentuate the desperate need to *account for* Chapman's crime, the impossibility of reducing it (as the prosecution had done) to a "monstrous exercise in upward mobility" ("Mark Chapman"). "I could not leave it at that," Gaines writes. "John Lennon's death was a stunning loss ... and my wish to know the reasons for his murder was like the wish, when a family member dies, to know exactly how, at what time, of what" — i.e., to *symbolize* the event. "In the Chapman case, no clinical or legal theory was adequate." In Lacanian terms the traumatic dimension of this crime relates to the *Che Vuoi?* — "What do you *want?*" (*Écrits* 690) — the unfathomable enigma of Chapman's *desire*. What did he *want* from us in killing Lennon? in thrusting Salinger's novel at us? in displaying his *Wizard of Oz* postcard on his hotel desk that morning? The killing is especially traumatic because it seems staged for our gaze, a message we're supposed to decipher, a call we're supposed to respond to. It is this abyssal, incomprehensible dimension of the Other's desire that Lacan had in mind when he spoke (in *Seminar VII*) of the neighbor as *Thing*.

Paul's own analysis — which, of course, is yet another borrowed *text* ("Graduation speech at Groton two years ago" [107]) — does not ultimately "account for" the connection between the novel and these killers. It rather uses the mystery of these connections as a launching pad for wide-ranging theorizations on the role of "imagination" in contemporary life, its broad references (to Freud, Jung, Chekhov, Beckett, Tolkein) functioning in turn to "tease the imagination and create a free play of interpretation" (Slethaug 84). The compelling quality of the speech consists not primarily in the direct insights it offers (there is hardly time to process these in the theatre) but in the mysterious "something more" to which it gestures — the *prospect* of deeper meanings, profounder insights concerning our very relation to "reality," to be found within the pages of Paul's thesis. And here we might supplement Paul's reading with a final Lacanian twist. Perhaps what we overlook, in searching *Catcher* for some deeper meaning between its lines — a meaning that could enable us to connect with Chapman's symbolic universe — is the book's symptomatic functioning *within* that universe, i.e., how the very *fantasy* of some deeper meaning in the book had enabled Chapman to cover over the gaps in his own reality. "I went down and laid in my cell," recalled the killer, "and I was thinking over why on earth would I kill anyone? What happened? What are the real reasons? ... And then it hit me, like a joyful thing, that I was called out for a special purpose, to promote the reading of the book" (qtd. in Gaines, "The Killer"). Chapman's symptom here performs the function of Lacanian *jouis-sense* ("enjoyment-in-meaning"): a proliferation of possible significations functions to mask an inherent gap or lack, covering over a derailing *blank space* in the subject's picture of reality.

"Cézanne," as Flan explains at a crucial point in the play, "would leave blank spaces in his canvasses if he couldn't account for the brush stroke, give a reason for the color" (118). If Guare's play is intent to explore "doorways," emphasizing the openings and links between seemingly disparate worlds, this dynamic is complicated by an engagement with "blank spaces," fundamental gaps in the picture, points of irremediable lack in the canvas of human connectivity. In this regard, what an intertextual reading can help accentuate is the "speculative" relationship established in this play between doorways and blank spaces. And perhaps it is here that we can find Guare's most vital commentary on the motif of "six degrees."[2]

Let us first explore more carefully the context of Flan's reference to these "blank spaces" in the works of Cézanne. Quoting and referencing texts of all kinds and indeed centering around a character whose persona is nothing *but* a mosaic of divergent texts, Guare's play culminates (most appropriately) in a crisis concerning the "textualization" of reality itself. The final moments of the play are marked by the unexpected depth of Ouisa's emotional response to her experiences with Paul, and her correlative refusal to make of him yet another text. "I will not turn him into an anecdote" (117), she says of her encounter with the boy. "How do we fit what happened to us into life without turning it into an anecdote with no teeth and a punch line you'll mouth over and over for years to come." Ouisa here contrasts the anecdotal text (a tale to be circulated among members of her social order, and indeed published by Flan in the *Times*) with the Real of the original experience — "How do we *keep* the experience?" (118). Fittingly, Flan will respond to this question through reference to yet another set of texts.

Flan is not generally credited with much depth of his own in these closing moments, yet his reference to Cézanne's blank spaces can in fact be understood as a meaningful and intelligent response to the dilemma Ouisa has identified when we consider these spaces in terms of Cézanne's own response to a crisis in representation. As Matthew Simms argues, these spaces in the painted surface record "the places where vision and intellect can and cannot interface productively with the spectacle of nature" (234). In their own way they register a struggle between experience and representation, "between the optical experience of the sunlight, reflection, gleam, and so forth, and the intellectual effort of building a harmony of colors on a canvas surface" (234). Flan gestures to the role of art as registering (*per negativum*) that which representation is powerless to directly capture, those points where the content of experienced reality exceeds or resists ordering within the structures of a representational medium. Blank spaces register the crisis or limitation *as such*.

For Gordon Slethaug and Mike Vanden Heuvel — both of whom approach the play in the context of "chaos theory" — what most defines the Kittredges is their proclivity for reducing and sterilizing the disorderly contingency of experience. Flan and Ouisa stand for "the practical ordering of reality" (Slethaug 86). Their existence, prior to the arrival of Paul, is defined by the maintenance of "unchanging stability" (Vanden Heuvel 238), even as they manifest "repressed desires" for something that would disrupt their orderly Paradise: "order is always primary, more desirable, more powerful than disorder" (236). Both critics find this ordering impulse reflected most directly in Flan's relation to artworks. What attracts him are the "structural qualities of Cézanne's paintings" (91), the degree of order they achieve and impose. His career as an art-dealer reduces art (in its potentially transformative intensity) to "a mere commodity, something to be bought and sold" (Slethaug 87) — it "renders even the most noisy and sublime artifacts comprehensible and quantifiable by placing them within an equivalent system of exchange that maintains equilibrium" (Vanden Heuvel 238). Yet Flan's references to Cézanne make explicit not simply his love for the structuring of reality but also (and more importantly) his attraction to the *unrepresentable*, to that which the paintings reflect as perpetually escaping, defying incorporation within a given structural organization ("That's why I love paintings"). He doesn't simply love structure — he loves the "problems" (118) inherent to the endless quest for structure, and he loves how paintings register these problems as such, grappling with them without ever fully resolving them: "The problems [Cézanne] brought up are the problems painters are still dealing with."

Indeed, far from simply reducing chaos, framing it into something that can reside aesthetically within the Kittredges' orderly apartment, these paintings introduce into Flan's world the *dis*orderly force correlative to what Lacan (in *Seminar XI*) calls the *objet a*. They are decidedly not reducible to "pieces of meat" (Guare 46), commodities in an economy of exchange enabling Flan to preserve his wealth and social status. More fundamentally they initiate and sustain an economy of *desire*, situating him in constant relationship to something which exceeds the frame of his existing realm, a sublime treasure which forever remains on the horizon. His perpetual pursuit of these paintings offers a perfect demonstration of the *metonymic* (and self-perpetuating) dynamic that defines Lacanian desire: "Tonight there's a Matisse we'll get and next month there's a Bonnard and after that —" (118). The very structural incompleteness of this line reflects the function of these artworks as "object-cause" of Flan's desire — they serve perpetually to disrupt homeostasis, introducing and holding open the space of a "something more" beyond present grasp. (We might ask: does Flan pursue paintings in order to make money from them, or does the money he makes enable him perpetually to pursue paintings?)

What Lacan's conception of desire helps to accentuate is the paradoxical way in which reality itself — the subject's identity and positioning within a consistent symbolic order — is held together *through* this relationship with a perpetually elusive, "disorderly" remainder. In insisting on the prominence of order over disorder in the Kittredges' world (desire for disorder being "repressed" in the interests of order), Slethaug and Vanden Heuvel tend to overlook the crucial way in which Flan's existing orderliness is maintained *as such* through its "short circuits" with the disorderly, with that which escapes the frame.

We can apply a similar logic apropos of Paul and the function of his story as *text* in the Kittredges' world. Initially identified with the pink shirt they give to him, Paul is a "burst of color," introducing something "chaotic, vital, and transformative" (Slethaug 88) into the homeostatic structuring of the Kittredges' social existence — "an exotic, imaginative life and an emotional, passionate colouration absent from their own" (87). Yet for Slethaug, the chaotic force that Paul introduces is ultimately gentrified through narrative: "When Ouisa and Flan tell the audience and their friends about the disruptive and disorderly arrival of Paul into their lives, their anecdotal account reduces it to order, just as they had earlier reduced great global cataclysms to conversational anecdotes" (90). We might well object that this particular anecdote, far from lacking "teeth" (as Ouisa herself puts it), has held us most forcefully in its grip, and that it continues to mystify and disturb long after we've seen the show. What we have here is not a straightforward example of how narrative, in its "desire to order" (Slethaug 91), tames the chaotic and contingent, stripping away the "vibrant" and "poignant" *life* correlative to experience in its "purity" (Plunka 199). This is not a mode of textualization that seeks containment, neatly packaging its referent and rendering it orderly, but one that seems to revel in the baffling, ultimately unrepresentable nature of that referent. The Kittredges' "anecdote," after all, is over two hours long, and what becomes especially apparent in performance is the *enjoyment* they take in the telling of it. Flan in particular is keen to *exaggerate* its disturbing elements: "He could've killed me. And you" (117). It is also Flan who insists on keeping the text of Paul incomplete and unresolved, *alive*. "He'll be back," he says, as though setting up a sequel. "We haven't heard the last of him. The imagination. He'll find a way" (119). Rather than reflecting narrative's gentrifying "desire to order," it is *as* text that the encounter with Paul most enables Flan to indulge his desire for *dis*order, opening and preserving the space of chaos in his universe. His textualization of Paul is not simply a withdrawal from the "Imagination" that the boy embodies — the story of this encounter permits chaos and disorder to function very potently for Flan *on the level of* imagination itself.

On one hand Paul is initially attractive to the Kittredges because he fits so perfectly into the framework of their social world, "because he has so cleverly simulated the Kittredges' interests, preferences, and tastes" (Slethaug 78). His Otherness as an African American is covered over, indeed rendered chic, by his erudition and refinement, his Harvard credentials and apparent connection with Poitier. Yet the *story* of Paul, on the other hand, becomes increasingly attractive (*as* a story) the more he exposes himself as markedly Other — gay, criminal, *unnameable* ("We didn't know Paul's name" [116]). What is ultimately revealed in their transformation of him into a text (to be circulated among members of their social order) is the paradoxical dynamic whereby such a *dis*orderly, non-symbolizable element can serve, for all its chaotic and disturbing force, to *reinforce* existing symbolic relations. It is *as* chaotic, *as* an ungraspable element in the picture defying all convenient integration, that Paul will serve as a vital social link. In writing the story for the *Times*, Flan is able to establish *connection* with the social world through the very strangeness of what has happened to him. This paradox is rendered even more conspicuously in Fred Schepisi's film version, in which the Kittredges' tale — while *accentuating* the incomprehensible mystery of their encounter with Paul — becomes the center-piece of important social functions and business deals, ensnaring desire and increasing the solidity of Flan's connection with his sphere.

We should note that this interdependent relation between order and disorder — the crucial sense in which Paul's bursting "color," for all its unexpected and disorderly otherness, may fulfill a vital structural function — has been alluded to in Flan's earliest references to Cézanne. The landscape he analyses for Geoffrey represents one of Cézanne's first attempts to use such a burst "to carry the weight of the picture": "A burst of color asked to carry so much" (14). Here again, a disorderly element ("bursting" into the field of vision) serves as the very structural principle of a picture's coherence and internal organization, holding its elements together.

As a *theatrical* experience, Guare's play encourages us to consider the "texualization" of experience from yet another angle. In directly enacting for us the content of the Kittredges' story, what the play complicates is Ouisa's very distinction between anecdotal re-telling and experience *as such*. A vital element of our own encounter with this play is the way the Kittredges' original experience and the Kittredges' narrativization *of* that experience become, in the theatre, *undecideable.* The play's framing strategy — its anecdotal presentation and tone, its fluid shifting between immediate enactment and commentary on displayed events — keeps constantly in question the ontological status of these re-enactments, foregrounding their ambiguity. Are we to take the scenes depicting Paul's visit as an "objective" rendering of what took place — do we have here a simple, neutral flash-back to what actually happened, or is it already a subjective filtering of Flan's and Ouisa's experience, a representation proffered (mediated, edited, *textualized*) for our benefit? At times the Kittredges drop the narration for long spells and enter into the scenes without distance, encouraging us to regard the enactments as unmediated "third-person" presentations of what took place; yet their interjections, directed "*To us*," function to reinstate the anecdotal atmosphere ("Six degrees, six degrees!" [94]). Indeed, key aspects of the enacted world prompt us actively to question whether we've been granted a window on the real: could the Kittredges' children really be so over-the-top in their excesses, or does our experience of them reflect Flan's and Ouisa's caricaturized presentation of their antics?

The most fitting response, in light of the paradoxes examined above, is to recognize the "truth" of this ambiguity as such, that is, how the ambiguity of our experience of the theatrical representation — its undecideability — reflects and illuminates the Real of the referent itself. The dynamic of this theatrical anecdote prompts us to question whether Ouisa's "experience" ever *had* an innocence prior to anecdotalization; it foregrounds the way in which original experience is, in Ouisa's world, always-already anecdotalized, lived with a view to its re-telling, experienced, that is, with regard to a *gaze* observing it. The opening moments of the play reflect *par excellence* this simultaneity of "immediate" experience and its narrativization for a third gaze. After the couple "*runs on stage, in nightdress, very agitated*" (3), Ouisa's first line is "Tell them!" Even as they are "shaking" from its impact, the characters' traumatic experience is being presented for the benefit of an observing gaze. In combining the Real of the event — lived and experienced *by* Flan and Ouisa — with the narrativization *of* the event, the play accentuates how the dynamic of narrativization is implicit in their experience as such, in its very immediacy. Put another way, what this structure encourages us to consider is how, as audience members, we occupy the place of a gaze that was included in their experience from the very beginning.

At stake, in this regard, is not simply the after-the-fact reduction of experienced reality through its textualization, but more importantly, the way in which immediate experience *as such* is supported and ordered through reference to what Lacanian psychoanalysis calls the big Other. For all the derailing disorder of their encounter with Paul, what remains firmly intact for the Kittredges, what retains its consistency, is the (gaze of) this big Other guaranteeing their identity, bestowing significance and coherence upon their lives and their social existence.

In this respect, I suggest we locate the Real of Ouisa's "experience" not primarily in the fullness or intensity of an encounter prior to its anecdotalization, but in the disruption of the anecdotal dynamic inherent *to* Ouisa's "real" experiences of the world. Perhaps, as Žižek continually asserts, the Real consists not (simply) in the substantial density of experience before it was mediated, textualized, reduced by symbolic structuring, but in the derailment of the very symbolic structures which determine what *appears* to us as "real," immediate experience (*Parallax* 25–26).

After Flan explains Cézanne's tendency to leave "blank spaces" in the canvas when unable to "account for" the brushstrokes or colors that would fill them, Ouisa replies, "Then I am a collage of unaccounted-for brushstrokes" (118). This response does, as many critics have asserted, acknowledge the role of disorder and randomness in life — Ouisa, like the Kandinsky, has her orderly and disorderly sides, and the two cannot be decisively separated. But we can understand the full extent of the transformation reflected in Ouisa by recognizing how this response subjects Flan's initial metaphor to an "anamorphic" inversion. The disjunction that Flan detects in Cézanne — a disjunction between the referent (the Real of "experience") and that which we can successfully capture, symbolize, represent in a text — is here transposed *into* the referent itself, reflecting the *self*-division or internal lack of what representation would seek to represent. Ouisa speaks here of "blank spaces" as pertaining not to a text that would (partially) represent reality, but as aspects of reality itself, defining her world on a fundamental level. As a "collage of unaccounted-for brushstrokes," her "life" is revealed as a succession of attempts to mediate or cover over gaps in the fabric of reality. In the terms deployed by Lacan in *Seminar XX*, reality itself is here presented as a fundamentally *non-all* canvas.

In this light, perhaps what is at stake in Ouisa's question of how we "*keep the experience*" is not simply the issue of how our representational texts and narrative versions of life inevitably reduce a prior fullness, failing to capture the Whole. If this were the case, Flan's strategy would be entirely appropriate. Blank spaces in the representational canvas leave open the place of the Real, registering the failure of any given text to adequately "fit in" all that we experience. Yet for Ouisa, the encounter with Paul is an experience *of* the non-all, the exposure of herself as a series of illegitimate flourishes plugging holes in a lacking canvas. And it is this exposure of *lack* that Flan's ("textualizing") response to the encounter with Paul does, by contrast, function to evade.

We can clarify what is at stake in this inversion by reconsidering the role in Guare's play of *love* and its particular significance apropos the motif of six-degree interconnectedness. Love, in many understandings, reflects *par excellence* the dynamic of connection, an overcoming of division. As Vanden Heuvel notes, many critical approaches to the play tend toward a sentimentalized vision of love as that which could overcome "the degrees of separation that fracture contemporary society" (240). Yet significantly, the non-all of Ouisa's world is presented not as a lack to be overcome or a wound to be healed *through* connection. Rather, it is the connection with Paul — or more specifically, the gesture of love that she extends to him — that *opens up* this self-division.

If Paul is a "doorway," he also confronts the Kittredges with a definitive blank space, a gap correlative to Lacan's *Che Vuoi?*— the Other's desire as an unfathomable and potentially threatening abyss. What did you *want* from us, sneaking in here and promising us roles in the movie-version of *Cats*? What did you *want* in talking to us about *Catcher*, and Beckett, and Chekhov, and *Star Wars*, and Freud? Perhaps the key difficulty for Ouisa is that Paul simply cannot be reduced, as Vanden Heuvel claims, to a "sponger," "parasiting food, sex, and status" (237) — his desire evades any such convenient symbolization. Even if he'd been looking to extort money, to steal paintings, to violate the apartment's occupants, that would be bad but it would be symbolizable — one could "account" for it in terms accessible to Ouisa. But what is potentially traumatic about Paul's desire is that it *exceeds* all these tangible things in the Kittredges' world, aiming at something in them "more than themselves," some hidden treasure he's posited within them. He doesn't simply sponge — he sends them pots of jam, he calls Flan his "father," he tells them that the few hours they spent together were the happiest he's ever had ...

What Ouisa cannot "account for," ultimately, is the very *violence* of Paul's desire for them, for their life, for their "Everlasting friendship" (99): "Everything we are in the world, this paltry thing — our life — he wanted it. He stabbed himself to get in here" (116–17). We find here the radical *asymmetry* that constitutes for Žižek the "traumatic" predicament of a loved one. We simply can never answer the question of what we are as an object for the other: "the other sees something in me and wants something from me, but I cannot give him what I do not possess — or, as Lacan puts it [in his eighth *Seminar*], there is no relationship between what the loved one possesses and what the loving one lacks" (*Metastases* 104).

Recognizing that she is simply "not enough" to warrant Paul's love (117), Ouisa responds to this deadlock through the *metaphorical* gesture of love, exchanging her status as loved one for that of the loving one: "*eromenos* (the loved one) changes into *erastes* (the loving one) by stretching out her hand and 'returning love'" (*Metastases* 103). "We'll be there," she affirms. "Paul. We love you" (115).

Crucial to note is how this dynamic resists a sentimentalized vision of love's power — love as that which could heal the wound of separation, overcoming the lack in Ouisa's life and bringing her into "reunion" with her "authentic self" (Rich). At stake, more fundamentally, is how the gesture of love *creates* disjunction, *uncovering* the space of lack in reality and disclosing Ouisa's internal deadlock. Love, here, is not that which could heal the non-all — enabling Ouisa, as Andreach argues, to establish a "self-reality-connection," a "bedrock" of solid "being" (63) — but that which reveals the non-all *as such*. Her exchange of her status as love-object for the status of *subject* is directly correlative to her exposure *as* a "collage of unaccounted-for brushstrokes." As Kenneth Reinhard puts it, "If the situation, the state of affairs, the status quo of a particular world, presents itself *as if* it were unified, love is what 'fractures' that imaginary unity, brings out the universal truth of disjunction in a particular situation" (68). (We should note that Ouisa does not perceive her relationship with Flan as disjointed — "We're a terrible match" [119] — until *after* her "experience" with Paul.)

I suggest that the challenge posed by *Six Degrees of Separation* resides in discovering, *in this very disjunction*, the seeds of a new, paradoxical mode of connection beyond one's existing symbolic coordinates. Ironically, in the play that coins the phrase, Guare simultaneously subjects the motif of six-degree interconnection to a type of speculative inversion: at stake here are not simply those connections ("doorways") that go initially unperceived behind an appearance of separation, but more fundamentally, those disjunctions (fundamental "blank spaces" in the canvas of reality) covered over by an appearance of *unity*. In this respect the play can be aligned not only with Žižek's Lacanian theorizations of the "Neighbor" but also with the work of theorists such as Alenka Zupančič, Eric Santner, and Alain Badiou who emphasize the potentials of what the latter terms "vital disorganization" (60). Central for these thinkers is the paradox of how encounters like those experienced by Ouisa, disrupting "our immersion in the practices and opinions of the social world we inhabit" (Santer 111), might serve as the source of a radically new subjective stance. At stake here, in Santner's words, is how a new fabric might be created "*out of a tear*": "the ways in which human subjects undergo tears in the fabric of their lives, tears that, in principle, allow not simply for new choices of objects of desire, but rather for the radical restructuring of the coordinates of desire, for genuine changes of direction in life" (110).

The "transcendent" dimension of this disorganizing *experience* is accentuated in Guare through a final intertextual connection. Ouisa's reference to the ceiling of the Sistine Chapel does of course evoke transcendent connection *per se*, "the hand of God touching the hand of man" (101), as well as the transcendence attainable through connection with art (Ouisa has literally touched

God as offered to her in this artwork). We should note, however, that her experience of this artwork becomes truly significant only retroactively. In itself, this experience was lived as an anecdote-to-be: "The workman said 'Hit it. Hit it. 'It's only a fresco.' I did. I slapped God's hand" (101). This initially innocuous gesture (done predominantly for the *story*) is something that *becomes* significant — acquires its "divine" dimension — only when Ouisa begins to perceive it from a radically new subjective stance.

Notes

1. In the playwright's own words, the title was a drawn from "a statistical theory that's gone around for a number of years" (qtd. in Bryer 82). The theory actually posited only 5.8 points of separation, but Guare "rounded it off" (83) in hopes of a better title.

2. The dynamic of "speculative" identity is developed by Žižek in his work on Hegelian paradoxes such as "the Spirit is a bone." See for instance chapter three of Žižek, *For They Know Not What They Do*.

Works Cited

Andreach, Robert J. *John Guare's Theatre: The Art of Connecting*. Newcastle: Cambridge Scholars Publishing, 2009. Print.

Badiou, Alain. *Ethics: An Essay on the Understanding of Evil*. Trans. Peter Hallward. London: Verso, 2001. Print.

Bryer, Jackson R. *The Playwright's Art: Conversations with Contemporary American Dramatists*. New Brunswick, NJ: Rutgers University Press, 1995. Print.

Gaines, James R. "Mark Chapman: The Man Who Shot Lennon." *People* 27.8 (1987): n. pag. Web. 3 Nov 2010.

_____. "Mark Chapman Part Iii [*sic*]: The Killer Takes His Fall." *People* 27.10 (1987): n. pag. Web. 3 Nov 2010.

Guare, John. *Six Degrees of Separation*. New York: Vintage Books, 1994. Print.

Lacan, Jacques. *Écrits*. Trans. Bruce Fink. New York: W.W. Norton, 2006. Print.

_____. *The Seminar of Jacques Lacan, Book VII: The Ethics of Psychoanalysis*. Trans. Dennis Porter. Ed. Jacques-Alain Miller. New York: W. W. Norton, 1992. Print.

_____. *The Seminar of Jacques Lacan, Book XI: The Four Fundamental Concepts of Psychoanalysis*. Trans. Alan Sheridan. Ed. Jacques-Alain Miller. New York: W. W. Norton, 1998. Print.

_____. *The Seminar of Jacques Lacan, Book XX: On Feminine Sexuality, the Limits of Love and Knowledge*. Trans. Bruce Fink. Ed. Jacques-Alain Miller. New York: W.W. Norton, 1999. Print.

McPhail, Mark. *Zen in the Art of Rhetoric: An Inquiry into Coherence*. Albany: State University of New York Press, 1996. Print.

Plunka, Gene A. *The Black Comedy of John Guare*. Newark: University of Delaware Press, 2002. Print.

Reinhard, Kenneth. "Toward a Political Theology of the Neighbour." *The Neighbor: Three Inquiries in Political Theology*. Ed. Kenneth Reinhard, Eric Santner and Slavoj Žižek. Chicago: University of Chicago Press, 2005. 11–75. Print.

Rich, Frank. "The Schisms of the City, Comically and Tragically." *New York Times* 15 June 1990, Theatre sec. Web. 3 Nov. 2010. Print.

Román, David. "*Fierce Love* and Fierce Response: Intervening in the Cultural Politics of Race, Sexuality, and AIDS." *Critical Essays: Gay and Lesbian Writers of Color*. Ed. Emmanuel S. Nelson. New York: Harrington Park, 1993. 195–219. Print.

Santner, Eric. "Miracles Happen: Benjamin, Rosenzweig, Freud, and the Matter of the Neighbor." *The Neighbor: Three Inquiries in Political Theology.* Ed. Kenneth Reinhard, Eric Santner and Slavoj Žižek. Chicago: University of Chicago Press, 2005. 76–133.

Simms, Matthew. "Cézanne's Unfinish." *Res* 36 (Autumn 1999): 226–42. Print.

"Six degrees of separation." *Wikipedia, The Free Encyclopedia.* 3 Nov. 2010. Web. 3 Nov. 2010. Print.

Slethaug, Gordon E. "Chaotics and Many Degrees of Freedom in John Guare's *Six Degrees of Separation.*" *American Drama* 11.1 (2002): 73–93. Print.

Vanden Heuvel, Mike. "From Paradise to Parasite: Information Theory, Noise, and Disequilibrium in John Guare's *Six Degrees of Separation.*" *Interrogating America Through Theatre and Performance.* Ed. William W. Demastes and Iris Smith Fischer. New York: Palgrave Macmillan, 2007. Print.

Zimmerman, David A. "Six Degrees of Distinction: Connection, Contagion, and the Aesthetics of Anything." *Arizona Quarterly* 55.3 (1999). 107–33. Print.

Žižek, Slavoj. *For They Know Not What They Do.* New York: Verso, 1991. Print.

_____. *Looking Awry.* Cambridge: MIT Press, 1992. Print.

_____. *The Metastases of Enjoyment.* New York: Verso, 2005. Print.

_____. *The Parallax View.* Cambridge: MIT Press, 2006. Print.

_____. *The Sublime Object of Ideology.* New York: Verson, 1989. Print.

"What there is behind us"

Susan Glaspell's Challenge to Nativist Discourse in Stage Adaptations of Her Harper's Monthly Fiction

SHARON FRIEDMAN

Critics and theatre artists have recognized Susan Glaspell's one-act plays and full-length dramas written between 1915 and 1922 for the Provincetown Players as a significant contribution to the little theatre movement that helped shape both a distinctly American aesthetic and a developing cultural nationalism. In recent years Glaspell scholars have discerned the intertextuality of her plays, novels and short stories that reveals a more nuanced portrait of the democratic nationalism she sought to encourage in her critique of conservative discourses of citizenship and nationhood emerging in this period. In her analysis of Glaspell's 1921 play *Inheritors*, Noelia Hernando-Real identifies its theme as the "necessary re-definition of the American self." She situates the play in the "ongoing national debate about the construction of American nationhood," dating back to the colonies, and played out on American stages. Citing S.E. Wilmer, Hernando-Real reminds us that drama that depicted "notions of what is national and what is alien" or "discussions about given discourses on Americanness" took on greater significance in periods of national crisis (185).

Interpreting Glaspell's treatment of American nationalism, Hernando-Real and other Glaspell scholars contextualize her work in the crisis period of World War I that heightened tensions over immigration and exacerbated rival ideologies: nativism and the eugenics movement, which fomented anti-immigrant sentiment; assimilation and "Americanization," which demanded undivided loyalty to nation; and cultural pluralism, which sought unity in difference. This paper argues that Glaspell's response to these discourses is rendered metaphorically in her short stories and expressed more explicitly in her drama, culminating in her scathing indictment of nativism and repressive American nationalism in her full-length play *Inheritors*.

The "Great War," following massive waves of immigration that had begun about 1880, aroused the anxieties of Americans who doubted the loyalties of the foreign born. At the same time, leading social scientists debated shifting views of heredity and race and their implications for defining a nation (Hattam 39). Additionally, the gradual shift from Lamarckian to Mendelian theories of heredity in the late nineteenth and early twentieth centuries raised questions about what physiological and behavioral characteristics were "fixed" genetically and what traits were subject to environmental factors and perhaps to alteration through socialization and assimilation. As Tamsen Wolff explains in her study of the "circulation" of ideas about heredity in early twentieth-century American drama, "the field of genetics took shape in a series of fits and starts, insights and misunderstandings" and during the early decades of the twentieth century scientific theories of heredity were constantly revised (1, 3).[1] Furthermore, the popularity of the American eugenics movement in the years leading up to and through the war relied on a simplified Mendelian theory of "distinct units of heredity" that functioned independently of environment, to warn against the dangers of hybridization and the potential of immigrant groups deemed inferior to pollute the nation's "blood." The eugenicists' project to "improve the human race through better breeding" offered pseudo scientific rationalizations for racist and nativist attitudes and policies. Their accounts of heredity pervaded public consciousness through tableaux, contests, and pageants, and pro- and anti-eugenicist ideas were debated in books, films, newspaper articles, and drama (3–5).[2]

The intersection of these events and theories fueled the anti-immigrant sentiment of nativists and the push for legislation restricting immigration, leading to the anti-immigration laws of 1917, 1921, and 1924 that effectively closed the border (Hattam 46). Concurrently, the Americanization movement sought to assimilate immigrants already settled in the United States and erase traces of any distinguishing cultural attributes that would engender divided loyalties. According to Victoria Hattam, author of *In the Shadow of Race,* "nineteenth-century concepts of race were expansive, often conflating notions of nationality, language, and culture under a general umbrella of race. By 1924 racial discourse had changed. Scholars and laypeople alike began to distinguish race from language, culture and nation, and it is from within this conceptual disarticulation that the term ethnic emerged" (21). The "dissagregation" of race from other social formations prompted scholars and public intellectuals to reconsider the basis of national unity, and as Hattam states, "how it could be fostered or undermined" (39). Some progressive era intellectuals took issue with the idea of full assimilation, referred to analogously as "the melting pot" (made famous by Israel Zangwill's 1908 play *The Melting Pot*). They argued for "cultural pluralism" as an "alternative axis of difference to those of race and nation," and maintained a loyalty to American nationhood that would at the same time "avoid the stultifying effects of standardization and homogenization" (60).[3]

Discourses of racial "otherness" are woven into Glaspell's critique of prejudice and exclusion in three works discussed in this paper: "Unveiling Brenda" (1916), a short story published in *Harper's Monthly Magazine*, the one-act play *Close the Book* (1917), and the full length *Inheritors* (1921), both plays written for the Provincetown Players. All three are set in the environs of mid-western colleges established to offer higher education for children of the farms and prairies and to transmit cultural and national values. All three incorporate characters aligned with tradition and dissent in their efforts to preserve family and community where these values are enacted and reaffirmed. Integral to the intertextuality that emerges when reading these works together (beyond the obvious parallels of scenario, setting, character and themes) is the concept of inheritance as it pertains not only to family, but also to group formations and ultimately the nation. These ideas become more explicit in the plays adapted from the stories, and more so with each successive work. Furthermore, a comparative analysis of the fiction and the plays suggests that Glaspell was acutely aware of her audiences. She transformed what Colette Lindroth calls "subversive" subtexts in her magazine fiction (259) to explicitly politicized conflicts staged for the avant-garde and politically engaged audiences of the Players in Greenwich Village, many of whom wrote for the radical journal *The Masses* or were active members of the Liberal Club, Heterodoxy (a feminist discussion group), or other organizations that espoused progressive politics and invited open debate of sensitive issues.

In both the story "Unveiling Brenda" and the one-act play apparently based on it, *Close the Book*, a seemingly light-hearted romance on a mid-western college campus is complicated by class and race prejudice. (The term "ethnicity" had not yet fully emerged).[4] The short story includes a feisty college student — a nascent "new woman" — who challenges masculine bombast as well as notions of belonging. Brenda, or Jhansi as she appears in the play version, takes pride in her purportedly "Gypsy" ancestry despite the snobbery of the local elite. Glaspell's adaptation of the story into a play for the Provincetown, however, sharpens and politicizes the young woman's rebellion as an outsider, parodies the student's own assumption that her "Gypsy blood" is the wellspring of her radical politics, and adds characters, plot turns, and dialogue that highlight the racial "othering" by those who would exclude her.

Amid the witty repartee of the characters in both story and play, the focus on the young woman's origins takes on larger meaning when one considers that these works were written at the height of America's involvement in the war, anti-immigrant sentiment, and the American eugenics movement.

To be clear, there are no references to the war, immigrants, or eugenics in either the *Harper's* story or one-act play, nor does the term "race" appear in the story. Nevertheless, the specter of a "Gypsy" renegade in the form of a young co-ed in a Midwestern university is sufficient to raise the anxieties of characters who, in varying ways, believe they are entrusted with family and community legacies.

The themes of nativism and allusions to intense nationalism are taken up explicitly in Glaspell's later full-length and aptly titled drama *Inheritors*. As Hattam points out, during this period the pervasiveness of "Americanization" was "buttressed at the presidential level by Theodore Roosevelt's and Woodrow Wilson's frequent anti-immigration appeals," including Roosevelt's assault on the "hyphenates" and his call for "100% Americanism." Wilson added "more muted" but still menacing calls for assimilation (45–46). Glaspell's play critiques the exclusionary politics of the nativists and their betrayal of democratic principles through powerful or in certain instances misguided characters that speak in Roosevelt's jingoistic language.

Glaspell had already critiqued metaphorically the concept of pure stock associated with nativism and eugenics in another *Harper's* short story called "Pollen" (1919) published two years before the production of *Inheritors*. The ambitions of the protagonist, a reclusive farmer obsessed with harvesting a perfect strain of corn, resonate metaphorically with early twentieth-century eugenics or "racial hygiene" movements, advocating population policies to control the reproduction of different groups. Glaspell's character Ira Mead gradually withdraws from a life-giving community whose imperfect fields he regards as a threat to the integrity of his breed. The farmer's zeal in cultivating his land and protecting his crop echoes the fervor of many eugenicists in their efforts to protect against the "permanent pollution of the national blood" carried by "defective" immigrants arriving in great numbers from abroad (Wolff 3, 170). Glaspell transposed this protagonist to *Inheritors* to underscore the profound alienation and dehumanization that ensues from this pursuit of purity in periods of xenophobic nationalism.

Patricia L. Bryan and Martha C. Carpentier assert that Glaspell was interested in the theories of evolution, natural selection, and the genetics of Darwin, Mendel, and Ernst Haeckel, which inform many of her novels and her plays, including *Inheritors* and *The Verge*, the latter also produced in 1921 (170). Indeed, Tamsen Wolff's in-depth analysis of *The Verge* examines Glaspell's confrontation with questions of "inheritance, transmission, mutation, and descent" through a radical female protagonist who experiments with creating a mutated hybrid plant that would transcend fixed forms.[5] However, Glaspell's allusions to these ideas conveyed through her characters' aspirations or prejudices in the stories and the plays also point to her concern for the dangers of "'playing God' with heredity"(Wolf 140), and applying these contested theories to human development, interpersonal relationships, community, and nation building.

In analyzing the discourses and intertexts that informed Glaspell's work, it is important to note at the outset that her writing includes an impressive range of genres, styles and themes: journalism (as a reporter and columnist), 50 short stories published by popular and literary journals, 14 plays (including *Alison's House*, for which she won Pulitzer Prize in 1930), and 9 novels. Her drama encompasses both social realism and modernist experimentation, moving between farcical comedy (e.g. *Close the Book*) and expressionist, poetic theatre (e.g. *The Verge*). However, in all of these forms, she demonstrates a close and often explicit engagement with various cultural developments that need to be placed in political and historical context. They call for an intertextual analysis that assumes, in Graham Allen's words that "all texts...contain within them the ideological structures and struggles expressed in society through discourse" (36).[6] In Glaspell's work, the subtlest representation of powerful ideas is shown to penetrate both casual and personal relationships. Glaspell biographer and critic Linda Ben-Zvi comments on her "uncanny ability" to present serious critiques of society in such a way that audiences and readers "are often unaware that they are being exposed to new ideas and positions, so seamlessly is the political woven into the very personal plots and lives" of her characters. In the plays the "radical" is "imbedded in the familiar" (275, 284).

Before composing "Unveiling Brenda," Glaspell had already forged a career as a journalist and published a short story collection *Lifted Masks* in 1912. Literary scholars note that her fiction frequently appeared alongside the work of several well-known authors — Ezra Pound, D.H. Lawrence, William Dean Howells, H. L. Mencken — and that her work was published in American magazines seeking "discerning, literate, and influential" readers (Lindroth, 258; Bryan and Carpentier 7). *Harper's*, in which "Unveiling Brenda" appeared, had reached its high point by the turn of the last century with its serialization of Henry James' *Washington Square* (1880) and Twain's *Personal Recollections of Joan of Arc* (1895–1896), and had turned from publishing primarily English authors to American fiction writers, signaling its attention to American culture and national issues (Perkins 168–169). The editors had created and responded to a particular kind of readership that would have eschewed sentimentality and a simple happy ending. In 1908, editor Henry Mills Alden stated that readers now preferred "scientific, historical, biographical, and critical writing," and noted that even in fiction, the preference was for "such imaginative literature as creates reality and reflects truth" (Alden qtd. in Perkins 169). In other words, the journal encouraged the genre of social realism that anticipated its changing emphasis after World War I to analysis of current affairs. At that time *Harper's* called itself, "a magazine of ideas" and "free and tranquil discussion" (*Harper's* qtd. in Perkins 169).

Glaspell's ability to present serious critiques of contemporary ideas in comic forms and to parody cherished beliefs with a double-edged irony aimed at several targets simultaneously, including her cohort of progressive artists and politicos in Greenwich Village, is easily discerned in "Unveiling Brenda." As social critique, who and what, we might ask, does Brenda represent, and what constitutes her veil? Brenda Munroe is an astute and candid student in handsome young Professor Peyton Root's English composition class — English 13 — which enjoys a popular following for all the wrong reasons at the openly disguised University of Iowa. Brenda, a simple farm girl in the back of the class, her brown braids resting on a green waist, distinguishes herself when she submits alternately humorous and reflective themes. Her essay "On the Pain of Teaching Dolts" punctures Peyton's bearing of self-importance as she notices his boredom and disdain for his mediocre students. Although her essay unsettles gendered power relations and the teacher-student hierarchy, it instantly establishes an unspoken bond between them.

Glaspell's urbane and witty third-person narrator manages to gently parody university culture, the intellectual aspirations of the socially privileged young professor from a respected family with the apt name of Root, as well as the exoticism attached to the mysterious farm girl Brenda who thinks that she is the abandoned child of "Gypsies." In a gently mocking tone aimed at the pretensions of both Peyton and his cohort the narrator notes that Peyton had studied at Harvard and Heidelberg, and hails from Des Champs, "a city which boasted as giddy a social life that ever scandalized a metropolis" (55). Peyton is described as a "nice, loveable fellow, who laughed a lot in spite of the fact that he took Walter Pater very hard," denigrated American literature, and taught it, as Brenda astutely notes in one of her themes, with an "oblique method" by way of the Greeks, Shelley, and the French poets. When his nonconformist ire is raised, he, predictably, turns to Nietzsche. Parodying the young professor's predilections and tastes, the narrator establishes her (or him)self as an enlightened observer who, like many *Harper's* readers, appreciates American fiction and spoofs the idolatry of academics toward English and European writers. At the same time, however, Glaspell also targets those who consider that idolatry "un–American."

Indeed, "Unveiling Brenda," "Close the Book," and *Inheritors*, all allude to an education which champions American over European literature as a means to socialize students to a nationalist ethos. Glaspell's satirical portrait of university culture suggests that she implicitly engages the ideological discourses of "difference" and American nationalism promulgated by educators of the period and which entered, in various ways, into curricular concerns and national consciousness.[7] The setting takes on further significance in Glaspell's depiction of a provincialism and prejudice that thwarts the traditions of inclusiveness in the founding of colleges for those previously denied higher education. Indeed, she is prescient in linking canon formation to politics and in recognizing the profound connections among institutions of higher learning, state funding, and the repression of dissent. When Peyton tells his American literature class that "American literature was a toddy with the stick left out," his comment manages to arouse the concern of a student reporter, the Des Champs paper, the chief of his department, and the "crabbed old regent from downstate" who voices his anxieties about what the taxpayers of that state will say about a professor who is teaching students to "despise their own literature" rather than "training Americans" (61). News travels fast. Although threats to academic freedom and American solidarity are dramatized explicitly in her full length play *Inheritors*, they are hinted at in this witty, satirical romance. As Lindroth observes in her reading of the stories, Glaspell conveys her points through "indirection — irony, understatement, metaphor, and the juxtapositions of opposites" (259).

The literary allusions in the story also suggest an implied reader sufficiently perceptive to engage what Lindroth sees as Glaspell's critique of "self-importance [and] mindless conformity" (259). As the story progresses, this critique of conformity extends to the community's attitudes toward difference. Presumably her *Harper's* readers would know the allusions to Pater's preoccupation with impressionism and his aestheticism ("Art for Art's Sake"), and to Nietzsche's repudiation of traditional morality and his quest for an ethics of "self-creation." They would, therefore, comprehend the narrator's good-humored jibes at young professor Root's quest for passionate engagement and intermittent rebellion — first in the books he consumes and then in his attachment to Brenda. This rebellion becomes most obvious when defending Brenda to those who deem her an "outsider."

The core of the story resides in Peyton's growing attraction for his student, his desire to gain her approval, and his admiration for her originality. (In 1916 it was apparently not frowned upon for male professors to escort young women students to campus dances and even to marry them.) His interest in her, however, provokes the class snobbery of Mrs. Shields, the sophisticated wife of the head of his department, and Peyton's confidante: "'She doesn't fit in,' said [Mrs. Shields], identified sarcastically by the narrator as "the U. of I's social leader" (60). In addition to referring to Brenda as the daughter of a milkman, Mrs. Shields declares her a rebel who makes no attempt to gain acceptance in campus sororities. Indeed, she has scorned them in a skit submitted to the *Iodia*, the campus magazine, entitled "Suppose they

Left me Out!" The rumor Mrs. Shields eventually discloses is that Brenda is an adopted daughter of Gypsies or a child the Gypsies had stolen — to which Peyton romantically and condescendingly replies:

> Strange, wild little thing! Dear little outsider! There was something about her gallant gaiety, something in the thought of her strange, bright aloneness made his throat tight. How he loved the untamed thing in her! ... the perpetual freshness, the spirited adventure [73–74].

Peyton's bathetic ode to "his strange girl" (replete with alliteration — "gallant gaiety") is key to Glaspell's witty parody of his paternalistic liberalism and romanticization of Brenda's alien roots.

When he follows Brenda home, however, Peyton is confronted with the rather stark reality of a rural farm, a mangy dog that waits for Brenda on the road home and a father concerned with selling a cow. The tone changes to one of poignancy as Brenda's adoptive mother tells him that Brenda has left home for Dakota to trace her true heritage. When Peyton finds her in Dakota, Brenda tells him forlornly that she is not a Gypsy, puncturing her romanticized image of herself as a rebel. Instead, she discovers that she is the daughter of a hard working boiler maker and Sunday school teacher who had contracted typhoid fever — "good and kind people" who had named her after a Christian missionary. The Gypsy story had been invented by a resentful neighbor boy. The veil of Brenda's outsider status — her stigma — socially inflicted and heroically borne, is lifted. With characteristic Glaspell irony and caustic humor, Peyton comes to the rescue, comforting Brenda because she is now an "insider."

Romantic and satiric in tone, the story concludes with a seemingly neat resolution of the conflict as it folds Brenda, still poor if not Gypsy, into the elite circles of the community through marriage. Brenda's nascent feminism in her confrontations with Peyton's authority in the classroom is muted when marriage is shown to be a shelter for her identity crisis. However, the echoes of class prejudice and the discourse of difference continue to disturb the less complacent reader long after the ironic resolution of the plot.

As Glaspell parodies the mythologizing of Brenda's "Gypsy" roots, she draws attention to the ways in which her "difference" becomes objectified. As an outspoken young woman, adopted daughter of the rural poor, she is associated with the rootlessness of both adoption in this period[8] and her supposed "Gypsy" origins. As such, she represents a threat to the campus community, deemed a bastion of advanced social thought, though one available only to the privileged.

The "Gypsy" in Brenda might be seen not only as a metaphor for the rootless, the non-conformist, and rebel, but also as an allusion to immigrants often termed "aliens" by nativists. Newcomers, especially those from eastern and southern Europe during this period, were viewed by many social commentators as inferior, lacking intelligence and motivation. However, others believed that these immigrants brought European radicalism with them to America and fomented labor unrest or resistance to government policies (Ambinder 780). In short, nativists feared that Eastern European immigrants would contaminate the pool of northwestern Europeans who had settled in America. Given that contamination and racial "mixing" is a pervasive concept associated with the nomadic "Gypsy," I would argue that Brenda functions as a metaphoric "alien" and racial "other" in Glaspell's story, especially given the potential for what the satirically named Mrs. Shields, community gatekeeper, alludes to as inappropriate in the Gypsy's romance with local aristocrat Peyton Root.

"Gypsies" (an exonym for Romani) have constituted a mythic presence in literature and folklore for hundreds of years, and Glaspell's metaphor of the Gypsy as rebel and alien might also signify the purported lure and danger in the racialized construction of the "Gypsies" in the western imagination. Even Mrs. Shields in "Unveiling Brenda" at first withholds the Gypsy story from Peyton for fear that he would find Brenda "picturesque" (73). Tracing the ideological ensemble of images in the context of a political and historical account of the Romani's persecution and marginality, Kate Trumpener argues that powerful western symbolism works in tandem with laws and policies of expulsion and imprisonment to associate the "Gypsy" with fear, danger, contagion, and disruption to civic order. Trumpener notes the paradoxical quality of their pariah status in the context of nationalism and culture: "Despite their self-containment, paradoxically, the Gypsies' wildness is highly contagious, as their arrival in a new place initiates and figures a crisis for Enlightenment definitions of civilization and national definitions of culture" (355). However, Trumpener also calls attention to the "bifurcation" of attitudes to the "Gypsy" among nineteenth-century authors: those who harbor anxieties for the "forces of civilization" threatened by the Gypsy presence, including the myths of stolen children (much like the rumor about Brenda) and "willing or resistant fellow travelers who seem to forget who they are" when following these bands; and those romanticists (like Peyton) who "celebrate in the Gypsies a community united by a love of liberty and a tradition of political resistance" (359).[9]

Trumpener's study of "Gypsies" in narratives of the west is germane for analyzing the figure of the counterfeit Gypsy in Glaspell's seemingly lighthearted scenario of a campus co-ed because it situates the romance of Brenda's origins in a history of literary symbolism satirized by Glaspell. Equally important to understanding this story is the racial prejudice toward "Gypsies" encoded in Mrs. Shield's warnings to Peyton about Brenda's "outsider" status. The discourse of the "racial other" is more explicitly scrutinized by Glaspell in her adaptation of the story into a satirical one-act play for the politicized audiences of the Provincetown Players.

In "Close the Book" anxieties about contamination are heightened. Brenda is given the more exoticized name Jhansi, and she is depicted as an outright rebel who demands a voice on campus and equality in marriage. She challenges the university's policies on free speech and is determined to violate every social practice related to conventional marriage and family traditions, especially those cherished by Peyton Root's family. Indeed, the play is set in the Root family home (*near* rather than *on* campus), albeit in their library filled with erudite books and portraits of distinguished Root elders. Peyton's grandmother is a descendent of "one of the most famous teachers of pioneer days" (17). The focus here is on genealogical inheritance, and Jhansi's "Gypsy" origin is at the core of the conflict. In the play, as in the story, social snobbery is on display, which does not preclude Jhansi and Peyton's haughty idealization of her outsider status. Jhansi, a campus radical, is more outspoken than Brenda, though her demands for free speech lack specific goals and context. Her politics are primarily channeled through campus leaflets about free speech and, more specifically, her confrontations with the Root family about the value of their lauded ancestry.

In depicting the Roots, Glaspell links their authority and power to major national institutions — military, state, bank, and university. Captain John Peyton was a revolutionary soldier, his descendant Richard gave money to found the university, and among the current family luminaries are their cousin, State Senator Byrd, and Uncle George, a banker and the President of the Board of Regents. Uncle George, ostensibly invited to an engagement dinner for Jhansi and Peyton, is really summoned to thwart Jhansi's wayward protests and protect Peyton's career jeopardized by his association with the "Gypsy." Peyton has already been denounced in a newspaper editorial as one of the "Untrue Americans" for his comment about American literature (again "the toddy with the stick left out"). Glaspell continues to parody university culture, its pretensions to humanism and, in the play, its deviation from the original Midwestern founders' value of democracy and educational opportunity. The sardonic grandmother Peyton asks, "What business has a professor of English to say anything about society? It's not in his department" (19).

Although the play adapts the basic scenario and witty tone of the short story, revealing in the course of events that Jhansi is really the daughter of devout Christian parents and not "Gypsies," the play compounds the irony: she turns out to be a poor relative of Senator Byrd. Peyton's sister, Bessie, like the messenger in *Oedipus*, brings what is supposed to be welcome news about Jhansi's true parentage, but Jhansi sees only disaster when Bessie tells her: "You must not stand outside society! ... You are one of us!" (23).

Of course, everyone is the target of Glaspell's satire, and when Senator Byrd enters with the large and authoritative book "Iowa Descendants of New England Families" (pointing up regional prejudices as well), further irony is at play. Jhansi and the family discover the skeletons in the closet of the distinguished Roots. All are leveled, and "Roots," both the family name and the genealogical concept, becomes inconsequential. Jhansi's fear of conformity by marriage to Peyton's illustrious family is somewhat alleviated, and Grandmother Peyton advises them to "Close that Book" and come in to dinner (30).

The resolution, though certainly consistent with comedy's restoration of the social order, also dismisses the genealogical concerns of Uncle George and Grandmother Peyton. However, this has prompted different responses to the play's social critique of race prejudice. Linda Ben-Zvi observes Glaspell's depiction of the "incipient racism in this 'all American family' who are fearful of the alien in their midst" (285). However, J. Ellen Gainor views the resolution of the scenario as "sidestepping" the issue of prejudice and miscegenation raised in the play and articulated in the dialogue. In her book, *Susan Glaspell in Context*, Gainor argues that although the play presents an uncompromising attitude toward free speech, "Glaspell's elimination of Jhansi's otherness suggests a conservatism that cannot be easily reconciled with the political liberalism suggested in the play's opening scenes" in which Jhansi urges Peyton to break free of traditions that bind him and take up her Gypsy heritage.[10] In the play's conclusion even the "note of class difference that has come to replace racial or ethnic distinction" is eliminated by the revelation of the undesirables among the Roots (71).

Gainor's astute reading points to what she sees as the ambivalence in the play's attitudes toward the issue of difference generally and intermarriage in particular, in a resolution that clearly retreats from confronting the subject directly. Furthermore, it mutes Jhansi's declarations of individual identity and radicalism by folding her into the family through marriage. Clearly, these are important concerns in interpreting Glaspell's treatment of otherness even in the comic genre. I would also agree with Gainor that the dialogue among the Roots is fraught with racist innuendos. However, like Ben-Zvi, I interpret Glaspell's rendering of "frank prejudice" in the dialogue as part of her critique, as well as her recurrent concern with what she sees as a developing provincialism and defensiveness in the Midwest, Glaspell's "roots." Although it is difficult to discern how harshly the play indicts this family without the sarcastic tone established by the urbane narrator of "Unveiling Brenda," I would argue that the playwright uses the dialogical structure of dramatic literature to point up their dissonances on race and inheritance that reflect the contradictions in ideologies during this period. In satirizing the Roots' perspectives as confused and contradictory, Glaspell undermines the authority of their racist discourse, and she questions their motivations in espousing their concerns.

One key example of this satirical banter is uttered by sardonic Grandmother Peyton's demand to exercise *her* right to free speech when she questions her daughter's (Peyton's mother) mission to "civilize the young woman": "I wonder how it is about gypsies. About the children. I wonder if it's as it is with the negroes.... It would be startling, woud'nt [sic]?— if one of them should turn out to be a real gypsy and take to this open road.... Quite likely, they'd do it by motor" (19). Clearly, Grandmother Peyton's wry allusion to nomads in automobiles undercuts the gravity with which other family members approach Jhansi's difference. However, in historicizing this dialogue, we might also discern Glaspell's astute and perhaps bold depiction of the languages of race that began to shift and destabilize in the late nineteenth and early twentieth centuries.

As Gainor observes, Grandmother Peyton's equation of "negroes and gypsies" suggests that Glaspell "was aware of the historical persecution of Gypsies as a dark or black race" and in this sense, the play indicts racial othering in its depiction of exclusionary attitudes toward Jhansi (68–69). However, Grandmother's remarks about racial inheritance in dialogue with her daughter's supposition that she can and will assimilate Jhansi, also reflects a distinction between "scientific" and "historic" races, pervasive in the late nineteenth century, and gradually transforming into distinctions (though not entirely parallel) between race and ethnicity in the twentieth century. These distinctions were integrally linked to concepts of culture and nation, particularly in campaigns to Americanize groups that scholars and government officials believed needed to be assimilated, as opposed to groups, such as blacks, who were perceived as having immutable qualities and therefore unassimilable.

Victoria Hattam traces the changing racial discourse from the late 1890s through the 1920s generated by scientists, political scientists and sociologists and their shifting formulations of the relations between the social and biological. As Hattam explains,

> One of the key distinguishing features of Lamarckianism was the notion of the heritability of acquired characteristics, which claimed that all human behavior could, over long periods of time, become habitual and ultimately heritable. Religion, language, nationality, and even institutions and social practices could become part of one's genetic makeup and, as such, could be passed on to future generations [24].

Lamarckian assumptions pervaded popular discourses as well. Hence, Grandmother Peyton's remark about Peyton and Jhansi's children taking to the open road might well reflect nineteenth-century Lamarkian views of race.

By 1913, as Hattam shows, "vestiges of an older race discourse" began to be replaced with a Mendelian frame in which "genetic notions of heredity buttressed a bright line distinction between races and other kinds of social solidarity" (39), though eugenicists continued to blur these lines. Uncle George's obsession with genealogy and fears that with Peyton's marriage, "we will have swallowed a gypsy" (20) reveals his anxiety about contamination, most pointedly through "mixed marriage" with an indigestible (unassimilable) "Gypsy," and suggests that he is expressing eugenicist views in his racialized construction of Jhansi. Glaspell has even the young rebel declare that her politics come from those Gypsies "right behind" her. "I am Jhansi, a child of the gypsies. I am a wanderer! I am an outlaw!" (25).

This shift in ideas about heredity informed attitudes toward immigrant groups in the context of anxieties over mass migrations and a heightened concern with national solidarity during the First World War. In other words, the concept of "'inherited tendencies'" associated with race versus "adaptation to 'local circumstances'" associated with groups based on national origin created distinct social problems in need of different solutions" (30). Racially defined groups linked by "body and blood" and seen as "homogenous and fixed," were distinguished from social groups linked by history and culture. The latter were seen as more malleable and assimilable (1–2).

Assimilation is precisely the tack taken by Peyton's mother, Mrs. Root, as she considers her options. Reared, as she notes, in "university circles," she says that she is "interested in *ideas*" (19). It may be these "ideas" that lead her to view Jhansi's "Gypsy" origins in social and historical rather than biological terms. However, fearful of the impact of Peyton's relationship with Jhansi on his career ("he used to be perfectly satisfied with civilization. But now he talks about society" [18–19]), she simultaneously espouses traditional gender roles and assimilationist views when she says of her prospective daughter-in-law: "She won't be in a position to say so much about freedom after she is married.... She won't be a gypsy after she's Peyton's wife. She'll be a married woman" (20). Marriage to the Roots, as Gainor notes, will "erase difference, at least to the outside world" (70). Glaspell's characters echo the discourses of a period that gradually began to distinguish between biology and culture, race and immigration. Mrs. Root clearly privileges a kind of protoethnic "Gypsy" above a racially conceived "Gypsy," though by no means does she consider Jhansie equal to the Roots.

The playwright, however, dismisses all these concerns and theories when the light banter among the skittish family members becomes moot with the discovery of Jhansi's relationship to Senator Byrd and the family's recognition that the genealogical book has little relevance for their pride or unity. Even Mrs. Root, in frustration, asks Peyton to stop reading from that "tiresome and obsolete book" (29). Rather than trying to comprehend genealogy, she says, "live well in the present — that is sufficient" (29). Perhaps this view defines Glaspell's ultimate resolution even as she eliminates "mixed marriage" as part of the family's present. Still, the playwright remains steadfast in linking power and politics to lingering genealogical concerns in the bluster of the patriarchs. Uncle George, reluctant to let go of the Book, reminds his cousin Senator Byrd that "one is democratic, of course, but when there is behind one what there is behind us, it enhances one's powers — responsibility — obligation" (27). No doubt the obligation he refers to is the preservation of what one political economist in 1894 called "blood, residence, and allegiance."[11]

Uncle George's allusion to "What there is behind us" is made explicit in Glaspell's serious full-length drama *Inheritors*, first produced for the Province-town Players in 1921 and revived in the 1926–27 season of Eva Le Gallienne's Civic Repertory Theatre. In *Inheritors* Glaspell fully explores the power of those who claim a traceable line of descent on American soil, ownership of the land, and connections to the state, and thus assume the privilege of defining what constitutes a culturally and politically unified nation. Although the central Acts of the play are set on a Midwestern college campus, the scenario differs from "Brenda" and "Close the Book." World War I moves to center stage, and the earnest young protagonist who defies her elders is about to be imprisoned for an act of civil disobedience. Rather than a faux "Gypsy" interloper, the rebellious college student, Madeline, is the granddaughter of the founders of Morton College, and she defies her own family. Her demand for free speech is exercised in defense of the rights of a conscientious objector to the war, as well as for several foreign nationals (considered racial others) who face deportation for campus protests. A more ethnically inflected "intermarriage" has already taken place in Madeline's family over twenty years earlier, and Glaspell focuses her attention on "difference," prejudice and exclusion in terms of civil rights and nationhood rather than on social acceptance.

This four-act drama, in the genre of social realism, spans 40 years (1879 to 1920), and Act I provides the back story of the college and its founding principles that Madeline attempts to reclaim under very difference circumstances. It traces the intersecting lives of two neighbors, Silas Morton and the educated nobleman Felix Fejevary, a refugee from the Hungarian War of Independence from Austria in 1848. Together, Morton and Fejevary establish Morton College for the children of the cornfields in a vision of inclusion rather than exclusion. Act One, set on the Morton farm in 1879 in the midst of July 4th celebrations, constitutes Glaspell's backward glance at moments of national pride interspersed with ambivalence about the means of achieving a unified nation. This seemingly patriotic reminiscence among the characters is shot through with anti-war sentiments, talk of dishonest dealings with the "Indians," and the need to look to the future to make it all worthwhile.

Structurally and characterologically, Act I traces the union between the Morton and Fejevary families, Madeline's ancestry. Her grandfathers fought together in the Civil War and envisioned a more peaceful development of the land for future generations. They have made their homes in the rolling prairie just "back of" the Mississippi River in Northwest Illinois, and their farms look out to a hill above the town that once belonged to the Indians, but now belongs to Silas. Rejecting the lucrative offer of a developer, Silas engages Felix in his vision of building a non-sectarian college on the hill for those with little opportunity for higher education. For Silas, it represents a kind of penance for his betrayal of the Indians who initially helped them. For Felix, it represents payment of his debt to America for giving him refuge. The college also represents the promise of democratic principles and enlightenment through higher learning that Silas has learned from Felix.

The marriage between Silas's son and Felix's daughter takes place without any signs of rancor, no doubt because of Fejevary's cultural capital and a more welcoming attitude among American settlers toward those seeking asylum from European wars of independence. Perhaps, this scene represents Glaspell's vision of a corrective to the xenophobia she depicts in the Acts set in 1920. However, the isolation of groups seen as biologically or historically "alien" hover over political conflicts presented in the play, both past and present. In their respective analyses of *Inheritors*, both J. Ellen Gainor and Noelia Hernando-Real point out that Glaspell humanizes Blackhawk and his tribe from whom Silas has wrested his land. Grandmother Morton, another of Glaspell's wise and feisty older women, who had fought the Indians, also remembers the Indians' generosity during times of hardship and imminent starvation. She understands their violent response to land grabs by the white settlers. Although she speaks in the nineteenth-century language of racial categories, she also recognizes the commonality among Native Americans and white settlers: "Red or White, a man's a man." Both she and her son Silas express remorse about the purchase of Blackhawk's land for far less than its worth and the sequestering of Native Americans on reservations. Above all, they recognize Blackhawk's claims to the land, even though it threatened the settlers' survival.

In linking past to present within the context of the play, however, Glaspell depicts the far less generous attitude toward the Indians voiced by the settlers' children. Fejevary Jr., Felix's Harvard educated son, justifies the Morton's victory over Blackhawk in his conflation of Darwin's *Origin of the Species* and the concept of "survival of the fittest" with social Darwinism. Where Darwin theorized that a change in the physical environment resulted in the perpetuation of some species and the demise of others ("natural selection"), he also implied that humans share a common ancestry. Social Darwinists, such as Herbert Spencer, applied these ideas to the social order, theorizing that individuals and races alike are engaged in a struggle for existence that leads inexorably to domination and hierarchy in society. Racial superiority was imputed to groups on the top and inferiority to those on the bottom. The ideology of social Darwinism was used to justify the treatment of Native Americans, blacks, immigrants, the poor and many other groups designated as innately inferior (Rosenblum and Travis 343; Steinberg 77). Fejevary Jr.'s racism in Act I foreshadows the jingoism of "100 per-cent American" that he espouses in Acts II and III when he assumes his privileged place in the community. Like Uncle George in "Close the Book," Fejevary Jr. becomes a banker, and advances socially to President of the Board of Trustees of Morton College and friend to State Senator Lewis, Chairman of the state appropriations committee.

When Act II of *Inheritors* shifts to 1920, granddaughter Madeline Fejevary Morton becomes the beleaguered "inheritor" of both American pioneer and immigrant (albeit educated upper class) traditions. However, more is at stake in her campus community than the curriculum and its focus on American literature to "train" its students in a nationalist ethos. The college must expel all who protest government policies, including professors who support the rights of dissenting students. In contrast to Jhansi's free-floating demand for free speech, Madeline's act of civil disobedience defends not only a conscientious objector to the war but also the rights of Hindu students (referred to by Senator Lewis as "the foreign element") to protest colonialism in India as well as the college's refusal to intervene in the government's decision to deport them. Deportation was the sword held over those who were seen as fomenting revolution. In this case, the Hindu students protesting British colonialism were perceived as incendiary revolutionists and a threat to America's alliance with England. As Linda Ben-Zvi reminds us, during this period opponents of the war confronted the Espionage Act, which placed tight restrictions upon political expression. This was especially true for those born outside of the United States, who also faced the Alien and Sedition Laws and could be deported for any statements made against the war or government policies, and branded as traitors, Bolsheviks or Reds (285). Ben-Zvi notes that when *Inheritors* opened in 1921, the Espionage and Sedition Acts had just been revoked, but they were in effect during the year that Glaspell wrote the play, and she risked prosecution for depicting these ideas on stage. Furthermore, the abuses she dramatizes were based on actual events (Ben-Zvi 288–289; Gainor 129–130).

In *Inheritors* the disruptive "aliens" are no longer metaphorical. They are referred to explicitly in Fejevary Jr.'s pejorative comments on Native Americans; in his son's racist slurs against the South Asian nationalists (called "dirty dagoes," "sissies" and "dirty anarchist[s]") whose encroachment on an American campus is seen by Fejevary Jr. and the Senator as a political contaminant; and in Madeline's father's demeaning attitude toward those "ignorant Swede[s]," the neighbors that he holds responsible for his wife's death. Madeline's mother contracted diphtheria in helping the afflicted family, and Ira Morton can not let go of his resentment or his association of the immigrant family with disease.

It is clear, however, that Glaspell shifts her focus in *Inheritors* from the social exclusion of the racial or ethnic "other" to the nativists' policies of exclusion in their claims to national solidarity and loyalty to the government. As noted, the Great War had provoked national fervor at home as well as abroad. Many feared disloyalty in groups harboring multiple cultural alliances, and they lobbied for restrictions on immigration. Others were engaged in institutional efforts to assimilate immigrants, particularly the children, already settled on American soil. Public representatives of specific immigrant groups who voiced their attachment to dual cultural identities negotiated their way through the poles of separatism, assimilation and cultural pluralism. As Hattam asserts, during the war years, the concept of nation was articulated in the language of inheritance (69), even if that inheritance entailed shared culture and allegiances.

Acts I and IV, set on the Morton Farm (the fourth Act in 1920), signify family inheritance and conflicted allegiance to the ties that bind. Acts II and III take place on the Morton College campus where these bonds are tested in terms of defining a national inheritance. The Great War has taken the lives of both Madeline's brother and Fejevary Jr.'s eldest son and is depicted as a catalyst for xenophobia, particularly toward the Hindu students. As in the earlier campus scenarios, Glaspell expands her critique of nativism to consider its implications for free speech and academic freedom. Abraham Lincoln, whose portrait hangs in the Morton farmhouse of Act I becomes a contested national icon for Morton College students in Act II, when the Hindu students quote him in arguing their cause. With characteristic Glaspell irony, her character Horace Fejevary — Felix, Jr.'s younger son and Madeline's dunce-like conservative cousin — upbraids the Hindu students for using Lincoln's speech in their revolutionary rhetoric. Once Horace actually reads the text of Lincoln's First Inaugural Address to Congress, specifically the passages in which Lincoln reiterates the rights of citizens to amend the Constitution, "dismember or overthrow it," he concludes that "Lincoln oughta have been more careful what he said." Senator Lewis concludes that in "quoting" Lincoln on behalf of Indian nationalism, the Hindus demonstrate that his speech is being "misapplied" (124). His misguided comments on Lincoln's lauded Address take a sinister turn when he threatens to dismiss Professor Holden for sympathizing with his dissident students. As the Senator proclaims, "We can get scholars enough. What we want is Americans" (119). Silas Morton's democratic vision has been reduced to mere catchphrases and anniversary celebrations of the college for fundraising.

Madeline emerges as the inheritor not only of her family's merged traditions and aspirations but also the conflicts between democratic values and repressive policies in the name of American nationalism. The core conflict of the play ultimately develops around her labored decision to abandon family and confront prison because she will not compromise her public support of the Hindu nationals, nor will she accept her uncle's offer to use his political influence to appease the courts. In no way, however, does Glaspell represent Madeline's defiance as flip or uncomplicated. In order to resist the law, Madeline must give up her powerful ties to her family. She must turn her back on the aunt who has been a mother to her after her own mother's death, and she must abandon her father whose disappointments and self-absorption threaten to consume her. However, Madeline achieves a kind of moral authority and a claim to full citizenship by becoming an exile in her own country. Unlike Brenda and Jhansi in Glaspell's earlier works, Madeline is the daughter of privilege, and therefore she does not require acceptance on any terms. In the play's conclusion she moves outside of the hallowed circle.

Hernando-Real interprets *Inheritors* as "Glaspell's original reply to the xenophobic national identity which, claiming to have its roots in the American pioneer past, was becoming one of the main weapons in the nationalistic struggle" (186). It is telling, then, that in the final scene of the play the playwright incorporates Madeline's father Ira's insularity as a contrapuntal motif to his daughter's act of civil disobedience on behalf of others. As noted, the character Ira Morton, transposed from Ira Mead of Glaspell's story "Pollen" is also obsessed with creating a perfect breed of corn. In "Pollen," however, Ira Mead comes to recognize that walling off his property to insure the reproduction of his pure breed has failed. He could not fully "direct" its procreation. His field is integrally connected to his neighbors' plots, and it is only by sharing his seed and his knowledge that he can protect his own produce. "Winds blew and carried seed. Winds blew and brought the life that changed other life" ("Pollen" 168). These other lives included Ira's neighbors who, in turn, had many gifts to offer the reclusive and taciturn Ira, among them conviviality, community, and ultimately love. (169). As the narrator tells us, the thought that released him "as wind releases life for other life" was, in Ira's words, "The corn ... men ... nations..." (169). In contrast, Ira Morton of *Inheritors*, Madeline's bereaved and defensive father, never achieves this recognition. He remains cut off from his community and even his daughter. However, in observing her father, Madeline comes to a profound understanding, much like the Ira of "Pollen": "The world is a — moving field. Nothing is to itself. If America thinks so, America is like father" (*Inheritors* 156).

The metaphor of a world perpetually changing and shifting ground, where nothing remains stagnant or isolated, might be interpreted as Glaspell's vision of an America continuously open to new social formations that involve the integration of all groups. Hernando-Real perceives in this vision a "utopian community of sharers from all social and ethnic backgrounds who work for the peaceful and fruitful evolution of their material and spiritual heritage," though never settling into the fixed structure of a "glorious mosaic" or even the brew of the "melting pot" imagined by assimilationists. Rather, the seeds of the nation "'blow and mix freely with the wind'" (Hernando-Real 198). I would add that in choosing the vegetative metaphor of hybridization and reproduction without design or intention, Glaspell clearly defies the social engineering associated with eugenicists.

Glaspell might also have been prescient about the future of a cultural pluralism that sought the preservation of groups defining themselves within the emerging discourse of ethnicities in a diverse nation. The metaphor of seeds that scatter with the wind suggests a cultural transformation that transcends any nationalist or cultural ethos that might thwart the impetus to continuously create new subjects and new communities in the changing landscape envisioned by her protagonist Madeline. Still, Glaspell is savvy in calling attention to the political, economic, and social conditions and ideologies that shape identities and fuel dreams, personal and collective, and that thwart or advance change. Her characters imagine "what there is behind us" to justify or bolster their visions of themselves within this socio-political web of associations. Mrs. Shields, Uncle George, and Felix Fejevary Jr. uphold their privileged positions by maintaining communities that they believe have thrived through exclusivity. Brenda, Jhansi, and Peyton Root romanticize "Gypsy" bloodlines and culture to escape stultifying communities that thwart their autonomy, only to objectify difference. Even the forward-looking Madeline imagines that her act of civil disobedience in the name of freedom and the protection of civil rights is inspired by Grandfather Fejevary's "gift from a field far off" (156) where inclusiveness and democracy prevail. "What there is behind us" will continue to be redefined by future generations who, like Madeline and perhaps Glaspell herself, envision a history that has shaped as well authorized their aspirations in the present.

Notes

1. Jean-Baptiste de Lamarck's theory of inheritance, which prevailed in the nineteenth-century, maintained that environmental forces "could alter human heredity and be transmitted through generations." In the early 1890s German biologist August Weismann challenged this

claim, arguing that hereditary material was "fixed in germ cells, unaffected by the processes of transmission or outside influences." In 1900 the re-discovery of Gregor Mendel's work with edible garden peas identified "distinct units of heredity" and focused on the stability of characteristics over generations" rather than the dominant "evolutionary theories at the same time, which focused on changes in characteristics" (1–3). See Tamsen Wolff, *Mendel's Theatre* for a full discussion of theories of heredity, the American eugenics movement and the link between eugenicists and theatre artists between 1910 and 1930. Wolff's thesis in examining the ramifications of heredity theory for the drama is that both are concerned with "visibility and spectatorship, the place of the past in the embodied present, and autonomous identity and agency" (6).

2. Wolff argues that the "eruption" of eugenic ideas responded to " the emergence of the United States as a dominant world power; unprecedented levels of immigration; mass African American migration to the Northern cities; the women's rights movement and especially the related issues of reproductive rights and sexual freedom; rapid urbanization; and World War I" (3). See "Introduction" for Wolff's summary of the premises of the American eugenics movement, the discourse of eugenics widely circulated by movies, books, the press, and drama during this period, including the use of ideas for progressive as well as conservative purposes, and its advancement of social policies such as "coercive sterilization." (1–13).

3. Hattam argues that it is critical to consider the terms race and ethnicity together because "ethnic identification has long been used as a counterpoint to race ... [and] establish[es] the boundaries and meaning of race" (1). Examining academic journals, government documents, political speeches and popular essays, she demonstrates the prevalence of ethnicity as a concept "tied to culture, plurality, malleability, and equality." Race, in contrast, was "seen as homogenous, fixed, and hierarchical — repeatedly tied to body and blood" (1–2). Between 1915 and 1935 scholars, government officials, and public intellectuals began to specify Jews and Mexicans as ethnic groups rather than races. Among the many social scientists and journalists that she cites, Hattam includes Horace Kallen, Louis Brandeis and Norman Hapgood (the editor of *Harper's Weekly*), who advanced the view of cultural pluralism. They claimed that "American democracy thrived on vigorous articulation of group particularity and difference." See Chapter 3, "fixing Race, Unfixing Ethnicity: New York Zionists and Ethnicity" for discussion of leading intellectuals and artists who contributed essays and art work to the *Menorah Journal*, especially during the interwar years debating "subnational identification and politics" (45–76).

4. Ethnic scholar Werner Sollors states that ethnicity in its noun form was not widespread until the 1940s and 1950s. Hattam sees this assertion as contributing to her argument that Jewish Intellectuals' efforts to carve out a position for ethnic groups in the 1910s and 1920s are early precursors to the discourse of ethnicity and race (Sollors cited in Hattam 46).

5. Wolff argues that in *The Verge*, Glaspell "consistently grapples with one concern that is deeply embedded in the discourses of eugenics: the possibilities of autonomous direction and mobility" (117). Although Glaspell depicts the protagonist's yearning to break out of established patterns and produce new forms, she also depicts her resistance to creating forms (in this case plants) that are "better" (more beautiful or useful) — an idea associated with the eugenicists' mission to breed for a selective type and to enlist women in their reproductive role.

6. Allen is also citing Julia Kristeva's essays "The Bounded Text" and "Word, Dialogue, Novel" in *Desire in Language*, ed. Leon S. Roudiez (New York: Columbia University Press, 1980) and M.M. Bakhtin, *The Dialogic Imagination: Four Essays*, ed. M. Holquist (Austin: University of Texas Press, 1981).

7. School boards as well as The Bureau of Education within the Department of the Interior are among the numerous organizations and institutions, private and public, listed by Hattam as involved in the campaign of Americanization.

8. See Carol J. Singley, *Adopting America*, Oxford: Oxford University Press, 2005) and Ellen Herman, *Kinship by Design: A History of Adoption in the Modern United States* (Chicago: Chicago University Press, 2008).

9. In her complex study of "Gypsies" in the narratives of the West, Kate Trumpener examines the conflation of cultural mythology and history, and argues that the post-enlightenment literary canon "sketches the historical evolution of an overtly political account of 'the Gypsies' into a literally autonomous literary one" (343).

10. For Gainor this contradiction "exemplifies the curious blend of conservatism and radicalism" that she sees in aspects of Glaspell's work and that of her Provincetown circle for whom "vestiges of Victorian morality" coexist with progressive politics (73). Gainor also notes that with *Close the Book* the Players "began its exploration of American attitudes toward the ethnic and racial Other," followed by the production of Eugene O'Neill's plays featuring nonwhite characters at the center (68).

11. In his two-part essay on "Assimilation of Nationalities in the United States," Richmond Mayo-Smith, professor of political economy at Columbia University, observed that "the progress of events has gradually destroyed the simplicity and obviousness of this conception," referring to nationality constituted by "blood, residence, and allegiance" (Mayo-Smith qtd. in Hattam 39–40).

Works Cited

Allen, Graham. *Intertextuality*. London: Routledge, 2000. Print.

Ambinder, Tyler. "Nativism." *Readers Companion to American History*. Ed. Eric Foner John A. Garraty. New York: Houghton Mifflin, 1991. 779–781. Print.

Ben-Zvi, Linda. "The Political as Personal in the Writing of Susan Glaspell." *Disclosing Intertextualities: The Stories, Plays, and Novels of Susan Glaspell*. Ed. Martha C. Carpentier and Barbara Ozieblo. Amsterdam: Rodopi, 2006. 275–294. Print.

Bryan, Patricia L. and Martha Carpentier, eds. *Her America: "A Jury of Her Peers" and Other Stories by Susan Glaspell*. Iowa City: University of Iowa Press, 2010.

Gainor, J. Ellen. *Susan Glaspell in Context*. Ann Arbor: University of Michigan Press, 2001. Print.

Glaspell, Susan. *The People*; and, *Close the Book*: two one-act plays. New York: F. Shay, 1918. 15–30. Print.

_____. *Inheritors*. Ed. C.W.E. Bigsby. Cambridge: Cambridge University Press, 2003. 103–157. Print.

_____. "Pollen." *Her America*. Ed. Patricia L. Bryan and Martha C. Carpenter. Iowa City: University of Iowa Press, 2010. 161–170. Print. Originally published in *Harper's Monthly Magazine* 138 (March 1919): 446–51. Print.

_____. "Unveiling Brenda." *Her America*. Eds. Patricia L. Bryan and Martha C. Carpentier. Iowa City: University of Iowa Press, 2010. 55–79. Print. Originally published in *Harper's Monthly Magazine* 133 (June 1916): 14–26.

Hattam, Victoria. *In the Shadow of Race*. Chicago: The University of Chicago Press, 2007. Print.

Hernando-Real, Noelia. "'E Pluribus Plurum': From a Unifying National Identity to Plural Identities in Susan Glaspell's Inheritors." Codifying the National Self: Spectators, Actors and the American Dramatic Text. Ed. Barbara Ozieblo and Mara Dolores Narbona-Carrin. Brussels: Peter Lang, 2006. 185–200. Print.

Lindroth, Colette. "America Unmasked: Cultural Commentary in Susan Glaspell's Short Fiction." *Disclosing Intertextualities: The Stories, Plays, and Novels of Susan Glaspell*. Ed. Martha C. Carpentier and Barbara Ozieblo. Amsterdam: Rodopi, 2006. 257–274. Print.

Perkins, Barbara M. "Harper's Magazine." *American Literary Magazines: The Eighteenth and Nineteenth Centuries*. Ed. Edward E. Chielens. Westport, CT: Greenwood Press, 1987. 166–171. Print.

Rosenblum, Karen E., and Toni-Michelle C. Travis, eds. *The Meaning of Difference*. 6th ed. New York: McGraw-Hill, 2011. Print.

Steinberg, Stephen. *The Ethnic Myth*. 3d ed. Boston: Beacon Press, 2001. Print.

Trumpener, Katie. "The Time of the Gypsies: A 'People without History' in the Narratives of the West." *Identities*. Eds. Kwame Anthony Appiah and Henry Louis Gates, Jr. Chicago: University of Chicago Press, 1995. 338–379. Print.

Wolff, Tamsen. *Mendel's Theatre*. New York: Palgrave Macmillan, 2009. Print.

About the Contributors

Kristin **Bennett** graduated from The College of New Jersey with M.A. and B.A. degrees in English language and literature. Her research interests include 19th century American and British literature, as well as prison literature and drama. She has taught English composition at Bucks County Community College and the Edna Mahan maximum security prison in New Jersey and has presented at the American Literature Association, Sigma Tau Delta, the Plymouth State University Medieval and Renaissance Forum, and the International American Drama conference at Kean University.

Annalisa **Brugnoli** is a Ph.D. (2009) and honorary fellow (2011) in North American studies at the University of Venice. Her dissertation was a study of the presence and signification of the shadow in O'Neill's plays. She has lectured on modern American theatre in Italy, Europe and the United States, and published extensively on Eugene O'Neill and American drama. Her scholarly interests also include Italian-American literature, Nathaniel Hawthorne and literary translation.

Drew **Eisenhauer** is a 2011 City of Paris Postdoctoral Research Fellow at the University of Paris, Diderot, where he is researching the French influences on plays about American bohemian artists and writers produced in the early twentieth century. His Ph.D. dissertation, "'Something Sweetly Personal and Sweetly Social': Modernism, Metadrama, and the Avant Garde in the Plays of the Provincetown Players," was completed in 2009. Eisenhauer also regularly presents papers at national and international conferences on American drama.

Ramón **Espejo Romero** is an associate professor of English at the University of Seville. For almost 15 years, he has been teaching American literature, mostly colonial and 19th century. His publications include work on American writers such as Anne Bradstreet, Edith Wharton, Herman Melville, Tom Wolfe and Paul Auster, as well as playwrights Eugene O'Neill, Arthur Miller and Edward Albee. He has focused on the way American playwrights have impacted Spanish theatre throughout the 20th century.

Herman Daniel **Farrell** III is an assistant professor of theatre at the University of Kentucky, where he teaches playwriting, theatre history and dramatic literature, including seminars on Eugene O'Neill. He received his B.A., *cum laude*, from Vassar College in 1983, a J.D. from New York University School of Law in 1989 and an M.F.A. in playwriting from Columbia University in 1994. Co-writer of the Peabody Award–winning HBO Film *Boycott*, his plays have been produced or developed in several venues, including Manhattan Theater Club, The Flea, New Dramatists, the

Eugene O' Neill Theater Center National Playwrights Conference and the Mac-Dowell Colony.

Sharon **Friedman** is an associate professor of modern literature and drama in the Gallatin School of New York University. Recent publications include an edited volume of essays, *Feminist Theatrical Revisions of Classic Works* (McFarland, 2009), and "The Gendered Terrain in Contemporary Theatre of War by Women" in *Theatre Journal* (Dec. 2010). Other essays have appeared in such publications as *American Studies, New Theatre Quarterly, Women and Performance, TDR, New England Theatre Journal, Text and Presentation, Susan Glaspell: Essays on Her Theatre and Fiction,* and *Codifying the National Self: Spectators, Actors and the American Text.*

Lisa Hall **Hagen** is an assistant professor of theatre history and dramaturgy at Utah Valley University. She holds a Ph.D. in theatre history and criticism from the University of Colorado, Boulder, as well as an M.A. in playwriting from Boston University and a B.A. in performance from San Francisco State University. She has published *Examining the Use of Safety, Confrontation, and Ambivalence in Six Depictions of Reproductive Women on the American Stage, 1997–2007.* Her research interests are focused on dramaturgy for sensitive audiences, Aliza Shvarts and an ethics of "realness" in performance.

Noelia **Hernando-Real** is an assistant professor of English and American literature at the Universidad Complutense de Madrid and vice president of the Susan Glaspell Society. Her publications include *Self and Space in the Theater of Susan Glaspell* (McFarland, 2011), "Drama and Cultural Pluralism in the America of Susan Glaspell's *Inheritors*" in *Interrogating America Through Theatre and Performance* (2007) and "E Pluribus Plurum: From a Unifying National Identity to Plural Identities in Susan Glaspell's *Inheritors*" in *Codifying the National Self: Spectators, Actors and the American Dramatic Text* (2006).

Jeffrey Eric **Jenkins** is the director of theatre studies in the drama department at New York University's Tisch School of the Arts, where he has taught theatre history, theory, and criticism since 1998. He is series editor of the *Best Plays Theater Yearbook* (eight volumes to date), an annual collection of commissioned critical essays and historical reference. Other publications include chapters in *Interrogating America Through Theatre and Performance* and *Angels in American Theater: Patrons, Patronage, and Philanthropy.*

Emeline **Jouve** is an assistant lecturer in the English department of the University of Toulouse II–Le Mirail, France. Her doctoral dissertation focused on the figure of the rebel in Susan Glaspell's plays. She has given papers at several international conferences in France, Spain and the United States, and has published articles on Susan Glaspell in French and American journals. She conducts research on how the dramatic medium can be used as a pedagogical tool for language learning and has directed several plays.

Franklin J. **Lasik** is a doctoral candidate at the University of Missouri, Columbia, where he has taught classes in acting, playwriting and script analysis, as well as scenic construction. He has also served as an actor, director and playwright, and is an active member of MU Improv. Among his research interests are theatre historiography, musical theatre, American drama, and American popular entertainment. He holds an M.A. in theatre from Ohio State University.

Rupendra Guha **Majumdar** is an associate professor of English at Delhi University. He has published *Central Man: The Paradox of Heroism in Modern American Drama* (2003) and four volumes of verse and has contributed to the *Encyclopedia of Modern Drama* (2007) and *The Essential Tagore* (2011). His research interests lie in all forms of narrative, linguistic and visual, ranging from the classical Greek/Latin/Sanskrit to present times and through the dynamics of performance.

Stephen **Marino** is an adjunct professor of English at St. Francis College and is the founding editor of *The Arthur Miller Journal* and former president of the Arthur Miller Society. His work on Miller has appeared in *Modern Drama, The South Atlantic Review, The Dictionary of Literary Biography* and *The Nevada Historical Quarterly*. He is the editor of *"The Salesman Has a Birthday": Essays Celebrating the Fiftieth Anniversary of Arthur Miller's Death of a Salesman* (2000) and the author of *A Language Study of Arthur Miller's Plays: The Poetic in the Colloquial* (2002).

Brenda **Murphy** is the Board of Trustees Distinguished Professor of English at the University of Connecticut. She has published a wide range of articles on American drama, theater, and performance. Among her 16 books are *The Provincetown Players and the Culture of Modernity* (2005), *Congressional Theatre: Dramatizing McCarthyism on Stage, Film, and Television* (1999), *Tennessee Williams and Elia Kazan: A Collaboration in the Theatre* (1992), *Understanding David Mamet* (2011), *O'Neill: Long Day's Journey Into Night* (2001), and, as editor, *Twentieth Century American Drama: Critical Concepts in Literary and Cultural Studies* (2006) and the *Cambridge Companion to American Women Playwrights* (1999).

Aurélie **Sanchez** is an assistant lecturer at the University of Toulouse le Mirail in France, finishing her Ph.D. dissertation on the chiaroscuro in Eugene O'Neill's late plays. She has participated in several conferences in France, Spain, Ireland and the United States, and has published articles on O'Neill's late plays in French journals, dealing with subjects that range from the Shakespearean influence on O'Neill to the "Americanness" of the author.

Jason **Shaffer** is an associate professor of English at the United States Naval Academy, where he teaches dramatic and early American literature and serves as dramaturg for the USNA drama program. He is the author of *Performing Patriotism: National Identity in the Colonial and Revolutionary American Theater* (University of Pennsylvania, 2007), and he has published in *Theatre Survey, Early American Literature*, and *Comparative Drama*. He is working on a history of the early evolution of celebrity in the United States.

Michael **Winetsky** is an intellectual historian, a cultural critic and a playwright. He received his Ph.D. in English (with a dissertation on Susan Glaspell) from the Graduate Center of the City University of New York in February 2011. Although trained as a Romanticist, he teaches and lectures mostly on American culture, and is an adjunct assistant professor of American studies at the College of Staten Island and adjunct assistant professor of English at the Borough of Manhattan Community College.

Sarah **Withers** is a doctoral candidate in the English Department at Indiana University, completing a dissertation on "Theatrical Properties: Inheritance and Modern American Drama." Her research interests include American drama, performance studies, gender and sexuality studies, as well as literary, legal and political discourses of inheritance. Her essay in this collection is an expansion of a presentation that received the Susan Glaspell Society's biannual award for best conference paper in 2011.

Graham **Wolfe** completed a Ph.D. in drama at the University of Toronto in 2010. His dissertation, "Encounters with the Real: A Žižekian Approach to the Sublime and the Fantastic in Contemporary Drama," won "Best Dissertation" at the Graduate Centre for Study of Drama. His articles have been published in journals including *Modern Drama, The Journal of Dramatic Theory and Criticism*, and *The International Journal of Žižek Studies* among others. He teaches courses in theatre and critical theory at the University of Toronto and Brock University.

Index

257

UNIVERSITY OF WINCHESTER
LIBRARY